Pioneering Healthcare Law

This book celebrates Professor Margaret Brazier's outstanding contribution to the field of healthcare law and bioethics. It examines key aspects developed in Professor Brazier's agenda-setting body of work, with contributions being provided by leading experts in the field from the UK, Australia, the US and continental Europe. They examine a range of current and future challenges for healthcare law and bioethics, representing state-of-the-art scholarship in the field.

The book is organised into five parts. Part I discusses key principles and themes in healthcare law and bioethics. Part II examines the dynamics of the patient–doctor relationship, in particular the role of patients. Part III explores legal and ethical issues relating to the human body. Part IV discusses the regulation of reproduction, and Part V examines the relationship between the criminal law and the healthcare process.

Offering a collaborative review of key and innovative themes in the field, the book will be of great interest and use to academics and students working in healthcare law and bioethics, and those working in health policy, law and regulation at both national and international levels.

Catherine Stanton is Lecturer in Law in the Centre for Social Ethics and Policy in the School of Law at the University of Manchester, UK.

Sarah Devaney is Senior Lecturer in Law in the Centre for Social Ethics and Policy in the School of Law, University of Manchester, UK.

Anne-Maree Farrell is Australian Research Council Future Fellow and Associate Professor in the Faculty of Law at Monash University, Australia.

Alexandra Mullock is Lecturer in Law in the Centre for Social Ethics and Policy in the School of Law, University of Manchester, UK.

Biomedical Law and Ethics Library
Series Editor: Sheila A.M. McLean

Scientific and clinical advances, social and political developments and the impact of healthcare on our lives raise profound ethical and legal questions. Medical law and ethics have become central to our understanding of these problems, and are important tools for the analysis and resolution of problems – real or imagined.

In this series, scholars at the forefront of biomedical law and ethics contribute to the debates in this area, with accessible, thought-provoking, and sometimes controversial, ideas. Each book in the series develops an independent hypothesis and argues cogently for a particular position. One of the major contributions of this series is the extent to which both law and ethics are utilised in the content of the books, and the shape of the series itself.

The books in this series are analytical, with a key target audience of lawyers, doctors, nurses and the intelligent lay public.

Available titles:

Human Fertilisation and Embryology
Reproducing regulation
Kirsty Horsey & Hazel Biggs

Intention and Causation in Medical Non-killing
The impact of criminal law concepts on euthanasia and assisted suicide
Glenys Williams

Impairment and Disability
Law and ethics at the beginning and end of life
Sheila A.M. McLean & Laura Williamson

Bioethics and the Humanities
Attitudes and perceptions
Robin Downie & Jane Macnaughton

Defending the Genetic Supermarket
The law and ethics of selection the next generation
Colin Gavaghan

The Harm Paradox
Tort law and the unwanted child in an era of choice
Nicolette Priaulx

Assisted Dying
Reflections on the need for law reform
Sheila A M McLean

Medicine, Malpractice and Misapprehensions
Vivienne Harpwood

Euthanasia, Ethics and the Law
From the conflict to compromise
Richard Huxtable

The Best Interests of the Child in Healthcare
Sarah Elliston

Values in Medicine
What are we really doing to patients?
Donald Evans

Autonomy, Consent and the Law
Sheila A.M. McLean

Healthcare Research Ethics and Law
Regulation, review and responsibility
Hazel Biggs

The Body in Bioethics
Alastair V. Campbell

Genomic Negligence
An interest in autonomy as the basis for novel negligence claims generated by genetic technology
Victoria Chico

Health Professionals and Trust
The cure for healthcare law and policy
Mark Henaghan

Medical Ethics in China
A transcultural interpretation
Jing-Bao Nie

Law, Ethics and Compromise at the Limits of Life
To treat or not to treat?
Richard Huxtable

Regulating Pre-Implantation Genetic Diagnosis
A comparative and theoretical analysis
Sheila A.M. McLean & Sarah Elliston

Bioethics
Methods, theories, domains
Marcus Düwell

Human Population Genetic Research in Developing Countries
The issue of group protection
Yue Wang

Coercive Care
Rights, law and policy
Bernadette McSherry & Ian Freckelton

Saviour Siblings
A relational approach to the welfare of the child in selective reproduction
Michelle Taylor-Sands

Human Population Genetic Research in Developing Countries
The issue of group protection
Yue Wang

Stem Cell Research and the Collaborative Regulation of Innovation
Sarah Devaney

The Voices and Rooms of European Bioethics
Richard Huxtable and Ruud Ter Meulen

The Legitimacy of Medical Treatment
What role for the medical exception?
Sara Fovargue and Alexandra Mullock

Regulating Risk
Values in health research governance
Shawn Harmon

The Jurisprudence of Pregnancy
Concepts of conflict, persons and property
Mary Neal

Autonomy and Pregnancy
A comparative analysis of compelled obstetric intervention
Samantha Halliday

Revisiting the Regulation of Human Fertilisation and Embryology
Kirsty Horsey

Pioneering Healthcare Law
Essays in honour of Margaret Brazier
Catherine Stanton, Sarah Devaney, Anne-Maree Farrell and Alexandra Mullock

End of Life Decision Making for Critically Impaired Infants
Resource allocation and difficult decisions
Neera Bhatia

Birth, Harm and the Role of Distributive Justice
Burdens, blessings, need and desert
Alasdair Maclean

Forthcoming titles include:

The Umbilical Cord Blood Controversies in Medical Law
Karen Devine

Revisiting Landmark Cases in Medical Law
Shaun D Pattinson

The Ethical and Legal Consequences of Posthumous Reproduction
Lewis Browne

About the series editor

Professor Sheila A.M. McLean is Professor Emerita of Law and Ethics in Medicine, School of Law, University of Glasgow, UK.

Pioneering Healthcare Law
Essays in honour of Margaret Brazier

Edited by
Catherine Stanton,
Sarah Devaney,
Anne-Maree Farrell
and Alexandra Mullock

LONDON AND NEW YORK

First published 2016
by Routledge
2 Park Square, Milton Park, Abingdon, Oxon, OX14 4RN

and by Routledge
711 Third Avenue, New York, NY 10017

Routledge is an imprint of the Taylor & Francis Group, an informa business

© 2016 editorial matter and selection, Catherine Stanton, Sarah Devaney, Anne-Maree Farrell and Alexandra Mullock; individual chapters, the contributors.

The right of Catherine Stanton, Sarah Devaney, Anne-Maree Farrell and Alexandra Mullock to be identified as editors of this work has been asserted by them in accordance with sections 77 and 78 of the Copyright, Designs and Patents Act 1988.

All rights reserved. No part of this book may be reprinted or reproduced or utilised in any form or by any electronic, mechanical, or other means, now known or hereafter invented, including photocopying and recording, or in any information storage or retrieval system, without permission in writing from the publishers.

Trademark notice: Product or corporate names may be trademarks or registered trademarks, and are used only for identification and explanation without intent to infringe.

British Library Cataloguing in Publication Data
A catalogue record for this book is available from the British Library

Library of Congress Cataloging-in-Publication Data
Pioneering healthcare law : essays in honour of Margaret Brazier / edited by Catherine Stanton, Sarah Devaney, Anne-Maree Farrell and Alexandra Mullock.
  pages cm. — (Biomedical law and ethics library)
 1. Medical laws and legislation. 2. Medical laws and legislation—Great Britain. I. Stanton, Catherine (Law teacher) II. Devaney, Sarah, editor. III. Farrell, Anne-Maree, 1964- editor. IV. Mullock, Alexandra, editor. V. Brazier, Margaret, honouree.
  K3601.P56 2016
  344.04'1—dc23
  2015020094

ISBN: 978-1-138-86109-1 (hbk)
ISBN: 978-1-315-71610-7 (ebk)

Typeset in Galliard
by Apex CoVantage, LLC

Printed and bound by CPI Group (UK) Ltd, Croydon, CR0 4YY

For Margot

Contents

Notes on contributors xiii
Acknowledgements xvii
Foreword xix
BRENDA HALE, BARONESS HALE OF RICHMOND, DBE, PC,
FBA, LLD, FRCPSYCH, DEPUTY PRESIDENT OF
THE SUPREME COURT OF THE UNITED KINGDOM

Margot Brazier: Editors' appreciation xxiii

1 **Pioneering healthcare law** 1
  ANNE-MAREE FARRELL, CATHERINE STANTON,
  ALEXANDRA MULLOCK AND SARAH DEVANEY

PART I
Key principles and themes in healthcare law 17

2 **Waxing and waning: The shifting sands of autonomy on the medico-legal shore** 19
  GRAEME T LAURIE AND J KENYON MASON

3 **Compulsory vaccination: Going beyond a civic duty?** 31
  NICOLA GLOVER-THOMAS AND SØREN HOLM

4 **The value of human life in healthcare law: Life versus death in the hands of the judiciary** 43
  ALEXANDRA MULLOCK AND ROB HEYWOOD

5 **Decisions at the end of life: An attempt at rationalisation** 55
  SHEILA A.M. McLEAN

6 **The past, present and future of EU health law** 67
  TAMARA HERVEY

7 Beyond medicine, patients and the law: Policy
   and governance in 21st century health law   78
   JOHN COGGON AND LAWRENCE O GOSTIN

PART II
Patient–doctor relations   89

8 (I love you!) I do, I do, I do, I do, I do: Breaches
   of sexual boundaries by patients in their relationships
   with healthcare professionals   91
   HAZEL BIGGS AND SUZANNE OST

9 When things go wrong: Patient harm, responsibility
   and (dis)empowerment   103
   ANNE-MAREE FARRELL AND SARAH DEVANEY

10 Critical decisions for critically ill infants: Principles,
   processes, problems   116
   GILES BIRCHLEY AND RICHARD HUXTABLE

11 The role of the family in healthcare decisions:
   The dead and the dying   129
   MONICA NAVARRO-MICHEL

PART III
Law, ethics and the human body   141

12 Exploring the legacy of the Retained Organs
   Commission a decade on: Lessons learned and
   the dangers of lessons lost   143
   JEAN V McHALE

13 Property interests in human tissue: Is the law
   still an ass?   156
   MUIREANN QUIGLEY AND LOANE SKENE

14 Law and humanity: Exploring organ donation using
   the Brazier method   168
   MARLEEN EIJKHOLT AND RUTH STIRTON

15 Sex change surgery for transgender minors:
   Should doctors speak out?   181
   SIMONA GIORDANO, CÉSAR PALACIOS-GONZÁLEZ
   AND JOHN HARRIS

16 The lawyer's prestige   189
    IAIN BRASSINGTON AND IMOGEN JONES

PART IV
Regulating reproduction   **197**

17 The science of muddling through: Categorising
    embryos   199
    MARIE FOX AND SHEELAGH McGUINNESS

18 Revisiting the regulation of the reproduction business   211
    DANIELLE GRIFFITHS AND AMEL ALGHRANI

19 Regulating responsible reproduction   223
    DAVID ARCHARD

20 Donor conception and information disclosure:
    Welfare or consent?   231
    ROSAMUND SCOTT

21 Are we still 'policing pregnancy'?   243
    SARA FOVARGUE AND JOSÉ MIOLA

PART V
The criminal law and the healthcare process   **255**

22 Vulnerability and the criminal law: The implications
    of Brazier's research for safeguarding people at risk   257
    KIRSTY KEYWOOD AND ZUZANNA SAWICKA

23 Revisiting the criminal law on the transmission
    of disease   268
    DAVID GURNHAM AND ANDREW ASHWORTH

24 Maternal responsibility to the child not yet born   280
    EMMA CAVE AND CATHERINE STANTON

25 Compromise medicalisation   292
    ROGER BROWNSWORD AND JEFFREY WALE

    Index   305

Contributors

Amel Alghrani, Senior Lecturer in Law, Liverpool Law School, University of Liverpool, UK.

David Archard, Professor, School of Politics, International Studies and Philosophy, Queen's University Belfast, UK.

Andrew Ashworth, Emeritus Vinerian Professor of English Law, Faculty of Law, University of Oxford, UK.

Hazel Biggs, Professor of Healthcare Law and Bioethics, Southampton Law School, University of Southampton, UK.

Giles Birchley, Wellcome Trust Research Fellow, Centre for Ethics in Medicine, University of Bristol.

Iain Brassington, Senior Lecturer, Centre for Social Ethics and Policy, School of Law, University of Manchester, UK.

Roger Brownsword, Professor of Law, Dickson Poon School of Law, King's College London and Professor of Law, University of Bournemouth, UK.

Emma Cave, Reader in Law, Durham Law School, University of Durham, UK.

John Coggon, Professor of Law and the Philosophy of Public Health, Southampton Law School, University of Southampton, UK.

Sarah Devaney, Senior Lecturer, Centre for Social Ethics and Policy, School of Law, University of Manchester and Co-Director of the Manchester Centre for Regulation & Governance (ManReg), UK.

Marleen Eijkholt, Assistant Professor Medical Humanities, Davidson College, USA.

Anne-Maree Farrell, Australian Research Council Future Fellow, Associate Professor, Faculty of Law, Monash University, Australia.

Sara Fovargue, Reader in Law, Law School, Lancaster University, UK.

Marie Fox, Professor of Socio-Legal Studies, Law School, University of Birmingham, UK.

Simona Giordano, Reader in Bioethics, Centre for Social Ethics and Policy, School of Law, University of Manchester, UK.

Nicola Glover-Thomas, Professor of Medical Law, Centre for Social Ethics and Policy, School of Law, University of Manchester, UK.

Lawrence O Gostin, Linda D and Timothy J O'Neill Professor of Global Health Law, Director of O'Neill Institute for National & Global Health Law, Georgetown University, USA.

Danielle Griffiths, Research Fellow, Institute for Science Ethics and Innovation, Faculty of Life Sciences, University of Manchester, UK.

David Gurnham, Associate Professor in Law, Southampton Law School, University of Southampton, UK.

Brenda Hale, Baroness Hale of Richmond, DBE, PC, FBA, LLD, FRCPsych Deputy President of the Supreme Court of the United Kingdom.

John Harris, Lord David Alliance Professor of Bioethics and Director, Institute for Science Ethics and Innovation, School of Life Sciences, University of Manchester, UK.

Tamara Hervey, Jean Monnet Professor of European Union Law, School of Law, University of Sheffield, UK.

Rob Heywood, Professor of Medical Law, University of East Anglia Law School, UK.

Søren Holm, Professor of Bioethics, Centre for Social Ethics and Policy, School of Law, University of Manchester, UK.

Richard Huxtable, Professor of Medical Ethics & Law, Centre for Ethics in Medicine, University of Bristol, UK.

Imogen Jones, Lecturer, Law School, University of Birmingham, UK.

Kirsty Keywood, Senior Lecturer, Centre for Social Ethics and Policy, School of Law, University of Manchester, UK.

Graeme T Laurie, Professor of Medical Jurisprudence, Director of the JK Mason Institute for Medicine, Life Sciences and the Law, School of Law, University of Edinburgh, UK.

Sheelagh McGuinness, Birmingham Fellow, Centre for Health Law, Science and Policy, University of Birmingham, UK.

Jean V McHale, Professor of Health Care Law, Director of Centre for Health Law, Science & Policy, Law School, University of Birmingham, UK.

Sheila A.M. McLean, Professor Emerita of Law and Ethics in Medicine, School of Law, University of Glasgow, UK.

J Kenyon Mason, Professor Emeritus of Forensic Medicine, School of Law, University of Edinburgh, UK.

José Miola, Professor of Medical Law, School of Law, University of Leicester, UK.

Alexandra Mullock, Lecturer, Centre for Social Ethics and Policy, School of Law, University of Manchester, UK.

Monica Navarro-Michel, Reader, Faculty of Law, University of Barcelona, Spain.

Suzanne Ost, Professor of Law, Law School, Lancaster University, UK.

César Palacios-González, Institute for Science, Ethics and Innovation, University of Manchester, UK.

Muireann Quigley, Professor of Law, Innovation and Society, Newcastle Law School, University of Newcastle, UK.

Zuzanna Sawicka, Consultant in Elderly Medicine, Pinderfields Hospital, Mid Yorkshire NHS Trust, UK.

Rosamund Scott, Professor of Medical Law and Ethics, Dickson Poon School of Law, King's College, London, UK.

Loane Skene, Professor, Faculty of Law, University of Melbourne, Australia.

Catherine Stanton, Lecturer, Centre for Social Ethics and Policy, School of Law, University of Manchester, UK.

Ruth Stirton, Lecturer in Healthcare Law, Sussex Law School, University of Sussex, UK.

Jeffrey Wale, Lecturer in Law, Department of Law, University of Bournemouth, UK.

Acknowledgements

We are very grateful to all the contributors who have enabled us to turn our vision of this festschrift into reality – and at remarkable speed. We are also extremely grateful for all the work done by those at Routledge, particularly Mark Sapwell who worked with us at the beginning of the project (and has now moved on to pastures new) and latterly Katie Carpenter and Olivia Manley, together with the publisher's reviewers who supported our proposal. Thanks also go to Tammy Hervey and her colleagues who generously hosted a workshop at the University of Sheffield for contributors to present their papers, together with Divine Banyubala for taking notes of the day's discussions. We are grateful too for Emma Cave's helpful comments on chapter 1, Sarah-Jane Brown's assistance with proofreading and Rodney and Vicky Brazier's guidance – particularly in the early stages when we were keeping the project a secret from Margot! On a project with four editors it is hard to apportion exact contribution and so we have taken the approach of naming the corresponding editor first and then the other editors in alphabetical order. Finally, we would all like to thank our families for their support throughout this process.

Foreword

Brenda Hale

BARONESS HALE OF RICHMOND, DBE, PC,
FBA, LLD, FRCPSYCH, DEPUTY PRESIDENT OF
THE SUPREME COURT OF THE UNITED KINGDOM

Remembering October 1968: my third year teaching Law at the University of Manchester, my second year delivering the lecture course in Constitutional and Administrative Law (still keeping barely two steps ahead of the class). Who should turn up in the lecture theatre (strategically placed, towards the back but in the centre) but this tiny slip of a girl, with an elfin face and ginger hair, still only 17 years old, and from the start asking the most penetrating and challenging questions? The great joy of university teaching, of course, is that the teachers learn as much from (some of) their students as the students learn from their teachers. The young Miss Jacobs (Margot then and ever since) was a joy to have in any class.

She was still a tiny slip of a girl, and not yet 21 years old, when she was appointed a lecturer in Law at the University of Manchester, straight after graduating, of course with an excellent first class degree, in the days when extracting first class marks from the Manchester examiners was like pulling teeth without an anaesthetic. Those were also the days when it was possible to gain an academic post in Law straight after graduating, something unheard of in this day and age. But they were also the days when it was possible to qualify as a barrister by private study without spending most of a year and a King's ransom attending the Bar Professional Training Course. This meant that many of the bright young graduates who started in Law teaching left after a year or two to go the Bar. We feared that Miss Jacobs might do the same, especially as she and a girlfriend shared a flat in the early days with two other young Law lecturers, both of whom eventually went off to very successful careers at the Manchester Bar.

Fortunately for the future of academic Law in Manchester, for generations of Manchester Law students, and for her many academic colleagues, not only in the Law but in other disciplines too, she decided not to heed the siren call of the Bar and to stay where she was. Perhaps her marriage, in 1974, to Rodney Brazier, who had joined the Law School in the same year as she did, but as a lecturer rather than a student, had something to do with it. Perhaps the birth of their daughter, my god-daughter Vicky, in 1979, had even more to do with it. Wanting to have a family was one of the reasons why I had given up trying to combine practice as a barrister with Law teaching a few years earlier. You can do them both for a while, at a relatively junior level, but it is not possible to combine a successful career at the provincial common law Bar with a successful career as an academic lawyer: something has to give.

Having determined upon an academic career, of course, Mrs Brazier did nothing by halves. Every young academic has to get their academic show on the road, to discover their niche and to develop it. It is a measure of the high regard in which Margot Jacobs was already held by one of the towering figures in the Law School of those days, Professor Harry Street, that very early on the Tort class was divided into two, with him taking one half and her taking the other. This was no mean feat on her part, because Street was one of the very few English Law teachers who espoused the American case method of teaching common law subjects. This makes demands upon the students, in terms of preparation and preparedness to talk in class, that many are too timid or too lazy to risk. So it takes special skills from the teacher to get them to engage and to engage successfully, as of course Margot Brazier did.

The experience was part of developing her into a first rank Tort lawyer, eventually becoming general editor of *Clerk & Lindsell*, the major doctrinal work on Tort Law to which all practitioners turn for the answers to their problems, and taking over the editorship of Street's own academic textbook on *Torts* after his sudden death in 1984. Doctrinal legal scholarship is, or ought to be, the foundation of all academic legal study. As Peter Birks has put it, 'there is no body of knowledgeable data which can subsist as a jumble of mismatched categories. The search for order is indistinguishable from the search for knowledge.'[1] Margot Brazier is, first and foremost, an excellent doctrinal lawyer. She could not be such a formidable critic of our humble judicial efforts were it not so. But there are at least two reasons why she is much more than that.

First, she has been at the forefront of the development of a new category of legal analysis, a new search for order among the jumble of mismatched categories. Like others in this book, I prefer to think of it as 'healthcare law' rather than simply 'medical law': the relationship between doctors and their patients is only a small part of a vast area of human and legal activity which has something to do with medicine and health. But saying that reveals the difficulty: doctrinal legal scholars have always, and rightly, been suspicious of categories labelled 'law and . . . ': 'law and social welfare', 'law and accounting', 'law and medicine', and so on. Where, they say, is the coherent conceptual framework which makes this a proper field of study, as opposed to a collection of more or less interesting instances? Without such a framework, is it not simply a non-law practitioners' tool, something they may need to know for professional purposes, but not a fit subject for academic study? Where do we find the underlying principles which enable lawyers to reason from one instance to the next?

---

1 *English Private Law* (OUP 2000) preface.

There are several kinds of answer to such questions. One is that a subject area becomes academically interesting once academics become interested in it – it is only the academics who can tease out the principles and begin to help the lawyers and the courts to reason from one case to the next. The development of the law of consent to medical treatment from *Sidaway*[2] to *Montgomery*[3] is surely an example of that. Another answer is that the contextual study of how the law works can reveal the discrepancies, the incoherence, the mismatch between how the law treats one situation and how it treats another which many might think comparable in principle. The law's intensely pragmatic approach to the status of gametes and embryos is surely an example of that. Yet, another answer is that the search for legal order is only part of the journey to understanding the law, let alone to developing it or moving it on to a better place. For that, the lawyer needs to develop an understanding of how the other actors think, feel and behave. The presence, or absence, of law in the thinking, feeling and behaviour of everyone involved in end-of-life decision-making is surely an example of that. Margot Brazier has written seminal work on these and many other topics discussed in this collection, which is not only a fitting tribute to her pioneering work, but also a demonstration of all that is exciting in the subject which she helped to create.

She has triumphantly provided all these kinds of answer to the sceptics' questions in the course of her academic career. She has shown how doctrinal legal rigour, combined with critical contextual thinking, and an acute understanding of many differing professional and personal perspectives, can advance a subject. She has been at the forefront of multi-disciplinary working in many areas. But she has done much more than that, because she has taken these academic virtues into the world outside the academy – as the editors put it, moving beyond the 'I think', which is the privilege of the academic, into the 'group think',[4] which is essential in building a consensus, and thus moving the law forward. Her work in chairing the Retained Organs Commission is but one example of her skills in achieving this, but it also exemplifies the values which she brings to all she does. It all adds up to what Marleen Eijkholt and Ruth Stirton call 'the Brazier method':[5] recognising the humanity of everyone involved in the delivery and receipt of healthcare, their strengths as well as their weaknesses, the reality of the dilemmas they face and the settings in which they face them.

It is a world in which those receiving care have responsibilities, to those providing the care, to themselves, to their families, as well as rights; in which parents and parents-to-be have responsibilities to one another, to themselves

---

2 *Sidaway v Board of Governors of the Bethlem Royal Hospital* [1985] AC 871.
3 *Montgomery v Lanarkshire Heath Board* [2015] UKSC 11, [2015] 2 WLR 768.
4 See the introductory chapter by Stanton, Devaney, Farrell and Mullock in this collection, at p. 5.
5 See the chapter by Eijkholt and Stirton in this collection, at p. 170.

and to their child or child-to-be; in which healthcare professionals have responsibilities to one another as well as to their patients and their patients' families. It is a world in which moral responsibility is at least as important, if not more important, than legal responsibility, a world in which the processes of the law cannot solve every problem, but human beings may stand a better chance of doing so. Margot Brazier is, and has been ever since I have known her, a frighteningly moral person.

My own journey led me from academic life in the University of Manchester to promoting the reform of the law at the Law Commission, to judging, first in Mental Health Review Tribunals, then part-time in the Crown and county courts, and eventually full-time in the higher courts. I often regret that Margot did not follow a similar path: had she done so, I might not now be bewailing the lack of female company on the Supreme Court. I can think of few academic lawyers who would be better qualified to serve on the Supreme Court bench . . . and, come to think of it, she is still quite young enough to do so!

Margot Brazier: Editors' appreciation

Sitting at a conference dinner in April 2014, the editors of this collection reflected on our immense good fortune to have worked with Margot Brazier. She has been, and continues to be, not only a pioneer in legal scholarship, both in the UK and internationally, but also a wonderfully wise colleague and friend to us and to so many others. Out of that conversation over dinner, this edited collection was born. We knew that the warmth and esteem in which Margot is held meant that there would be no shortage of contributors. To try to include as many as possible, we decided to reflect the collaborative approach which has been characteristic of Margot's work. As a result, the contributions to this book cross disciplines, academic institutions and even continents. Indeed, their number attests to the high esteem in which Margot is held as an academic, colleague and friend. In the paragraphs that follow, we offer a short appreciation of Margot, reflecting on her scholarship, teaching and achievements both at the University of Manchester (Manchester) and beyond.[1]

Margot and Manchester

Margot first came to Manchester to study law as an undergraduate. She completed her degree, graduating in 1971. Her initial career plan was to go to the Bar, but, given her relative youth at the time, she decided she would wait a couple of years before doing so. In this interim period, she joined the Faculty of Law (now School of Law) as a lecturer. An added attraction of taking up this position was that it gave her the opportunity to work with Professor Harry Street, a leading jurist whose work she much admired. This career decision would also have a key impact upon Margot's personal life, as she would subsequently marry one of her colleagues, Rodney Brazier, in 1974. Together, the Braziers have remained at the heart of the School of Law at Manchester for over 40 years. Although Margot did go on to qualify as a barrister, she did not

---

1 We would like to thank Margot for agreeing to be interviewed by Sarah Devaney and Alexandra Mullock, two of the editors of the collection, about her academic life, teaching and research.

end up going to the Bar. Margot's change of heart can be attributed to the birth of her daughter, Vicky. At that time (and arguably still), it was very difficult to combine motherhood with the life of a barrister, and fortunately Margot was very much enjoying her work at Manchester and so she set her sights on a career in academia.

Early research

Margot's early research was in the field of tort and, in particular, professional negligence.[2] As a result of her expertise in this area, she became co-editor of *Clerk & Lindsell on Torts* and *Street on Torts*.[3] It was her work in tort that led to her reading North American case law on medical malpractice and 'informed consent'. Such reading provided the initial spark that would lead to her growing interest in law and medicine and her subsequent pioneering work in what is now known as healthcare law. Margot also drew inspiration from the work of Peter Skegg, whom she describes as a key influence in her early work in the burgeoning field. In particular, she recalls reading his work on the law relating to dead bodies,[4] and she admired the way in which he wove a critical understanding of the underlying issues with the practicalities of the law: a skill at which Margot herself is so adept.[5]

A commitment to collaboration

In 1983, a seminal meeting took place. At a Manchester philosophy seminar on the topic of 'test tube babies', Margot met John Harris.[6] They discovered they shared a number of common interests, and a highly influential academic collaboration and partnership began. Together with colleagues, Tony Dyson and Mary Lobjoit, they came together to develop a Masters (MA) degree in healthcare ethics and law, which would run across the four Manchester faculties of which they were then members.[7] In 1986, the Centre for Social Ethics and Policy (CSEP) was founded to create a base for the MA, as well as to develop teaching and research in the area. Margot recalls that the MA's first intake comprised four full-time students – two nurses, a doctor and a lawyer – together

---

2 See M Brazier, 'Surveyors' Negligence – A Survey' (1981) Conv 96.
3 Both remain seminal texts in the field, now in their 21st and 13th editions, respectively, at the time of writing.
4 See PDG Skegg, 'Human Corpses, Medical Specimens and the Law of Property' (1975) 4 Anglo-Am L Rev 412.
5 See J Montgomery, 'The Compleat Lawyer – Medical Law as Practical Reasoning: Doctrine, Empiricism and Engagement' (2012) 20 Med L Rev 8.
6 Now internationally renowned bioethicist, Professor John Harris, Lord David Alliance Professor of Bioethics, Director of the Institute for Sciences Ethics and Innovation, University of Manchester.
7 For an overview, see M Brazier, A Dyson, J Harris and M Lobjoit, 'Medical Ethics in Manchester' (1987) 13 JME 150.

with three part-time students, all of whom were doctors. The MA, together with its distance-learning version, continues to flourish at Manchester. Two of the editors of this collection, together with hundreds of lawyers, doctors and academics are grateful graduates. Over time, CSEP has become an internationally renowned research centre in healthcare law and bioethics, attracting significant national and international research funding, as well as highly talented researchers and students.

A passion for teaching

Many academics have a preference for their role as either a teacher or researcher. Margot has always been passionate about both these aspects of her work. Those of us who have been taught by her have been fortunate to enjoy the fascinating and lively discussions she facilitates. This has often taken place through the use of exotic and colourful examples from case law or the 'real world', in which she selects members of her student audience to star! Margot also brings great humour to her teaching, and great compassion. No matter how busy, she always makes time to see her students individually. Deservedly, her enthusiasm, wit, and great kindness have brought Margot many teaching accolades over her 40-year plus career. Although she has taught across a number of areas of law, she has focused primarily on tort and healthcare law. In the latter field, she has been responsible for the design and delivery of numerous innovative course units. While healthcare law and related course units may be an accepted part of both undergraduate and postgraduate law curricula nowadays, Margot has pointed out that this was not always the case.

In the early 1980s, Manchester law students' growing interest in social issues led Margot to propose the teaching of a new course unit, 'Law, Medicine & Ethics'. This new course unit was designed to harness such interest and combine it with good legal training covering elements of tort, criminal, public and property law, encouraging students to critically examine issues across several legal areas. Not all of her colleagues were convinced that the proposal had merit at the time. Margot recalls that she faced strong opposition to running the unit and there was much debate at Faculty Board about whether it should be introduced. In the end, she obtained approval from the Board to run the elective unit by a single vote. However, it came with a caveat which was it would only run if 20 students enrolled. Happily, 80 students registered in its first year, and in its current incarnation remains one of the most popular undergraduate elective units for Manchester law students; so much so that a further elective unit has been added. Essential reading for such course units is Margot's textbook, *Medicine, Patients and the Law*.[8] Since it was first published in 1987, it has proved to be a wonderful resource for students and healthcare practitioners alike. While

---

8   Originally sole-authored by Margot, it is now co-written with Emma Cave, with the 6th edition in progress at the time of writing.

retaining the detail and high-level critique that such study requires, it remains accessible to a lay audience and a seminal work in the field.[9]

Leader, colleague and friend

This collection highlights the immense contribution Margot has made, and continues to make, to the field of healthcare law and to public policy.[10] In recognition of this, she has received a large number of honours and awards. They include an OBE (1997), Fellow of the Academy of Medical Sciences (2007), Queen's Counsel (honoris causa) (2008), Halsbury Legal Award for Academic Contribution (2013), and Fellow of the British Academy (2014). However, no appreciation of Margot's work would be complete without an acknowledgement of the immense contribution she has made to the lives of so many of us, both professionally and personally. We know she has provided encouragement and guidance to many, whether as colleagues or students. As female academics, we want to acknowledge with gratitude the support Margot has given us as a valued colleague, mentor and friend in pursuing our academic careers: she is indeed a 'paradigmatic female role model'.[11] She has always shown concern not just for our professional development but also for our wellbeing and that of our families. Margot is respected, valued and, most importantly, loved by many.

---

9 See M Brazier and E Cave, 'Why We Wrote . . . *Medicine, Patients and the Law*' (2008) 3 Clin Ethics 205.
10 See also 'Across the Spectrum of Medical Law: A Special Issue in Honour of Margaret Brazier' (2012) 20(1) Med L Rev 1–156.
11 Ibid, L Gostin, 'Foreword in Honour of a Pioneer of Medical Law: Professor Margaret Brazier OBE QC FMEDSCI', 4.

1 Pioneering healthcare law

Anne-Maree Farrell, Catherine Stanton, Alexandra Mullock and Sarah Devaney

Introduction

This collection of essays examines a range of current and future challenges for healthcare law, representing state-of-the-art scholarship in the field. It draws inspiration from the pioneering and highly influential work of one of the outstanding leaders in the field, Margaret Brazier. Brazier has led the way not only in terms of her intellectual rigour but also in her commitment to critically examining how law works (or does not work) in healthcare practice. This is evidenced in the diversity and qualitative depth of her scholarship, as well as in her extensive contributions to public policy and law reform. In this chapter, we explore the evolution and development of healthcare law, identifying Brazier's distinctive contribution to the field. We then provide an overview of the structure of the collection, which has been organised around five key areas in Brazier's scholarship, before offering some brief concluding comments.

The evolution and development of healthcare law

The study of law and its relationship to medicine was the central focus of early scholarship in the emerging field of what would become known as medical law in the 1980s. It drew predominantly on tort law, contract law and the criminal law which touched on, or otherwise sought to interpret, this relationship. Most of the interesting early cases in medical law emanated from North America, with English jurisprudence lagging far behind.[1] This began to change with a number of important cases decided by appellate courts. This included the well-known case of *Sidaway* where the House of Lords engaged in substantive analysis of the law of consent in medical treatment for the first time.[2] This landmark decision was subsequently critiqued in a seminal paper by Brazier, marking her place as a leading and influential thinker in this new field of legal study.[3]

---

1 I Kennedy, 'The Patient on the Clapham Omnibus' (1984) 47 MLR 454.
2 *Sidaway v Board of Governors of the Bethlem Royal Hospital* [1985] AC 871.
3 M Brazier, 'Patient Autonomy and Consent to Treatment: The Role of the Law?' (1987) 7(2) LS 169.

Much of the focus in medical law has been on examining the issues of autonomy and self-determination as encapsulated in the law of consent and further developed in line with human rights jurisprudence.[4] It has involved philosophical and conceptual analysis, together with the application of rights-based principles,[5] to inform a legal framework for regulating the relationship between doctors and patients.[6] Notwithstanding scholarly engagement with 'de-medicalisation' arguments,[7] the relationship between law and medicine, in particular doctor–patient relations, has been and will continue to be a core aspect of study in the field underpinned by engagement with (philosophical) bioethical critique.[8]

However, it is possible to discern a number of conceptual and analytical shifts within the field over time to encompass a broader examination of the role of law in health and medicine at both national and supranational levels. First, there were calls for a greater focus on the law governing the design and delivery of healthcare, rather than just the relationship between law and medicine.[9] Second, human rights principles became more explicitly part of scholarly thinking and analysis following the adoption of the *Human Rights Act 1998* and subsequent jurisprudence.[10] Third, the contribution of private law has clearly diminished over time. This has taken place as a result of the upsurge in public law, regulation and governance which intersects in increasingly diverse ways with health systems, services, technologies and delivery.[11] In this regard, the influence of European Union law on Member States' health systems has grown exponentially in recent years.[12] Fourth, there is growing scholarly interest in examining ethical, legal and social issues affecting health at the population level, both nationally and globally.[13] Finally, there has been a greater preparedness by scholars working

---

4 For an overview, see C Foster, *Choosing Life, Choosing Death: The Tyranny of Autonomy in Medical Ethics and Law* (Hart 2009); S McLean, *Autonomy Consent and the Law* (Routledge 2010).
5 Indeed, it has been argued that 'medical law is a subset of human rights law', see I Kennedy and A Grubb, *Medical Law* (3rd edn, Butterworths 2000) 3.
6 See J Montgomery, 'The Compleat Lawyer – Medical Law As Practical Reasoning: Doctrine, Empiricism, and Engagement' (2012) 20 Med L Rev 8, 10.
7 See for example S Sheldon, *Beyond Control: Medical Power and Abortion Law* (Pluto Press 1997).
8 For an overview of the relationship, see J Miola, *Medical Ethics and Medical Law: A Symbiotic Relationship* (Hart 2007).
9 J Montgomery, 'Time for a Paradigm Shift? Medical Law in Transition' (2000) 53(1) CLP 363.
10 See for example E Wicks, *Human Rights and Healthcare* (Hart 2007); T Murphy, *Health and Human Rights* (Hart 2013).
11 M Brazier and N Glover, 'Does Medical Law Have A Future?' in D Hayton (ed), *Law's Futures* (Hart 2000); AM Farrell et al., 'Regulatory "Desirables" for New Health Technologies' (2013) 21(1) Med L Rev 1–171 (special issue).
12 T Hervey and J McHale, *European Union Law: Themes and Implications* (CUP 2015).
13 J Coggon, *What Makes Health Public? A Critical Evaluation of Moral, Legal, and Political Claims in Public Health* (CUP 2012); L Gostin, *Global Health Law* (Harvard UP 2014).

in the field to incorporate theoretical insights and methodological approaches from a range of other disciplines, including feminist studies, sociology, regulatory studies and the behavioural sciences.[14]

While arguments have been put forward over time regarding the use of terminology to describe the field,[15] as well as its appropriate 'jurisdiction',[16] we would argue that the days of debating whether it should be recognised as a discrete sub-discipline within the legal academy are now over. In the 21st century, the study of law and regulatory governance involving health, (bio)medicine and related technologies is clearly thriving, producing rigorous and innovative scholarship together with engagement in policy debates and law reform. This has been in no small measure due to the outstanding scholarship and leadership shown by Brazier.

Brazier: Academic scholarship and contribution to healthcare law

In the context of her scholarship, Brazier's pioneering and distinctive contribution lies firmly within the field of healthcare law. We use this descriptor advisedly here: much of her work has focused on examining ethical, legal and social issues in healthcare, particularly as they involve and impact upon patients and their families. In adopting this focus, recurring themes in her scholarship in this area have included how we should conceptualise autonomy and responsibility.[17] In doing so, Brazier demonstrates the multi-disciplinary approach evident in other areas of her work, drawing on the work of ethicists and philosophers.[18] For Brazier, autonomy is not an opportunity for individuals to seek to satisfy their preferences without concern for others. Exercising autonomy and being responsible for the choices we make involves consideration of how our choices will impact on others.[19] Thus, although Brazier is known for her championing of

---

14 See for example R Fletcher et al., 'Legal Embodiment: Analysing the Body of Healthcare Law' (2008) 16 Med L Rev 321; M Quigley, 'Nudging for Health: On Public Policy and Designing Choice Architecture' (2013) 21 Med L Rev 588. On the use of qualitative research methodologies, see for example B Farsides and R Scott, 'No Small Matter for Some: Practitioners' Views on the Moral Status and Treatment of Human Embryos' (2012) 20(1) Med L Rev 90; chapters by Birchley and Huxtable, Farrell & Devaney in this collection.
15 See for example Montgomery (n 9), D Morgan, *Issues in Medical Law and Ethics* (Cavendish 2001) ch 1; T Hervey and J McHale, *Health Law and the EU* (CUP 2004) ch 1.
16 K Veitch, *The Jurisdiction of Medical Law* (Ashgate 2007).
17 See for example M Brazier, 'Liberty, Responsibility, Maternity' (1999) 52 CLP 359; M Brazier, 'Do No Harm – Do Patients Have Responsibilities Too?' (2006) 65(2) CLJ 397.
18 See for example Brazier (2006) (n 17).
19 Ibid 400–1. See further JK Mason, 'Autonomous Humanity? In Tribute to Margaret Brazier' (2012) 20(1) Med L Rev 8; the chapter by Laurie and Mason in this collection where they suggest that a better description of Brazier's approach would be 'humane autonomy' instead of 'autonomous humanity'.

enhanced patient autonomy, she recognises that this comes with responsibility in terms of a partnership in healthcare decision-making with doctors and other healthcare professionals. Although optimistically committed to realising the ideal of the 'therapeutic alliance',[20] she maintains a healthy scepticism, as well as a keen critical eye, as to how abstract ethical principles and pronouncements from medico-legal elites may clash with the day-to-day reality of the clinic.

While understanding of the difficulties and pressures that doctors face in the professional cultures and institutional environments in which they work,[21] she nevertheless places the 'humanity' of key actors in healthcare (in particular patients and their families) at the forefront of her analysis of legal and ethical conundrums in clinical practice. 'Humanity' is a recurring theme in and across key areas of Brazier's research. It is employed as a useful heuristic device for both conceptual analysis[22] and what has been described as her unique methodological approach.[23] In the former case, the term seeks to capture the complexity and interconnected nature of relationships in healthcare settings and how they play out in decision-making, treatment and outcomes. While not exhaustive, it includes human vulnerabilities, foibles and preferences, as well as providing the basis for claims about the importance of partnership, respect and dignity in healthcare settings.

In the latter case, Montgomery neatly sums up the 'key characteristics' of Brazier's methodological approach, drawing upon one of her seminal papers on informed consent and the law:[24]

> A concern with the role of law in facilitating effective healthcare, as well as protecting patients' rights; an interest in the reliability of the assumptions made about the reality of clinical practice [so as to ensure that policy draws on a firm evidence base]; a healthy cynicism about the consequences of legal interventions; an awareness of the need to develop tailored responses [that fully address the problem at hand, rather than just relying on 'hard' law].[25]

---

20 H Teff, 'Consent to Medical Procedures: Paternalism, Self-Determination or Therapeutic Alliance?' (1985) 8 LQR 432.
21 This is evidenced in some of Brazier's scholarship examining the impact of criminalisation of doctors for medical malpractice, see M Brazier and N Allen, 'Criminalizing Medical Malpractice' in C Erin and S Ost (eds), *The Criminal Justice System and Health Care* (OUP 2007); M Brazier and A Alghrani, 'Fatal Medical Malpractice and Criminal Liability' (2009) 25 PN 51.
22 See for example M Brazier, 'Retained Organs: Ethics and Humanity' (2002) 22 LS 550; Mason (n 19).
23 Montgomery (n 6) 10, 12–14; see also Eijkholt and Stirton in this collection.
24 Brazier (n 3). Note that Gostin views Brazier's 'rigorous scholarship' on informed consent as contributing to the concept becoming the 'most robust legal idea in medicine and health care during the late twentieth century': see L Gostin, 'Foreword in Honour of a Pioneer of Medical Law: Professor Margaret Brazier OBE QC FMEDSCI' (2012) 20(1) Med L Rev 1, 2.
25 Montgomery (n 6) 11–12.

Brazier's approach is in contrast to other leading scholars in the field who could be said to have focused on a more 'top-down' approach to principles-based development, which is abstracted from the day-to-day reality of the clinic and the lives of patients and their families.[26] Instead, Brazier employs this distinctive approach to confront some of the more difficult ethical and legal dilemmas that arise in the clinic. While revealing an empathetic understanding of the humanity of key actors, this is never done at the expense of intellectual rigour in tackling what Biggs et al. have described as the 'hard questions: questions that challenge her own views and moral position'.[27] Brazier has never been intellectually shy in rising to such a challenge, nor in asking her fellow scholars to do likewise.[28]

Brazier: Public service engagement and leadership

Healthcare law often deals with issues affecting life and death (and much in-between) that are strongly contested and directly engage with the public and political spheres. Indeed, we would suggest that one of the more rewarding aspects of working in this field is that it offers both challenges and opportunities to contribute to, or otherwise have an impact upon, policy-making and law reform in relation to such issues. However, we suggest it requires a certain disposition and approach to be successful in such engagement. In academia, we are encouraged to engage in 'I think': putting forward our own arguments on particular issues, as well as unpacking and critiquing those of others. We develop high-level conceptual and analytical skills in so doing, underpinned by experience and expertise in our respective fields. If we choose public engagement, then a different paradigm for analysis and decision-making presents itself. Academics must participate more in 'group think': this may involve conflict, catharsis, collaboration and (hopefully) consensus. Brazier is that relatively rare phenomenon in academia: not only is she an outstanding scholar who has made a pioneering contribution to her field, but she has also made an equally outstanding contribution as a public intellectual and leader in policy debate and law reform.

In terms of the skill set required for this latter work, what can we glean from Brazier's leading roles in bodies examining surrogacy,[29] human tissue/organs retention[30] and neonatal medicine?[31] First, you must have an in-depth

---

26 Montgomery (n 6) 10, 12–14.
27 H Biggs et al., 'Editorial for Across the Spectrum of Medical Law: A Special Issue in Honour of Margaret Brazier' (2012) 20(1) Med L Rev 6.
28 Brazier issued such a challenge when she took on the role of Editor-in-Chief of the *Medical Law Review*, the leading peer-reviewed journal in the field, see M Brazier, 'Editorial: Times of Change?' (2005) 13(1) Med L Rev 1.
29 *Surrogacy: Review for health ministers of current arrangements for payments and regulation – Report of the review team*, Cm 4068 (Department of Health 1998).
30 See Retained Organs Commission, *Remembering the Past, Looking to the Future: The Final Report of the Retained Organs Commission including the Summary Accountability Report for 2003/2004* (Department of Health 2004).
31 Nuffield Council on Bioethics, *Critical Care Decisions in Fetal and Neonatal Medicine: Ethical Issues* (Nuffield Council on Bioethics 2006).

understanding of the law but you must also understand its limitations and retain a healthy scepticism regarding its interpretation and application in practice. Second, you must have an appreciation of the diverse ways in which law can be used as a mechanism of social control; this may require a range of soft and hard legal options to be employed for the purposes of consensus building, effective reform and desired behaviour change. Third, you must incorporate values-based analysis that draws on a sound evidence basis. This requires taking account of the real life experiences of those who work within (or work around) the law as it stands.[32] Fourth, you must recognise the importance of a multi-dimensional approach to the process of policy and law reform. This includes consultation and respect for differing stakeholder views; an appreciation of the importance of being listened to and heard; the ability to show due deference to, and to work within, imposed terms of reference; and the capacity to proceed in a timely and productive manner towards a specified outcome. Through her public service leadership, Brazier has offered a principled, yet pragmatic way forward in healthcare policy and law reform that has had a significant impact upon law on the books, as well as law in practice. This makes her an exemplary role model for healthcare law scholars.[33]

Structure and key themes

The structure of this collection is organised around five key areas in Brazier's research. They are: key principles and themes in healthcare law and practice; patient–doctor relations; human tissue; reproduction; and the criminal process and healthcare practice. We asked contributors to engage (collaboratively where possible) with Brazier's scholarship either directly in terms of analysis or to otherwise use it as a springboard for engagement with their chosen topic. We have been amazed, and indeed inspired, by the breadth and depth of scholarship evident in the 24 chapters that form the substantive part of this collection. Not only is it a testament to the impressive range of topics in healthcare law with which Brazier has engaged over her long academic career, but it also makes clear what an intellectually engaging and innovative field of academic study healthcare law has come to be in the century.

Part 1: Key principles and themes in healthcare law

The first part of the collection engages with some of the theories and principles which underpin Brazier's work. As noted previously, this has included an exploration of the concepts of autonomy and responsibility. In their chapter, Laurie

---

32 Montgomery (n 6) 22–4.
33 In summarising the key aspects of Brazier's approach to public service engagement and leadership, we have drawn on Montgomery (n 6) 20–8, D Archard, 'Margot Brazier: Making a Difference' (2012) 20(1) Med L Rev 45, and the chapter by McHale in this collection.

and Mason draw on this work in order to critically reflect upon the meaning and scope of these two concepts, which they see as 'inseparable'. They argue that autonomy should be seen as 'tempered by the responsibilities to others that it implies'. It is an argument that is explored in the familial context (an area which has been of enduring scholarly interest for Brazier) by looking at two paradigmatic examples: the parent–child relationship and the genetic relationship.

The responsibilities generated by different relationships have also been considered by Brazier in the context of public health. In a seminal paper co-authored with her Manchester colleague, John Harris, they focused on the responsibilities of individuals in the context of communicable disease and the challenges this posed for the law in seeking to balance rights and responsibilities in this area.[34] Drawing inspiration from this paper, Glover-Thomas and Holm adopt a similar approach, combining both ethical and legal critique in examining the contested issue of vaccination. Against a backdrop of lower rates of immunisation leading to outbreaks of vaccine-preventable diseases such as measles, the authors question whether it could be morally justifiable to introduce mandatory vaccination. Their analysis focuses on the risks, benefits and burdens of routine vaccination to both individuals and society. They conclude that although it may be hard to introduce a strict mandate, whereby sanctions are applied for a failure to comply, the difficulty of controlling disease in an age of global travel means that 'reflection is needed about whether coercion may offer the way forward'.

Brazier's work has also touched on the ethically and legally challenging area of the law's approach to end-of-life decision-making. In high profile cases from *Bland*[35] to *Nicklinson*,[36] the courts have had to navigate this difficult territory against a backdrop of principles such as the sanctity of life, inviolability, autonomy and dignity. Writing together, Brazier and Suzanne Ost have suggested that the introduction of a new term, 'reverence for life', might 'bridge the gaps between the different philosophical attitudes'[37] and so facilitate better decision-making at the end of life. This suggestion is discussed in the chapter by Mullock and Heywood, who consider that the term has the potential to be developed further as a compromise between opposing philosophical positions and, in so doing, could provide a coherent approach for the law to adopt in this highly contested area. The thorny issue of end-of-life decision-making also emerges in McLean's chapter, which focuses on assisted dying. As McLean points out, although Brazier has largely avoided directly confronting the issue, much of her work does indirectly engage with concerns such as autonomy and

---

34 M Brazier and J Harris, 'Public Health and Private Lives' (1996) 4 Med L Rev 171.
35 *Airedale NHS Trust v Bland* [1993] AC 789.
36 *R (Nicklinson and another) v Ministry of Justice, R (AM (AP)) v DPP* [2014] UKSC 38.
37 M Brazier and S Ost, *Bioethics, Medicine and the Criminal Law Volume 3: Medicine and Bioethics in the Theatre of the Criminal Process* (CUP 2013) 89.

end-of-life decision-making, which are central to assisted dying. While 20 years ago Brazier urged caution and compromise rather than legal change,[38] McLean asks whether the evolution of the law and related social developments might have persuaded Brazier to change her mind on the issue.

The evolution and future of medical/healthcare law is important to Brazier. Writing in 2000, she and Glover considered whether medical law had a future, concluding that it did and that 'law's relationship with medicine and health will continue to provide fertile ground for scholars in 2050'.[39] Inspired by Brazier and Glover's work, Hervey considers the future of EU health law. She argues that whereas EU law is often seen to embody competition and consumerism, it also encompasses the protection of human rights and the promotion of solidarity and equality. While some EU health law already reflects these latter values and shows concern for the health of those in other parts of the world, Hervey suggests that there is significant potential for the EU and its laws to have a global impact by engaging with health issues at the population level. Coggon and Gostin also focus on the future of 'health' law. Drawing on their respective research in public health law and ethics, they argue that there is still a role for 'medical' law, with its focus on patients, doctors and others engaged in healthcare. However, for those concerned with health more broadly, discussion of the provision of healthcare can only provide part of the analysis. The authors therefore call for a broader disciplinary approach which takes account of a wider range of (public and private) actors, institutions and governance arrangements which influence health and wellbeing.

Part II: Patient–doctor relations

Brazier's research has also focused on the patient–doctor relationship, in particular the role of patients and the recurring themes of autonomy and responsibility.[40] In their chapter, Biggs and Ost take up the theme of responsibility, focusing on the issue of maintaining sexual boundaries in the patient–doctor relationship. Although healthcare practitioners have professional and ethical obligations to maintain such boundaries with their patients, they argue that patients who deliberately initiate such breaches should also accept some degree of moral responsibility. How we should conceptualise patient responsibility is further developed in Farrell and Devaney's chapter, in light of Brazier's suggestion that the 'empowerment of patients . . . brings responsibilities'.[41] They focus on the notion of empowerment as a key variable influencing the relationship between patient autonomy and responsibility. Drawing on findings from empirical research, they argue that there is a need to further expand upon Brazier's challenge to re-think the moral and legal dimensions of

---

38 M Brazier, 'Euthanasia and the Law' (1996) 52(2) *British Medical Bulletin* 317.
39 Brazier and Glover (n 11), 387.
40 Brazier (2006) (n 17).
41 Ibid 401.

patients' responsibilities by recognising the influential role played by cultures and practices in healthcare systems which act as barriers to patient empowerment.

For very young patients, the responsibilities of parents rather than the patient become crucial. Drawing on Brazier's academic scholarship and policy work relating to the care of neonates,[42] Birchley and Huxtable discuss the difficulties such cases can present. If parents and clinicians cannot agree on the 'best interests' of an infant, the case may be taken to court. Birchley and Huxtable echo Brazier's views that the adversarial nature of court processes can 'encourage rather than diffuse, conflict', as well as being financially and emotionally costly.[43] The authors therefore consider whether the use of Clinical Ethics Committees might offer a useful alternative forum for exploring ethically problematic issues that arise in such cases. In the final chapter in this section, Navarro-Michel builds on Brazier's call for more co-operative partnerships between patients and healthcare professionals.[44] She argues that the role of the family in healthcare decision-making, even for patients with capacity, should be regarded more positively. She suggests that we might learn from aspects of the Spanish approach where instead of viewing familial influence as potentially problematic, it is instead accorded great respect and significance.

Part III: Law, ethics and the human body

The consideration of legal and ethical challenges relating to the human body has been a recurring theme both in Brazier's research and in her public service engagement. As we entered the new millennium, the discovery that human tissue had been retained at The Royal Liverpool Children's Hospital and other locations in the UK caused a public outcry. It also led to great personal distress for those affected, in particular parents who found that their deceased children's organs had been kept without their knowledge or consent.[45] As a result of these events, the Retained Organs Commission was established in 2001, with Brazier as its Chair. Its remit was wide and included providing advocacy for affected families; management of the return of organs held by the National Health Service (NHS); and providing advice on law reform in the area.[46]

---

42 M Brazier, 'An Intractable Dispute: When Parents and Professionals Disagree' (2005) 13 Med L Rev 412. See also (n 31) above and also the subsequent professional guidelines which largely adopted the recommendations of the Nuffield Council Report: BAPM, The Management of Babies Born Extremely Preterm at Less than 26 Weeks of Gestation (2008) Arch Dis Child – FNN Online first: published October 6 2008.
43 Brazier (n 42).
44 Brazier (n 3).
45 D Madden, '"Not Just Body Parts and Tissues" – Organ Retention, Consent and the Role of Families' (2012) 1 Socio-Legal Studies Review 1.
46 Department of Health, Retained Organs Commission <http://webarchive.nationalarchives.gov.uk/+/www.dh.gov.uk/en/Aboutus/MinistersandDepartmentLeaders/ChiefMedicalOfficer/ProgressOnPolicy/ProgressBrowsableDocument/DH_501600> (accessed 25 March 2015).

The Commission's valuable work and its findings fed into the enactment of the Human Tissue Act 2004, which now regulates the acquisition, retention and use of human tissue in England. In her chapter, McHale reflects upon the work of the Commission and its legacy, drawing upon interviews with Brazier and other former members of the Commission. McHale highlights the many challenges the Commission faced and the role it played in promoting respect and the importance of consent, which is now embodied in the 2004 Act. She argues that they are principles which both healthcare professionals and other stakeholders must continue to take into account in order to ensure that lessons learned from the work of Brazier and the Commission are not lost.

As in other areas of her research, Brazier has been keen to examine the principles (or the lack thereof) underlying the law relating to human tissue. In 2002, she criticised the lack of generalisable principles governing the circumstances in which the common law should recognise property rights in biomaterials. In her typical style, she commented that: 'If that represents the law, [then] the law is an ass.'[47] In their chapter, Quigley and Skene ask if this is still the case. Following a review of the relevant law, they conclude that the law is not as 'asinine' as it once was. However, they caution that developments in biotechnology may mean that there will be continuing challenges for the law in this area.

In a chapter that embraces Brazier's unique approach to some of the most challenging dilemmas in healthcare law, Eijkholt and Stirton argue that Brazier's contribution to the legal academy warrants greater jurisprudential attention. Identifying a 'Brazier Method' for resolving ethical and legal dilemmas concerning organs and other human tissue, they consider how her appreciation of, and respect for, the humanity of all parties enhances the quality of solutions proposed. Indeed, in a theme that runs through the collection, they recognise Brazier's commitment to seeking a mutually acceptable and reasoned compromise to such dilemmas where possible. They argue that the way in which Brazier places the humanity of key actors at the centre of proposals for a pragmatic solution has the potential to be applied beyond the field of healthcare law. They suggest that the importance of Brazier's work lies in the fact that she never lets us forget that legal dilemmas and challenges are not just academic exercises, but are firmly rooted in the lives of 'real', often vulnerable, people.

The final two chapters in this section focus on Brazier's interest in legal and ethical issues relating to human bodies, whether living or dead.[48] Giordano, Palacios-González and Harris explore the issue of sex change surgery for transgender minors, in circumstances where current authoritative guidelines recommend that it should only be performed on adults. They argue that where it is in the patient's best interests to have the surgery, doctors should be allowed to proceed with it, though they suggest they should first seek the

---

47 Brazier (n 22) 563.
48 S McGuinness and M Brazier, 'Respecting the Living Means Respecting the Dead Too' (2008) 28(2) OJLS 297.

approval of their peer professional body or the courts. Drawing on Brazier's penchant for generating lively scenarios through which to examine legal and ethical dilemmas, the last chapter in this section, by Brassington and Jones, invites readers to consider a number of important questions raised by Christopher Priest's novel *The Prestige*.[49] The book's plot includes a device that allows the magician to create a 'copy' of himself in another part of the theatre. The original version is left in the device, 'as if dead', thus raising questions about the moral and legal status of the 'source' bodies created during his shows and how they should be treated. This leads the authors to examine whether they are dead bodies subject to the legal requirement for a lawful and decent burial, or, alternatively, whether they exist in a form of vegetative state with consequent legal personality.

Part IV: Regulating reproduction

Brazier has written extensively on the law and reproduction, in circumstances where her oft-remarked-upon prescience about contested issues and future directions in the law is particularly noticeable. In her seminal paper, 'Regulating the Reproduction Business?',[50] which was written almost a decade after the Human Fertilisation and Embryology (HFE) Act 1990 had come into force, Brazier noted that there had been 'little conceptual depth' underpinning law in this area. Notwithstanding this position, a regulatory system was in place, perhaps suggesting that 'pragmatism has its advantages'.[51] Several chapters draw out themes from this paper, discussing their continuing relevance. This is despite the fact that both science and the legislation have evolved since Brazier's paper was published.

Fox and McGuinness reflect on distinctions which have been drawn between embryos, such as classing them as 'reproductive' or 'research' in order to create legal categories such as 'permitted' and 'unpermitted'. In so doing, the law has been able to regulate so that, for example, hybrid embryos can be created for research but cannot be implanted for reproductive purposes.[52] Fox and McGuiness see this as an example of the pragmatism of the law in this area, as highlighted by Brazier. The theme of pragmatism is also alluded to by Griffiths and Alghrani in their chapter examining human fertilisation and embryology law. They critically reflect on Brazier's observation that the law had 'little conceptual depth',[53] arguing that this remains the case today. Drawing on the examples provided by surrogacy and mitochondria replacement (MR), they discuss the law's inconsistencies: for example, that those conceived using donated gametes have a right to find out information about the donor, whereas no donor information will be available for those benefitting from the donation

---

49 C Priest, *The Prestige* (Gollancz 2011).
50 M Brazier 'Regulating the Reproduction Business?' (1999) 7(2) Med L Rev 166.
51 Ibid 167.
52 HFE Act 1990 (as amended), s 4(6).
53 Brazier (n 50) 167.

of mitochondrial DNA. Given that the UK has been the first country to allow MR in humans, and the fact that surrogacy is on the rise, they conclude that 'perhaps such pragmatic inconsistencies have their advantages'.

Another of Brazier's seminal papers was published in 1999. In 'Liberty, Responsibility, Maternity',[54] she argued that reproduction should be morally responsible and that the interests of the future child in having a 'decent life'[55] should be taken into account in such decision-making. Although Brazier does not demand the enforcing of any such moral obligations with regulatory measures, Archard suggests in his chapter that there are moral distinctions to be drawn between regulating the choices of the fertile and the infertile. This leads him to argue that in contrast to the cost of regulating the fertile, 'the costs of legally preventing the infertile from being irresponsible procreators are not so great as to outweigh the harms they might otherwise cause to the future child'. Scott also focuses on assisted reproduction and cites Brazier's observation that 'all too often crucial issues of individual rights, the balance between individual rights and public policy, and issues of conflicting rights are skated over'.[56] Scott explores such conflicting interests in the context of the licencing requirement under the HFE Act 1990 (as amended) that clinics must give information about 'the importance of informing any resulting child at an early age that the child results from the gametes of a person who is not a parent of the child'.[57] She explores whether this requirement should be considered part of the operation of the 'welfare' clause[58] or of the consent process, and whether it should be deemed a moral and/or legal requirement.

Concerns about child welfare are also at the heart of Brazier's conviction that reproduction brings responsibility which extends to a woman's conduct in pregnancy, once she has decided to carry that pregnancy to term. She cannot justify causing harm to the child in utero any more than to any of her children who have been born.[59] Yet, Brazier argues, this moral responsibility should not lead to legal responsibility because: '[w]e need to rediscover means of supporting and encouraging responsible choice without inevitably allowing the heavy boots of the law to trample over private choices'.[60] To explore whether these 'heavy boots' are still evident today, Fovargue and Miola consider a line of 'enforced caesarean' cases from the 1990s to the present. They analyse several recent cases where the delivery options of women being treated under the Mental Capacity Act 1983 were considered. They note the prescience of a comment made by Brazier in a paper published following *St George's Healthcare NHS*

---

54 Brazier (1999) (n 17).
55 Ibid 373.
56 Brazier (n 50) 167.
57 HFE Act 1990 (as amended), s 13(6C)(a).
58 Ibid s 13(5).
59 M Brazier, 'Parental Responsibilities, Foetal Welfare and Children's Health' in C Bridge (ed), *Family Law Towards the Millennium: Essays for PM Bromley* (Butterworths 1997) 272.
60 Brazier (1999) (n 17) 391.

Trust v S,⁶¹ where she noted that 'the conclusion, or news of a conclusion, to the story is premature ... in terms of legal analysis because other issues where liberty and procreative responsibility conflict remain to be resolved'.⁶² They conclude that Brazier's analysis is still valid today since '[t]he question of *how* we address moral duties to the foetus without seeing them leak into legal ones remains unanswered'.

Part V: The criminal law and the healthcare process

In recent years, Brazier's principal research has focused on the role of the criminal law in the healthcare process.⁶³ In yet another example of Brazier's impressive intuition, her collaborative work on this topic, which considered extending the scope of the offence of wilful neglect to protect all patients,⁶⁴ is now reflected in recently adopted legislation in the area.⁶⁵ Having established that the role of the criminal law in healthcare has been much neglected, Brazier's recent scholarship on the topic has provided the inspiration for the chapters in this section. In the first chapter, Keywood and Sawicka review Brazier's scholarship which touches on the issue of patient (or individual) vulnerability. They suggest that themes found in Brazier's early writing on the issue continue to resonate in her more recent work on the role of the criminal law in healthcare. They examine the new offence of ill-treatment and wilful neglect by care workers and care providers, together with pre-existing offences under the Mental Capacity Act 2005 and the Mental Health Act 1983. They argue that while use of the criminal law will provide some safeguards for the vulnerable, the focus on such offences must not detract from 'the importance of other legal domains acting to foster resilience in the structures, environments and circumstances of those who are rendered vulnerable in their health and social care encounters'.

Reflecting on Brazier's work on the criminalisation of breaches of healthcare obligations,⁶⁶ the chapter by Gurnham and Ashworth suggests that those who cite her work in support of widening the remit for criminalising the sexual transmission of disease do so without fully appreciating the nuances of her analysis. Exploring the recent English Court of Appeal judgment in *R v Golding*,⁶⁷ which confirmed that recklessly transmitting herpes contravenes section 20 of the Offences Against the Person Act 1861, they argue that the Court failed

---

61 *St George's Healthcare NHS Trust v S, R v Collins, ex parte S* [1998] 3 WLR 936, CA.
62 Brazier (1999) (n 17) 359–60.
63 See for example, Brazier and Ost (n 37).
64 There are pre-existing offences under the Mental Capacity Act 2005 concerning those lacking capacity, and under Mental Health Act 1983 for those with a mental disorder. See A Alghrani, M Brazier, AM Farrell et al., 'Health Care Scandals in the NHS: Crime and Punishment' (2011) 37(4) JME 230.
65 Criminal Justice and Courts Act 2015, ss 20–25.
66 Brazier (2006) (n 17).
67 [2014] EWCA Crim 889.

to address important concerns associated with imposing criminal liability, such as fault, harm and causation. Gurnham and Ashworth suggest that such wider policy issues should be addressed by a Supreme Court ruling on the case or examined in detail by the Law Commission as they consider this area of law.[68]

The reach of the criminal law is also the theme of the chapter by Cave and Stanton where they reflect on Brazier's work on the issue of maternal responsibility. They consider its continuing relevance in the context of the recent English Court of Appeal judgment in *CP Criminal Injuries Compensation Authority*,[69] which generated debate as to whether the criminal law has a role to play in regulating the conduct of pregnant women. Cave and Stanton reflect on Brazier's analysis, agreeing with her perspective that the application of the criminal law is not appropriate in this context. Although the Court of Appeal closed the door on the potential criminalisation of maternal conduct in some circumstances, the authors argue that further clarification of the law is needed. Finally, Brownsword and Wale reflect on Brazier and Ost's discussion of the Abortion Act 1967 where they suggest that 'medicalisation plays a useful if often criticised role in mediating between the polarized extremes of bioethical debate . . . offer[ing] a way forward that is less than intellectually first class, but better than the practical alternatives'.[70] Through this process, which Brownsword and Wale term 'compromise medicalisation', the medical profession is entrusted with the role of protecting the compromise agreed by the legislature. They argue that the compromise established by the 1967 Act has not held and that important lessons should be drawn from this experience when considering the use of 'compromise medicalisation' in other highly contested areas, such as the legalisation of assisted suicide.

Conclusion

This collection provides an opportunity to reflect on the past, present and future(s) of healthcare law. Brazier was there at its beginning, has played a seminal role in its development, and has been so prescient about its future directions that one might wonder where she keeps her crystal ball. She has written widely across many of the key topics that have underpinned theoretical and analytical developments within the field, which is attested to in the breadth and depth of the scholarship presented in the chapters that comprise this collection. Recurring themes of Brazier's work have included autonomy and responsibility, which have been accompanied by a keen understanding and recognition of the importance of taking account of the humanity of those involved at the intersection of ethics, law and social mores in healthcare practice. This has been

---

68 See Law Commission, *Reform of Offences Against the Person: A Scoping Consultation Paper*, Consultation Paper No. 217 (TSO 2014). Submissions in response to the paper had just closed at the time of writing.
69 [2014] EWCA Civ 1554
70 Brazier and Ost (n 37) 262–3.

underpinned by a methodological approach which takes account of such humanity in seeking to forge an acceptable compromise between a range of stakeholder views which is both principled and practical in its application.

This collection is also a testament to the fact that Brazier's scholarship and public service leadership springs from a truly open and inquiring mind, as well as a compassionate heart. Her pioneering spirit continues to demonstrate to others that they need not flinch from exploring challenging questions, and that to do so in a sensitive manner is not to shy away from robust intellectual enquiry. Having forged a groundbreaking path in the study and application of healthcare law, she delights in encouraging and joining others in their forays into considering what its future holds. For Brazier, that now involves going back in time to examine historical conceptions about the human body.[71] As always, the underlying aim is to challenge us to think more deeply and critically about key issues and rationales that underpin healthcare law scholarship, as well as its application in practice. The search for new frontiers goes on, and the mapping of unchartered intellectual territory awaits her incisive analysis. Pioneering work never ends; there is clearly much yet to come.

---

71 See Brazier and Ost (n 37); M Brazier, 'The Body in Time' (2015) 7(2) Law Innovation and Technology (in press).

Part I
Key principles and themes in healthcare law

2 Waxing and waning
The shifting sands of autonomy on the medico-legal shore

Graeme T Laurie and J Kenyon Mason

Introduction

This chapter must begin with a confession, or, at least, the confirmation of an open secret. We share with Margaret Brazier a deep scepticism about the law's ability to give appropriate and meaningful moral force to the fundamental ethical principle of respect for autonomy. This will come as no surprise to any reader familiar with Brazier's work, or indeed ours. In this chapter, however, we want to combine forces (with the passive and unknowing input of Brazier by way of her scholarship) to argue that autonomy must come with responsibility. More particularly, this chapter focusses on autonomy within the family and the responsibilities that we all owe to each other within the family unit as genetically, and more socially, defined.

This choice of context is apt for a number of reasons. First, it reflects much of the scholarly contribution that Brazier has made over the decades to both medical law and family law. Second, the familial context provides a setting like no other in which to confirm John Donne's oft-quoted aphorism that 'no man is an island'. This is something that the law seems signally incapable of grasping, although there is development as we argue below. Third, family relationships provide us with a particularly acute example of our necessarily social selves; we are dealing here not only with interconnections of individuals but also with pluralities of autonomies. Self-evidently, navigating such a social space cannot be done by reference to autonomy alone, yet the law often persists in a worldview that purports to do precisely this. We will demonstrate this through two paradigm examples of family relationships: the parent–child relationship and the genetic relationship. We will argue that medical law as it relates to the family can be best justified, and given greatest moral force, if we see autonomy as something that can be, and is, *tempered* by the responsibilities to others that it implies.

Brazier on autonomy and responsibility

Brazier began her 2006 contribution to the *Cambridge Law Journal* with the following quote:

> Towards the end of his judgment in *R. v. Collins and Ashworth Hospital Authority ex p. Brady*, Kay J. (as he then was) delivered the following

homily: 'it would seem to me a matter of deep regret if the law has developed to a point in this area where the rights of a patient count for everything and other ethical values and institutional integrity count for nothing'.[1]

Brazier went on to argue that Kay J. *may* have been right. She lamented the dominance of autonomy that has arisen in medical law in the last few decades at the expense of other ethical imperatives such as beneficence, non-maleficence and justice. This trend has been well documented by many scholars.[2] Margot's ethical normative standpoint came easily: '[p]atients, people, have responsibilities to others which we neglect at our peril.'[3] However, her qualification as to the correctness of the honourable judge in *Brady* came not from ethical vacillation, but from the law itself: 'determining when the law should step in to enforce such responsibilities is much more difficult.'[4]

Let us begin with the points on which we agree with Brazier. Her position, as she herself points out, developed from the thinking of ethicists and philosophers such as Faden and Beauchamp,[5] and O'Neill,[6] who have long argued for a far richer notion of autonomy than is found in the current law of either the United Kingdom (UK) or the United States (US). Thus, elaborating on Faden and Beauchamp's view of autonomy as encompassing 'privacy, voluntariness, self-mastery, choosing freely, choosing one's own moral position and *accepting responsibility for one's choices*',[7] Brazier argued that this last point, naturally, requires at least consideration of how one's choices will affect others. This is a quite modest demand, and one that is fairly incontrovertible so far as it represents a defensible moral position. However, the question Brazier asked was whether the law should attempt to enforce such a position, or rather, whether it should provide remedies if (moral) responsibilities are not discharged – and, here, we take some issue. This is not because it is a bad question per se, but we suggest that it asks the *wrong kind* of question about the relationship between autonomy and responsibility. To have responsibility does not necessarily imply (or require) the availability of a legal remedy – which, in turn, implies that someone else has a right. Rather, it can imply that there is an imperative for a

---

1 M Brazier, 'Do No Harm – Do Patients Have Responsibilities Too?' (2006) 65(2) CLJ 397–422, 397.
2 See, for example, C Foster, *Choosing Life, Choosing Death: The Tyranny of Autonomy in Medical Ethics and Law* (Hart 2009), and J Herring and C Foster, 'Welfare means Relationality, Virtue and Altruism' (2012) 32(3) LS 480.
3 Brazier (n 1) 398.
4 Ibid.
5 R Faden and T Beauchamp (in collaboration with N King), *A History and Theory of Informed Consent* (CUP 1986).
6 O O'Neill, *Autonomy and Trust in Bioethics* (CUP 2002). And see O O'Neill, 'Some Limits of Informed Consent' (2003) 29 JME 4.
7 Faden and Beauchamp (n 5) 7.

richer – and thicker[8] – concept of autonomy itself. Brazier comes close to recognising this in her Cambridge article when she writes: '[m]y responsibilities may not translate into legal obligations. What identifying my ethical responsibilities may do is identify the limits of the obligation owed to me.'[9] It is this limiting or reconceptualising of the autonomy right – rather than the imposition of a (legal) responsibility – that we will now explore, beginning with the parent–child relationship.

Autonomy and the parent–child relationship

We have discussed Brazier's preoccupation with the interface between the legal and humanitarian aspects of autonomy elsewhere under the heading of autonomous humanity.[10] On reflection it probably would have been better to refer to 'humane autonomy', thus emphasising the close links between what we see as her unique brand of autonomy and what has become known as 'relational autonomy' or, more specifically, 'caring autonomy'.[11] It is trite to remark that circumstances alter cases, and one of the difficulties in accepting either of the latter concepts lies in their inconsistency. Somewhere along the line, its protagonists must allow room for a balancing argument between, on the one hand, the entrenched legal reliance on individualistic autonomy as a baseline and, on the other, the strong human instinct to care for our fellows. What living relationship is more powerful than that of parent and child? Mighty few. Our contribution in this respect is to suggest that, counter to the legal dynamic and the majority of discussion in the literature that are both focussed on recognising the growing autonomy of the maturing child, we must also recognise the equal importance of the developing responsibilities that come with this tenet. Thus, just as autonomy develops and we are more self-reliant, so too do our responsibilities accumulate, and we must be more cognisant of our immediate significant others and the impact of our choices on them.

As to autonomy per se, there is no dispute as to the upper end of the scale. Once a child has passed the age of 18, he or she becomes a legal adult and assumes individual autonomy and, given mental capacity, full sole responsibility for decisions as to health care.[12] It is clear, however, that development of capacity

---

8 See, for example, J Husted, 'Autonomy and a Right Not to Know' in R Chadwick, M Levitt, and D Shickle (eds), *The Right to Know and the Right Not to Know: Genetic Privacy and Responsibility* (CUP 2014), 24.
9 Brazier (n 1) 413.
10 J K Mason, 'Autonomous Humanity? In Tribute to Margaret Brazier' (2012) 20 Med L Rev 150.
11 For which, see K Löhmus, *Caring Autonomy: European Human Rights Law and the Challenge of Individualism* (CUP, 2015). For criticism of the distinction of relational autonomy, see S McLean, *Autonomy, Consent and the Law* (Routledge 2010) 214.
12 Family Law Reform Act 1969, s 1.

to make decisions for oneself is the result of a process. Essentially, then, the question of responsibility for the healthcare management of the maturing child resolves itself into the nature of the autonomy of the adolescent – and this has been one of Brazier's major target subjects.[13]

Although her seminal paper is now somewhat dated, we regard both the judicial and the statutory approach to adolescent autonomy as still unclear, and this is largely due to difficulties – and laxity – in definition. What is adolescence? Most certainly, it is not a single moment in time; it is a series of moments – a transitional time – and as such it is better thought of as a process of transition than as a stable state of being. Indeed, many adults would regard adolescence per se as being distinctly unstable! Thus, this period has been helpfully defined as 'the process of developing from a child into an adult'.[14] Given this, there is no logical distinction to be made between a child and an adolescent – the frequent allusion to the age of 16 in both English and Scots family law represents no more than a legal convenience dictated by the quest for clarity and certainty. Does it assist in the context of medical treatment, or does it merely cause confusion in the fields of parental responsibility and control of the legal minor as represented by the nearly-but-not-quite 16-year-old, or the even less clear liminal space[15] between 16 and 18? This uncertainty is, perhaps, best expressed in the Family Law Reform Act 1969 where s 8(1) empowers the consent of the 16-year-old to medical treatment while s 8(3) retains the effectiveness of any consent which would have been effective before the enactment of s 8(1) – which, as we have argued elsewhere, we believe is, basically, a reference to the parental responsibilities for legal minors.[16] The vast majority of medico-legal commentators, Brazier and ourselves included, deprecate the use of a calendar age as a measure of capacity – what matters is the patient's ability to understand the issues involved. We argue that this ability to understand includes the responsibility to appreciate the consequences of decisions on immediate significant others, most particularly family members. But how, then, have the courts grappled with this apparent conflict of interests introduced by statute? And is the problem, which distils into one between the individual autonomy of *children* and the caring autonomy of parents, finally resolved? We think not.

It is well-established that a review of the topic must start with *Gillick*,[17] where the rights of a *child*, who is deemed to be capable of understanding the process and its likely consequences, to consent to medical treatment were confirmed,

---

13 M Brazier and C Bridge, 'Coercion or Caring: Analysing Adolescent Autonomy' (1996) 16 LS 84.
14 *Concise Oxford English Dictionary* (11th edn, revised 2008) 17.
15 A 'liminal space' is a space in-between, deriving from the Latin *limen*, meaning threshold. See A van Gennep, *The Rites of Passage* (Routledge and Kegan Paul 1960), especially chapter 5 (Birth and Childhood) and Wellcome Trust Senior Investigator Award No. WT103360MA, University of Edinburgh.
16 JK Mason and GT Laurie, *Mason and McCall Smith's Law and Medical Ethics* (9th edn, OUP 2013) para 4.61.
17 *Gillick v West Norfolk and Wisbech AHA* [1985] 3 All ER 402, HL.

albeit by the narrowest of overall judicial support. It is equally well-known that the majority of resultant academic opinion was to the effect that the *Gillick* rule was, at least, undermined by the allied decisions in *Re R*[18] and *Re W*.[19] Enough ink has been spread over these cases as to render a further detailed description of them otiose in the present context. It is, however, relevant that we summarise our own, perhaps minority, view as to how far, if at all, they affect *Gillick*. We believe that they carry different messages. Insofar as locking and unlocking doors involves activity, Lord Donaldson's metaphor in *Re R* of multiple key holders to consent to treatment of minors certainly raises the implication that parents may legally interfere with the wishes of the mature – or *Gillick*-competent – minor, at least when it comes to refusal of treatment and care. The analogy was, however, replaced in *Re W* by that of the flak-jacket, the donning of which is a purely passive, protective exercise. Yes, the metaphorical ack-ack gunner is the litigious child, but we take issue with Brazier, who concluded that Lord Donaldson impliedly 'condemns' hospitals for accepting the protection offered.[20] Rather, he is opening the way to conscientious medical practice in the case of a vulnerable patient. *Re W* resolves a medical dilemma and *Gillick* is, thereby, undisturbed.

Clearly, then, whether or not the doctor accepts the proffered 'flak-jacket' depends to a large extent on the severity of the condition to be treated – and the end of the line is to be found in a clinical choice between life and death where the courts will, in general, prefer professional expertise to the autonomy of the *Gillick*-competent minor.[21] In fact, if our analysis is correct, the courts *need* be involved only rarely – when both the competent minor and his or her parents refuse treatment against strong medical advice,[22] or when parents plead responsibility and insist on treatment in the face of competent minor refusal. We suggest that there are ways to resolve these apparent conflicts that reduce the superficial dichotomisation of the issues at stake. If parents and child are in agreement as to the correct course of action, we have, arguably, an instance of 'family autonomy'. This is not a concept that is recognised by the British courts, but it has held sway in Ireland and has been deployed by the Supreme Court to support resistance to state-endorsed interference in family life.[23] This is not to suggest that this can never be overridden but, rather, that the unity of the family sets up a strong *prima facie* presumption – bolstered by the plurality of

---

18 *Re R (a minor) (wardship: medical treatment)* [1992] Fam 11.
19 *Re W (a minor) (medical treatment)* [1992] 4 All ER 627.
20 Brazier and Bridge (n 13) 87.
21 See, for example, the high profile case of *Re M (child: refusal of medical treatment)* [1999] 2 FLR 1097 – refusal of a heart transplant. And, in general, see E Cave, 'Maximisation of Minors' Capacity' (2011) 23 CFLQ 41.
22 For which, see the paradigmatic Jehovah's Witness case of *Re E (minor)* [1993] 1 FLR 386.
23 G Laurie, 'Better to Hesitate at the Threshold of Compulsion: PKU Testing and the Concept of Family Autonomy in Eire' (2002) 28(3) JME 136.

autonomies raised in one voice – that necessitates overwhelming evidence of benefit both to the child and to the family unit, before it can be legitimately set aside.

Contrariwise, where there is apparent conflict between parents and child, this is usually viewed as an expression of parental responsibility *versus* child autonomy. It need not be thus. For example, to encompass holistically the role of autonomy it might be preferable to consider the caring autonomy of the parents *together with* the individual autonomy of the child. Alternatively, we might consider the responsibilities of the parents towards their child with the responsibilities of the child towards his or her parents. What, we might ask, precisely are these responsibilities? At base, they are a duty to care about the consequences of our decisions on others, and to take this into account in decision-making. The common feature here – whether we cast the issues as autonomies *or* responsibilities – is the bond of care within the family unit. We suggest, moreover, that it is preferable to level the playing field by identifying what is at stake and thereby comparing like-with-like – for example considering, simultaneously, the range of responsibilities and the pluralities of autonomies. In turn, this can help to reveal shared concerns rather than contentious conflict. To do so might further assist in keeping the courts out of family life.

The child incapax

This still leaves open – indeed, raises – the question of parental *responsibility* for assuming the autonomous mantle of children who are unable to express themselves by reason of incapacity. This is a wide aspect of autonomy that involves the whole spectrum of the parent–child relationship, including that of the child *in utero*. It is now self-evident, for example, that a competent woman is under no obligation to alter her lifestyle for the benefit of her foetus,[24] nor has she an obligation to undergo treatment for that purpose.[25] But what if the maternal–foetal conflict is of a social – e.g. religious – rather than a medical nature? At what point does a maternal decision as to her foetus or neonate become irresponsible?[26] In the UK, a foetus has no legal rights until it is born alive, and this is also a tenet of European human rights law. But, what of the pregnant woman who chooses to continue pregnancy? What obligations does she owe to her *future* child? Indeed, what obligations do parents, in general, owe to their children as, hopefully, *future* autonomous persons?

---

24 *Re F (in utero)* [1988] Fam 122, and more recently *CP (a child) v Criminal Injuries Compensation Authority* [2014] EWCA Civ 1554.
25 *St George's Healthcare NHS Trust v S* [1998] 3 All ER 673.
26 This question should not be confused with the decision to terminate pregnancy within the law. We might, better, consider: at what point does government interference with foetal or neonatal autonomy become unacceptable? See S McLean and JK Mason, 'Our Inheritance, Our Future: Their Rights?' (2005) 13 Int J Child Rights 255.

Once again, we contend that autonomy and responsibility are inseparable concepts.²⁷ The relationship can be seen as one of ebb and flow, the *temporary* immaturity of the person being a strong influence on the force of the tide. As our maturity deepens, so our entitlement to recognition of autonomy strengthens. This fluid continuum, is not, however, one that law tends to recognise as robustly as it could. Law compartmentalises us into status silos of 'parenthood' and 'childhood', refusing to see that these are contingent states. The implications for responsibility and autonomy of recognising this are profound. Even so, there is now little doubt as to the common law understanding of responsibility for the welfare of the infant. Baker J. has recently expressed this without equivocation:

> It is a fundamental principle of family law in this jurisdiction that responsibility for making decisions about a child rest with his parents. In most cases, the parents are the best people to make decisions about a child and the State – whether it be the court, or any public authority – has no business interfering with the exercise of parental responsibility unless the child is suffering or is likely to suffer significant harm as a result of the care given to the child not being what it would be reasonable to expect a parent to give.²⁸

These words arose in the unusual case of Ashya King, whose parents found themselves at the uncomfortable end of both family and criminal law for seeking to act on their own view of their child's best interests by removing him from the UK in a desperate attempt to seek effective treatment.²⁹ The invocation of wardship jurisdiction and the European Arrest Warrant violently disrupted the family dynamic in this case. Our analysis suggests that the family-faced-with-futility scenario should not lightly be labelled in the category of abusers. This is because we argue here that parental responsibility should not be seen solely as provision of immediate term care; instead it should be viewed also as a charge to promote the chance of *future* autonomy. This extrapolation of Brazier's arguments, we wager, would lead many observers to take a very different view of such a troubling case and of the parent–child relationship more generally.

Responsibilities to autonomous others

It is a further truism that the bonds of family do not necessarily bind as tightly once the parenthood–childhood dynamic is a thing of the past. But, equally axiomatically, family ties connect us to others beyond the vertical maternal/

---

27 Thus emphasising the oft-forgotten fact that children develop increasing responsibility to their parents as they mature.
28 *Ashya King (a child), Re* [2014] EWHC 2964 (Fam), per Baker J at para 31.
29 Leading Article, 'Hard Cases', (2014) *The Times*, 2 September, 28.

paternal relationship. Horizontal connections to siblings, cousins, and even relatives-in-law, have moral meaning for a variety of reasons, but few are so potentially powerful as the genetic ties between us. This example provides the focus for the second half of this chapter, in which we intend to do no more than emphasise the reality that *some* forms of genetic information – such as highly predictive, recessive or dominant treatable disorders – can have significant consequences for our immediate family. This is true both in terms of the health and well-being of blood relatives who might have an interest in knowing 'familial' genetic information, and also for those related through law or by the common enterprise of continuing the family – that is, that future reproductive choices can also found claims to an interest in knowing familial genetic information.

We have argued elsewhere about the rights and responsibilities relating to genetic information, and we will not repeat those arguments.[30] Our contribution here is to suggest that ethics, professional guidance and, even, law are far more in alignment about giving effect to the responsibilities arising from the generation of genetic knowledge than the 'tyranny of autonomy'[31] caricature might lead us to believe. Brazier argued that 'a family member holding information crucial to the good health of his or her relatives owes an ethical obligation to consider sharing that information'.[32] This is extensively supported in the clinical[33] and ethical literature,[34] and it is a view with which we take little issue. However, and once again, whither the law in all of this? Brazier considered whether there is a legal *obligation* to share genetic information, examining, first, whether there is a duty of care in negligence to family members likely to be affected by genetic disease,[35] and second, whether there is a professional duty or discretion to disclose.[36] In typical prescient fashion, Brazier noted:

> If it is *my* relatives who are of [sic] risk because of *our* heritage, the responsibility to act to protect those family members is primarily mine. Professionals can and should inform and advise me to assist me to discharge my ethical

---

30 See G Laurie, *Genetic Privacy: A Challenge to Medico-legal Norms* (CUP 2002), and more recently, G Laurie, 'Recognizing the Right Not to Know: Conceptual, Professional, and Legal Implications' (2014) 42(1) J Med Law and Ethics 53, and G Laurie, 'Privacy and the Right Not to Know: A Plea for Conceptual Clarity', in Chadwick, Levitt, Shickle (n 8) 38.
31 We borrow here from the excellent title of C Foster, *Choosing Life, Choosing Death: The Tyranny of Autonomy in Medical Ethics and Law* (n 2).
32 Brazier (n 1) 410.
33 B Rahman et al., 'To Know or Not to Know: An Update of the Literature on the Psychological and Behavioral Impact of Genetic Testing for Alzheimer Disease Risk' (2012) 16(8) Genetic Testing and Molecular Markers 1, and J Hodgson and C Gaff, 'Enhancing Family Communication About Genetics: Ethical and Professional Dilemmas' (2013) 16 Journal of Genetic Counselling 16.
34 N Hallowell et al., 'Balancing Autonomy and Responsibility: The Ethics of Generating and Disclosing Genetic Information' (2003) 29 JME 74; M Parker and A Lucassen, 'Genetic Information: A Joint Account?' (2004) 329 BMJ 165.
35 We first considered this in G Laurie, 'Obligations Arising from Genetic Information – Negligence and the Protection of Familial Interests' (1999) 11 CFQ 109.
36 Brazier (n 1) 412–413.

responsibilities. I cannot shuffle off responsibility to them.³⁷ [emphasis in original]

More recently, this has been confirmed as a matter of everyday practice by the Joint Committee on Medical Genetics that has pointed out:

> there are significant practical hurdles in contacting a range of relatives who may be difficult to identify and locate. For these reasons, current UK genetic practice largely leaves the onus of communication with the individual first diagnosed.³⁸

Legal attention on the relevant rights and responsibilities has also increased since Brazier's own analysis, becoming bolder in the conviction that law *could* be made to enforce familial responsibilities. Thus, for example, we have Fay arguing for a common law duty of care on the part of clinicians when there is 'effective treatment' for an 'identifiable victim', i.e. first order family members at highest risk.³⁹ Similarly, Foster et al. have suggested that the balancing of human rights considerations under the Human Rights Act 1998 between Article 8 (right to respect for private and family life) and Article 10 (freedom of expression) – would 'mandate' that a version of a 'joint account model'⁴⁰ of familial genetic information be deployed.⁴¹ But, of course, herein lies the rub. The only UK case to consider the question – *ABC v St George's Healthcare NHS Foundation Trust* [2015] EWHC 1394 (QB) – refused to recognise autonomy and responsibility as inherently connected for fear of legal uncertainty.

Further afield, and in the context of data protection legislation, the European Article 29 Data Protection Working Party has indicated that:

> To the extent that genetic data has a family dimension, it can be argued that it is 'shared' information, with family members having a right to information that may have implications for their own health and future life . . . The precise legal consequences of this argument are not yet clear. At least two scenarios can be imagined. One is that other family members could

---

37 Ibid 413.
38 Royal College of Physicians, Royal College of Pathologists and British Society of Human Genetics, *Consent and Confidentiality in Clinical Practice: Guidance on Genetic Testing and Sharing Genetic Information* (2nd edn, 2011) https://www.rcplondon.ac.uk/sites/default/files/consent_and_confidentiality_2011.pdf (accessed February 2015).
39 M Fay, 'Informing the Family: A Geneticist's Duty of Care to Disclose Genetic Risks to Relatives of the Proband' (2011) 27(2) Prof Neg 97.
40 See Parker and Lucassen (n 34). Foster et al. suggest a modified version that reflects the communitarian and feminist-based argument in R Gilbar and S Barnoy, 'Disclosure of Genetic Information to Relatives in Israel: Between Privacy and Familial Responsibility' (2012) 31 New Gen and Soc 391.
41 C Foster, J Herring and M Boyd, 'Testing the Limits of the 'Joint Account' Model of Genetic Information: A Legal Thought Experiment' (2014) JME, Published Online First: 25 June 2014, doi:10.1136/medethics-2014–102142.

also be considered as 'data subjects' with all the rights that follow from this. Another option is that other family members would have a right of information of a different character, based on the fact that their personal interests may be directly affected. However, in both scenarios further options and conditions would have to be considered to accommodate the various conflicts that are likely to arise between the different claims of family members, either to have access to information or to keep it confidential.[42]

The Icelandic Supreme Court has already recognised the interest that a family member has in having a say over a deceased relative's personal data for the potential implications this might have for him or her.[43] Moreover, the current draft proposals for a European Data Protection Regulation now expressly mention 'genetic data' as a sub-set of 'personal data' to be protected,[44] albeit that they do not attempt to resolve the responsibility dilemma highlighted by the Article 29 Working Party (above). Our preference would be for express acknowledgement of the familial nature of (some) genetic information in *both* of the respects that we have argued for above, viz, not only that family members might have 'rights' as data subjects (albeit in a modified form), but also that the exercise of any rights with respect to 'personal' data can be curtailed if processing is necessary in the 'vital interests' of a family member. At present, the Data Protection Directive and the draft General Data Protection Regulation allow processing in the interests of a data subject or of the public interest, but this is insufficiently specific in the context of our present discussion. To incorporate this proposal would bring legal recognition to a social and medical reality that uniquely affects the family unit.[45] But, equally,

---

42 Article 29 Data Protection Working Party, *Working Document on Genetic Data* (2004) <http://ec.europa.eu/justice/policies/privacy/docs/wpdocs/2004/wp91_en.pdf> (accessed February 2015).
43 For discussion, see R Gertz, 'Is it "Me" or "We"? : Genetic Relations and the Meaning of "Personal Data" under the Data Protection Directive' (2004) 11(3) Euro J Health Law 231. Note, however, the provisions of the European Data Protection Directive do not extend to the personal data of deceased persons.
44 Draft Regulation of the European Parliament and of the Council on the protection of individuals with regard to the processing of personal data and on the free movement of such data (Brussels, 25.1.2012, COM(2012) 11 final), draft Articles 4(1), 4(10), 9(1), and 33(2).
45 For an excellent account on data, see M Taylor, *Genetic Data and the Law: A Critical Perspective on Privacy Protection* (CUP 2012). On inconsistencies between data and tissue, see G Laurie and S Harmon, 'Through the Thicket and Across the Divide: Successfully Navigating the Regulatory Landscape in Life Sciences Research' in E Cloatre and M Pickersgill (eds), *Knowledge, Technology and Law* (Routledge 2014) 121. The Article 29 Group has recently confirmed its view that 'health data also include "information derived from the testing or examination of a body part or bodily substance, including biological samples" [reflecting the draft General Data Protection Regulation]', see Letter from the Article 29 WP to the European Commission, DG CONNECT on mHealth <http://ec.europa.eu/justice/data-protection/article-29/documentation/other-document/index_en.htm> (5 February 2015).

we caution against putting too much faith in law, as the next example demonstrates.

Some jurisdictions have attempted to give legal effect to the responsibilities that vex us. We have discussed the position at common law in some of the US elsewhere.[46] More recently, Australia has legislated to amend its Privacy Act 1988 to allow disclosures of genetic information to family members for similar motives outlined herein.[47] The law now permits a healthcare organisation to disclose genetic information where it:

> reasonably believes that the use or disclosure is necessary to lessen or prevent a serious threat to the life, health or safety (whether or not the threat is imminent) of an individual who is a genetic relative of the individual to whom the genetic information relates . . . (s 5, introducing Schedule 3.2.1(e) to the Guidelines for National Privacy Principles about genetic information).

This move has, however, been subject to sustained criticism.[48] Technical and practical issues of drafting and legislative interplay have meant that actual action on information available to healthcare professionals is restricted, while definitional and ethical concerns plague the legislation. For example, what precisely does the term 'genetic' encompass, and is this different from 'familial' information? Furthermore, what will constitute a 'serious threat', and what of non-genetic relatives whose reproductive choices might also be impacted with significant downstream implications for future persons? Finally, and to return to an issue that has occupied us for many years, what about the important claim that some people would prefer *not* to know? We should be very careful in the climate of this discussion not to suggest that the relationship between responsibility and autonomy necessarily means that there is *always* a responsibility to attempt to *promote* autonomy. As our chapter title suggests: just as the moon has its influence on the tides, so too must we face the consequences of recognising more responsibilities when it comes to autonomies. Legal attempts to proscribe on the vagaries may be doomed to failure.

Conclusion

Our conclusion on this discussion of the interplay between medical law and family law neatly mirrors the position that Brazier has outlined in her work, and which we identify above: 'If it is *my* relatives who are of [sic] risk because

---

46 Mason and McCall Smith's *Law and Medical Ethics* (n 16) ch 7.
47 See the Privacy Legislation Amendment Act 2006.
48 W Bonython and B Arnold, 'Disclosure "downunder": Misadventures in Australian Genetic Privacy Law' (2014) 40 JME 168, and M Otlowski, 'Australian Reforms Enabling Disclosure of Genetic Information to Genetic Relatives by Health Practitioners' (2013) 21(1) J Law Med 217.

of *our* heritage, the responsibility to act to protect those family members is primarily mine.'[49] As we have argued, these responsibilities are essentially a *communal/familial* consideration, not restricted to genetic relations. Moreover, we favour only a marginal role for law in achieving this. As the last example demonstrates, even if we try to give effect to responsible conduct when it comes to promoting the autonomy of others, there is no substitute for taking moral responsibility for the ones we love. We sincerely hope that Brazier would agree.

49 Brazier (n 1) 413.

3 Compulsory vaccination
Going beyond a civic duty?

Nicola Glover-Thomas and Søren Holm

Introduction

In 1996, Margaret Brazier and John Harris published a paper, *Public Health and Private Lives*, which considered the legal and moral dilemmas surrounding the control of infectious disease posed for society.[1] In particular, they considered just how far society should enforce an obligation not to expose others to infection and argued that such obligations should be driven by a strong moral duty to protect others from harm. Indeed, they suggested that, in principle, where reckless transmission of disease occurred, it should be seen as part of a wider interpretation of reckless endangerment of others' safety. In the years following the publication of the paper, the tensions inherent within public health law discourse between the rights of individuals and the broader rights of the public has received relatively little attention. Yet, arguably, a number of debates have emerged over this time which have provoked further discussion within wider policy circles. One such debate centres on the increasingly significant global threat posed by reduced levels of immunisation against vaccine-preventable disease, leading to new outbreaks of measles becoming more commonplace.[2] This chapter considers this very threat and asks whether the adoption of a compulsory vaccination programme in the United Kingdom (UK) could ever be morally justified, and if it could, whether it should translate into a legal obligation.

Vaccination is one of the oldest, most important and effective tools in the public health toolbox.[3] Smallpox was eradicated by vaccination, and there is hope that polio will be eradicated as well in the not too distant future. In the UK, there is a comprehensive childhood vaccination programme covering a range of diseases, as well as specific vaccination programmes targeting the elderly

---

1 M Brazier and J Harris, 'Public Health and Private Lives' (1996) 4 Med L Rev 171.
2 The United States (US) was declared free of measles in 2000 by the Centers for Disease Control. However, a major nationwide outbreak of measles, with the main transmission of disease happening at Disneyland in California, is ongoing at the time of writing this chapter.
3 In this chapter, 'vaccination' refers to any immunisation against a communicable disease.

and other at-risk populations.[4] Ensuring adequate vaccination of children across the globe is also a major WHO target.[5] Most vaccination programmes are voluntary and require the consent of the person being vaccinated or, in the case of children, the consent of a parent or guardian before vaccination takes place. However, there are situations where there may be a case for compulsion or coercion, either because there is a public health crisis or because the goals of the vaccination programme cannot be achieved without a very high take-up of the vaccination. There is historical precedent for compulsory vaccination in a situation of perceived public health crisis. For example, vaccination against smallpox was compulsory in England between 1853 and 1907.[6]

Even in countries where vaccination is in principle voluntary there may be specific groups, for example healthcare professionals or teachers, that are strongly encouraged to be vaccinated and where official encouragement may border on coercion. For instance, UK medical doctors are advised by the General Medical Council to be 'immunised against common serious communicable diseases.'[7] A doctor who is not vaccinated against common serious communicable diseases and who harms their patients by transmitting the disease in question may thus face professional censure. There are also well-known examples where one group of people are vaccinated primarily to benefit another group. For example, the rubella component of the measles, mumps and rubella (MMR) vaccine is primarily incorporated in the vaccine to protect foetuses against the teratogenic effects of infection during pregnancy. Rubella (German measles) is in itself a mild disease, and we would not vaccinate against it just as a childhood disease. Boys receiving the MMR vaccine function as a conduit to the principal objective of herd immunity against rubella.

Vaccination reduces cases of infectious diseases by protecting the individual who has been vaccinated and by diminishing the likelihood of disease proliferation. As long as an adequate number of people have been vaccinated with a sufficiently effective vaccine, the transmission of disease can be slowed, or completely abolished. How large a proportion of the population that needs to be vaccinated to achieve a population effect varies from disease to disease.[8] In the UK, it is recommended that at least 95% of children receive both the MMR vaccine and booster to achieve herd immunity.[9] Recent measles outbreaks

---

4   See, for example, the 2013–14 Immunisation Schedule for England <www.gov.uk/government/uploads/system/uploads/attachment_data/file/227651/8515_DoH_Complete_Imm_schedule_A4_2013_09.pdf> (accessed 3 February 2015).
5   World Health Organization (WHO), *Global Vaccine Action Plan 2011–2020* (WHO 2013).
6   The Vaccination Act 1853 introduced compulsory vaccination of children. It was not until the Vaccination Act 1907 that it became possible for parents to self-certify an objection to vaccination of their children.
7   General Medical Council, *Good Medical Practice* (General Medical Council 2013).
8   For an overview of vaccine controversies and their consequences, see P Davies, S Chapman and J Leask, 'Antivaccination Activists on the World Wide Web' (2002) 87 Arch Dis Child 22.
9   W Moss and D Griffin, 'Global Measles Elimination' (2006) 4 Nature Reviews Microbiology 900; see also WHO, *Measles: Fact Sheet No. 286*, November 2014 <www.who.int/mediacentre/factsheets/fs286/en/> (accessed 3 February 2015).

in the UK have all been in localities or groups with much lower vaccination rates.[10]

Contemporary medical ethics and medical law strongly favour the competent individual's right to choose, but might there be scope for coercion in relation to specific vaccinations, now or in the future? In order to answer this question we need to consider the individual and collective benefits as well as the side effects of vaccination in more detail. We need to develop a coherent account of citizens' mutual obligations in a modern welfare state with a comprehensive health care system, such as that found in the UK. In this chapter, we briefly outline the individual and societal benefits, risks and burdens associated with vaccination and then provide an ethical and legal analysis of whether coercion or compulsion can be justified and, if so, in what circumstances. The analysis primarily focuses on the mundane circumstances of routine vaccination, since this is the context where the argument is most evenly balanced.

The benefits of vaccination

The individual benefits of vaccination are easily identified. Being vaccinated against a particular infectious disease provides some degree of protection against becoming infected, or developing a serious infection with that particular disease. The degree of protection differs widely between different vaccinations, even in immune competent individuals. Smallpox vaccination was almost 100% effective, whereas the protection offered by vaccination against tuberculosis is much smaller.[11]

The societal benefits of having an adequately vaccinated population are also clear, with herd immunity offering the strongest example of vaccination-linked benefits. Herd immunity occurs when the vaccination of a sufficiently large portion of the population creates a wider coverage of immunity for the rest of the populace, particularly for those without immunity. This creates a measure of protection for the population as a whole because it makes it more difficult for the disease to spread as there are fewer individuals left vulnerable to infection. It is important to note that the group of unvaccinated people consists of not only those who have chosen not to be vaccinated but also those who cannot be vaccinated. These include individuals who are immune compromised and cannot be vaccinated with a live vaccine, and those who are too young to be vaccinated. Protection of those who cannot be vaccinated can only be achieved by adequate vaccination in the general population. By vaccinating certain groups who hold particular roles, such as healthcare workers, we may also be able to protect others.

---

10 S Ghebrehewet, G Hayhurst, A Keenan, H Moore, 'Outbreak of Measles in Central and Eastern Cheshire, UK, October 2008–February 2009' (2013) 141 Epidemiology and Infection 1849; V Baugh, J Figueroa, J Bosanquet and others, 'Ongoing Measles Outbreak in Orthodox Jewish Community, London, UK' (2013) 19 Emerging Infectious Diseases 1707.
11 G Colditz, T Brewer, C Berkey and others, 'Efficacy of BCG Vaccine in the Prevention of Tuberculosis: Meta-Analysis of the Published Literature' (1994) 271 JAMA 698.

The risks and burdens of vaccination

All vaccination programmes create burdens for those who choose to be vaccinated. They may have to allocate time to being vaccinated, and many vaccinations are delivered by injection which causes some pain and discomfort. These burdens are often small for the individual, but they fall on a large group and have to be taken into account in any cost–benefit estimation. Different vaccinations have different risks. Those vaccinations that are part of the standard programmes for children or the elderly have been used for a long time, and we therefore have very good estimates of the risks, which are very small.[12] In contrast, risks associated with new vaccines that are used to respond to new epidemics are more difficult to predict in advance. The now proven connection between the H1N1 Pandemrix (pandemic flu) vaccine and the occurrence of narcolepsy was, for instance, completely unexpected and probably unpredictable.[13] However, even though the risks are small, they are still important because we have no reason to believe that those who suffer the side effects are the same as those who would have had a severe case of the disease if they had not been vaccinated.

Reciprocity, autonomy and the public good

A vaccination programme which manages to significantly reduce the propagation of a disease in vaccinated and unvaccinated groups is a public good. This should be understood in the everyday sense and in the more restricted economic sense. In other words, it is a good that is non-excludable and non-rivalrous. The unvaccinated cannot be excluded from the benefit, and one person having the benefit does not prevent others from having it. The public good is created by a combination of the government offering the vaccination programme and a sufficient number of people agreeing to the vaccination. Both the vaccinated and the unvaccinated benefit from the existence of the public good, but is this sufficient justification for compulsion or coercion? This may be particularly problematic where some of those who have a vaccination only do so because they are compelled or coerced, and then they suffer harm that they would not otherwise have suffered. If respect for the autonomous individual is the supreme principle in a liberal society, as it is sometimes claimed to be, it seems that we cannot compel or coerce. But perhaps this conclusion is too hasty, primarily because it ignores the context in which these choices are made.

Individuals may have duties towards others in their community based on reciprocity, or they may have duties as citizens in a society with a comprehensive

---

12 M Maglione, L Das, L Raaen and others, 'Safety of Vaccines Used for Routine Immunization of US Children: A Systematic Review' (2014) 134 Pediatrics 325.
13 M Partinen, O Saarenpää-Heikkilä, I Ilveskoski and others, 'Increased Incidence and Clinical Picture of Childhood Narcolepsy Following the 2009 H1N1 Pandemic Vaccination Campaign in Finland' (2012) 7 PloS ONE e33723.

healthcare system.[14] Let us consider these two options. Obligations in reciprocity arise because I benefit from the actions of others in ways that create an obligation on me to reciprocate, either towards them personally or towards the group to which we belong.[15] I clearly benefit from other people in my community being vaccinated. It reduces my risk of being infected, because there will be fewer infected people around. Is this a benefit that creates a duty of reciprocation? Not if everyone has chosen to be vaccinated purely for their own benefit (i.e. to reduce their own risk of being infected). But, if a significant proportion of those who choose vaccination do so partly to reduce community risk, then I may have a duty to reciprocate their community-minded action.

Routine vaccination happens in a context of a healthcare system which promotes a vaccination programme, a planned sequence of vaccinations to achieve particular public health goals. In many healthcare systems, even those that have a large component of private payment, the childhood vaccination programme is delivered to everybody for free. Moreover, in publicly funded healthcare systems those who do fall ill will be cared for by such systems. So a wide range of obligations may emerge from this. Seen from the view of the collective, many vaccination programmes generate resources because the benefits created far outweigh the costs spent.[16] Participating in a vaccination programme therefore provides an opportunity for citizens to benefit society by participating in a very low-risk activity. This may in itself produce an obligation to participate. In the present context the question is whether there is an obligation to be vaccinated, and if so, to what extent?

Obligations may be generated interactionally, in the interactions between the health care system and the citizen as a participant in the system. For example, parents rely on the healthcare system for monitoring their children during the first years of life, and they rely on the system to deal quickly and efficiently with the childhood diseases, scrapes and scratches that will almost inevitably occur. Is it then not reasonable for the system also to rely on the parents to act prudently in a range of circumstances, such as securing the kettle in the kitchen[17] and availing themselves of the childhood vaccination programme? As noted above, taking up the offer of vaccination does create a small burden, and some very minimal risk, but it significantly eases the burden on the health care system, both financially and operationally during times of peak demand. For those who choose to participate in the system and accept its benefits, it is contended that there is an obligation to participate in recommended vaccinations.

---

14 L Becker, *Reciprocity* (2nd edn, University of Chicago Press 1990); A Viens, 'Public Health, Ethical Behavior and Reciprocity' (2008) 8(5) The American Journal of Bioethics 1; J Harris and S Holm, 'Is There a Moral Obligation Not to Infect Others?'(1995) 311 BMJ 1215.
15 Becker (n 14).
16 F Zhou, A Shefer, J Wenger and others, 'Economic Evaluation of the Routine Childhood Immunization Program in the United States, 2009' (2014) 133 Pediatrics 577.
17 W Holmes, B Keane and H Rode, 'The Severity of Kettle Burns and the Dangers of the Dangling Cord' (2012) 38 Burns 453.

To what extent should the state intervene to promote or protect the public good?

The tension between private individual rights and those of the collective influences how governments act to promote or protect the public good. In assessing the legitimacy of state intervention, we need to understand what stimulates and influences this balancing exercise. This dilemma is characteristically assessed through a consideration of the harm principle which provides that competent adults should have freedom of action unless they pose a risk to others.[18] If there is a risk of serious harm to other persons or property, then does this provide sufficient justification for measures to be undertaken in order to minimise that harm?

It is in this context that coercive vaccination measures, which value the protection of the public good over individual choice, need to be viewed. As discussed above, vaccination programmes are often voluntary, relying upon the individual to recognise the value of vaccination for his own health and that of the collective.[19] A community is more likely to perceive voluntary measures positively. Nevertheless, for the benefits of vaccination to be achieved, sufficient take-up is essential to enable adequate immunity across the community. However, considerable distrust and perceived risk surrounding vaccines remains and presents a formidable challenge. Widespread take-up of vaccines is necessary for universal vaccination programmes to be successful, yet history suggests that public confidence is precarious.[20]

Various levels of state intervention are legitimised in different parts of the world. Whether it be the required wearing of seatbelts or control over recreational drug use, these interventions seek to modify and control behaviour that is regarded as affecting the individual alone.[21] It may be difficult to regard as justifiable laws that seek to challenge an individual's behaviour which will have no impact upon others, yet implicit in this is the recognition that there are few activities that individuals can pursue which do not have the potential to affect others. Paternalistic interventions, which limit individual choice, are commonly justified on the basis that individuals do not have the capacity to fully appreciate what is in their own interests. Vaccination controversies, such as that surrounding the MMR vaccine in 1998, where publication of a fraudulent research paper in the *Lancet* linking the MMR vaccine with the increased prevalence of digestive

---

18 J Raz, 'Autonomy, Toleration and the Harm Principle' in S Mendus (ed), *Justifying Toleration: Conceptual and Historical Perspectives* (CUP 2009).
19 Vaccine European New Integrated Collaboration Effort (VENICE) *Report on First survey of Immunisation Programs in Europe*, 2007 <http://venice.cineca.org/Report_II_WP3.pdf> (accessed 3 February 2015).
20 P Stephanie, 'Vaccination and Other Altruistic Medical Treatments: Should Autonomy or Communitarianism Prevail?' (2000) 4 Med Law Int 223.
21 C Sunstein and R Thaler, 'Libertarian Paternalism Is Not an Oxymoron' (2003) 70 U Chi L Rev 1159, 1162.

disorders and autism spectrum disorders in children,[22] clearly signal that behavioural choices can be profoundly influenced.[23] Thus, in defence of paternalistic intervention, and in order to protect both the individual from themselves and the health of the collective, interventionist public health mandates are sometimes regarded as necessary.[24]

How far is it appropriate to constrain individual interests in autonomy?

From the compulsory vaccination perspective, several European countries and the United States (US) lead the way with the law being harnessed as a tool to maintain the public's health. Several types of vaccination policy exist, with some exerting considerable control through assertive and comprehensive mandatory programmes, while others focus upon indirect encouragement/coercion. For example, in the US, state laws requiring vaccinations for children and proof of a completed immunisation profile, or a vaccination exemption, prior to enrolment in a public or private school are common.[25] Vaccination policies, which are not grounded in compulsion, often rely upon systems underpinned by strong recommendations, assertive educational programmes and nudging the behaviour of the individual towards the willing acceptance of vaccination.[26]

Compulsion within the public health sphere has become a more dominant feature over recent years, despite the absence of a vaccination mandate in the UK. For example, statutory powers to control infectious disease have existed within England since the Public Health Act 1848 and are governed now by the Public Health (Control of Disease) Act 1984, together with the Health Protection (Notification) Regulations 2010. Prior to the Health and Social Care Act 2008, statutory detention powers only applied to specified diseases, with powers also given to local authorities to seek compulsory removal and detention of a person meeting the disease criteria in England, Wales and Northern Ireland. The 1984 Act has since been significantly amended by Part 3 of the Health and Social Care Act 2008, expanding the remit of compulsory treatment and confinement to contamination risks and health threats to the

---

22 F Godlee, J Smith and H Marcovitch, 'Wakefield's Article Linking MMR Vaccine and Autism was Fraudulent' (2011) 342 BMJ 7452.
23 L Guillaume and P Bath, 'A Content Analysis of Mass Media Sources in Relation to the MMR Vaccine Scare' (2008) 14 Health Informatics Journal 323.
24 A Cappelen, O Mæstad and B Tungodden, 'Demand for Childhood Vaccination – Insights from Behavioral Economics' (2011) 37 Forum for Development Studies 349, 350–51.
25 A Ciolli, 'Mandatory School Vaccinations: The Role of Tort Law' (2008) 81Yale J Biol Med 129; see also J Hodge and L Gostin, 'School Vaccination Requirements: Historical, Social, and Legal Perspectives' (2001/2002) 90 Kentucky Law Journal 831, 867 <www.publichealthlaw.net/Research/PDF/vaccine.pdf> (accessed 27 January 2015).
26 See R Thaler and C Sunstein, *Nudge: Improving Decisions About Health, Wealth, and Happiness* (Penguin 2009); Cappelen and others (n 24) 362.

public at large.[27] The scope of these powers has also been expanded and now allows for the legitimate isolation and restraint of individuals, as well as the seizure of property. The 'all hazards' approach lies at the heart of this legislative health protection mandate, with a significant public health hazard acting as the determining factor in decision-making, rather than a narrowly construed list of specified infectious diseases.[28]

The justification for this kind of aggressive intervention sits squarely within the public health agenda of collective protection and social justice; after all, many of the notifiable diseases within the Public Health (Control of Disease) Act 1984 are highly contagious and have high mortality rates if left untreated. Despite the draconian nature of these powers, the overarching objective of protecting the majority has been, and continues to be, the central rationale as pointed out by Brazier and Harris.[29] Likewise, the assessment of risk to identify perceived public health hazards, instead of relying upon identifiable evidence of disease, indicates a shifting political trend favouring the health needs of the collective, a move that reflects a global swing towards a communitarian agenda. The legitimacy of infectious disease control powers was tested in the European Court of Human Rights in *Enhorn v Sweden* in 2005, where an HIV-positive man who unknowingly infected another and failed to attend legally required medical appointments was later isolated in hospital under compulsion. This response was deemed disproportionate to the suspected risk and was found to be in breach of his Article 5 right to liberty.[30] But, does the *Enhorn* decision indicate a judicial willingness to constrain the extent of intervention for infectious disease? The use of coercion may be generated not by the failure or refusal by the infected person to comply with a treatment regime, but rather by the nature of the disease itself.[31] Diseases such as HIV and Hepatitis B do not spread through airborne transmission, and control of infection can be maintained well if medical advice and protocols are followed.

In the UK, the Health and Social Care Act 2008 has moved risk determination to centre stage. Infectious disease control has been an increasingly overt public health priority, with new outbreaks of previously vaccine-controlled

---

27 The Health Protection (Notification) Regulations (2010 SI 2010/659), the Health Protection (Local Authority Powers) Regulations 2010 (SI 2010/657) and the Health Protection (Part 2A Orders) Regulations 2010 (SI 2010/658).
28 Health and Social Care Act 2008, Pt 3. The 'all hazards' approach encompasses infection and contamination of any kind and enables public authorities to respond to modern day health hazards more effectively. See International Health Regulations (2005); WHA58.3 Revision of the International Health Regulations <www.who.int/ihr/about/FAQ2009.pdf > (accessed 3 February 2015).
29 Brazier and Harris (n 1).
30 *Enhorn v. Sweden* [2005] ECHR 56529/00.
31 R Coker, 'Tuberculosis, Non-Compliance and Detention for the Public Health' (2000) 26 JME 157.

diseases taking place.[32] Moreover, newly emerging diseases continue to raise global concerns, with SARS, H5N1 avian influenza and, more recently, MERS (Middle East respiratory syndrome) and Ebola being on the WHO radar.[33] Given this shift towards risk determination in relation to infectious disease control, there is scope, despite the *Enhorn* decision, for aggressive intervention to be justified once identification and magnitude of risk is ascertained.[34] There is a universal aspiration to minimise the probability of risk and the severity of harm which may accrue from insufficient herd immunity. Would compulsory vaccination provide a legitimate solution to these problems?

Compulsory vaccination programmes

The word 'mandate' can be given numerous definitions and interpretations. A mandate is generally understood as being a command or an order and exhibits two key features: it requires individuals to be subject to or do something, and it often involves a penalty when compliance is not forthcoming. A penalty can take many forms, ranging from significant financial or custodial penalties to indirect penalties. An example of the latter is exclusion from state school entry when a child does not have a complete immunisation profile.

Whether a system is a truly mandatory one depends largely on how easy it is to avoid or reject the mandate. Where opt-outs are available within the system but in practice are difficult to apply for and obtain, one could argue that this makes the system mandatory because avoidance is so difficult. In the contemporary vaccination context, enforcement of mandates rarely involves the positive use of penalties.[35] In the US, access to the public education system depends upon a child having a full immunisation profile; however, opting out of vaccination is an easy undertaking.[36] Moral persuasion is also used as a means of indirect encouragement to comply. In Sweden and Finland during the H1N1 pandemic between 2009 and 2010, mass compliance with the vaccination programme was bolstered by considerable moral persuasion.[37]

---

32 V Jansen, N Stollenwerk, H Jensen and others, 'Measles Outbreaks in a Population with Declining Vaccine Uptake' (2003) 301 Science 804.
33 WHO, *Influenza at the Human-Animal Interface (HAI)* <www.who.int/influenza/human_animal_interface/en/> (accessed 3 February 2015). On July 2014, the WHO met to determine whether coronavirus (which causes MERS) should be considered a 'public health emergency of international concern,' see <www.who.int/csr/disease/coronavirus_infections/update_20130709/en/index.html> (accessed 3 February 2015).
34 K Calman and G Royston, 'Risk Language and Dialects' (1997) 315 BMJ 939.
35 M Wynia, 'Mandating Vaccination: What Counts as a "Mandate" in Public Health and When Should They Be Used?' (2007) 7 (12) American Journal of Bioethics 2.
36 D Salmon, S Teret, C MacIntyre and others, 'Compulsory Vaccination and Conscientious or Philosophical Exemptions: Past, Present and Future' (2006) 367 Lancet 436.
37 N Goldstein and R Cialdini, 'Using Social Norms as a Lever of Social Influence' in A Pratkanis (ed), *The Science of Social Influence: Advances and Future Progress* (Psychology Press 2007).

One of the most compelling and oft-cited arguments for embracing a compulsory programme is the notion that it will enhance herd immunity.[38] Herd immunity is susceptible to failure because it is dependent upon immunisation rates remaining adequate. In the UK and elsewhere, outbreaks of vaccine-preventable disease have emerged over recent years. For example, the year 2008 saw the highest number of recorded confirmed cases of measles (1370) in England and Wales since disease monitoring was introduced in 1995.[39] Where outbreaks do occur, unvaccinated children and young adults have so far been particularly affected. However, with the lowering of immunity across the population, it will make others increasingly vulnerable to infection, such as babies too young to be vaccinated. Although there is fear that herd immunity is collapsing,[40] it can be attained if a programme of mandatory vaccination is in place. Yet, justifications for the use of compulsion seem to be set firmly within a utilitarian framework, rather than from any value derived by the individual.[41]

The argument that there can be little legitimacy in eliciting the use of penalties against those who inadvertently spread disease is one grounded in moral values.[42] Howsoever, is this argument as effective when applied to preventive mechanisms to control disease? If an individual refuses to ensure their children are vaccinated, could it be argued that the decision to reject vaccination is effectively the same as harming others? Harris and Holm argue that when an individual is infected with a disease that is vaccine preventable, then this could be equivalent to causing harm to that other person.[43] As van Delden and others suggest: '[t]his does not imply an obligation not to become ill, but does lead to a prima facie duty not to infect someone when one knows this can be

---

38 T John and R Samuel, 'Herd Immunity and Herd Effect: New Insights and Definitions' (2000) 16 European Journal of Epidemiology 601.
39 Health Protection Agency, *Vaccine Coverage and COVER (Cover of Vaccination Evaluated Rapidly)*, 2011 <www.hpa.org.uk/Topics/InfectiousDiseases/InfectionsAZ/VaccineCoverageAndCOVER/> (accessed 3 February 2015); Outbreak of Measles in Wales Nov 2012 – July 2013, Report of the agencies which responded to the outbreak (Abertawe Bro Morgannwg University Health Board, Powys Health Board, Hywel Dda Health Board and Public Health Wales), October 2013 <www.wales.nhs.uk/sitesplus/888/news/29688> (accessed 3 February 2015).
40 Over 20 years ago, MMR first dose uptake in England was at 92%. This had dropped to 79% by 2003 in the wake of the Wakefield research: see Health Protection Agency, 'COVER programme: January to March 2003' (2003) 91 CDR Weekly (Online) 465. By 2012–13, MMR coverage in England for children reaching their second birthday had risen to 92.3%, although this is still below the WHO target of at least 95% coverage.
41 R Field and A Caplan, 'A Proposed Ethical Framework for Vaccine Mandates: Competing Values and the Case of HPV' (2008) 18 Kennedy Institute of Ethics Journal 111.
42 R Bennett, 'Is There a Case for Criminalising Vertical Transmission of the Human Immunodeficiency Virus (HIV) from Mother to Child?' (2013) 1 Journal of Medical Law and Ethics 121.
43 Harris and Holm (n 14) 1215.

prevented.'[44] Is this the same as Brazier and Harris' argument that we all have a moral responsibility to avoid reckless endangerment of others in relation to infectious disease?

A responsibility to not harm others is one that has a wide spectrum for interpretation; moreover, it has the potential to be overly oppressive.[45] So does the duty to not cause harm justify use of compulsion in vaccination programmes? The answer to this question may depend upon what risks of harm may stem from the vaccination itself, and this may itself countermand any arguments in favour of the vaccination mandate.[46] No intervention is entirely free from risk.[47] Side effects from vaccination tend to be mild and transitory.[48] Rarely, an allergic reaction may occur resulting in a rash. Very rarely, an anaphylactic reaction may ensue quickly after the vaccine has been administered, which may prove life threatening. Sometimes significant risks associated with vaccination can and do materialise.[49] When this does occur, it does little to bolster and reinforce the message that vaccines are safe and should be administered for the public good.

Conclusion

In this chapter we have briefly considered vaccination's benefits, risks and burdens to both the individual and the collective. From this we have then deliberated over whether a compulsory vaccination mandate can ever be a justifiable response to ensure public health needs are met. Despite the benefits which flow from vaccination, the risks must not be ignored, yet neither should they be determinative in the decision to maintain protection. The recent examples of disease outbreak in the UK and elsewhere should be a stark reminder to us of the devastation posed by a virulent disease. Living in a world where the threat of disease for many has a very minor impact upon daily activities means that the vaccination programmes around the world are largely working and public health protection is being maintained. This is good news. However, there is also a risk that the success of vaccination programmes enables misconceptions about vaccination safety to emerge.

---

44 J van Delden, R Ashcroft, A Dawson and others, 'The Ethics of Mandatory Vaccination against Influenza for Health Care Workers' (2008) 26 Vaccine 5562.
45 M Verweij, 'Obligatory Precautions Against Infection' (2005) 19 Bioethics 323.
46 'Tackling Negative Perceptions Towards Vaccination' (2007) 7 Lancet Infectious Diseases 235.
47 K Malone and A Hinman, 'Vaccination Mandates: The Public Health Imperative and Individual Rights' in R Goodman, R Hoffman, W Lopez and others (eds), *Law in Public Health Practice* (OUP 2003); R Chen and B Hibbs, 'Vaccine Safety: Current and Future Challenges' (1998) 27 Pediatric Annals 445.
48 K Stratton, C Howe and J Johnston, 'Adverse Events Associated with Childhood Vaccines Other Than Pertussis and Rubella: Summary of A Report from the Institute of Medicine' (1994) 271 JAMA 1602.
49 H Nohynek, J Jokinen, M Partinen and others, 'AS03 Adjuvanted AH1N1 Vaccine Associated With an Abrupt Increase in the Incidence of Childhood Narcolepsy in Finland' (2012) 7 PLoS ONE e33536.

A vaccination mandate in the strictest sense, where failure to comply results in sanction, is difficult to achieve. It may be deemed morally repugnant to penalise children by preventing them from accessing an education, or to impose a prison term or fine as a way of encouraging people to comply with vaccination programmes. Setting individual rights and autonomy to one side, and recognising the need to place collective health needs at the forefront of decision-making, is accepted practice in certain situations.[50] Autonomy is not absolute.[51] International legal regulations have moved the goalposts, with an 'all hazards' approach being applied to health protection.[52] Pivotal within many vaccination systems has been the voluntary acceptance and cooperation of individuals. However, reliance on voluntariness has left such systems vulnerable to controversy, latent mistrust and scaremongering. With the shape of global travel and distribution networks changing, disease control is increasingly difficult. On balance, a wholly voluntary vaccination programme may no longer be tenable, and reflection is needed about whether coercion may offer the way forward.

---

50 M Brazier, 'Patient Autonomy and Consent to Treatment: The Role of the Law?' (1987) 7 LS 169.
51 A McCall Smith, 'Beyond Autonomy' (1997) 14 Journal of Contemporary Health Law & Policy 23.
52 van Delden and others (n 44) 5564.

4 The value of human life in healthcare law
Life versus death in the hands of the judiciary

Alexandra Mullock and Rob Heywood

Introduction

Understanding and interpreting the value of human life has troubled ethicists, theologians, philosophers and lawyers since the dawn of time. The academic literature concerning the issue is voluminous.[1] Some prefer to use the language of sanctity of life,[2] whereas others suggest that this is misleading and instead refer to the inviolability of life.[3] In their recent work, Margaret Brazier and Suzanne Ost suggest a new term which they argue may be more appropriate when attempting to navigate the murky waters of the meaning of life and the value that should be attached to it.[4] They introduce the term *reverence for life*, which 'might bridge the gaps between the different philosophical attitudes'[5] that infuse the debate concerning the acceptability of various end-of-life decisions. In this chapter we analyse evolving academic and judicial conceptions regarding the value of life in the context of dilemmas in end-of-life law.[6]

The delicate moral and ethical questions which underpin the meaning and value of life have taken centre stage in a number of high-profile cases[7] in which

---

1 See J Keown, *The Law and Ethics of Medicine: Essays on the Inviolability of Human Life* (OUP 2012); R Dworkin, *Life's Dominion: An Argument About Abortion and Euthanasia* (Alfred Knopf 1993); J Harris, *The Value of Life* (Routledge 1985); G Williams, *The Sanctity of Life and the Criminal Law* (Faber and Faber 1957).
2 See G Williams, ibid.
3 See Keown (n 1).
4 M Brazier and S Ost, *Bioethics, Medicine and the Criminal Law Volume 3: Medicine and Bioethics in the Theatre of the Criminal Process* (CUP 2013).
5 Ibid 89.
6 'End-of-life law' encompasses both criminal and medical law principles. See J Coggon, 'Assisted Dying and the Context of Debate: "Medical Law" versus "End-of-Life Law"' (2010) 18(4) Med L Rev 541.
7 See *R (Nicklinson and another) v Ministry of Justice, R (AM (AP)) v DPP* [2014] UKSC 38, [2014] 3 WLR 200; *Aintree University Hospitals NHS Foundation Trust v James* [2013] UKSC 67, [2014] AC 591; *W v M* [2011] EWHC 2443 (Fam), [2012] 1 WLR 1653; *R (Purdy) v DPP* [2009] UKHL 45, [2010] 1 AC 345; *Pretty v United Kingdom* (2346 / 02) [2002] 2 FLR 45; *Airedale NHS Trust v Bland* [1993] AC 789.

it is clear that judges have sometimes struggled to separate the moral arguments from the legal ones. Attempting to explain and understand their decisions by reference to a coherent judicial interpretation of the value that should be attached to human life has therefore become something of a challenge. Brazier and Ost suggest that adopting their language of reverence for life may be helpful in allowing us to rationalise the judgments which have touched on end-of-life. They suggest that cases should 'rest on a strong presumption in favour of reverence for life',[8] but then further indicate that 'the presumption is not and should not be irrebuttable'.[9]

Drawing on the work of Brazier and Ost, this chapter explores some of the conceptual difficulties inherent in assessing the value and importance that one should attach to human life. Following that, consideration is given to the situations in which it may be permissible to end life without offending certain core values and beliefs. We then explore how judges have come to understand and interpret the meaning and value of life by reference to a number of recent cases. We conclude by highlighting some of the problems that have been left in the wake of contemporary case law and identify a number of unanswered questions which need to be addressed.

Conceptual difficulties with the value and importance of human life

One of the main problems when discussing the value of human life is the eclectic terminology that pervades the debate. The term sanctity of life is commonly used in the literature and also in the case law.[10] This, as Brazier and Ost point out, is a 'misnomer as a description of how the criminal process in England does and should approach the value of lives'.[11] Sanctity of life invokes religious connotations that do not sit squarely with modern conceptions of the role, aim and purpose of the criminal law. As Jackson states, the 'idea that God alone should have the power to decide the moment of an individual's death'[12] is incongruous in a society which is no longer dominated by religious values and beliefs. The parlance of sanctity tends to give the impression that life should be preserved at all costs, a belief that is sometimes referred to as vitalism.[13] In view of the sanctity of life being so closely aligned with religious beliefs, it has become possible for legal scholars to hone in on its weaknesses, identifying the fact that

---

8 Brazier and Ost (n 4), 90–91.
9 Ibid.
10 See Williams (n 1). The sanctity of human life is discussed at length in the House of Lords' decision in *Bland* (n 7). More recently, see the judgment of Lord Neuberger in *Nicklinson* (n 7), [90]–[98].
11 Brazier and Ost, (n 4), 83–84.
12 E Jackson and J Keown, *Debating Euthanasia* (Hart 2012) 37.
13 Keown (n 1), 4.

religion no longer dictates the contours of the criminal law.[14] Thus, deploying the language of sanctity to argue against assisted dying is susceptible to attack.

Supporters of vitalism aside, very few scholars have tried to articulate an argument that supports preservation of life at all costs. Keown embraces the term 'inviolability of life',[15] removing the debate from the domain of religion and placing it within the framework of the common law and human rights by recognising the intrinsic value of life itself. In so doing, Keown constructs a robust argument against allowing doctors to intentionally kill patients, which he claims is neither based in religion nor inconsistent with fundamental principles of law. His criticism of those who elide the concepts of sanctity and inviolability is that they ignore key principles which are crucial to his argument.[16]

The inviolability of life principle prohibits intentional killing by act or omission. It follows that a doctor cannot intentionally shorten the life of his patient by undertaking a positive act to hasten death, and equally is prohibited from withholding or withdrawing treatment, *with intent to shorten life*.[17] Accordingly, Brazier and Ost seek to distance themselves from the language of inviolability because they suggest it is 'a more absolute command allowing no exception'.[18] Yet if one remains true to the inviolability ideology, this may not be an accurate interpretation. While the inviolability of life principle recognises no exceptions, it is perhaps misleading to say it is absolute in the sense that it holds that life should be preserved at all costs. The inviolability of life principle, as conventionally understood, permits the withholding and withdrawing of life-prolonging treatment which is not worthwhile because it is futile or too burdensome for the patient. Thus, even though it would be wrong to withhold treatment because the patient's *life* was thought to be worthless, it would be acceptable to withhold treatment based on the fact that the *treatment itself* was deemed to be worthless, provided that the only intention of the doctor in withdrawing or withholding the treatment was to alleviate the patient's pain and suffering, with death being an unintended yet foreseen consequence of that act.[19] This position was described by David Price as a 'sop',[20] in which Keown concedes some ground where a patient is being sustained in the most hopeless of situations, while at the same time still being able to present what is, *prima facie*, an internally consistent argument that, in real terms, maintains an unduly restrictive approach to end-of-life decision-making.

There are other more pragmatic concerns. First, the inviolability principle holds the doctrine of double effect in too high a regard, without considering

---

14 Williams (n 1).
15 Keown (n 1), 5–22.
16 Ibid 13–16; 332–335.
17 Ibid 12.
18 Brazier and Ost (n 4), 89.
19 Keown (n 1), 12.
20 D Price, 'Fairly *Bland*: An Alternative View of a Supposed New "Death Ethic" and the BMA Guidelines' (2001) 21 Legal Studies 618, 638.

the practical implications of the later House of Lords' decision in *R v Woollin*.[21] There are now some situations in which foresight of a virtually certain consequence *may* amount to intent, and as this question rests on the interpretation of a jury, any doctors seeking to rely on double effect must surely be advised that they are traversing the most uncertain of legal terrains. Second, determining the question of futility is not straightforward. For every convincing argument in favour of suggesting that a treatment is in fact futile, a convincing counter-argument can be raised.[22] This frequently allows the supporters of the inviolability principle to argue the case for justifiably sustaining a patient. Finally, where the question converges on 'treatment', there is always room for disagreement as to what may actually amount to treatment.[23] Nonetheless, in theory at least, the inviolability principle is only absolute in the sense of the intrinsic value it affords to human life itself, but is not absolute in that it does not rule out completely withdrawal of treatment in certain cases.

The cases in which the inviolability principle would condone certain end-of-life decisions made by doctors are narrow. Some scholars therefore encourage the assessment of quality of life considerations when determining end-of-life questions, and for others the idea of the intrinsic value of human life is rejected altogether.[24] Thus it becomes evident that views are polarised.

This is where the recent work of Brazier and Ost becomes most relevant, because their use of 'reverence' purports to adopt a compromise between the extreme positions. Their proposal focuses on a presumption in favour of reverence for life, by which they mean the intrinsic value of human life itself. Nevertheless, they concede that this presumption is capable of being rebutted in appropriate circumstances.[25] It is not the first time that the idea of compromise per se has been posited in the field of end-of-life decision-making,[26] but the aspect of Brazier and Ost's work that marks it out as being especially interesting is the manner in which they feel compromise could be achieved.

Accommodation, exception or rebuttable presumption?

Those who remain committed to the inviolability of life principle have always been critical of the House of Lords' decision in *Bland*.[27] This criticism, it is claimed, is based on the reasoning and not the outcome. Keown suggests that

---

21 *R v Woollin* [1999] 1 AC 82.
22 See R Mohindra, 'Medical Futility: A Conceptual Model' (2007) 33 JME 71; N Jecker and R Pearlman, 'Medical Futility: Who Decides?' (1992) 152 Arch Intern Med 1140; See also Sir Alan Ward's analysis in *Aintree University Hospitals NHS Foundation Trust v David James and Others* [2013] EWCA Civ 65, [35].
23 For discussion see Keown (n 1), 330–332.
24 See Jackson and Keown (n 12) and also Harris (n 1).
25 Brazier and Ost (n 4), 91.
26 For an interesting discussion see R Huxtable, *Law, Ethics and Compromise at the Limits of Life: To Treat or Not to Treat?* (Routledge 2013).
27 Keown (n 1), 328–356.

their Lordships focused their minds on the wrong question when they considered whether the patient's *life* itself was worthwhile, rather than assessing the question of whether or not the *treatment* being provided was worthwhile. He argues that the correct questions that should be asked in withdrawal cases are: 'is tube-feeding "treatment" and, if so, is it worthwhile?'[28] However, even if these 'correct' questions had been asked in *Bland*, there is a convincing argument that the treatment should still have been withdrawn. Yet would the supporters of the inviolability of life ever truly admit this and accept *Bland* as a humane decision? One suspects not. The argument would undoubtedly have been put forward that the artificial nutrition and hydration (ANH) was not treatment but rather 'basic care' which can never be withdrawn, or, if ANH *is* treatment, that the threshold for futility was not met.

To suggest that ANH is not medical treatment is a particularly weak argument that has been judicially dismissed.[29] Yet the futility question is delicately poised and difficult to deal with. The issue becomes even more vexed when considering futility from the perspective of benefits versus burdens.[30] The assessment of the benefits versus burdens of treatment is actually a useful starting point in the context of assessing futility, but some would argue the calculation should not be confined solely to treatment per se and so the assessment of benefits and burdens will not always be as clear-cut as it was in *Bland*. In recent times, the courts have been faced with a number of challenging scenarios. Where the patient is in a minimally conscious state, the assessment of futility demands a more detailed forensic examination from a judge. The fact that the patient is receiving some benefit from the treatment is much easier to identify than in, say, a patient in a persistent vegetative state, but whether or not the burdens of the treatment outweigh the benefits is a different matter. In cases such as *W v M* and *Aintree*,[31] judges have adopted varied approaches to the question of futility, with some placing emphasis on only the benefits of treatment as a reason for preserving life, and others implementing a more expansive balancing exercise yielding a rather different result.

To categorise the withdrawal of treatment cases as exceptions to the inviolability of life principle may be misleading. Its supporters would simply suggest that, if correctly reasoned, withdrawal of life-sustaining treatment where the treatment itself is deemed futile is not ruled out and can thus be accommodated within the principle. Judges have nonetheless been slow to explain and justify the decisions in which they have permitted withdrawal of treatment by reference to acting within the margin of acceptability recognised by the classic inviolability principle. Equally, the situations in which they could actually do so, if they thought it appropriate, are limited to withdrawal type cases and, for this reason,

---

28 Ibid 340.
29 *Bland* (n 7).
30 This approach is advocated by Keown. Ibid 12.
31 *W v M*; *Aintree* (n 7).

it may be necessary to identify actual exceptions to recognising the intrinsic value of life.

Inclusive of, but not limited to, withdrawal of treatment cases, there are those at the opposite end of the spectrum to the inviolability principle who suggest it is appropriate to consider factors pertaining to the patient's quality of life.[32] From this reasoning a strong argument emerges in favour of greater flexibility within the law that not only allows passive withdrawal of treatment, but also the intentional and active shortening of a patient's life in certain circumstances. This approach is still problematic for some, though, because to distance oneself from recognising *any* intrinsic value to human life is too radical a step.[33]

Brazier and Ost's suggestion of a rebuttable presumption in favour of the intrinsic value of life, in the form of reverence for life, could therefore act as a happy medium.[34] Reverence would certainly be wider in scope than the permissible withdrawal scenarios accommodated within the inviolability principle; it could conceivably be extended to permit active intervention, encompassing cases such as *Pretty*, *Purdy*, and, more recently, *Nicklinson*.[35] Tensions will naturally surround the concept of a 'rebuttable presumption'. Some thought would need to be given to the precise nature and type of evidence that may be required in order to rebut the presumption in favour of reverence for life. There would need to be convincing evidence that the plight of the patient did fall within one of those 'hard' cases in which there was a solid justification for permitting a patient's life to be shortened, whether by passive or active assistance, and regardless of whether it was accompanied by a direct intention to shorten life. Identifying those 'hard' cases is where the difficulty will lie, but certainly the recent decisions in *W v M*, *Aintree* and *Nicklinson*,[36] to which we now turn our attention, are strong candidates for falling within this category.

Recent judicial interpretations of the value of life

The cases of *W v M*, *Aintree* and *Nicklinson* compelled members of the judiciary to consider how the 'sanctity' principle should be interpreted.[37] We now assess how the presumption that human life has intrinsic value was regarded in the context, and against the conflicting issues, of each case.

---

32 See L Doyal, 'Dignity in Dying Should Include the Legalisation of Non-Voluntary Euthanasia' (2006) 1 Clinical Ethics 65; P Singer, *Practical Ethics* (2nd edn, CUP 1993); Harris (n 1).
33 This seems to be a key reason as to why Brazier and Ost have sought to develop their reverence for life argument.
34 Brazier and Ost (n 4), 90–91.
35 *Pretty*, *Purdy*, *Nicklinson* (n 7).
36 *W v M*; *Aintree*; *Nicklinson* (n 7).
37 Ibid.

W v M

In this case, Baker J prioritised the sanctity of life in the face of compelling evidence that M, who was in a minimally conscious state (MCS), would not wish to be kept alive in such a condition. We have both (separately) argued that this narrow evaluation gave too much weight to the intrinsic value of M's life in the best interests balancing exercise,[38] and too little to her past wishes and feelings,[39] the views of her family,[40] and also the grim reality of life at the lower limits of MCS. In the absence of a legally binding advance decision to refuse life-sustaining treatment (AD), which would have rebutted the presumption of preserving life, Baker J felt that the evidence of M's sister and partner regarding M's wishes (that she would not wish to be kept alive in a state of total dependency) was insufficient to justify withdrawing ANH. The main reason given was that in contrast to a person in a vegetative state, a minimally conscious person is capable of experiencing life, whatever that might mean for *that* person.[41] Baker J indicated that the presumption in favour of preserving life should only (definitely) continue if M's clinical condition remained stable. He intimated that if future, even trivial, infection threatens M's life, it might be appropriate not to treat her. This tells us that the presumption can be highly opportunistic and will depend upon 'the window of opportunity' for permitting and achieving death.[42] Accordingly, for Baker J, the appropriate window for rebutting the presumption for preserving M's life in the absence of a binding AD would be if an infection struck and the treatment to be withheld is not ANH, or at least not only ANH.

Aintree

This case concerned a best interests evaluation to determine whether treatment should be *withheld* from a patient in MCS.[43] Unlike M, however, the evidence suggested that the patient, David James, initially experienced a greater degree

---

38 See R Heywood, 'Withdrawal of Treatment from Minimally Conscious Patients' (2012) 7(1) Clinical Ethics 10; A Mullock, 'Deciding the Fate of a Minimally Conscious Patient: An Unsatisfactory Balancing Act?' (2012) 20(3) Med L Rev 460.

39 Section 4(6) of the Mental Capacity Act 2005 requires the decision-maker to 'consider, as far as reasonably ascertainable, the person's past and present wishes and feelings . . . and the beliefs and values that would be likely to influence his decision'.

40 Section 4(7) of the Mental Capacity Act 2005. For an interesting discussion see S Halliday, C Kitzinger and J Kitzinger, 'Law in Everyday Life and Death: A Socio-Legal Study of Chronic Disorders of Consciousness' (2014) Legal Studies, DOI: 10.1111/lest.12042.

41 The evidence produced painted an uncertain picture about M's quality of life, including evidence of suffering, distress and some contentment. Some have questioned the assumption that something is better than nothing in this context, for example, S Ashwal, R Cranford, 'The Minimally Conscious State in Children' (2002) 9 Seminars in Pediatric Neurology 19.

42 See C Kitzinger and J Kitzinger, 'The "Window of Opportunity" for Death after Severe Brain Injury: Family Experiences' (2013) 35(7) Sociology of Health & Illness 1095.

43 The treatment in question was not ANH but invasive support for circulatory problems, renal replacement therapy and CPR (in the event of cardiac arrest).

of consciousness before rapidly deteriorating to the point at which death seemed imminent. At the point at which he had a sufficient degree of response and awareness, the evidence indicated that he might have expressed a wish for treatment to continue in order to prolong his life. With or without treatment, however, the clinical evidence indicated that Mr James was approaching the end of life, and indeed he died before the Supreme Court considered his case. Considering the decision of Jackson J in the Court of Protection, (broadly) in favour of continuing treatment,[44] and the subsequent Court of Appeal decision which overturned Jackson J's decision,[45] the Supreme Court sat as a panel of five,[46] reaching a unanimous decision delivered by Lady Hale.

Confirming that the 'strong presumption that it is in a person's best interests to stay alive'[47] is not an absolute position, Lady Hale scrutinised the approach to the best interests test in order to establish a more coherent principle regarding its possible rebuttal. Lady Hale agreed with the Court of Appeal's decision that it was not in Mr James' best interests to have the treatments because by the time the case had reached them his health had significantly deteriorated. However, she held that their reasoning and approach to the best interests test had been wrong. Rather, Jackson J had been correct in his broad approach, which considered the question of futility from a subjective rather than primarily objective perspective, taking greater account of the patient's apparent wishes and what he might regard as a worthwhile treatment. A treatment that delivers 'some benefit' to the patient, even if it does not affect the underlying disease, might be regarded as worthwhile despite its limited clinical value. The nuances of the particular treatments, however, led Lady Hale to the conclusion that Jackson J had overlooked some aspects of the consequences and burdens of some of the treatments. Moreover, notwithstanding the subjective influence upon the question of futility, objective clinical appraisal of the burdens of each treatment remained necessary and that as patients, 'we cannot always have what we want'.[48]

Reflecting on *W v M*, an approach which offers some elements of a substituted judgment, would clearly mitigate a judicial preference for prioritising the preservation of life in the face of evidence that the patient would choose otherwise.[49] When we cannot be certain what the patient actually prefers, we will often only have their past, competent preferences to guide us, and as *Aintree* confirms, the judiciary should not feel free to ignore this evidence.

---

44 *Aintree* [2012] EWHC 3524 COP.
45 *Aintree* [2013] EWCA Civ 65.
46 *Aintree* (n 7), Lord Neuberger, Lady Hale, Lord Clarke, Lord Carnwath and Lord Hughes.
47 *Aintree* (n 7), [35].
48 Ibid [45]. This supports the decision in *R (Burke) v General Medical Council* [2005] EWCA Civ 1003 CA.
49 Substituted judgment is employed in some US jurisdictions. See *In re Quinlan* (1976) 355 A.2d 647; *Cruzan v Director Missouri Department of Health* (1990) 110 S Ct 2841 (USA Supreme Court).

As one of us has argued in more detail,[50] a more expansive evaluation that considers the wider social issues together with a more nuanced approach to questions of futility and intolerability is necessary to avoid an overly medical, paternalistic approach.

As we will now see in relation to assisted dying, the dilemma over preserving life is less troubled, at least in some respects, when we know unquestionably that a person wants to die, provided that they can act alone. Yet for a person seeking active help to die no lawful help is available unless they travel abroad to a permissive jurisdiction, and so once again resolving the tension between preserving life and respecting autonomy becomes profoundly challenging.

Nicklinson

The high profile case of *Nicklinson* concerned important questions regarding the current law in England and Wales relating to assisted suicide, and particularly the ongoing development and possible expansion of the right to autonomy under Article 8 of the European Convention on Human Rights.[51] The appellants failed in their attempt to persuade the majority of the Supreme Court that the blanket ban on assisting a suicide was incompatible with Article 8(1). However, in addition to those dissenting,[52] three justices occupying what might be regarded as the middle ground suggested that a future attempt might be successful if Parliament failed to consider the ongoing interference with autonomy in end-of-life issues,[53] which is firmly established under Article 8.[54] A number of the justices reflected on the diverse legal and moral arguments that have shaped this debate, including the importance of the value of life.

Lord Neuberger considered various dimensions to the 'sanctity' or 'primacy' principle, as he put it, and how it relates to the ban on assisted suicide. In relation to the life of a person seeking to die, he argued that the decriminalisation of suicide had 'substantially undermined' the principle:

> if the primacy of human life does not prevent a person committing suicide, it is difficult to see why it should prevent that person seeking assistance in committing suicide.[55]

---

50 R Heywood, 'Moving on from *Bland*: The Evolution of the Law and Minimally Conscious Patients' (2014) 22(4) Med L Rev 548.
51 *Nicklinson* (n 7). See also *Pretty v UK* (Application 2346/02)(2002) 35 EHRR 1, and *R (on the application of Purdy) v Director of Public Prosecutions (Society for the Protection of Unborn Children Intervening)* [2009] UKHL 45.
52 Lady Hale and Lord Kerr.
53 See the judgments of Lord Neuberger, Lord Wilson and Lord Mance.
54 See *Haas v Switzerland* (2011) 53 EHRR 33, *Koch v Germany* (2013) 56 EHRR 6, and *Gross v Switzerland* (2014) 58 EHRR 7.
55 *Nicklinson*, [90].

Furthermore, in so far as the objection to legal assisted dying rests on concern over preserving *other* human lives, Lord Neuberger suggested that it does little more 'than replicate concerns about the lives of the weak and vulnerable'.[56] Lord Neuberger was even persuaded by an expansive argument previously used by another assisted dying litigant, Debbie Purdy.[57] Agreeing that concerns about legal change based on the sanctity of life can be reversed, he pointed out that evidence shows that 'some people with a progressive degenerative disease feel themselves forced to end their lives before they would wish to',[58] while still able to act alone. Thus, Lord Neuberger argued, the blanket ban 'may serve to cut short their lives'.[59]

The importance of the value of life emerged repeatedly and, coincidentally, Lord Sumption spoke of 'reverence for human life for its own sake'.[60] Lady Hale alluded to the religious foundation of the principle, stating that 'respect for the intrinsic value of all human life is probably the most important value in Judaeo-Christian morality'.[61] This, she suggested, should absolutely justify refusing to oblige a person to help another to commit suicide, but it would not 'so obviously justify prohibiting those who freely judged that, in the circumstances of a particular case, there was no moral impediment to their assisting suicide.'[62]

Such willingness to open the door to rebutting the presumption in favour of life, for a person whose Article 8 rights are engaged and who requires assistance in suicide, seems to represent a significant development in judicial thinking. By weighing the presumption for life against other fundamental ethical concerns (mainly autonomy, but also dignity), several members of the Supreme Court have provided possible guidance for Parliament.[63]

Unanswered questions: Where next?

Coherent and ethically sound principles have developed in relation to certain questions about life and death. We know conclusively that a competent adult has an inviolable right to refuse life-sustaining treatment.[64] This right to die via

---

56 Ibid. Lord Kerr agreed with Neuberger regarding the logic of using the sanctity argument to prevent those who need assistance whilst those able to act independently are not prevented ([358]).
57 *R (on the application of Purdy)* (n 51).
58 Ibid [96].
59 Ibid.
60 Ibid [209].
61 Ibid [311].
62 Ibid.
63 For example, House of Lords Bill 24 (2013), which would legalise physician-assisted suicide for terminally ill, mentally competent people who are expected to die naturally within six months. At the time of writing the Bill is in Committee Stage, see Hansard (7 November 2014).
64 *B v NHS Trust* [2002] 2 All ER 449.

withdrawal can extend to those who create a legally valid AD and to those in a vegetative state.[65] However, rebutting the presumption in favour of life for those in MCS or a similar condition will often hinge on a best interests evaluation, which has been subject to significant judicial discretion. The decision in *Aintree* has confirmed that the test as to what is a worthwhile treatment should be influenced by the patient's wishes, but ultimately the circumstances in which the presumption of preserving life might be rebutted will be influenced by numerous objective factors as well. Within the factors considered for a best interests balancing exercise, the Mental Capacity Act 2005 urges decision-makers to consider the past wishes of the patient.[66] Moreover, questions of the burdens and benefits of treatment, together with assessing the experiences of the patient, unavoidably, and rightly, involve certain quality of life determinations. The principle of preserving life needs to reflect these wider concerns in a coherent and principled fashion.

This applies equally to active measures which foreshorten life. As Lord Neuberger and Lady Hale indicated in *Nicklinson*, it is time for other ethical concerns to be regarded as equally or potentially even more important than traditional 'sanctity' considerations. Notwithstanding vital factors linked to the preservation of life, such as protecting the vulnerable, and the avoidance of the slippery slope, the recognition of the autonomous right of the competent individual to choose death, in order to avoid terrible suffering, should lead to a more nuanced and sensitive approach from the law.

Conclusion

As Brazier and Ost state, we sit on a 'perilous perch' regarding the endless battles about the intrinsic value of life.[67] Religious dogma enshrining the 'sanctity' of life invokes connotations that do not reflect the concerns of a pluralistic society. Furthermore, as Price argued, while it is laudable to seek to avoid devaluing certain lives, sanctity may be a 'hazardous distraction', and '[r]espect for specific patients not the sanctity of life is the proper legal and ethical guide'.[68] While the concept of sanctity has evolved to encompass the alternative principle of inviolability, this too provides a limited and theoretically flawed approach to this dilemma. Inviolability purports to cast off religious baggage yet causes confusion over possible interpretations of treatment and futility, and it suffers from too heavy a reliance on double effect, which may be seen as a 'sop'[69] rather than a sound way to limit any tendency towards vitalism. Both concepts

---

65 Note that exceptions may be permitted, e.g. for religious faith: *Ashan v University Hospitals Leicester NHS Trust* [2006] EWHC 2624.
66 Mental Capacity Act 2005, s 4 (6) (a)–(c).
67 Brazier and Ost (n 4), 83.
68 D Price, 'My View of the Sanctity of Life: A Rebuttal of John Keown's Critique' (2007) 27(4) Legal Studies 549, 565.
69 Price (n 20).

offer an incoherent and sometimes highly discretionary approach which has generally encouraged an overly paternalistic attitude. Searching for an alternative, 'respect' for life seems inadequate for a strong presumption in favour of life. Lord Neuberger's reference to 'primacy' might be useful in providing a simple numerical expression conveying importance while avoiding being value-laden, yet we question whether a term devoid of ethical significance is desirable. Does the concept of reverence for life assist us then in finding a principled compromise and a more coherent approach?

Inevitably, there may be cynicism about the addition of yet another ambiguous term into the never-ending debate concerning the intrinsic value of human life. It could be argued that Brazier and Ost are simply using the term to 'fudge' a gap between their own differences concerning end-of-life decision-making and how, if indeed at all, the law should be reformed. There is also the pragmatic question of whether in fact reverence would change anything at all in terms of outcomes in these hard cases. Due to constraints in space, some of these questions cannot be answered here, and they will indeed need to be addressed in the future. It suffices to say at this point that we are of the view that Brazier and Ost mean reverence for life to be something more than just a linguistic alternative. The idea has a much greater potential in so far as it conveys importance to humanity, offering a less absolute position which reflects the rebuttable presumption for preserving life in a way that might be developed as a coherent compromise between sanctity, inviolability and concerns about autonomy, dignity and the quality of life.

5 Decisions at the end of life
An attempt at rationalisation

Sheila A.M. McLean

Introduction

This may seem a somewhat strange topic for inclusion in this book, given that it is not an area that has formed a major part of Margaret Brazier's important contribution to research and publications in medical law. That is not, however, to say that she has been silent on this subject. For example, as far back as 1996, she published a short article entitled 'Euthanasia and the law'[1] in which she reflected on the arguments in favour of legalisation, concluding amongst other things, that:

> Regulating, formalising, active euthanasia when a significant number of professionals and laypersons deplore such a move will have one certain result. The law will interfere more not less in the final stages of the professional's relationship with his patient.[2]

Further, in at least two of her books,[3] she deals specifically with end of life decisions, albeit from a perspective different from that which will be outlined here. What is clear, however, is that Brazier has turned her mind to end of life decisions, because these form an important plank of medico-legal inquiry. Equally, because much of the debate in this area revolves around issues of autonomy, medical practice and the role of the state – matters on which she has written extensively – it is arguable that the choice of topic is not as odd as it might at first appear.

End of life decisions come in a variety of forms and are, or can be, taken by a variety of people. Space precludes consideration of every aspect of this topic. However, what follows will focus on the conceptual and legal devices applied

---

1 M Brazier, 'Euthanasia and the law' (1996) 52(2) British Medical Bulletin, 317.
2 Ibid, at 324.
3 See, for example, M Brazier and E Cave, *Medicine, Patients and the Law*, (5th edn, London: Penguin Books, 2011); M Brazier and S Ost, *Bioethics, Medicine and the Criminal Law Volume III: Medicine and Bioethics in the Theatre of the Criminal Process* (Cambridge: Cambridge University Press, 2013).

in the principal arenas of debate, from which generalisable principles can hopefully be elucidated and extended throughout the entire area. Specifically, this chapter is concerned with the question as to whether or not assisted dying decisions (including both assisted suicide and voluntary euthanasia) can be so clearly delineated from other decisions that lead to death as to justify being treated differently by the law.

The role and relevance of autonomy

Before turning to specific issues, it is worth beginning by addressing the fundamental principle that underpins both agreement and disagreement on end of life decision-making; most importantly, the role and relevance of autonomy. What is meant by autonomy, and what its acceptable consequences are, is basic to our understanding of the legitimacy or otherwise of choices made. It is probably unexceptionable to claim that people have a real and important interest in how they die – perhaps, even, when they die. As populations age, the end stages of people's lives are increasingly prolonged, often accompanied by chronic and/or disabling conditions, and are not always comfortable or dignified. As Patel says:

> Many people have come to view a degenerative dying process as a fate worse than death itself. They dread a difficult and protracted dying process in some medical institution, with the ultimate specter of prolonged suspension in a helpless state sustained by a variety of tubes and machines.[4]

The downside (if it can be called that) of increasing longevity, medical advances and enhanced care provision is that all too often people's lives end in prolonged suffering, whether physical or existential. Many people would choose to forego these experiences, even if this means a shorter life. Their ability to do so will depend on a number of factors, at least some of which are outside their direct control. For example, the law categorises certain end of life decisions as essentially mere aspects of acceptable medical practice, whereas others are seen as criminal offences. This categorisation rests on a variety of explanations ranging from cultural or social sensitivities to legal principles and, sometimes, to fine (and arguable) distinctions.

In a liberal, western democracy, the essence of liberalism, according to Max Charlesworth, is 'the moral conviction that, because they are autonomous moral agents or persons, people must as far as possible be free to choose for themselves, even if their choices are, objectively speaking, mistaken'.[5] Autonomy, then, presumptively trumps other interests. Of course, exceptions can be, and often are, required. Thus, for example, my right to free speech is limited by the rights of

---

4 K Patel, 'Euthanasia and Physician-Assisted Suicide Policy in the Netherlands and Oregon: A Comparative Analysis' (2004) 19(1) Journal of Health & Social Policy, 37, at 38.
5 M Charlesworth, *Bioethics in a Liberal Society* (Cambridge: Cambridge University Press, 1993), at 4.

others not to be defamed. It is, however, in delineating those restrictions and limitations on autonomy that we begin to see how some of the fine distinctions referred to above become significant. Moreover, autonomy itself is not a simple concept. For some, autonomy is simply self-rule. That is, the individual, *qua* individual and assuming legal competence, is free to make self-regarding decisions, the only caveat – derived in large part from the work of John Stuart Mill[6] – being that liberty can be restricted when the decision taken causes third-party harm. Still others would define autonomy in a more relational manner. On this understanding of autonomy, other-regarding decisions are important. In other words, as we are all products of our environment, so we should have regard to those around us when exercising our choices and decisions.[7] Whichever account is the more appealing, each definition encapsulates acceptance of the authority of individuals to choose and to act. The important characteristic of an autonomous decision on either account is that it is made without external force or pressure by a competent individual, and that it expresses the genuine, authentic interests of that person.

For a variety of reasons, people may feel unwilling or unable to continue to exist in whatever condition they find themselves. For some people the preferred option to continued suffering is death. The reasons for choosing death may be many and varied, but they may also amount to a decision that is recognisably autonomous. Where this is the case, it might be asked why such decisions should not be encapsulated in the general expectation that autonomous decisions should be respected? If autonomy is the overriding principle, then surely it should trump any other (opposing) interests? As Lord Donaldson said in the case of *Re T*:

> The patient's interest consists of his right to self-determination – his right to live his own life how he wishes, even if it will damage his health or lead to his premature death. Society's interest is in upholding the concept that all human life is sacred and that it should be preserved if at all possible. It is well established that in the ultimate the right of the individual is paramount.[8]

Despite this assertion, and while – as we will see later – some choices for death are respected by the law, requests for assisted suicide or euthanasia, even if they can be categorised as fully autonomous, are not. To a large extent, the rationale for this distinction is said to relate to the fact that both assisted suicide and euthanasia involve third parties – usually physicians – whereas suicide (not a crime) is an act carried out by individuals themselves, unaided. Since consent is not a defence to killing, the act of providing assistance is *prima facie* a criminal offence.

---

6   *On Liberty* (London: Longman, Roberts & Green, 1869).
7   For further discussion, see SAM McLean, *Autonomy, Consent and the Law* (London: Routledge-Cavendish, 2010).
8   *Re T* (1992) 9 BMLR 46, at 59.

Is assistance in dying always criminalised?

There are, however, a number of situations in which end of life decisions are made – and respected – in which the individual is not the sole person complicit in the final act (or omission). Take for example, cases where individuals wish to have life-sustaining treatment removed. Just such a situation arose in the case of *Ms B*,[9] when a woman who was dependent on a ventilator requested that it be removed. Her expectation – indeed her hope – was that she would subsequently die; she chose, effectively, death over a quality of life she regarded as unacceptable. In the face of her doctors' refusal to comply with her wishes, the case was litigated. The words of Dame Butler-Sloss are worthy of repetition here:

> If mental capacity is not in issue and the patient, having been given the relevant information and offered the available options, chooses to refuse the treatment, that decision has to be respected by the doctors. Considerations that the best interests of the patient would indicate that the decision should be to consent to treatment are irrelevant.[10]

These words broadly echo those of Lord Goff in the case of *Airedale NHS Trust v Bland*[11] where he too indicated that in the face of a competent, autonomous decision, the principle of self-determination (or autonomy) trumps even the principle of the sanctity of human life.

To be sure, Ms B would not have chosen death over life had she not been in the situation in which she found herself, but it was precisely because of that – to her, intolerable – situation that she made an autonomous decision for death. Acting on her expressed wishes, no doctor would be held liable either in civil or criminal law. This conclusion in what would otherwise appear to be clinical complicity – if not direct involvement – in the patient's death might seem strange given that we have already made the point that the consent of the individual does not provide a defence in the case of a killing. However, it is reached by way of a number of arguments, the validity of which, it will be argued, is somewhat dubious. One such argument rests on the alleged distinction between acts and omissions.

Broadly speaking, we are liable for the consequences of our acts, but not always for those following an omission. For example, were we to attack someone, (an act) liability would follow; on the other hand, were we to avoid assisting someone who is being attacked (an omission), in the absence of a pre-existing duty of care no such liability would attach. It is, therefore, important to assess the purported distinction between acts and omissions, and this arises quite specifically in relation to the question as to whether or not withholding treatment

---

9 *Re B (adult: refusal of treatment)* (2002) 65 BMLR 149.
10 Ibid, at para 174
11 (1993) 12 BMLR 64, at 111–112.

(an omission) is in any meaningful way different from withdrawing treatment (an act). In common sense terms, the former is said to be equivalent to letting die, the latter to killing.

Does this apparent difference actually have any consequences in law? In reality, it does not. Physicians are free to withhold (an omission) or withdraw (an act) treatment – assuming justification and appropriate medical practice – without in either case being culpable. In this situation, and even although there clearly is a pre-existing duty of care between doctor and patient – which would normally mandate accountability for both acts and omissions – neither act nor omission is criminalised provided it is deemed to be in the patient's best interests. The case of Anthony Bland,[12] previously referred to, shows that even some members of the judiciary have concerns about whether or not such a distinction is tenable. Lord Mustill, for example, expressed 'acute unease . . . due in an important part to the sensation that however much the terminologies may differ, the ethical status of the two courses of action is for all relevant purposes indistinguishable'.[13] Further, Price points out that '[e]ven if the treatment refusal is an omission, it is the cause of death where this is the known, inevitable consequence of the patient's decision'.[14] So, withholding life-sustaining treatment and withdrawing life-sustaining treatment both predictably result in death, as would the provision of treatment designed to do so. Grayling points to the somewhat convoluted logic that strives to retain what I have called elsewhere a distinction without a difference:

> Lawyers and doctors distinguish between withholding treatment with death as the result, and giving treatment that causes death. The first is considered to be permissible in law and ethics, the second is not. But in fact there is no difference between them; for withholding treatment is an act, based on a decision, just as giving treatment is an act, based on a decision.[15]

So, if we cannot simplistically rely on the acts/omissions 'distinction' to conclude on the 'rightness' of behaviour that brings about death, is there any additional or alternative basis on which we can reasonably do so? One way is to advert to the question of intention. The doctor's actions, or omissions, can be differentiated from criminal behaviour because she or he does not intend to kill in these circumstances. Evidence of intention is generally a prerequisite of successful prosecution, and the assumption is that doctors always act in the best interests of their patients. They cure or palliate; they do not kill. However, simple reflection on the case of *Ms B* must surely lead to the conclusion that the act (or omission) of removing the ventilator foreseeably led to Ms B's death,

---

12 *Bland*, ibid.
13 *Bland*, n 11, at para. 132.
14 D Price, 'Assisted Suicide and Refusing Medical Treatment: Linguistics, Morals and Legal Contortions' (1996) 4(4), Medical Law Review, 270, at 287–288.
15 A Grayling, 'Right to die' (2005) 330 BMJ, 799, at 799.

and it must be remembered that 'there are cases where simply having foresight about a particular event is sufficient to ground moral responsibility'.[16] The doctor knew that Ms B's death would follow removal of the ventilator – indeed, this was one reason for refusing her request in the first place. Yet, not only does the law permit such an act, any doctor who refuses to comply with the patient's wishes will be liable to prosecution for assault. As Orentlicher points out, 'many treatment withdrawals reflect an intent to die . . . When physicians discontinue life-sustaining treatment for these patients, they are doing so to facilitate an intent to die.'[17] In such facilitation, arguably they are at least complicit in the death. Moreover, in the case of *Bland*,[18] where the court authorised the removal of assisted nutrition and hydration (ANH) from a young man in a persistent (or permanent) vegetative state, Lord Goff made it clear that even when the intention to kill is there, it may still be possible to approve the act in question. He did not doubt that 'the whole purpose of stopping artificial feeding is to bring about the death of Anthony Bland'.[19] Thus, in this case, where the intention was clearly to bring about the death – interestingly of an individual who was in no position to express an opinion, far less an autonomous one – policy seems able to circumvent the prohibition on killing.

The difficulty – if not impossibility – of accurately determining intention is also evidenced by research into the practice of terminal or palliative sedation. In this scenario, a patient suffering from refractory (that is, otherwise uncontrollable and untenable) symptoms may be sedated either temporarily or permanently. In the latter case, which is an increasingly common way of managing end of life situations,[20] De Graeff and Dean report that, '[t]he use of sedation for the relief of symptoms at the end of life is open to abuse. There are data from several countries indicating that administration of sedating medication, ostensibly to relieve distress, but with the manifest intent of hastening death, is commonplace.'[21] As Smith notes, '[i]ntentions are neither easy to determine nor . . . simplistic'.[22] While it may be argued that '[i]n palliative sedation the intention is to relieve refractory symptoms, never to kill the patient',[23] when it is accompanied by the withholding of ANH, as it often is, then this may

---

16 SW Smith, *End of Life Decisions in Medical Care: Principles and Policies for Regulating the Dying Process* (Cambridge: Cambridge University Press, 2014), at 83.
17 D Orentlicher, *Matters of Life and Death: Making Moral Theory Work in Medical Ethics and the Law* (Princeton and Oxford: Princeton University Press, 2001), at 35.
18 *Bland*, n 11.
19 (1993) 12 BMLR 64, per Lord Goff at 127.
20 For discussion, see S Sterckx, K Raus and F Mortier (eds), *Continuous Sedation at the End of Life: Ethical, Clinical and Legal Perspectives* (Cambridge: Cambridge University Press, 2013), Introduction.
21 A De Graeff and M Dean, 'Palliative Sedation Therapy in the Last Weeks of Life: A Literature Review and Recommendations for Standards' (2007) 10(1) Journal of Palliative Medicine, 67, at 77.
22 SW Smith, *End-of-Life Decisions in Medical Care Principles and Policies for Regulating the Dying Process* (Cambridge: Cambridge University Press, 2014), at 83.
23 B Broeckaert, 'Palliative Sedation, Physician-Assisted Suicide, and Euthanasia: "Same but Different"?' (2011) 11(6) The American Journal of Bioethics, 62, 63.

well be an example of a situation where foresight and intention are difficult to separate. Failure to provide ANH will foreseeably, but also intentionally, bring about death; otherwise, save where ANH itself can be shown to be harmful, there would be no rationale to withhold it.

If intention is an insufficient basis on which to judge behaviour, and the alleged distinction between acts and omissions is also of dubious value, on what grounds can the law continue to permit 'assistance' in death in some cases and not in others? This is a difficult question to answer.

Why not legalise assisted death?

While what has gone before might suggest that the devices used to distinguish between lawful and unlawful assistance in dying are based on fictions and sometimes tortuous reasoning, there are, of course, other arguments that are levelled against legalisation of assisted dying. One primary objection relates to what I earlier called cultural sensitivities. In a culture that values the sanctity of life (whether for religious or other reasons), surely it cannot be permissible deliberately or foreseeably to bring about the death of another person? To an extent, this question has already been addressed. While the law rightly will seek to uphold the sanctity of life, courts have declared the state's interest in so doing to be secondary to the right of individuals to act in a self-determining or autonomous manner, and we have already seen examples of situations in which a choice for death – with assistance, whether active or passive – is respected in law.

Nor is it inevitable that legalising assisted dying would breach the harm principle already referred to. In their study, Georges *et al.* found that relatives of those having an assisted death (that is, those most likely to be affected or 'harmed') felt that an assisted death:

> mainly contributes to the quality of the end of the patients' life because their wishes are respected and further suffering is prevented. It also appeared that knowing how one's own wishes and requests for euthanasia will be treated generated feelings of trust and control, thus possibly contributing favorably to the quality of the end of the patient's life.[24]

Far from causing harm, for individuals making the, undoubtedly difficult, decision to seek an assisted death, important values are protected when their request is respected. These include 'control, maintenance of independence and self-determination [which] are, for many people, important aspects of a good death'.[25]

---

24 J Georges, D Bregje, B Onwuteaka-Philipsen, M Muller, G van der Wal, A van der Heide and P van der Maas, '"Relatives" Perspective on the Terminally Ill Patients Who Died after Euthanasia or Physician-Assisted Suicide: A Retrospective Cross-Sectional Interview Study in the Netherlands' (2007) 31(1) Death Studies, 1, at 12.
25 J Rietjens, A van der Heide, B Onwuteaka-Philipsen, P van der Maas and G van der Wal, 'Preferences of the Dutch general public for a good death and associations with attitudes towards end-of-life decision-making' (2006) 20 Palliative Medicine, 685, at 690.

However, other forms of harm might emerge. For example, some fear the development of a so-called slippery slope in which permitting assisted dying will result in many more deaths, some of them not freely chosen. This argument takes two forms: the logical and the empirical. The logical argument is described by Burgess: 'the real worry ... must be of a slide through habituation into wholesale killing of a kind the reformers never contemplated legalising.'[26] The empirical form of the slippery slope argument 'does not allege that the consequences are inevitable but that they will happen in practice because safeguards to prevent it either cannot be designed or will not work'.[27] Should any such slope appear, this would be a strong argument against legalisation; however, there is no such empirical evidence. Even if the categories of candidates for assisted dying expand, or the numbers of assisted deaths increase, this does not inherently mean that the slope has been stepped upon. Rather, it may simply mean that the system is actually working and those states which have legalised assisted dying are increasingly comfortable that the safeguards in place are sufficient.

There are, of course, other arguments against legalisation of assisted dying. Some are rooted in religious or philosophical concerns. Steinbock argues that 'laws against suicide and mercy killing have developed from religious doctrine'.[28] The belief that 'only God has the right to determine when a person will die, or that committing suicide is a blasphemous rejection of God's gift of life'[29] is one held in good faith by many people, and is an unarguable proposition for those who believe it. However, this begs the question as to whether or not their beliefs should be imposed on others. In the US case of *Compassion in Dying v State of Washington*, this telling point was made:

> Those who believe strongly that death must come without physician assistance are free to follow that creed, be they doctors or patients. They are not free, however to force their views, their religious convictions, or their philosophies on all other members of a democratic society, and to compel those whose values differ from theirs to die painful, protracted, and agonizing deaths.[30]

Dworkin puts it even more simply and starkly, saying, '[m]aking someone die in a way that others approve, but he believes a horrifying contradiction of his life, is a devastating, odious form of tyranny.'[31]

Finally, opponents of legalisation challenge the extent to which a seemingly autonomous decision may in fact be forced by third parties or external circumstances. The fear is that relatives or others (perhaps even doctors) will put pressure

---

26 J Burgess, 'The great slippery-slope argument' (1993) *JME*, 169, at 171.
27 M Freeman, 'Death, dying and the Human Rights Act' (1999) 52 Current Legal Problems, 218, at 233–234.
28 B Steinbock, 'The case for physician assisted suicide: not (yet) proven' (2005) 31 *JME*, 235, at 236.
29 Steinbock, ibid.
30 79 F 3d 790 (9th Cir 1996) 810, at 839.
31 R Dworkin, *Life's Dominion: An Argument about Abortion and Euthanasia* (London: HarperCollins, 1993), at 217.

on the ill or vulnerable person (often conceptualised as elderly or disabled) to ask for an assisted death, thereby liberating an inheritance or getting rid of a burden. This is a genuine fear and would be of great concern were it to occur. However, proponents of legalisation do not argue that just *any* apparent decision for an assisted death should be respected; only one which is shown to be competent and autonomous would be acceptable. Given that the law judges issues of competence and autonomy on a regular basis in other areas, surely it is capable of doing so here?[32] In fact, the likelihood is that any legislation to decriminalise assisted dying would be bound by careful caveats and restrictions, many more, in fact, than any that currently circumscribe, for example, the right to choose death by refusing treatment. Second, if manipulation is possible in the case of assisted deaths, it is also possible in other end of life decisions which are currently accepted. As Dworkin says, '[i]f a physician can manipulate the patient's request for death, he can manipulate the patient's request for termination of treatment.'[33] The same can be said of relatives or other third parties.

What's the difference?

What we have seen here is that, in a number of circumstances, an individual may prefer death to continued existence – not in the abstract, but in the face of the reality of suffering. What people want is a 'good death'. Evidence suggests that the reasons for this preference are subtle and complex. Rietjens *et al.* for example, found that:

> Items that were considered important for a good death by the large majority of respondents included the possibility to say goodbye to loved ones (94%), dying with dignity (92%), being able to decide about treatment at the end of life (88%), and dying free of pain (87%). Items that were less often considered important were dying at home (65%), not being a burden on relatives (65%), being prepared for death (63%), being conscious until death (61%), and not depending on others (60%).[34]

Raus, Sterckx and Mortier also claim that – where available – people 'choose PAS [physician assisted suicide] not in order to avoid pain, but mainly because they want to avoid further indignity, and they value the opportunity to control the manner in which they die'.[35] Even opponents of legalising assisted dying will

---

32 As Lady Hale recently suggested in *R (Nicklinson & Anor) v Ministry of Justice; R (AM) v DPP* [2014] UKSC 38, at 314.
33 G Dworkin, 'Public Policy and Physician-Assisted Suicide', in G Dworkin, RG Frey and S Bok (eds), *Euthanasia and Physician-Assisted Suicide: For and Against* (Cambridge: Cambridge University Press, 1998), 64, at 67.
34 J Rietjens, A van der Heide, B Onwuteaka-Philipsen, P van der Maas and G van der Wal, 'Preferences of the Dutch general public for a good death and associations with attitudes towards end-of-life decision-making' (2006) 20 Palliative Medicine, 685, at 687.
35 K Raus, S Sterckx and F Mortier 'Is Continuous Sedation at the End of Life an Ethically Preferable Alternative to Physician-Assisted Suicide?' (2011) 11(6) The American Journal of Bioethics, 32, at 35.

surely recognise, and sympathise with, these aspirations. While, as we have seen, there are some cases in which death can legitimately be chosen (suicide, refusal of treatment, court-endorsed removal of treatment), others, where individuals equally legitimately wish to control their death, are regarded as illegitimate. Problematically, the most common situation where a decision for death is not respected is where a competent individual makes an autonomous choice. At the very least this must seem paradoxical, if not cruel.

Yet, it may be argued, the deliberate and knowledgeable involvement of, say, a doctor, in the patient's death flies in the face of the legal prohibition on killing, which is highly valued. What has been argued here is that this is a fundamental obfuscation of the similarities between, for example, treatment withdrawal and assisted dying. As has been said, '[t]o say that the patient's illness, rather than the withdrawal of life-sustaining treatment "causes" the patient's death simply means that a court will not hold the physician liable for the death. Legal causation is a question of policy, not mechanical connection.'[36]

Equally, efforts to demonstrate significant differences between 'acceptable' end of life decisions and assisted dying tend to fail. Complicity in a chosen death can occur either by act or omission; probably most would admit this, given the frailty of the acts/omissions doctrine and the difficulties of establishing intention. Policy and context are flimsy bases on which to criminalise autonomously chosen decisions.

We have also seen that the voluntariness of a choice for an assisted death is sometimes called into question where the patient requires active assistance. Yet, the very same inquiry needs to be made where the route to an assisted death is via refusal or rejection of life-sustaining treatment. In the case of *Ms B*, the only question addressed was her competence, not whether her decision was free and truly informed. For Jackson, it is 'illogical' to assert that 'Ms B was competent to request that she be disconnected from artificial ventilation, but that we could never make the identical assessment with a sufficient degree of certainty if Ms B had needed more active intervention in order to bring her life to an end'.[37]

Recognition of the possibility that the differential treatment of specific end of life decisions is a matter of policy rather than strictly applied legal principles forces consideration of the consequences of this policy. The words of Lord Browne-Wilkinson in the *Bland* case provide a poignant description of these consequences:

> How can it be lawful to allow a patient to die slowly, though painlessly, over a period of weeks from lack of food but unlawful to produce his immediate death by a lethal injection, thereby saving his family from yet another ordeal to add to the tragedy that has already struck them? I find

---

36 Notes, 'Physician Assisted Suicide and the Right to Die with Assistance' (1991–92) 105 *Harv L Rev* 2001, at 2029.
37 E Jackson, 'Whose Death is it Anyway?: Euthanasia and the Medical Profession', in J Holder, C O'Cinneide and M Freeman (eds), (2004) 57 *Current Legal Problems*, 415, at 439.

it difficult to find a moral answer to that question. But it is undoubtedly the law.[38]

But is it 'good' law? Can it be right that the sanctity of life 'is only jealously guarded when the issue in question is the right of a competent individual to choose his or her own death with the assistance of a third party'?[39] Or can we agree that '[f]rom the patient's perspective, the line the law currently draws between lawful and unlawful life-shortening practices makes very little sense'?[40]

Looking to the future

Interestingly, Puppinck and de La Hougue have recently identified what they see as a shift within the European Court of Human Rights which may have significance in those member states of the Council of Europe that have not yet legalised assisted dying.[41] In an extensive review of cases considered by the Court, they detect a move away from strict adherence to Article 2's right to life in the European Convention on Human Rights,[42] towards an interpretation of Article 8 (the right to private and family life) which seems more amenable to recognition of a rights-based approach to end of life decisions. Their examination of recent cases before the Court leads them to conclude that '[t]he court has made no secret of the moral foundation of its approach: it acts from an individualistic conception of dignity, which implies a right to quality of life, in particular against old age and decay'.[43]

In the case of *Haas v Switzerland*,[44] the applicant sought to commit suicide with a physician-provided prescription, which was declined. He argued that the state should be compelled to provide him with 'the medical means of committing suicide without pain and without a risk of failure'.[45] The Court's position was that 'an individual's right to decide by what means and at what point his or her life will end ... is one of the aspects of the right to respect for private life within the meaning of Article 8 of the Convention'.[46] In *Koch v Germany*,[47] the emphasis shifted from the individual's need to prove that the state should provide assisted dying, to the need for the state to justify its failure to do so.

---

38 *Bland*, n 11 at 131.
39 S McLean and S Elliston, 'Death, Decision-Making and the Law' (2004) Juridical Review, 265, at 269.
40 Jackson, n 36, at 433.
41 G Puppinck and C de La Hougue, 'The right to assisted suicide in the case law of the European Court of Human Rights' (2014) 18(7–8) The International Journal of Human Rights, 735.
42 Which forms the basis of the UK's Human Rights Act 1998.
43 Puppinck and de La Hougue n 41, at 746.
44 (App. No. 31322/07) ECHR 20 January 2011.
45 Puppinck and de La Hougue, n 41, at 739.
46 *Haas*, n 44, at para 51.
47 (App. No. 497/09) ECHR 19 July 2012.

Finally, in *Gross v Switzerland*,[48] the Court was concerned with more procedural matters, but declared that:

> in an era of growing medical sophistication combined with longer life expectancies, many people are concerned that they should not be forced to linger on in old age or in states of advanced physical or mental decrepitude which conflict with strongly held ideas of self and personal identity.[49]

According to Puppinck and de La Hougue, '[t]he main consequence of this case is to transfer the practice of assisted suicide from the medical domain to civil liberties'.[50]

Conclusion

To an extent, moves within the United Kingdom also seem to have re-evaluated the status of autonomy at the end of life. Most notably, both legislative[51] and court-based[52] developments seem to demonstrate a perceived need for revision and clarification of the law at the end of life. For proponents of legal change, these initiatives may not go far enough, but they may provide a measure of comfort for those who, for their own autonomous reasons, wish lawfully to die with assistance. In a society that values liberty, autonomy and freedom to act where no harm to others is shown, individual decisions should be respected even when they conflict with the opinions held (however firmly) by others. Most importantly, they should be protected against 'the tyranny of pluralism, i.e., the majority vote of elected representatives of the people themselves'.[53] While law reform in the UK may be incremental rather than dramatic, and may maintain some of the distinctions and sophistry criticised here, any movement to respect autonomous decisions at the end of life can be welcomed.

Would anything argued for here change Brazier's early resistance to law reform?[54] Perhaps not, but much has changed since 1996, and, at the very least, we have learned that the law is both in need of clarification and capable of respecting autonomy without sacrificing the vulnerable.

---

48 (App. No. 67810/10) ECHR 12 May 2013.
49 Ibid, at para 58.
50 Puppinck and de La Hougue, n 41, at 743.
51 Assisted Dying Bill [HL] 2014–15; Assisted Suicide (Scotland) Bill 2013.
52 *Nicklinson*, n 32.
53 J Safranek and S Safranek, 'Assisted Suicide: The State versus The People' (1997) 21 Seattle University Law Review, 261, at 265.
54 Brazier, n 1.

6 The past, present and future of EU health law

Tamara Hervey

Introduction

In 2000, Margaret Brazier and Nicola Glover considered the future of medical law.[1] One of the perhaps unforeseen futures of medical law at that time was its European Union (EU) version. This chapter reflects on the past, present and future of EU health law. It is inspired by, and responds to, Brazier and Glover's approach, substantive content and analysis. Brazier and Glover characterise their approach as involving 'a degree of hyperbole and a great deal of crystal ball gazing'.[2] While this chapter includes some of the latter, it attempts to avoid the former. Rather, it offers an analysis of the direction of travel of EU health law which eschews the almost catastrophising tendencies within some discussions,[3] particularly those from the health law and policy community.[4]

The past and present of EU health law

This chapter implies that 'EU health law' is a meaningful analytical category. Whether this is the case was certainly disputed, and doubts continue. Over ten years ago, with encouragement from Margaret Brazier, Jean McHale and I explored the important and interesting *interfaces* between EU law and the ways in which it constrains and empowers state actors, and individuals, within the EU's Member States, on the one hand, and health law, on the other.[5] Others

---

1   M Brazier and N Glover, 'Does Medical Law Have a Future?' in D Hayton (ed), *Law's Futures* (Hart 2000).
2   Ibid 372.
3   For references, see T Hervey and J McHale, *EU Health Law: Themes and Implications* (CUP 2015).
4   In that regard, it is based on my work with Jean McHale, and I wish to express full credit here for the fruitfulness of that collaboration, especially as McHale is not a named co-author in this particular chapter. For a full account of our current collaborative efforts, see Hervey and McHale (n 3).
5   T Hervey and J McHale, *Health Law and the European Union* (CUP 2004) 4–5. On the word 'and' in such contexts, see T Murphy, 'Repetition, Revolution and Resonance: An Introduction to New Technologies and Human Rights' in T Murphy (ed), *New Technologies and Human Rights* (OUP 2009).

have continued in that vein,[6] assisting those concerned with health to understand the implications of EU law for their activities. EU health policy work takes a similar approach. The metaphor of 'patchwork' abounds.[7]

The relevant legal provisions constitutionally 'belong' to different domains, principally those of the internal market, social affairs, public health, enterprise, and economic and trade policy. This constitutional dispersion suggests that there is insufficient coherence in EU health policy for EU health law to exist. Much here also depends on what is considered to fall within the scope of EU health law. Should we have a narrow focus on cross-border medical treatment, the migration of patients and professionals within the EU? Should we include EU regulation of pharmaceuticals and medical devices? Should we also encompass public health protection and the promotion of good health, through, for instance, the regulation of tobacco, alcohol, food, air and water quality, road safety and health and safety at work? With too broad a focus, all of EU law (indeed all of law) is potentially health law. An approach that sees the core function of the relevant law as determining whether it is part of EU health law is most appropriate here. De Ruijter expresses this particularly well:

> If EU agricultural policy aims to create a European market for milk, it is agricultural policy. However European Union health policy is adopted when, in the context of creating a market for milk, mandatory testing for bovine tuberculosis is implemented at EU level.[8]

Space precludes a full defence of the implication that 'EU health law' now exists and will continue to do so into the future. Indeed, Brazier and Glover noted that 'medical law' would not have featured in a 'Law's Futures' collection published in the middle of the 20th century, but referred briefly to thriving scholarship, litigation and legislation, rather than embarking on an extended defence of the existence of medical law. Similarly, EU health law is the subject of scholarship, litigation and legislation, which expresses its principles and focuses on particular themes. This is in addition to promoting an understanding of the field as structurally coherent and distinct.[9]

---

6 See for example L Hancher and W Sauter, *EU Competition and Internal Market Law in the Health Care Sector* (OUP 2012); J Van de Gronden et al. (eds), *Health Care and EU Law* (Springer 2011); E Mossialos et al. (eds), *Health Systems Governance in Europe: The Role of EU Law and Policy* (CUP 2010).
7 H Vollaard, 'The Making of a European Healthcare Union: Insights from Comparative Federalism' Journal of European Public Policy (forthcoming); T Hervey and B Vanhercke, 'Health Care and the EU: The Law and Policy Patchwork' in Mossialos et al. (n 6); W Lamping, 'European Integration and Health Policy: A Peculiar Relationship' in M Steffen (ed), *Health Governance in Europe: Issues, Challenges and Theories* (Routledge 2005).
8 A de Ruijter, *A Silent Revolution: The Expansion of EU Power in the Field of Human Health* (PhD thesis, University of Amsterdam 2015) 59.
9 For further discussion, see T Hervey, 'Telling Stories about European Union Health Law: The Emergence of a New Field of Legal Enquiry' Comparative European Politics (forthcoming).

The present and future of EU health law

Brazier and Glover identify four interconnected themes through which they explore the future of medical law. The first is 'law's relationship with medicine and science'.[10] Discoveries about the human body, and its capacities for healing and regeneration, as well as in materials technologies, such as nanotechnology, raise profound challenges for law. Which medical 'advances' should be authorised, protected from criminal prosecution, and paid for by public health systems, and which should not, are questions for medical law. For Brazier and Glover, these questions can be navigated using human rights reasoning, but human rights law itself does not necessarily reach an appropriate balance between individual desires and collective responsibilities.

Second, Brazier and Glover trace the shift from medical law (essentially private law) to health law (essentially public law). There are significant consequences of this move for national health systems based on solidarity models. Where access to novel (and inherently more risky) treatments is enhanced, through the loosening of criminal or tort law's grip on healthcare professionals' ability to provide such treatments, and then things go wrong:

> The NHS is left to deal with the consequences. The cost to the public purse is increased because the private market procedures, which NHS clinicians might have declined to perform, have catapulted the consumers into incontrovertible *illness* . . . [T]he NHS picks up the burden of privately funded care.[11]

Changes in conceptions of (ill-)health are Brazier and Glover's third theme. They discuss the implications of human desires or preferences being expressed as health needs:[12] consequently, 'medicine in all its forms is just another good to be bought freely in the marketplace'.[13] The 'marketisation' of health alters relationships between healthcare professionals and patients/consumers. Healthcare professionals are no longer gatekeepers to healthcare. Indeed, they are no longer in continuing, one-to-one, loyalty-based relationships with patients.[14]

Finally, Brazier and Glover consider changes in care structures for the vulnerable elderly and those with mental ill-health (many elderly people fall into both categories). The blurring of boundaries between healthcare and social care has implications for healthcare law. Most worrying is that the 'evidence that on occasion "carers" do not care is also ignored'.[15] For one writing in the UK in

---

10 Brazier and Glover (n 1) 372.
11 Ibid 378.
12 Ibid 374.
13 Ibid 375.
14 Ibid 380.
15 Ibid 387.

2015, this is perhaps the most poignant and prescient of Brazier and Glover's observations in 2000.[16]

In the context of EU health law, all four of these themes have been associated with an implicit (or sometimes explicit) movement towards a less desirable position than the status quo. EU health law, it is felt,[17] undermines or compromises the health law that we know. It focuses on the bringing to market of new health technologies, using law to support scientific developments that may well enhance the EU's global economic performance, through developing its internal market, and hence the ability of Europe-based enterprises to compete globally. But this aspect of EU health law does not necessarily support ethical principles[18] or the health needs of Europe's (or the world's) most vulnerable. EU health law changes relationships between healthcare professionals and patients for the worse, because it brings into those relationships undesired principles of consumerism, competition and related concepts of liberalism (freedom to trade, freedom to consume). It 'marketises' medical services, by seeing them as 'factors of production'. EU health law thereby grants a privileged constitutional position to freedom to receive and provide medical services, requiring those who seek to restrict such freedom to cast their position as the exception to the rule.[19]

---

16 See for example R Francis, *Report of the Mid Staffordshire NHS Foundation Trust Public Inquiry* (HM Government Stationery Office 2013); R Francis, *Independent Inquiry into Care Provided by Mid Staffordshire NHS Foundation Trust* (HM Government Stationery Office 2010); C Newdick and C Danbury, 'Culture, Compassion and Clinical Neglect: Probity in the NHS after Mid Staffordshire' (2013) JME (doi:10.1136/medethics-2012–101048); C Newdick, 'From Hippocrates to Commodities: Three Models of NHS Governance' (2014) 22 Med L Rev 162.

17 See Hervey and McHale (n 3) for examples.

18 See for example M Flear, 'Clinical Trials Abroad: The Marketable Ethics, Weak Protections and Vulnerable Subjects of EU Law' in Alberta Albors-Llorens et al. (eds), *Cambridge Yearbook of European Legal Studies, Vol 16 2013–2014* (Hart 2014); G Bache, M Flear and T Hervey, 'The Defining Features of the European Union's Approach to Regulating New Health Technologies'; AM Farrell, 'Risk, Legitimacy, and EU Regulation of Health Technologies' and E Stokes, 'Something Old, Something New, Something Borrowed: Emerging Health Technologies and the Continuing Role of Existing Regulations' in M Flear et al. (eds), *European Law and New Health Technologies* (OUP 2013); AM Farrell, *The Politics of Blood: Ethics, Innovation and the Regulation of Risk* (CUP 2012); M Lee, 'Risk and Beyond: EU Regulation of Nanotechnology' (2010) 35 EL Rev 799; H Roscam, 'Patients' Rights in a Technology and Market Driven-Europe' (2010) 17 EJHL 11; J McHale, 'Nanomedicine and the EU: Some Legal Ethical and Regulatory Challenges' (2009) 16 MJ 65; A Mahalatchimy, 'Access to Advanced Therapy Medicinal Products in the EU: Where Do We Stand?' (2001) 18 EJHL 305.

19 See for example Hancher and Sauter (n 6) 53–83, but see 133–137; W Gekiere, R Baeten and W Palm, 'Free Movement of Services in the EU and Health Care' in Mossialos et al. (n 6); M Hartlev, 'Diversity and Harmonisation. Trends and Challenges in European Health Law' (2010) 17 EJHL 37; C Newdick, 'The European Court of Justice, Transnational Health Care, and Social Citizenship – Accidental Death of a Concept?' (2009) 26 Wis Int'l LJ 845; C Newdick, 'Preserving Social Citizenship in Health Care Markets – There May be Trouble Ahead' (2008) 2 MJLH 93; C Newdick, 'Citizenship, Free Movement and Health Care: Cementing Individual Rights by Corroding Social Solidarity' (2006) 43 CMLR 1645; G Davies, 'The Process and Side-effects of Harmonisation of European Welfare States', (2006) Jean Monnet Working Paper 2/06 <www.jeanmonnetprogram.org/papers/06/060201.pdf> (accessed 20 January 2015).

Access to the EU's market in medical services is strengthened; the idea of medical services as expressing care relationships is diminished. EU law also affects social care.[20] If it is hard to call to account '"carers" who do not care' in a *national* context, then it is significantly more difficult to do so in a cross-jurisdictional context. The consequences of conflict-of-laws, with all its complexities, and the practicalities of bringing litigation, or changing accountability structures in other ways, such as through alternative dispute resolution, make it almost impossible for EU law to protect the vulnerable.

Although there is some truth in these conclusions, none is defensible in its strongest form.[21] This is because EU health law has its own special characteristics and specific legitimacy, separable from those of EU economic law. Although EU health law strongly embodies the themes of consumerism, and competition within a market, those are not the only themes of EU health law. EU health law also embodies solidarity as the underlying basis of health systems in Europe, and the European commitment to the value of equality of treatment according to medical need. Take, for instance, the jurisprudence of the Court of Justice of the EU (CJEU) on free movement of services and freedom of establishment of health institutions.[22] Considered impressionistically, the CJEU appears to be increasingly willing to disrupt national health systems by allowing access to extra-jurisdictional institutions or actors.

---

20 T Hervey, A Stark, A Dawson et al., 'Long-Term Care for Older People and EU Law: The Position in England and Scotland' (2012) 34 J Soc Wel & Fam L 104.
21 The arguments outlined here are explained in much greater detail in Hervey and McHale (n 3).
22 On hospitals, see *Geraets-Smits/Peerbooms* C–157/99, EU:C:2001:404; *Müller-Fauré/van Riet*, C-385/99, EU:C:2003:270; *Inizan*, C-56/01, EU:C:2003:578; *Watts* EU:C:2006:325; *Stamatelaki*, C-444/05, EU:C:2007:231; *Commission v France (Major Medical Equipment)*, C-512/08, EU:C:2010:579 (and now see Directive 2011/24/EU on the application of patients' rights in cross-border healthcare [2011] OJ L88/45, Article 8 which consolidates these rulings); *CBI*, T-137/10, EU:T:2012:584; *Asklepios Kliniken*, T-167/04, EU:T:2007:215. On national health insurance institutions, see *AOK Bundesverband* EU:C:2004:150; *Commission v Slovenia (Non-Life Insurance)*, C-185/11, EU:C:2012:43; *AG2R Prévoyance*, C-437/09, EU:C:2011:112. On pharmacies, see *DocMorris*, C-322/01, EU:C:2003:664; *Commission v Germany (Hospital Pharmacies)*, C-141/07, EU:C:2008:492; *Commission v Italy (Pharmacies)*, C-531/06, EU:C:2009:315; *Neumann-Siewert*, C-171/07 and C-172/07, EU:C:2009:316; *Pérez/Gómez*, C-570/07 and C-571/07, EU:C:2010:300; *Venturini*, C-159/12, C-160/12 and C-161/12, EU:C:2013:791; *Susisalo*, C-84/11, EU:C:2012:374; *Sam McCauley Chemists*, C-221/05, EU:C:2006:474. On laboratories, see *Commission v France (Biomedical Laboratories I)*, C-496/01, EU:C:2004:137; *Commission v Belgium (Clinical Biology Laboratories)*, C-221/85, EU:C:1987:81; *Commission v France (Biomedical Laboratories II)*, C-89/09, EU:C:2010:772; *Commission v Luxembourg (Laboratory Analyses and Tests)*, C-490/09, EU:C:2011:34. On blood and human tissue institutions, see *CopyGene*, C-262/08, EU:C:2010:328; *Future Health Technologies*, C-86/09, EU:C:2010:334; *De Fruytier*, C-237/09, EU:C:2010:316. On dental clinics, see *Kohll* EU:C:1998:171; *Doulamis*, C-446/05, EU:C:2008:157; *Hartlauer*, C-169/07, EU:C:2009:141. On opticians and ophthalmologists see *MacQueen*, C-108/96, EU:C:2001:67; *Commission v Greece (Opticians)*, C-140/03, EU:C:2005:242; *Ker-Optika*, C-108/09, EU:C:2010:725. See Hervey and McHale (n 3) chapters 9–11.

In this regard, the CJEU is criticised for paying insufficient attention to the role of national health (insurance) systems in securing equitable access to healthcare, and promoting solidarity between healthy and less healthy people, and across generations, within a particular Member State. The frequently articulated fear is that the future of EU health law thus implies a market-based system for health care services within EU Member States – EU health law inexorably moves health systems towards liberalism.[23] But the CJEU does not go this far. A closer scrutiny of the jurisprudence shows a different trajectory. The CJEU differentiates between institutions and also types of healthcare or service. Where an institution or service is seen by the CJEU to be close to the 'heart' of the national health system, such as in the case of public/national health insurance, hospitals, laboratories or blood services, the CJEU does not follow the consumer and competition-led logic of internal market law. Rather, EU health law respects the 'special place' of health systems, and does not treat them simply as an expression of actors engaging within a market.[24]

Bringing healthcare services provided through national health systems within the scope of EU health law does involve conceptualising healthcare as a consumer service. As noted above, the very structure of EU law can set the desires of an individual consumer of healthcare services (patient) against the priorities of a national health system, with the former as the rule and the latter as the exception. But EU health law does not treat health services as essentially identical to other consumer services. It recognises that healthcare rarely operates as a 'one-shot' *caveat emptor* transaction. Rather, it takes place in the context of trust-based relationships, which are often ongoing. Even elective surgery may involve periods of aftercare, where lines between health and social care may be blurred.[25] Patients frequently do not directly contract with healthcare institutions or professionals at all – provision is mediated through insurers who may direct individuals to specific providers, or through a nationalised health service, where the choice of provider may be very limited indeed. EU health law does not entirely replace relationships of solidarity, trust and a professional ethic of care with those of consumer relations.[26] EU health law recognises the need to secure financial sustainability of national health systems, especially in the context of fiscal austerity.[27] It also recognises that 'rights' to healthcare are not only consumer rights, or even patient rights, but are also human rights.[28]

---

23 For examples, see Hervey and McHale (n 3).
24 See the case law cited above (n 22) and discussion in Hervey and McHale (n 3).
25 In some cases these are necessary for the remainder of a patient's life, for example organ transplant patients must continue taking immune suppressants to prevent organ rejection.
26 See for example the more recent cases of *Commission v Spain (Emergency hospital care)* Case C-211/08 EU:C:2010:340; *Elchinov*, C-173/09, EU:C:2010:581; *Non-hospital Medical Care*, C-255/09, EU:C:2011:695; and the consolidation of the principles inherent in these cases in Directive 2011/24/EU (n 22).
27 See also S Greer, 'The Three Faces of European Union Health Policy: Policy, Markets, Austerity' (2014) 33 Policy and Society 13.
28 See further de Ruijter (n 8).

EU health law 73

Respect for principles of solidarity, equality and human rights protection in EU health law is not limited to the jurisprudence of the CJEU. Many aspects of EU health legislation also embody these themes. The Patients' Rights Directive 2011/24/EU is only the most high profile example. Other examples include exclusions for the health sector in EU public procurement and competition law;[29] and protection of health rights in EU migration law.[30] EU legislation, including internal market legislation, also often embodies ethical principles.[31] The logic of EU economic law implies that we should expect a movement towards convergence on a European standard for ethically controversial medical treatments, for instance, abortion or euthanasia, as well as on ethics in medical research.[32] But such a movement has not taken place. The outcomes of relevant litigation,[33] and, more importantly, the overall lack of such litigation, because of the narrow framing of those outcomes, demonstrate that the consumerising effects of EU internal market law do not undermine ethical settlements expressed in national law.[34]

---

29 See for example Directive 2014/24/EU on public procurement [2014] OJ L94/65; Regulation 360/2012/EU on the application of Articles 107 and 108 of the Treaty on the Functioning of the European Union to de minimis aid granted to undertakings providing services of general economic interest [2012] OJ L114/8.
30 See for example Directive 2013/33/EU laying down standards for the reception of applicants for international protection [2013] OJ L180/96; Directive 2011/95/EU on standards for the qualification of third-country nationals or stateless persons as beneficiaries of international protection, for a uniform status for refugees or for persons eligible for subsidiary protection, and for the content of the protection granted [2011] L337/9; Directive 2011/36/EU on preventing and combating trafficking in human beings and protecting its victims, and replacing Council Framework Decision 2002/629/JHA [2011] OJ L101/1.
31 See for example Regulation 536/2014/EU on clinical trials on medicinal products for human use, and repealing Directive 2001/20/EC [2014] OJ L158/1; Directive 2010/63/EU on the protection of animals used for scientific purposes [2010] OJ L276/33; Directive 2010/53/EU on standards of quality and safety of human organs intended for transplantation [2010] OJ L207/14; Directive 2005/28/EC laying down principles and detailed guidelines for good clinical practice as regards investigational medicinal products for human use, as well as the requirements for authorisation of the manufacturing or importation of such products [2005] OJ L91/13; Directive 2004/23/EC on setting standards of quality and safety for the donation, procurement, testing, processing, preservation, storage and distribution of human tissues and cells [2004] OJ L102/48; Directive 2002/98/EC setting standards of quality and safety for the collection, testing, processing, storage and distribution of human blood and blood components and amending Directive 2001/83/EC [2003] OJ L33/30; Regulation 141/2000/EC on orphan medicinal products [2000] OJ L18/1.
32 See for example *Brüstle*, C-34/10, EU:C:2011:669.
33 See *SPUC v Grogan*, C-159/90, EU:C:1991:378. No other litigation involving abortion has so far reached the CJEU. Other relevant cases have been considered by national courts alone, see for instance: *AG v Open Door Counselling Ltd* [1988] 2 CMLR 443; *AG v X* [1992] 2 CMLR 277.
34 This is also the case for the law of the European Convention on Human Rights (not covered in this chapter), where the Strasbourg Court continues to respect national margins of appreciation in such contexts.

Many aspects of EU health law also support the reduction of risk of harm. These include legislation on pharmaceuticals and medical devices,[35] and legislation which impedes a liberal or even libertarian approach to protection of health and prevention of disease. Well-known examples include tobacco regulation;[36] less well-known ones include regulation of food and genetically modified organisms.[37] Nothing in EU health law *requires* Member States to adopt liberal, or market-based, approaches in the law which governs their health systems. EU competition and free movement law are used not only to achieve economic efficiency and free trade in a narrow sense. They also support a range of other objectives, including promoting social and ethical goals. The EU's legislature, its administrative authorities, and its court find ways to respect the distinctive features of European health systems.

The existence, and continued existence, of EU health law as an organising category – EU health law's present and future – allows the articulation of principles and values, which emerge from health law as it is understood in the EU's Member States. These are expressed in EU health law's themes of consumerism and freedom. But they are also expressed in themes of solidarity, equality, access to healthcare, protection from harm, and respect for human

---

35 See for example Directive 2005/62/EC implementing Directive 2002/98/EC as regards Community standards and specifications relating to a quality system for blood establishments [2005] OJ L256/41; Directive 2005/61/EC implementing Directive 2002/98/EC as regards traceability requirements and notification of serious adverse reactions and events [2005] OJ L256/32; Directive 2005/28/EC (n 31); Directive 2004/23/EC (n 31); Directive 2002/98/EC (n 31); Directive 2001/104/EC amending Council Directive 93/42/EEC concerning medical devices [2002] OJ L6/50, and the proposed amendments in Commission, 'Safe, effective and innovative medical devices and in vitro diagnostic medical devices for the benefit of patients, consumers and healthcare professionals' COM (2012) 540 final; Commission, Proposal for a Regulation of the European Parliament and of the Council on medical devices, and amending Directive 2001/83/EC, Regulation (EC) No 178/2002 and Regulation (EC) No 1223/2009' COM (2012) 542 final; Commission, Proposal for a Regulation of the European Parliament and of the Council on *in vitro* diagnostic medical devices COM (2012) 541 final; Directive 2001/83/EC of the European Parliament and of the Council of 6 November 2001 on the Community code relating to medicinal products for human use [2001] OJ L311/67.
36 Directive 2014/40/EU on the approximation of the laws, regulations and administrative provisions of the Member States concerning the manufacture, presentation and sale of tobacco and related products and repealing Directive 2001/37/EC [2014] OJ L127/1; Directive 2003/33/EC on the approximation of the laws, regulations and administrative provisions of the Member States relating to the advertising and sponsorship of tobacco products [2003] OJ L152/16.
37 See for example Regulation 1924/2006/EC on nutrition and health claims made on foods [2007] OJ L12/3; Regulation 109/2008/EC amending Regulation 1924/2006/EC on nutrition and health claims made on foods [2008] OJ L39/14; Regulation 116/2010/EU amending Regulation 1924/2006/EC of the European Parliament and of the Council with regard to the list of nutrition claims [2010] OJ L37/16; Regulation 1829/2003/EC on genetically modified food and feed [2003] OJ L268/1.

rights. The future of EU health law will undoubtedly include consumerism and free trade within markets. But those themes will only be part of its future.

The future of EU health law

The vast majority of existing literature on EU health law is 'inward facing'. It is concerned with the effects of EU law *within* the EU's Member States. But global trade, and its effects on communicable and non-communicable diseases, is arguably *more* important for health. Such global trade patterns include the off-shoring of clinical trials and the availability of novel and experimental treatments for those desperate and wealthy enough to travel anywhere to receive them. It is easier to market novel (and often untested, or even downright fake[38]) health technologies across the globe using the internet. New structures of international health service providers, accredited in the global North/West, but located in the global East (and sometimes South), are emerging. Communicable disease control is more difficult in the context of increased availability of global aviation transport, and global markets in alcohol, food, and tobacco. Climate change exacerbates global poverty and scarcity of food and water. Many in the global South do not have access to essential medicines.[39] All these phenomena create important challenges for EU health law. It is at least as important for EU health law to consider these challenges as it is to question whether migrant patients *within* the EU can receive healthcare in another Member State. EU health law's future – and its next big challenge – will involve a much stronger focus on its global dimensions ('EU external health law').[40]

Some of the EU's internal health law already has *de facto* implications for health elsewhere in the world. A good example is the EU's clinical trials legislation,[41] which in practice applies to all clinical trials where future marketing authorisation will be sought within the EU. But much of EU internal health law shows insufficient concern for the health of those outside the EU. For instance, the CJEU has held that EU tobacco legislation on the presentation and labelling of tobacco products (including, for instance, adopting graphic health warnings on cigarette packets), as opposed to legislation on the composition of tobacco products, does not apply outside of the EU.[42] Another example,

---

38 Directive 2011/62/EU amending Directive 2001/83/EC on the Community code relating to medicinal products for human use, as regards the prevention of the entry into the legal supply chain of falsified medicinal products [2011] OJ L174/74.
39 See for example Regulation 953/2003/EC to avoid trade diversion into the European Union of certain key medicines [2003] OJ L135/1; Regulation 1568/2003/EC on aid to fight poverty diseases (HIV/AIDS, tuberculosis and malaria) in developing countries [2003] OJ L224/7.
40 Hervey and McHale (n 3).
41 (n 31).
42 *R v Secretary of State for Health, ex parte British American Tobacco and Imperial Tobacco Ltd*, C-491/01, EU:C:2002:741.

internally applicable EU law on organs,[43] is based on human rights protection, solidarity and equality. It embodies a legal commitment to non-commodification of the human body, and allows Member States significant discretion to secure high human rights standards, thus setting itself apart from an approach based on liberal trade and consumer choice.

In contrast, there is almost no externally applicable EU law on human organs.[44] The EU has left such matters to the Council of Europe, which, given the EU's now-developed human rights law,[45] reveals a serious limitation of current EU health law. Access to essential medicines provides a third example. Given disparities of economic and political power between the global North/West and the global South, the world trading system (in particular global intellectual property law), as interpreted and applied in practice, fails to promote fairness, respect for human needs and rights, or transparency. Although it would be legally competent to do so, the EU does little in practice to redress these deficiencies, and to the extent that it participates at all, it conflates access to essential medicines with research and intellectual property protection.[46]

The EU's global trade law is based on liberalism, but with important counterpoints. Liberal trade laws, supporting and encouraging global mobility of capital, products and labour, have significant negative effects on health. For instance, the abilities of least developed or developing countries to provide high quality healthcare for their populations may be reduced where healthcare professional migration to developed countries is facilitated by global health law.[47] Counterfeit or falsified medicines may circulate more easily, and where attempts to control this phenomenon are focused on intellectual property rights, the safety of patients in the global South may be more compromised than that of patients in the global North/West. More seriously, equality of access to essential medicines between South and North may be detrimentally affected.

But there are also significant opportunities for EU health law to have positive effects on global health. Particularly where free trade and fair competition can be aligned with delivering life-enhancing health innovations for patients outside

---

43 (n 31, n 35).
44 The only area of EU external relations law that might apply is the human rights conditionality clauses of the EU's trade agreements.
45 See further S Peers et al. (eds), *The EU Charter of Fundamental Rights: A Commentary* (Hart 2014).
46 For instance the EU's 'third generation', 'TRIPS-plus' agreements, including free trade agreements, and 'Economic Partnership Agreements' all seek to secure detailed provisions on patent law and enforcement of intellectual property law more generally. See further Hervey and McHale (n 3) chapter 17.
47 See for example IG Cohen (ed), *The Globalization of Health Care: Legal and Ethical Issues* (OUP 2013); YYB Chen and C Flood, 'Medical Tourism's Impact on Health Care Equity and Access in Low- and Middle-Income Countries: Making the Case for Regulation' (2013) 41 J Law Med Ethics 286; I Glinos, 'Going Beyond Numbers: A Typology of Health Professional Mobility Inside and Outside the European Union' (2014) 33 Policy and Society 25.

the EU, but also where EU health innovation law requires ethical or human rights protections, EU external health law embodies, and will continue to embody, values that are expressed within health systems inside the EU. There is scope for EU health law to 'export' those values elsewhere.

Conclusion

Brazier and Glover concluded their reflections on the future of medical law with three questions: (1) 'Will the law develop a capacity to define and enforce an entitlement to *basic* health care sufficient to ensure that those who are ill can obtain treatment?'; (2) will 'the community . . . recognise that a responsibility to treat the sick requires some sacrifice of individual wants'?, and; (3) will such a capacity and recognition be based on a notion of basic human rights?[48] Whatever the answer to those questions, and whether 'the community' concerned is regional, national, European or global, EU health law will now be part of the process through which the answer is reached. Those interested in the future of healthcare law must also be interested in the future of EU health law. The contributions of EU health law will be based not only on the consumerism and market competition commonly associated with EU law. They will also express values of solidarity, equality, dignity and respect for human rights – for all of these are the themes of EU health law.

48 Brazier and Glover (n 1) 388.

7 Beyond medicine, patients and the law
Policy and governance in 21st century health law

John Coggon and Lawrence O Gostin

Introduction

Margaret Brazier's contribution to shaping the field of medical law has been inestimable, not least in her celebrated, ground-breaking textbook *Medicine, Patients and the Law*.[1] Throughout her career she has pushed the boundaries, focusing not simply on law and medicine, but on the wider legal and policy problems of health protection, whilst balancing health with other social and ethical values. In this chapter, we examine mainstream medical law and consider how concerns for law and health have necessarily led to an expansion of that field. We do so with reference to our respective approaches to public and global health law and ethics.

Our argument is that there are two analytical shifts that should characterise future work by health law scholars. First, there needs to be a keen awareness and understanding of modes of governance that move far beyond what are generally considered to be *legal* measures: we need to look at policy, regulation, the impact and practices of non-state actors (e.g. industry and civil society), and the influence of multiple regimes and sectors (e.g., agriculture, transportation and the environment). Second, we need to take account in our analyses of the potential impacts not just of medicine but also of public health measures and the socio-economic determinants of health (e.g. income, education and gender equality).

Health and law 1: Bringing law to medicine and patients

Various accounts may be given of the emergence and rapid growth of medical law as a field of study in the United Kingdom (UK). Although law had not been entirely alien to the practice and governance of medicine prior to the 1970s, the work of pioneering legal scholars such as Brazier and the activity – some

---

1 The first edition of this work was published in 1987. At the time of writing, the book is in its fifth edition, now co-authored with Emma Cave: M Brazier and E Cave, *Medicine, Patients and the Law* (5th edn, Penguin 2011). For an authors' perspective on the rationale behind the work, see M Brazier and E Cave, 'Why We Wrote. . . *Medicine, Patients and the Law*' (2008) 3(4) Clinical Ethics 205.

might even say activism – of the courts since that time have brought sweeping changes to the regulation of medicine.[2] We would not wish to suggest that there has been a single guiding mantra or mission that has motivated medical lawyers or judges. However, it is not too much of a broad brush approach to suggest that a great deal of the work of medical law as it emerged, and as it continues to exist today, has focused most keenly on the ethically motivated task of protecting patients' autonomy. Though sometimes characterised as unthinking and simplistic,[3] that project has entailed a focus both on limiting professional powers and on empowering patients.

In this sense, we might present much of the theoretical development of medical law in the UK as having taken place in two main areas. First, medical law has put constraints on professional practice through externally imposed standards. Landmark developments here include the courts' progressive 'demedicalisation' of the best interests standard, which is applied under law in cases of patients who lack capacity;[4] the imposition of professional standards of care that are not understood merely by reference to what is accepted by a body of practitioners,[5] and which may include the regulatory force of the criminal law;[6] and the impact of the Human Rights Act 1998. Second, medical law has evolved to assure and strengthen patient empowerment. This has most notably arisen in the galvanisation of the medical–ethical principle of patient autonomy, particularly in relation to the development of legal principle (for example causation in clinical negligence claims[7]) to ensure the provision of information in the process of gaining consent; and legal principles in capacity law that afford decision-making powers to minors[8] as well as for adults. Particularly in the case of adults, this has been informed by a broad and deferential value-agnosticism, assuring rights to give or refuse consent for any or no reason.[9]

The general overarching theme that emerges is that medical law has developed (in large part, although we acknowledge not universally),[10] to privilege individual

---

2 K Veitch, *The Jurisdiction of Medical Law* (Ashgate 2007).
3 C Foster, *Choosing Life, Choosing Death: The Tyranny of Autonomy in Medical Ethics and Law* (Hart 2009).
4 See the emerging doctrine in the following legal developments: *Re F (Mental patient: Sterilisation)* [1990] 2 AC 1; *Airedale NHS Trust v Bland* [1993] AC 789; *In re A (Medical Treatment: Male Sterilisation)* [2000] 1 FCR 193; *Ahsan v University Hospitals Leicester NHS Trust* [2006] EWHC 2624 (QB), [2007] PIQR P19; *Aintree University Hospitals NHS Foundation Trust v James* [2013] UKSC 67, [2014] 1 All ER 573; Mental Capacity Act 2005, s 4.
5 *Bolitho v City and Hackney Health Authority* [1998] AC 232 (HL).
6 M Brazier and S Ost, *Bioethics, Medicine and the Criminal Law* (CUP 2013).
7 *Chester v Afshar* [2004] UKHL 41; [2004] 4 All ER 587.
8 *Gillick v West Norfolk and Wisbech AHA* [1986] AC 112.
9 *In Re T (Adult: Refusal of Treatment)* [1993] Fam 95; *In Re MB (Medical treatment)* [1997] 2 FLR 426; *Ms B v An NHS Hospital Trust* [2002] 2 All ER 449; Mental Capacity Act 2005, s 1(4).
10 Cf J Coggon, 'Varied and Principled Understandings of Autonomy in English Law: Justifiable Inconsistency or Blinkered Moralism?' (2007) 15(3) Health Care Analysis 235.

patient choice. It thus secures for individuals greater freedom from unwelcome interference and a firm recognition of value pluralism.[11] The situation is not that professional opinion counts for nothing. Nor is it that individual autonomy trumps all. The law continues to recognise the expertise needed for the medical component of a clinical decision.[12] Furthermore, it maintains a distinction between 'negative' rights to refuse treatment, which it will respect,[13] and 'positive' rights to demand interventions, which are not guaranteed.[14] It should be emphasised too that there are growing critiques of the primacy of autonomy in medical law: not least in Brazier's scholarship, which pushes for a focus in medical law on patients' responsibilities as well as their rights.[15] Nevertheless, medical law has in great part served to limit state and professional powers to interfere with individual patients' freedom, even where doing so would be (perceived to be) for their own good, or to ensure that they behave ethically.[16]

As well as having pushed a moral and social mission, medical law has expanded since Brazier began working in the field, both in its outlook and scope.[17] It has grown to cover questions such as enhancement,[18] body modification,[19] reproductive freedoms,[20] genetic-[21] and nano-[22] technologies and so on. Much of the ground-breaking work on these and other areas has been conducted by Brazier and other scholars based at the Centre for Social Ethics and Policy (CSEP) at the University of Manchester, including many people working under Brazier's mentorship. Notwithstanding its expanded horizons, however, it remains arguable that medical law as a field has still kept a fairly narrow

---

11 J Coggon, 'Assisted Dying and the Context of Debate: "Medical Law" *versus* "End-of-Life Law"' (2010) 18(4) Med L Rev 541.
12 *R (Burke) v General Medical Council* [2005] EWHC Civ 1003, [2006] QB 273.
13 *In Re T (Adult: Refusal of Treatment)* [1993] Fam 95; *Ms B v An NHS Hospital Trust* [2002] 2 All ER 449.
14 *Pretty v UK* [2002] 35 EHRR 1; *R (Nicklinson) v Ministry of Justice; R (AM) v Director of Public Prosecutions* [2014] UKSC 38, [2014] 3 WLR 200; *R (Burke) v GMC* (n 12).
15 M Brazier, 'Do No Harm – Do Patients Have Responsibilities Too?' (2006) 65(2) CLJ 397; J Coggon, 'Would Responsible Medical Lawyers Lose Their Patients?' (2012) 20(1) Med L Rev 130; cf JK Mason, 'Autonomous Humanity? In Tribute to Margaret Brazier' (2012) 20(4) Med L Rev 150. See also M Brazier and J Harris, 'Public Health and Private Lives' (1996) 4(2) Med L Rev 171.
16 Brazier (n 15).
17 Veitch (n 2).
18 See N Hyder and J Harris, 'The Criminal Law and Enhancement – None of the Law's Business?' in A Alghrani, R Bennett and S Ost (eds), *The Criminal Law and Bioethical Conflict: Walking the Tightrope* (CUP 2012).
19 See for example M Latham, 'The Shape of Things to Come: Feminism, Regulation and Cosmetic Surgery' (2008) 16(3) Med L Rev 437.
20 See S Walker, 'Potential Persons and Welfare of The (Potential) Child Test' (2014) 14(3) Med L Int'l 157.
21 See S Chan and M Quigley, 'Frozen Embryos, Genetic Information and Reproductive Rights' (2007) 21(8) Bioethics 439.
22 See S Holm, 'Does Nanotechnology Require a New "Nanoethics"?' in J Gunning and S Holm (eds), *Ethics, Law, and Society – Volume III* (Ashgate 2007).

'jurisdiction', focusing on the practice of medicine and aiming primarily to secure patients' rights and empowerment. There are, of course, notable exceptions, perhaps most obviously in de-medicalisation theses, such as those surrounding abortion law.[23]

The general point stands, though, and continues to do so even given directed enlargements of the field by scholars such as Jonathan Montgomery, who have argued that study must focus not just on doctors and patients, but look as well to wider health care systems and actors.[24] Such theorists have sought to expand our inquiry into healthcare law. Of course, we should not forget that Brazier's work does account for social, professional, and institutional contexts, and not simply the practice of medicine narrowly conceived.[25] Yet even allowing for the expansions noted here, medical law and healthcare law continue to operate with a predominant focus on patients.[26] They keep the practical focus of concern, and thus the persons who are subject to analysis, within the healthcare sector. In other words, in relation to English law, academics in medical law and healthcare law may fairly be said to be generally concerned with matters that fall within the purview of the Department of Health, rather than other government departments.

Having offered the above characterisation, our aim is to contrast that predominant means of studying law and health with the growing areas of scholarship that look beyond questions regarding medicine, patients and the law, and move away from the remit of the Department of Health. In the remainder of this chapter, we critically outline and defend academic and practical agendas that take us further than the spaces presented in the majority of textbooks on medical law and healthcare law. Our vision is of a field that spans across sectors, and is concerned with citizens' rights, rather than those of the more narrowly conceived concept of the patient. We aim, furthermore, to emphasise the need for health law scholars to engage with modes of governance that involve regulatory techniques other than those that may technically be designated as 'law', as well as modes of public control that are employed by 'private' actors, such as large corporations, philanthropies and non-governmental organisations. Through bodies such as the General Medical Council and the British Medical Association, medical lawyers are clearly alive to the regulatory function of softer mechanisms of governance.[27] However,

---

23 See S Sheldon, *Beyond Control: Medical Power and Abortion Law* (Pluto Press 1997); Coggon (n 11); S Ost, 'The De-Medicalisation of Assisted Dying: Is a Less Medicalised Model the Way Forward' (2010) 18(4) Med L Rev 497.
24 J Montgomery, *Health Care Law* (2nd edn, OUP 2002).
25 Like Ken Mason, we would cite organ donation policy as a particularly strong example of Brazier's work speaking beyond medicine, patients and law. See for example M Brazier, 'Retained Organs: Ethics and Humanity' (2002) 22(4) LS 550; S McGuinness and M Brazier, 'Respecting the Living Means Respecting the Dead Too' (2008) 28(2) OJLS 297.
26 See for example Mason and Laurie's textbook, where public health is raised and addressed still in terms of *patient* rather than citizen: JK Mason and G Laurie, *Mason & McCall Smith's Law and Medical Ethics* (8th edn, OUP 2010) 29.
27 As well as Brazier's own work, see for example J Miola, *Medical Ethics and Medical Law: A Symbiotic Relationship* (Hart 2007).

as we expand our inquiry across sectors, and indeed globally, the legal and governance tools become more diffuse in practice, and philosophically much more difficult to contain within a robust theory.[28] We thus outline how we see the field growing and why it is necessary, and indeed good, that it should do so. We frame our analysis around the two modes of expansion just noted: working with an understanding of health law that spreads across sectors, and with an understanding that engages a very broad range of 'public' or social controls.

Health and law 2: Beyond medicine, beyond patients, beyond the law

Both authors of this chapter are involved in academic projects that push the scope and agendas of health law and ethics far beyond medicine and healthcare. We will speak shortly to the field of global health law, but begin by outlining our respective characterisations of (national) *public health* law, reflecting on their rationales. As the chapter progresses we will reflect on how these areas relate to medico-legal studies.

Our definitions of public health law

Gostin has defined public health law as follows:

> Public health law is the study of the legal powers and duties of the state, in collaboration with its partners (e.g. health care, business, the community, the media, and academe), to ensure the conditions for people to be healthy (to identify, prevent, and ameliorate risks to health in the population), and of the limitations on the power of the state to constrain for the common good the autonomy, privacy, liberty, proprietary, and other legally protected interests of individuals. The prime objective of public health law is to pursue the highest possible level of physical and mental health in the population, consistent with the values of social justice.[29]

Coggon, by contrast, offers a briefer characterisation of public health law, which may be read in conjunction with his parallel definition of public health ethics:

> [P]ublic health law entails those aspects of law, policy, and regulation that bear on the health status (howsoever understood) of their subjects.[30]

---

28 See J Coggon, 'Global Health, Law and Ethics: Fragmented Sovereignty and the Limits of Universal Theory' in M Freeman, S Hawkes and B Bennett (eds), *Law and Global Health* (OUP 2014).
29 L Gostin, *Public Health Law – Power, Duty, Restraint*, (2nd edn, University of California Press 2008) 4.
30 J Coggon, *What Makes Health Public? A Critical Evaluation of Moral, Legal, and Political Claims in Public Health* (CUP 2012) 90–1.

[Public health ethics refers to] the critical ethical evaluation of questions concerning possible, actual, and proposed public health measures.[31]

Our respective definitions of public health law have both been advanced with rationales that explain and aim to justify the concerns and approaches of the proposed conceptions of the subject. If we begin with Gostin's definition, various features can be highlighted.[32] First is the idea of *the state's* power, and duty, to protect people's health. This legal power is understood with due consideration both for the general importance of health as a basic component of human functioning, and for legal and democratic constraints against governmental activity. As such, it advances a mandate for measures – including coercive measures – to safeguard and promote health. Within legal limits, individuals and corporations may be compelled by this governmental mandate in order to serve the common good.

A second feature in Gostin's definition is the focus on the state's 'partners'. These are broadly conceived. An important observation is that Gostin therefore embraces, *within* the concept of public health *law*, the health impacts and governance functions of non-state actors (as noted, the examples that he gives are healthcare, business, the community, the media and academia). In this sense, his definition is less concerned with a 'purist' account of law and instead focuses on an analysis of legal, regulatory *and* socio-economic functions of coordination as they do, can and should impact on health. Furthermore, Gostin emphasises three additional features. Public health lawyers recognise the importance of focusing on populations rather than individuals (or individual patients). They are also alive to the role and impact of communities on health, noting as previously mentioned that this entails actors whose norms and functions are not standardly considered as part of 'the law'. Within his definition, there is also an ethical commitment, specifically to a concept of social justice; that is to say that for Gostin, public health law is not a neutral academic pursuit but rather a mission-led enterprise.

Coggon's definition, which was developed during his time working at CSEP at the University of Manchester alongside scholars including Brazier, is much shorter, although it is no less broad-reaching. Again, it does not limit itself to a narrow or strict concept of law. Rather, it includes wide mechanisms of social control and governance.[33] In Coggon's definition, the concern is with measures that may impact on health, regardless of the (actual or imputed) motivation of the regulator. In this sense, Coggon's definition may be considered a more detachedly academic one than that of Gostin: whilst Gostin's characterisation of the field refers to 'the study of . . . ', it goes on to present a particular practical agenda. In contrast, Coggon's definition relates to concerns for health as it may be impacted by structured social norms and practices, but with a neutrality as

---

31 Ibid 93.
32 For greater detail, see Gostin (n 29) part I.
33 Coggon (n 30) chs 4 and 5.

regards the motivation or aims of the person who may engage in (or resist) public health law or practice. So it may include a pro-health scholar, such as Gostin (i.e. a scholar who advocates for a position that uses law and policy as tools that should be used to ameliorate health), but also includes scholars who are sceptical of the justification, rationale, methods or agenda of pro-health theorists.[34]

Justifications for, and in, our concepts of public health law

Expansive definitions of public health, and by implication public health ethics and law, have been criticised for, amongst other things, attempting to bring too much into their domain.[35] This is a problem not faced by mainstream medical law. Can we claim coherence and legitimacy to the fields of public health ethics and law? In thinking about justifications for the very expansive definitions that we have provided, it is useful to begin by emphasising a contrast between practical and academic aims.

The central issue in public health ethics and law is in defining when the health or health-affecting status or activity of a person or agent is the business of others, and especially when it is the business of the state.[36] In addressing this, the academic asks *what makes health public?* This apparently simple question opens up an array of arguments in political theory concerning how responsibilities and freedoms are properly defined and allocated in a structured society with central, state-sponsored governance mechanisms.[37]

In contrast, the activist asks the more practical question: *how, in a given instance, can health be made public?* Here, the concern is with developing an argument that a health concern should be made the subject of policy; for example, that smoking in a public place is not a purely private choice, but one that has public implications and thus should be subject to regulatory oversight or even interference.[38] In both instances, we would argue that related justifications concerning practical coherence and a normatively valid rationale are present.[39] Medicine is a sufficiently important institution that there is significant

---

34 So Coggon sees libertarian philosophical theorists such as Petr Skrabanek, or libertarian legal theorists, such as Richard Epstein, as participants in public health ethics and law, notwithstanding that they argue *against* the legitimacy of (much) state activity directed to improving health. See for example P Skrabanek, *The Death of Humane Medicine and the Rise of Coercive Healthism* (St Edmundsbury Press 1994); R Epstein, 'In Defense of the "Old" Public Health' (2004) 69(4) Brook L Rev 1421.
35 See especially M Rothstein, 'Rethinking the Meaning of Public Health' (2002) 30 Journal of Law, Medicine and Ethics 144.
36 See Coggon (n 30) introduction.
37 Global health law is discussed below, and the question of how we explore the question 'what makes health public?' at a global level is explored in Coggon (n 28).
38 Cf J Coggon, 'Morality and Strategy in Politicising Tobacco Use: Criminal Law, Public Health, and Philosophy' in AM Viens, J Coggon and A Kessel (eds), *Criminal Law, Philosophy and Public Health Practice* (CUP 2013).
39 See also T Ruger, 'Health Law's Coherence Anxiety' (2008) 96(2) Geo L J 625.

merit in examining its practices and considering how governance mechanisms do and should relate to it. This is similarly so with other matters that impact on health. Just as scholars may be justifiably concerned that patients can rightfully access good medicine whilst enjoying protections from unwarranted practices, so scholars may be interested in other means of protecting health in society and the constraints that may be put on these.

Given academic and activists' concerns, and the wider rationales for the field, which are caught in our respective representations and analyses of public health law, it is unsurprising that we have independently argued for the acute relevance of political context.[40] This political context may usefully be compared with, but also differentiated from, the medical lawyer's concern with *ethics*.[41] A paper by Gostin and colleagues outlines the distinctive nature of the normative challenges within public health law:

> This broad vision [of public health, and thus public health law] is politically charged. Critics express strong objections: Why should health be a primary social undertaking when compared with other competing priorities? Why should private actors take responsibility for the public's health? Are public health agencies going beyond their legitimate scope by supporting fundamental changes in the socioeconomic environment?[42]

Within the confines of the practice of medicine, our concerns often focus on patient autonomy because there is a need to ensure that patients are respected as persons who are, within limits, entitled to decide for themselves how they live their lives, and on what basis they do so. In the philosophical imagining of medical–ethical problems, we can generally conceive of a universe that contains two people: first, the person who (potentially) might benefit from healthcare; and second, the person with expertise and licence to provide it.[43]

But if our concern is with health more generally, healthcare provides only a part of the relevant context. As such, autonomy cannot, or at the very least possibly cannot, tell the whole of the normative story. Having explained the basis of our reasons for holding this position, in the next section we will seek to explain why we believe that scholars and activists interested in health and law ought to work within a broader agenda. We will furnish these considerations with reflections drawn from our more recent scholarship on global health, principally, Gostin's book on global health law.

---

40 Gostin (n 29) ch 1; Coggon (n 30) part II.
41 See also Coggon (n 11).
42 L Gostin, J Boufford and R Martinez, 'The Future of the Public's Health: Vision, Values, and Strategies' (2004) 23(4) Health Affairs 96–7.
43 Some questions in medical law, such as confidentiality in cases where a patient poses a risk to others, or macro-decision making, such as in relation to resource allocation, clearly require a broader ethical framing.

Governance, health, and practical priorities

There is not space here to outline the complex and important new field of global health law in full.[44] However, it is worth noting that in a global context there is an even greater need to emphasise the governance roles of non-state actors and to look across governmental sectors. It is for this reason that Gostin has employed the use of the concept of *governance for global health*, as opposed to the more standardly understood idea of global health. It is useful to draw here from a particular aspect of Gostin's book, which goes to the heart of justifying projects and priorities in health and law. He offers the following philosophical thought experiment, whose utility we would stress is not limited to questions in a global setting. The aim is rather to demonstrate a universal claim: namely, that health lawyers' (and others') focus should be on more than assuring access to medicine. Gostin says:

> Among the three essential conditions for good health, global health actors have focused intently on the provision of health care, often neglecting or deemphasizing the other two major conditions for health and well-being [i.e. there has been a focus on health care, to the neglect of public health and the socio-economic determinants of health] . . .
>
> Does this tacit prioritization of medicine make sense, given finite resources? To get some purchase on this question, consider a thought experiment loosely modelled on the political philosopher John Rawls's 'veil of ignorance.' Suppose – without knowing your life's circumstances (young/old, rich/poor, health/ill/disabled, or living in the global South or global North) – you were forced to choose between two stark options for the future of global health.
>
> Under option one, provision of health care would be strongly prioritized. You could see a health care professional whenever you wanted to, attend high-quality clinics and hospitals, and gain access to advanced medicines. This scenario would achieve the ideal of universal health coverage but would be highly oriented toward medical care – leaving gaps in population-level public health services and the social determinants of health. Universal health coverage would best serve the interests of individuals already ill and suffering, but it would have limited impact in preventing illness, injury, and early death.
>
> Under option two, scarce resources would be directed primarily toward population-level prevention strategies. As a result, everyone would live in an environment in which they could turn on the tap and drink clean water; breathe fresh, unpolluted air; live, work, and play in sanitary and hygienic surroundings; eat safe and nourishing food; be free from infestations of malarial mosquitoes, plague-ridden rats, or other disease vectors; not be exposed to tobacco smoke or other toxins; and not live in fear of avoidable injury or violence. This scenario would make unsparing use of public health measures but would offer no assurance of medical treatment.

---

44 L Gostin, *Global Health Law* (Harvard UP 2014); Coggon (n 28).

Blinded to your life's circumstances, and facing these two stark options, there are compelling reasons for choosing option two – and I believe most people would prefer to live in a safe, habitable environment. If the day-to-day circumstances of your life do not allow for the maintenance of good health, medical treatments cannot fill the gap.[45]

If, as we expect to be the case, this thought experiment resonates with readers, it suggests important reasons to advance concerns beyond the medical domain. Scholars in health and law are interested in questions of validity, whether in a narrower context of medical ethics or a wider one of social justice. This subject of concern is not the central one of jurisprudes' analyses of legal validity: i.e. what is law, and how do we identify legal, as opposed to non-legal, norms?[46] Rather, the concern is with how the law and other governance mechanisms might legitimately safeguard people's health, whilst also ensuring respect for other important values.

An important point to be drawn out here is that, whether we are thinking about health because we want to optimise the health of members of a population, or because we have (say, libertarian) concerns about the legitimate role of government and its activities undertaken in the name of health, we need to address many more normative questions than are found simply within the medical context or that are resolvable simply by reference to respecting individual choices.[47] These normative questions bring added complexity, a couple of which we will highlight explicitly.[48] First, complexity comes because of the need to account not just for people but also for institutions, and actors such as private corporations, community groups and charities. Complexity comes, furthermore, because when 'the population is the patient', we are often speaking to justifications for interventions that will only confer a possible or statistical benefit to any identifiable individual person.[49] Unlike standard questions concerning the patient in medical law, it is not possible to approach justification through consent. Or, if it is, then it requires a mechanism such as a deliberative democracy approach,[50] although that clearly does not provide the same quality of consent as one achieves when obtaining individual consent.

---

45 Gostin (n 44) 419–20.
46 Cf HLA Hart, *The Concept of Law* (2nd edn, OUP 1997); J Finnis, *Natural Law and Natural Rights* (OUP 1980).
47 Cf R Epstein, 'Let the Shoemaker Stick to His Last: A Defense of the "Old" Public Health' (2003) 46(3) Perspectives in Biology and Medicine S138; L Gostin and M Bloche, 'The Politics of Public Health: A Response to Epstein' (2003) 46(3) Perspectives in Biology and Medicine S160.
48 See further Gostin (n 44); Coggon (n 28).
49 Cf G Rose, 'Sick Individuals and Sick Populations' (1985) 14 International Journal of Epidemiology 32; B Charlton, 'A Critique of Geoffrey Rose's "Population Strategy" for Preventive Medicine' (1995) 88 Journal of the Royal Society of Medicine 607; L Gostin, 'Public Health: The Population as Patient' in C DeAngelis (ed), *Patient Care and Professionalism* (OUP 2014).
50 See B Jennings, 'Frameworks for Ethics in Public Health' (2013) IX(2) Acta Bioethica 165.

These and other complexities are indeed challenging. In some aspects, the resources to respond to them feature already in policy arguments in medical law scholarship. They are coming to do so more fully still in the public health ethics and law literatures.[51] In any case, health law scholars need to grapple with the fundamentals of social justice and political morality, and consider how these fundamentals impact on our understandings of justifiable health law and policy.[52] In so doing, we suggest that a move beyond 'hard law', beyond the medical, and beyond patients properly so called, is inevitable.

Conclusion

With public health law's focus on populations, its emphasis on preventing disease and promoting health as opposed simply to remediating ill health, and with its focus on health impacts across sectors and beyond governmental controls, do we find ourselves in a position where we would argue against the continuation of medical law? The answer is – we hope unsurprisingly – no! There is a clear role for medicine and health care within a state that is committed, amongst other things, to wider public health agendas.[53]

As already seen, Gostin's definition of public health law explicitly includes engagement with healthcare. In addition, his work speaks clearly to the importance of synergies between actors in medicine and in public health.[54] The choice suggested in the Rawls-inspired thought experiment quoted above is not intended really to suggest an either/or binary. Most readers of Gostin's book will be lucky enough to live in countries that assure healthy environments *and* accessible healthcare. And that is what states should aim to do. As such, there is important – morally important – work for medical lawyers, as well as for those of us who examine the wider questions and concerns highlighted here. Neither of our definitions of public health law could ignore the role of healthcare and, thus, the rights and duties of doctors, patients, and other actors in that sphere.

Our concern is not, therefore, to do away with medical law. We wish, instead, to ensure that due emphasis is placed upon questions that normatively should be of interest to health lawyers, whether they are concerned with maximising individual liberty or seek to optimally safeguard human flourishing, welfare, wellbeing, rights and so on. Brazier has herself made important contributions to these wider debates.[55] We hope in this chapter to have demonstrated why a broader analytical terrain for health lawyers is, if challenging to traverse, nonetheless vitally important ground to cover.

---

51 For a review, see Coggon (n 30) ch 8.
52 Reviewing theories of justice and political morality has not been a specific concern in this chapter, but they are vital and the subject of ongoing research for each of us.
53 Gostin (n 49).
54 Ibid.
55 See especially Brazier and Harris (n 15).

Part II
Patient–doctor relations

8 (I love you!) I do, I do, I do, I do, I do

Breaches of sexual boundaries by patients in their relationships with healthcare professionals

Hazel Biggs and Suzanne Ost

Introduction

In a seminal paper published in 2006 ('Do No Harm'),[1] Margaret Brazier contended that consideration of patients' rights has been prioritised without similar consideration being paid to any duties they might owe. Some nine years on, arguably little has changed. It is true that a certain level of patient responsibility is recognised in relation to patients behaving appropriately whilst receiving healthcare (they should not behave violently or aggressively towards staff),[2] and patients' responsibilities regarding truth telling and ill-health perceived to be self-inflicted have increasingly attracted academic interest.[3] However, there has been scant analysis of the duties that patients should owe healthcare professionals (HCPs), especially in the particular context of this chapter: sexual boundary breaches.[4]

Such breaches are typically defined in the literature as being perpetrated by HCPs rather than patients: '[a] breach of sexual boundaries occurs when a healthcare professional displays sexualised behaviour towards a patient or carer'.[5] Unsurprisingly, therefore, doctors' duties in this regard are clearly and succinctly

---

1 M Brazier, 'Do No Harm – Do Patients Have Responsibilities Too?' (2006) 65 CLJ 397, (hereafter 'Do No Harm').
2 As reflected, e.g. in notices on display in NHS hospital wards and waiting rooms stating that aggressive, abusive or violent behaviour towards employees will not be tolerated.
3 See, e.g. D Resnik, 'The Patient's Duty to Adhere to Prescribed Treatment: An Ethical Analysis' (2005) 30(2) J Med Phil 167; K Sharkey and L Gillam, 'Should Patients with Self-Inflicted Illness Receive Lower Priority in Access to Healthcare Resources? Mapping out the Debate' (2010) 36 JME 661.
4 Analysis of patient-initiated breaches tends to focus on HCPs' experiences of such behaviour rather than on the matter of patients' responsibilities. See for example N Farber, D Novack, J Silverstein et al., 'Physicians' Experiences with Patients who Transgress Boundaries' (2000) 15 Journal of General Internal Medicine 770.
5 Council for Healthcare Regulatory Excellence, *Clear Sexual Boundaries between Healthcare Professionals and Patients: Responsibilities of Healthcare Professionals* (CHRE 2008) 3. The definition continues by defining sexualised behaviour as 'acts, words or behaviour designed or intended to arouse or gratify sexual impulses or desires'.

stated in General Medical Council (GMC) Guidance, which requires that they 'must not pursue a sexual or improper emotional relationship with a current patient'.[6] Similarly, the Nursing and Midwifery Council (NMC) advises nurses and midwives that 'they must not engage in any sexual activity with any person in their care or make any sexual advances verbally, physically or by innuendo'.[7] In demanding that HCPs do not breach sexual boundaries with their patients, these regulatory bodies hold HCPs to account for failing to act ethically. HCPs who ignore this responsibility can face professional sanction by the GMC or the NMC and may also breach the criminal law and/or face civil law liability if their actions constitute a sexual offence, battery or (sexual) harassment.

Patients who instigate such conduct are not held to similar standards in the way explored by Brazier in 'Do No Harm'. Yet research has demonstrated that sometimes the *patient* is the initiator of sexual boundaries breaches. In one study, 77% of participants (female doctors) had experienced some form of sexual harassment by a patient;[8] in another, 75% of the participants (psychiatric trainees) had experienced unwanted sexual contact from patients.[9] Nurses and nursing students seem particularly susceptible to patient-initiated sexual boundary breaches, with 90% of participants reporting at least one instance of sexual harassment from patients in a study published in 2003.[10]

Informed by Brazier's concerns about the potential imbalance between patients' rights and HCPs' responsibilities, this chapter argues that although the need to maintain sexual boundaries in HCP–patient relationships is a matter of professional accountability, if such breaches are deliberately initiated by the patient, they too should bear some moral responsibility. We begin by considering HCPs' and patients' moral responsibility, arguing that the HCP–patient relationship involves reciprocal obligations, and then consider what this means for patient-initiated sexual boundary breaches. Whilst we would hold patients to account for boundary breaches which they know to be inappropriate, we go

---

6 GMC, *Maintaining a Professional Boundary Between You and Your Patient* (GMC 2013) [4] <http://www.gmc-uk.org/guidance/ethical_guidance/21170.asp> (accessed 25 February 2015).

7 NMC, *Maintaining Boundaries* (NMC 2012) <http://www.nmc-uk.org/Nurses-and-midwives/Regulation-in-practice/Regulation-in-Practice-Topics/Maintaining-Boundaries-/> (accessed 25 March 2015).

8 See S Phillips and M Schneider, 'Sexual Harassment of Female Doctors by Patients' (1993) 329(26) New Eng J M 1936. See also Farber, Novack, Silverstein et al. (n 4).

9 J Morgan and S Porter, 'Sexual Harassment of Psychiatric Trainees: Experiences and Attitudes' (1999) 75 Postgraduate Medical Journal 410–413. See also J McComas, C Hébert, C Glacoomin et al., 'Experiences of Student and Practising Physician Therapists with Inappropriate Patient Sexual Behaviour' (1993) 73(11) Physical Therapy 762 (80.8% of participants had experienced inappropriate patient sexual behaviour).

10 G Bronner, C Peretz and M Ehrenfeld, 'Sexual Harassment of Nurses and Nursing Students' (2003) 42(6) Journal of Advanced Nursing 637. See also S Finnis and I Robbins, 'Sexual Harassment of Nurses: an Occupational Hazard' (1994) 3 Journal of Clinical Nursing 87.

on to suggest that they should be ascribed a lower level of moral responsibility than HCPs. We briefly consider the potential criminal consequences that might flow from some sexual boundary breaches and conclude by suggesting practical mechanisms that might help to avoid the occurrence of patient-initiated sexual boundary breaches in the HCP–patient relationship.

HCPs' and patients' moral responsibility to avoid sexual boundary breaches

Encounters between HCPs and patients, which occur in private by necessity, and frequently require close physical contact, present opportunities for sexual boundaries to be breached. In this context, patients' vulnerability has long been a concern of medical law and ethics, even in an age when patient autonomy is paramount, due to the relative power of the HCP.[11] Thus, sexual boundary breaches between HCPs and patients should not happen, and it is primarily the responsibility of the HCP to ensure that they are avoided. Consequently, professional guidance holds HCPs to account even if it is the patient who initiates sexual behaviour. For example, guidance from the Canadian College of Physicians and Surgeons of Newfoundland and Labrador states that:

> It is the responsibility of the physician to recognize that patient participation in or purported patient consent to boundary violations does not lessen a medical practitioner's responsibility to avoid boundary violations . . . A medical practitioner must not . . . respond sexually to any form of sexual advance by patients.[12]

On the face of it, this professional imperative seems common sense and straightforward. However, if we envisage a scenario where, during an appointment with her GP involving an intimate examination, a patient named Sandra initiates consensual sexual activity with him and then claims to have fallen in love with him, the position might become more complex.

Sandra could argue that she did not in fact know that initiating sexual behaviour with her GP was inappropriate, and such ignorance may seem reasonable given that patients are not commonly advised about appropriate sexual boundaries, whilst doctors' sexual boundary breaches are frequently publicised in media news reports. It might be contended that if such doctor-initiated breaches are publicised, the public comes to understand that such behaviour is wrong and, by implication, that it would be wrong for a patient to set about trying to

---

11 See for example NMC (n 7); W Tschan, 'Abuse in Doctor–Patient Relationships' (2013) 178 Key Issues in Mental Health 129 and, more generally, H Brody, *The Healer's Power* (Yale University Press 1992).
12 College of Physicians and Surgeons of Newfoundland and Labrador, *Guideline – Boundary Violations and Misconduct of a Sexual Nature*, introduction and [1] <https://www.cpsnl.ca/default.asp?com=Policies&m=361&y=&id=9> (accessed 25 February 2015).

engage a doctor in that behaviour. Yet, provided that the doctor consents, it is not unreasonable to expect that at least some patients will perceive patient-initiated breaches as less wrongful, or at least as less concerning, given that such breaches attract so little publicity and the patient owes no professional duty to refrain from such breaches. With this in mind, we might not consider that Sandra has violated her moral responsibility, just that she has inappropriately. However, the NHS Constitution lays out responsibilities such as treating NHS staff with respect[13] which, although there is nothing explicit within it relating to sexual boundary breaches, would encompass this kind of conduct. Such an approach is also adopted in the Royal College of Surgeons' code of patient responsibilities and the American Medical Association's Opinion on patient responsibilities in its Code of Medical Ethics.[14] More specifically, albeit exceptionally, NHS Scotland's *Charter of Patient Rights and Responsibilities* states that '[y]ou must not be involved in any . . . sexual . . . harassment or abuse towards staff'.[15]

Where conclusive guidance is lacking, there is a fairly persuasive argument that we should not hold Sandra to account for initiating this breach of sexual boundaries (that is, we should not ascribe *retrospective* responsibility to her) because there has been a failure to provide her with the information she needs to take *prospective* responsibility for her actions.[16] This is particularly so in the light of research conducted by Gartrell et al., who comment that:

> Some patients, because of their vulnerability, may interpret their physician's professional caring as personal intimacy and even initiate sexual advances. It is the physician's responsibility, however, to prevent the harm that may result from physician patient sexual contact.[17]

Ascribing responsibility to the patient becomes more problematic still if, alongside Sandra's ignorance of these guides to patient responsibilities, the GP responds positively to her advances or even encourages it. By doing so, the doctor misleads her about what is appropriate, in addition to failing in his

---

13 Department of Health, *The NHS Constitution* (Crown 2013) 11.
14 The Royal College of Surgeons of England Patient Liaison Group, *Patient Rights and Responsibilities* (Royal College of Surgeons of England 2005); American Medical Association, *Code of Ethics 2014–15*, Opinion 10.02 <http://www.ama-assn.org/ama/pub/physician-resources/medical-ethics/code-medical-ethics/opinion1002.page?> (accessed 25 February 2015).
15 NHS Scotland, *The Charter of Patient Rights and Responsibilities* (Scottish Government 2012) 17.
16 On whether we should ascribe prospective and retrospective responsibility to patients, see M Kelley, 'Limits on Patient Responsibility' (2005) 30 J Med Phil 189, 198.
17 N Gartrell, N Milliken, W Goodson et al., 'Physician-patient Sexual Contact: Prevalence and Problems', (1992) 157 Western Journal of Medicine 139, 142.

professional duty, and Sandra may legitimately be confused about the appropriate boundaries that should be maintained between HCP and patient.

The position would be more complicated, however, if Sandra then threatens to make an allegation that the doctor has sexually assaulted her because he refuses to engage in such conduct with her again at her next appointment. Here there is a strong implication that Sandra has deliberately manipulated the situation and ought to be held morally responsible for her actions even if the doctor has been lax in upholding his professional obligations.

Whilst avoidance of sexual boundary breaches is *primarily* the doctor's responsibility because he is acting in a professional capacity in the doctor–patient relationship,[18] Sandra's behaviour suggests that she should bear some moral responsibility if she is initiating behaviour that she knows to be inappropriate in the context of this relationship. Just as there are examples of doctors who sexually exploit patients by abusing the doctor–patient relationship,[19] Sandra has utilised this relationship for her own ends, ends which are unrelated to the objective of advancing her health. She has 'negotiat[ed] a form of power as control',[20] exploiting the doctor and impairing his autonomy through her subsequent threats. Whilst her threats may not prevent the doctor from behaving autonomously in response to her demand, at least to some degree, they are a form of coercion that push him in a direction which his refusal suggests he would not have chosen in their absence.[21]

It may therefore seem wholly reasonable to hold Sandra morally responsible for her actions in this situation. In a pluralistic society individuals should generally take responsibility for their actions and be answerable for their conduct, reflecting Brazier's view in 'Do No Harm' that the communitarian nature of the NHS justifies ascribing patient responsibility.[22] By acting intentionally, knowingly or negligently, we are then morally responsible for our behaviour.[23] Indeed, Brazier, writing elsewhere with one of us, has noted that taking responsibility for one's actions is a defining feature of a person, the key to an individual's

---

18 A matter we consider further in the next section.
19 See *Norberg v Wynrib* [1992] 2 SCR 226; Department of Health, *The Kerr/Haslam Inquiry: Full Report* (Cm 6640) (HMSO 2005).
20 T McGuire, D Dougherty and J Atkinson, '"Paradoxing the Dialectic": the Impact of Patients' Sexual Harassment in the Discursive Construction of Nurses' Caregiving Roles' (2006) 19(3) Management Communication Quarterly 416, 442.
21 A more detailed consideration of how acting under the coercion of a threat can affect autonomy is not possible here. For an account of why an individual acting under duress as a consequence of another's threat is suffering from impaired autonomy because he relinquishes control of his compliant action to his threatener, see J Taylor, 'Autonomy, Duress and Coercion' (2003) 20(2) Soc Phil & Pol'y 127.
22 See J Gardner, 'The Mark of Responsibility' (2003) 23(3) OJLS 157, 161.
23 F Miller, R Troug and D Brock, 'Moral Fictions and Medical Ethics' (2010) 24(9) Bioethics 453, 457–458.

moral agency,[24] and Gauthier has drawn attention to the significance of moral responsibility for others:

> Moral responsibility as a virtue begins with the individual but then moves outward to the impact of individual choices and actions and important relationships and the society, as well.[25]

Nevertheless, perhaps even in this situation, the imbalance of power between doctor and patient should be enough to prevent us from holding Sandra responsible. The quotation from Gartrell et al. above certainly suggests that patients who initiate sexual advances do so because they are vulnerable. But is this true in every case of patient-initiated sexual behaviour? We have argued elsewhere that whilst in some cases, patients will be vulnerable[26] and that the imbalance of power in the physician–patient relationship can be exacerbated by a sexual imbalance of power where the doctor is male and the patient female, it is surely an over-generalisation to categorise the entire (female) patient population as vulnerable.[27] And even if we were to view Sandra as vulnerable because of her status as a female patient, '[v]ulnerability . . . does not confer automatic innocence of wrongdoing on the vulnerable'.[28]

The need to recognise that patients have responsibilities too is the thrust of Brazier's argument in 'Do No Harm', an argument which, according to Coggon, 'can be reduced to the straightforward claim that if patients are to be respected as moral agents, this entails their being beholden to the demands of morality'.[29] Further, Draper and Sorell accuse medical ethics of being 'one-sided. It dwells on the ethical obligations of doctors to the exclusion of those of

---

24 M Brazier and S Ost, *Medicine and Bioethics in the Theatre of the Criminal* Process (CUP 2013) 199–200. On moral agency, see T Beauchamp and J Childress, *Principles of Biomedical Ethics* (7th edn, OUP 2013) 72–73.
25 C Gauthier, 'The Virtue of Moral Responsibility and the Obligations of Patients' (2005) 30 J Med Phil 153, 159.
26 See the example provided in K Stephens, 'Brisbane doctor "shamelessly exploited" patient through affair', (2013) *Brisbane Time*s, 11 December <http://www.brisbanetimes.com.au/queensland/brisbane-doctor-shamelessly-exploited-patient-through-affair-20131210–2z41e.html> (accessed 25 February 2015). We also note that it is generally accepted that all the patient population is vulnerable in the context of sexual behaviour in the therapist–patient relationship and the phenomenon of transference. See for instance J Bouhoustos, J Holroyd, H Lerman et al. 'Sexual Intimacy Between Psychotherapists and Patients' (1983) 14 Professional Psychology: Research and Practice 185.
27 S Ost and H Biggs, '"Consensual" Sexual Activity between Doctors and Patients: A Matter for the Criminal Law?', in A Alghrani, R Bennett and S Ost (eds), *The Criminal Law and Bioethical Conflict* (CUP 2012) 109.
28 H Draper and T Sorell, 'Patients' Responsibilities in Medical Ethics' (2002) 16(4) Bioethics 335, 339.
29 J Coggon, 'Would Responsible Medical Lawyers Lose Their Patients?' (2012) 20(1) Med L Rev 130, 132.

patients.'[30] In medical law and ethics, protecting autonomy is the predominant way in which patients are respected as moral agents, but it is questionable whether this moral agency should be devoid of an inherent 'reciprocity of obligation', for which Brazier and Lobjoit have argued elsewhere.[31] On this construction, patients' autonomy and their responsibility for their behaviour must go hand in hand;[32] both are integral aspects of being a moral agent, and patients must accept the existence of their moral responsibility to ensure reciprocity of obligation in their relationships with HCPs.

One model of the doctor–patient relationship, the mutuality model, offers an apposite framework for recognising that patients as well as doctors have moral responsibility in the context of this relationship. This model is: 'characterized by the active involvement of patients as more equal partners in the consultation . . . in which both parties participate as a joint venture'.[33] It thus recognises the autonomy of both parties but also implicitly recognises responsibility because it requires both parties to undertake to work together to achieve goals related to the patient's health. This could not be achieved if both doctor and patient fail to act responsibly and to take responsibility for their behaviour.

Recognising that patients as moral agents are responsible for their actions, and viewing the relationship between a patient and HCP as one of mutuality and thereby recognising that it involves shared obligations, has significant implications for breaches of sexual boundaries by patients. An important factor here when deciding whether to hold Sandra accountable is whether she was acting as an autonomous moral agent in her encounter with her doctor. Clearly, if she has manipulated the situation to try to coerce the GP into pursuing a relationship with her, she has acted deliberately and must shoulder some responsibility. But if Sandra has wrongly interpreted the doctor's intentions in the way described by Gartrell et al.,[34] her ability to act autonomously may be compromised.

What does this mean for patients who instigate sexual boundary breaches?

Patients have a moral responsibility to avoid instigating any breach of sexual boundaries with their doctor or nurse. This responsibility is born out of the need to respect the HCP's role, and also to recognise that a patient has the same professional relationship with the HCP as do his or her other patients,

---

30 Draper and Sorell (n 28), 335.
31 M Brazier and M Lobjoit, 'Fiduciary Relationship: An Ethical Approach and a Legal Concept?' in R Bennett and C Erin (eds), *HIV and AIDS Testing, Screening and Confidentiality* (OUP 1999) 196 and 199.
32 Brazier (n 1) 409; Draper and Sorell (n 28) 338.
33 M Morgan, 'The Doctor–Patient Relationship' in G Scrambler (ed), *Sociology as Applied to Medicine* (Elsevier 2008) 49–65, 54.
34 See above (n 17).

and all are entitled to the same level of care and respect. Any sexual boundary breaches that are unwanted by HCPs violate their bodily autonomy and could cause them to suffer harm, for example by way of emotional distress and professional sanction. Moreover, such breaches may well have a negative effect for the particular patients who initiate them since it could lead to their HCPs treating them in a different way to their other patients by distancing themselves from them, to the detriment of their care.[35] In consensual cases, the HCP could also treat the particular patient differently from others by prioritising that patient's needs over others. The consequences for other patients could be that they have their appointments with the HCP cancelled or the HCP could fail to show them the same level of care and commitment.[36] Requiring patients to respect professional boundaries in the same way as HCPs should is essentially demanding that patients follow the four principles of biomedical ethics espoused by Beauchamp and Childress: non-maleficence, beneficence, autonomy and justice.[37] Holding patients to account for their sexual boundary breaches in this way imposes no greater moral demands on them than we currently do, for, as Brazier notes, '[m]oral obligations to respect the autonomy of others, to do no harm, to seek to do good and to deal justly with others, attach to each and every one of us in our professional and our daily lives'.[38]

There would be no doubt about the wisdom of this statement if we applied it to a situation where a drunken patient (Pete) makes advances to a nurse charged with treating him for injuries sustained as a result of his intoxication. If he touches the nurse without her consent or subjects her to offensive, lewd language, his disregard of his moral responsibility is as blatant as it would be in any other context involving subjecting another to one's unwanted sexual advances. This could lead us to conclude that Pete's failings are greater than Sandra's violation of her responsibility for initiating consensual sexual activity with her doctor. Assuming that the GP has consented, Sandra appears not to have violated his autonomy, his right to consent,[39] in the way that Pete does if he touches the nurse inappropriately. We might perceive Sandra's culpability to be lessened because of the doctor's complicity, but professional guidance, as noted above, does not concede this point. Although we have suggested that patients should hold some moral responsibility for the maintenance of sexual boundaries with their HCPs, and would hold patients to the four principles that Beauchamp and Childress argue medical professionals are bound by, the HCP–patient relationship is clearly not mutual to the extent that the *level* of moral responsibility ascribed to patients matches that we require of

---

35 As documented in McGuire, Dougherty and Atkinson (n 20).
36 See P Bratuskins, H McGarry and S Wilkinson, 'Sexual Harassment of Australian Female General Practitioners by Patients' (2013) 199(7) Medical J of Aust 454.
37 Beauchamp and Childress (n 24).
38 Brazier (n 1) 401.
39 See for example M Dempsey and J Herring, 'Why Sexual Penetration Requires Justification' (2007) 27(3) OJLS 4671.

HCPs. Alongside the obvious power imbalance in the relationship, doctors, for example, are bound by their professional codes of conduct and bound to follow professional guidance. They are also made aware of their responsibilities to maintain sexual boundaries with their patients as part of their training,[40] as are nurses[41] and other HCPs. In a more general context, Draper and Sorell provide a useful analogy, comparing doctors to drivers and patients to pedestrians:

> like drivers . . . [doctors] have to pass examinations for professional qualifications that require knowledge of, or even evidence of, ethical conduct. Patients are like pedestrians. They do not have to pass a test to qualify as patients, but how they behave affects others involved in the health care system.[42]

It is the HCP's professional role which gives rise to the responsibility to maintain boundaries, because this responsibility underlines and expresses the crucial value of trust in the profession.[43] HCPs, and doctors in particular, epitomise what Moline has referred to as our paradigm professionals,[44] individuals who act for the good of their clients, who are committed to take the trust placed in them seriously. It is two aspects of being a professional which we suggest give rise to this responsibility. First, we require HCPs to embrace a shared culture of professionalism[45] in the sense of upholding the reputation of the healthcare profession. Second, we expect doctors to exhibit professionalism in a personal moral sense, and we have a higher expectation of doctors as rational moral agents than we do of patients,[46] placing our trust in them not to succumb to any temptation to breach sexual boundaries.

To avoid undermining the value of trust in the healthcare profession, HCPs who breach the sexual boundaries are held responsible and regularly brought to account by way of their regulatory bodies' disciplinary procedures. In this way, we assess HCPs' responsibility for their actions by taking into account a distinct, more demanding set of values adopted by the profession.[47] In the

---

40 In a more general context, see Kelley (n 16) 197.
41 See the news story published in 2008 on the Royal College of Nursing's website at <http://www.rcn.org.uk/development/students/getinvolved/news_stories/sexual_145boundaries146_to_be_part_of_all_nurse_training> (accessed 25 March 2015).
42 Draper and Sorell (n 28) 336–337.
43 F Turoldo and M Barilan, 'The Concept of Responsibility: Three Stages in its Evolution Within Bioethics' (2008) 17 Cambridge Quarterly of Healthcare Ethics 114.
44 J Moline, 'Professionals and Professions: A Philosophical Examination of an Ideal' (1986) 22(5) Soc Sci Med 501.
45 As discussed in the report on the failings at the Mid Staffordshire Trust. See Robert Francis, *Report of the Mid Staffordshire Foundation Trust Public Inquiry* vol 3 (Crown 2013) 1382.
46 Turoldo and Barilan (n 43) 116; A Tauber, *Patient Autonomy and the Ethics of Responsibility* (MIT Press 2005) 12.
47 Brazier and Ost (n 24) 204–205.

case of nurses, for instance, the value of trust and the duty to care are emphasised:

> A nurse or midwife breaching any sexual boundary . . . damages public trust . . . The professional judgement of the nurse or midwife may be impaired when boundaries are crossed or breached, resulting in the nurse or midwife losing objectivity regarding the care and treatment of the person. As a result the nurse or midwife may not be able to meet the requirements of the professional code to 'make the care of people your first concern.[48]

Similarly, the GMC has determined to uphold standards of professional conduct even where the consensual nature of a HCP's sexual relationship with a patient's carer is seemingly evidenced by their subsequent marriage.[49] This seems to draw a line designed to avoid any suggestion of impropriety and reflects the strict role-related responsibility that we demand of doctors. However, there should be room to recognise that in some circumstances, such as very remote communities with only one GP, it might be problematic, or even unrealistic to uphold an absolute prohibition on such relationships.

Any breach of sexual boundaries by a HCP is thus always a serious matter for the professional party, even where it is apparently consensual, but the ramifications for the patient who instigates such conduct are rather less certain. The obvious lack of professional responsibility attached to the patient makes it difficult to hold patients who breach their moral responsibility towards HCPs accountable, and, '[s]o far, those calling for increased patient responsibility have not adequately addressed what a robust account of patient responsibility, with consequences attached to performance and failure, would mean for patients and patient choice'.[50] However, failing to outline and uphold repercussions for patients who ignore their moral responsibility could give the impression that although sexual boundary violations are discouraged, such violations will not be taken too seriously. As a consequence, patients may then fail to accept causal accountability for their actions.[51]

Whilst it is clear that the moral responsibility of patients is always of a lower level than HCPs, there are situations where the patient should be called to account for their conduct and its consequences. For example, a patient such as Pete, who makes inappropriate and unwelcome sexual advances to a HCP including physical touching, may legitimately face criminal sanctions for common assault. Similarly, if Sandra has deliberately pursued her GP and follows that up with the threat to expose his conduct for her own ends, she will cause him emotional harm that may amount to a criminal assault under the Offences against the Person Act 1861 s 47.[52] It is also arguable, though contentious,

---

48 NMC (n 7).
49 BMJ News, C Dyer, 'GP who married widower shortly after patient's death is suspended for six months' (2013) 347 BMJ f6841.
50 Kelley (n 16) 191.
51 On patients' causal responsibility, see Gauthier (n 25) 159.
52 *R v Burstow, R v Ireland* [1997] UKHL 34.

that her coercion of the doctor in this situation vitiates his apparent consent and so amounts to a sexual offence.[53]

Where the offence to the HCP falls short of physical conduct but nevertheless causes alarm or distress, it may fall within the remit of the Protection from Harassment Act 1997 (PHA), as amended. In particular, s 7(2) criminalises repeated attempts to impose contact and unwanted communications on a person/victim where this could be expected to cause distress or fear in a reasonable person. Harassment also encompasses 'causing alarm or distress' under s 2 of the PHA, which may apply to Sandra if she persists in her attempt to continue the sexual relationship under the threat that she will allege sexual assault against the doctor if he refuses. There is an evidential burden to demonstrate that the specific conduct was calculated to cause distress as well as being unreasonable and oppressive, and dicta in *Plavelil*[54] indicates that such allegations can be oppressive even where they can be readily rebutted. A single such incident or allegation may, however, be insufficient to constitute harassment, because harassment is regarded as a number of related incidents that amount to a course of conduct. Where there is, or has been, a course of conduct that amounts to a breach of s 1(1) of the PHA, this may be regarded as stalking contrary to s 2A(1) of the PHA or s 4A(1)(b)(i) where it involves fear of violence or s 4A(1)(b)(ii) if it provokes serious alarm or distress.

It does not necessarily follow, of course, that moral responsibility for acting in a certain way results in legal responsibility, a matter which Brazier grapples with in 'Do No Harm',[55] but where it does, unwanted sexual advances that might amount to an offence should be reported to the police, not least to avoid any escalation towards stalking or harassment. Where this kind of behaviour by a patient falls short of criminal conduct, however, it might be possible to impose sanctions similar to the practical consequences faced by patients who act violently or aggressively towards staff.[56] In those kinds of situations, HCPs can, for example, legitimately refuse to treat such a patient and ensure that their conduct is noted in their records to alert other staff. Similarly, patients might be removed from a GP's patient list and reallocated to another practice. Of course, every patient is entitled to NHS treatment, and will be likely to present for treatment at some future time, so in the case of breaches of sexual boundaries it might be necessary to ensure that all HCPs are accompanied, or chaperoned, during every subsequent healthcare encounter with that patient.[57]

---

53 For discussion of possible criminal liability for consensual sexual boundary breaches (albeit in relation to doctors rather than patients), see Ost and Biggs (n 27).
54 *Plavelil v Director of Public Prosecutions* [2014] EWHC 736 (Admin).
55 Brazier (n 1) 411. See also H Fingarette, *On Responsibility* (Basic Books 1967) 42.
56 See for example the policy outlined at <http://southseamedicalcentre.co.uk/help.html> (accessed 25 February 2015).
57 In a more general context, see Draper and Sorell (n 28) 351. See also the GMC's *Intimate Examinations and Chaperones* guidance (GMC 2013) <http://www.gmc-uk.org/guidance/ethical_guidance/21168.asp> (accessed 25 February 2015).

Conclusion

None of the arguments presented in this chapter should be seen as challenging the ethical position that HCPs should always be expected to maintain the sexual boundaries between them and their patients and resist any patient-initiated attempts to breach these boundaries. However, the best way to avoid occurrences of patient-initiated sexual boundary breaches in the HCP–patient relationship is to ensure that patients are aware of their responsibilities and the reasons why certain boundaries in this relationship should be maintained. Patients can only take moral responsibility if there is no doubt about what their obligations are in relation to maintaining sexual boundaries with HCPs. It has been suggested by others that HCPs should be the ones who inform patients about appropriate boundaries.[58] Whilst this may be appropriate, up to a point, making HCPs responsible for informing patients about such boundaries might seem at odds with their obligations to provide treatment and care, and could be misconstrued by patients. Moreover, ensuring that each patient has been advised as to appropriate boundaries will place further strain on the limited time available for one-to-one interactions with patients.[59]

Instead, guidance should be given to patients by way of notices and information leaflets in GP practices, hospitals and clinics. All new patients could be provided with documentation outlining all of their responsibilities, including in relation to the nature of their relationships with HCPs, so that there is no doubt. Information could also be provided online by the NHS, just as some GP practice websites provide information regarding their policies on violent and aggressive behaviour towards staff, for instance.[60]

In short, the avoidance of sexual boundary breaches requires patients as well as HCPs to take moral responsibility for their actions according to a growing view of 'patient ethics'[61] and in a broadly similar way to that envisaged by Brazier in her seminal article, 'Do No Harm'.

58 Bronner, Peretz and Ehrenfeld (n 10) 643; M Pathé, P Mullen and R Purcell, 'Patients who Stalk Doctors: their Motives and Management' (2002) 176 Med J of Aust 335, 337.
59 See also Gauthier (n 25) 163.
60 See the example provided above (n 56).
61 Coggon (n 29), 133.

9 When things go wrong
Patient harm, responsibility and (dis)empowerment

Anne-Maree Farrell and Sarah Devaney

Introduction

In 'Do No Harm – Do Patients Have Responsibilities Too?',[1] Margaret Brazier examined the relationship between morality and law in the context of patients' responsibilities. She argued that patients have moral obligations, not wholly defined by legal parameters, which should be taken account of in the context of the patient–doctor relationship, as well in the healthcare system more generally. In this way, she sought to challenge widely accepted notions of patient autonomy and responsibility in the existing bioethics and healthcare law literature. Brazier noted that the patient's position in healthcare, and the legal framework which governs it, have moved on from the 'Dark Ages where the patient's duty was to be patient' and where 'recipients of medical care were infantilised'.[2] She identified distinct consequences of this shift in the context of a publicly funded healthcare system, such as the National Health Service (NHS) in the United Kingdom (UK), emphasising that patient responsibility exists in a communal context in which the actions of patients, healthcare providers, institutions and the community are intertwined. As she put it, it is in essence 'a model of collaboration between doctors and patients, between the well and the sick, and between patients and patients'.[3] With this model, she suggests that 'empowerment of patients . . . brings responsibilities'.[4]

In this chapter, we engage with Brazier's interpretation of the relationship between patient autonomy and responsibility in situations where patients suffer harm as a result of healthcare treatment. We focus on the notion of *empowerment* as a key variable influencing this relationship. We argue that interactions between patients and healthcare professionals are socially and institutionally embedded, with power asymmetries structuring such interactions. Underpinned by the 'competence gap',[5] as well as patients' vulnerability due to ill-health and

---

1 M Brazier, 'Do No Harm – Do Patients Have Responsibilities Too?' (2006) 65(2) CLJ 397.
2 Ibid 401.
3 Ibid.
4 Ibid.
5 D Lupton, *Medicine as Culture: Illness, Disease and the Body in Western Society* (Sage 2003) 113.

unfamiliarity with the institutional healthcare environment, paternalism features strongly in such interactions, often leading to poor communication, mistrust and the use of blame strategies when patients suffer harm. Patients' family and friends often act as advocates on their behalf as they attempt, with mixed success, to navigate professional and institutional cultures that are defensive and largely unresponsive to their concerns about healthcare quality and safety. In the circumstances, we need to further expand upon Brazier's challenge to rethink the moral and legal dimensions of patients' responsibilities, by recognising the influential role played by cultures and practices in healthcare systems which act as barriers to patient empowerment.

In order to elucidate these arguments, we first explore how empowerment influences the relationship between patient autonomy and responsibility in healthcare settings. We examine patients' experiences of receiving treatment in the NHS and how empowerment – or conversely disempowerment – features in their recounting of such experiences, focusing on themes of vulnerability, trust and blame. We then offer concluding comments on what such findings may mean for claims made about patients' duties and obligations in the healthcare law and bioethics literature. Our examination of patients' experiences draws on select findings from a pilot study examining clinical negligence claiming.[6] As part of the study, individuals who had sought legal advice and/or pursued legal action arising out of harm caused through clinical negligence in the NHS were interviewed. Such individuals were accessed via a law firm in the north of England, which has a substantial legal practice in this area. Research ethics approval for the study was obtained from the University of Manchester.

Following a screening process by the firm, they sent information sheets, consent forms and reply paid envelopes to their clients on two separate occasions in relation to files closed between January 2006 and June 2009. Once signed consent forms were returned, 30 semi-structured interviews were conducted mostly by telephone (some in person) to elicit their experiences regarding first, accessing and receiving treatment for the condition or illness which gave rise to (potential) clinical negligence claims, and second, the process of making clinical negligence claims. The findings set out in this chapter draw on analysis undertaken in relation to the first aspect, and it is for this reason that we use the term 'patients' rather than 'claimants'. Coding reliability was assessed and confirmed using a sample of five transcribed interviews, and

---

6 The pilot study, *Making Amends? An Empirical Study of Clinical Negligence Claiming in England*, was funded by the Nuffield Foundation Social Sciences Small Grant Scheme. The Principal Investigator on the grant was Dr Angela Melville, with Co-Investigators Professor Frank Stephen and the two authors of this chapter. We acknowledge the work and support of our fellow investigators on the project, as well as research assistants Tammy Krause and Jamie Irving. We also gratefully acknowledge the financial support of the Nuffield Foundation.

saturation was reached after 25 interviews. As the law firm had conducted an initial screening of those who were to be contacted, we make no claims as to the representativeness of the sample. Quotations used in the body of this chapter are not representative of all interviews conducted, but instead reflect themes identified by the authors using iterative thematic analysis,[7] in order to address key arguments made here.

Between patient autonomy and responsibility: The role of empowerment

Remaining the focus of extensive academic discussion,[8] the autonomy of patients to make decisions about their treatment has been upheld and defended by the courts[9] and enshrined in legislation to facilitate its expression through consent.[10] It has been suggested that there are important tangible benefits associated with promoting such an approach, such as greater patient satisfaction, increased adherence to treatment regimens and better health outcomes overall.[11] As Brazier has pointed out, this increased focus on, and support for, patient autonomy necessitates a more critical reflection on the notion of patient responsibility.[12] However, defining what we mean by responsibility in the healthcare context is complex.[13]

It has been suggested that a useful way of identifying patients' responsibilities is by viewing them as co-producers of health services. Patient responsibility exists in the context of interactions between doctors and patients, as well as between other healthcare professionals and patients. Account must also be taken of the responsibilities patients may have to third parties, institutions and the community as a whole in terms of accessing and receiving healthcare services. Viewed in this way, they contribute to care and prevention strategies through

---

7 G Guest, K MacQueen and E Namey, *Applied Thematic Analysis* (Sage 2012).
8 See for example, M Brazier, 'Patient Autonomy and Consent to Treatment: the Role of the Law? (1987) 7(2) LS 169; A MacLean, *Autonomy, Informed Consent and Medical Law: A Relational Challenge* (CUP 2009); C Foster, *Choosing Life, Choosing Death: The Tyranny of Autonomy in Medical Ethics and Law* (Hart 2009); J Coggon and J Miola, 'Autonomy, Liberty and Medical Decision Making' (2011) 70(3) CLJ 523; S McLean, *Autonomy, Consent and the Law* (Routledge 2010); M Donnelly, *Healthcare Decision-Making and the Law* (CUP 2014).
9 *Re T (Adult: Refusal of Medical Treatment)* [1993] Fam. 95, 102 (CA); *Airedale NHS Trust v Bland* [1993] AC 789 (HL); *St George's NHS Hospital Trust v S* [1999] Fam. 26, CA; *Ms B v An NHS Hospital Trust* (2002) EWHC 429 (Fam); *Chester v Afshar* [2005] 1 AC 134; *Montgomery v Lanarkshire Health Board* [2015] UKSC 11.
10 See Mental Capacity Act 2005.
11 M Stewart, 'Towards a Global Definition of Patient-Centred Care' (2001) 322 BMJ 444, 445.
12 Brazier (n 1) 398–9, 404.
13 G Dworkin, 'Voluntary Health Risks and Public Policy' (1981) 11(5) Hastings Center Report 26; D Wikler, 'Who Should Be Blamed for Being Sick?' (1987) 14(1) Health Education Quarterly 11.

mutual participation and shared decision-making.[14] Other commentators have expressed the view that it is preferable to speak of health responsibilities rather than patient responsibilities,[15] because focusing primarily on patients' responsibilities can potentially open the door towards promoting health inequity and create opportunities for victim blaming. This may be particularly problematic for disadvantaged individuals, who find themselves held responsible for social and environmental factors which may be largely beyond their control.[16]

Differing conceptions of patient responsibility within the NHS may also be gleaned from a range of institutional and legal sources. From the 1990s onwards, a series of guidelines and charters were developed within the NHS, with the aim of identifying the roles, obligations and responsibilities of patients, healthcare professionals and institutions within the NHS.[17] Patients and their families are encouraged under the NHS Constitution to be aware of a number of responsibilities, including providing feedback, whether positive or negative, on treatment provided.[18] In legal terms, it is well established that no contractual relationship exists between NHS patients and their healthcare providers.[19] This necessarily structures the extent to which legal rights and duties attach to all parties. Opportunities under English law for holding patients responsible for harm suffered through medical treatment have largely been limited to well-established principles under tort law, including on occasion holding patients (partially) responsible for the harm on the grounds of contributory negligence.[20]

Against this background of academic and policy discourse, how then should we understand the notion of empowerment as a phenomenon which connects patient autonomy and responsibility? The shift towards autonomy implies greater power being accorded to patients in terms of choice, decision-making and management of their health. In a treatment context, however, paternalism still appears to be a major driver of interactions between patients and healthcare professionals. This is often underpinned by the 'competence gap',[21] as well as poor

---

14 S Buetow, 'The Scope for the Involvement of Patients in Their Consultations with Health Professionals: Rights, Responsibilities and Preferences of Patients' (1998) 24 JME 243; Institute of Medicine, Committee on Quality of Health Care in America, *Crossing the Quality Chasm: A New Health System for the 21st Century* (National Academies Press 2001).
15 H Schmidt, 'Patients' Charters and Health Responsibilities' (2007) 335 BMJ 1187.
16 Ibid 1188.
17 The NHS Constitution for England (26 March 2013) <www.gov.uk/government/publications/the-nhs-constitution-for-england> (accessed 6 February 2015).
18 Ibid. Available data shows that patients do not feel empowered to provide feedback on poor care in medical treatment: see Healthwatch England, *Suffering in Silence: Listening to Consumer Experiences of the Health and Social Care Complaints System* (October 2014).
19 M Brazier and E Cave, *Patients Medicine and the Law* (5th edn, Penguin Books 2011) [7.2].
20 See for example *Pidgeon v Doncaster HA* [2002] Lloyd's Rep Med 130.
21 Lupton (n 5).

communication skills on the part of healthcare professionals.[22] Notwithstanding aspirational claims about empowerment in the context of patient-centred care, the findings from empirical research suggest that 'power asymmetry' persists in interactions between patients and healthcare professionals. This may be difficult to avoid in publicly funded healthcare systems, such as the NHS, where rationing of healthcare resources and medicines is inevitable.[23] In the circumstances, it has been suggested that a more realistic way forward is to focus on how best to strike a balance between paternalism and autonomy in such interactions.[24] In practice, this may translate into the need for ongoing negotiations between patients and healthcare professionals to navigate treatment processes and likely health outcomes,[25] particularly where such patients have chronic conditions.[26]

Despite lively academic and policy debates on what should be the preferred approach, the findings from inquiries into recent NHS scandals involving serious and fatal failings in healthcare quality and safety have made it painfully clear that power asymmetry remains alive and well in the treatment and care of patients (and their families).[27] Such findings call into question the very idea of empowerment as an everyday reality for patients within the NHS. This appears to be further reinforced when things go wrong in treatment and patients suffer harm. The evidence from such inquiries is that patients feel vulnerable, disempowered and subject to professional and institutional cultures and practices which are defensive and not sufficiently responsive to their concerns about healthcare quality and safety issues.

In order to address such failings, the UK government has recently instituted a raft of legal and other reforms to embed new cultures and practices to better promote patient-centred care and safety in the NHS.[28] These now include

---

22 A Pilnick and R Dingwall, 'On the Remarkable Persistence of Asymmetry in Doctor/Patient Interaction' (2011) 72 Social Science & Medicine 1374, 1376; *Al Hamwi v Johnston* [2005] EWHC 206.
23 N Crisp, 'Patient Power Needs to Be Built on Strong Intellectual Foundations: An Essay by Nigel Crisp' (2012) 345 BMJ e6177.
24 Pilnick and Dingwall (n 22) 1381.
25 S Hor, N Godbold, A Collier et al., 'Finding the Patient in Patient Safety' (2013) 17(6) Health 567, 576.
26 A Mol, *The Logic of Care: Health and the Problem of Patient Choice* (Routledge 2008); A Coulter, V Entwistle, A Eccles et al., 'Personalised Care Planning for Adults with Chronic or Long-Term Conditions' (2015) 1 Cochrane Database Syst Rev CD010523.
27 *Report of the Mid Staffordshire NHS Foundation Trust Public Inquiry* (Chair: Mr Robert Francis QC), HC 947 (TSO 2013); Department of Health, National Advisory Group for the Safety of Patients in England, *A Promise to Learn – A Commitment to Act: Improving Patient Safety in England* (August 2013); Professor Sir Bruce Keogh, *Review into the Quality of Care and Treatment Provided by 14 Hospital Trusts in England: Overview Report* (16 July 2013); Department of Health, *Hard Truths: The Journey to Putting Patients First. The Government Response to the Mid Staffordshire NHS Foundation Trust Public Inquiry*, Cm 8777–1, Vols I and II (January 2014).
28 T Richards, A Coulter and P Wicks, 'Time to Deliver Patient Centred Care' (2015) 350 BMJ h530.

improved patients' complaints processes;[29] independent regulatory audits of how such processes are handled;[30] a statutory duty of candour;[31] and the creation of new criminal offences of ill treatment and wilful neglect.[32] Although such reforms are to be welcomed, only time will tell whether they will actually bring about desired changes. In the next section of the paper, we present select findings from our empirical research that examined, inter alia, patients' experiences of receiving treatment in the NHS where things went wrong and they suffered harm. Our findings focus on three key themes that emerged from patient interviews: vulnerability, trust and blame, and how they contributed to patient disempowerment.

Vulnerability

Feelings of vulnerability was a prevalent theme throughout patient interviews. This was constituted in a number of ways. First, vulnerability was a corollary of suffering physical and/or mental illness. Although experienced by patients with chronic and acute conditions, feeling vulnerable appeared to be particularly strong where the onset of symptoms was unexpected or sudden:

> If I got to the hospital and I thought something wasn't right and I approached the nurse the answer I got was he's been fine all day he's not complained of having a tummy ache or he's not complained of a headache but when you've had a stroke and you're so seriously ill like he was he's not going to complain because he didn't know how to.
>
> (C06)

Second, it was important to patients and their families that they were shown due respect and dignity by their treating healthcare professionals and within

---

29 House of Commons Health Committee, *Complaints and Raising Concerns*, Fourth Report of Session 2014–15, HC 350 (TSO 2015); House of Commons Public Administration Select Committee, *Inquiry into NHS Complaints and Clinical Failure* <www.parliament.uk/business/committees/committees-a-z/commons-select/public-administration-select-committee/inquiries/parliament-2010/nhs-complaints-and-clinical-failure/> (accessed 25 March 2015).
30 Local Authority Social Services and National Health Service Complaints (England) Regulations 2009, SI 2009 No. 309.
31 Health and Social Care Act 2008 (Regulated Activities) Regulations 2014; Care Quality Commission, Regulation 5: Fit and Proper Persons: Directors and Regulation 20: Duty of Candour, Guidance for NHS Bodies, (November 2014); *Joint Statement from the Chief Executives of Statutory Regulators of Healthcare Professionals: Openness and Honesty – the Professional Duty of Candour* <www.gmc-uk.org> (accessed 25 March 2015).
32 Criminal Justice and Courts Act 2015, ss 19, 20. Department of Health, Strategy and External Relation Directorate/Quality Regulation, *New Offences of Ill-Treatment or Wilful Neglect: Government Response to Consultation* (June 2014).

wider institutional settings. Feelings of vulnerability increased if this did not happen:

> They wouldn't close his eyes they wouldn't, they wouldn't stop doing that on his chest and they did that all the way to the hospital and I begged them not to just to leave him in peace and then they wouldn't even cover his face when he went through A and E and all these people were just looking at him and he'd died and I thought it was just so cruel, I just thought that was so cruel and undignified.
>
> (C08)

Third, such feelings were exacerbated by paternalistic attitudes adopted by healthcare professionals in consultations with patients and in the treatment provided to them:

> There's still one per cent of them who believe that they're two steps above everybody else and so don't discuss anything with you and just go and get on and do it.
>
> (C20)

> I wish I'd had a recorder the last time I saw him because he was just so rude and the way he spoke to me, just so detrimental, it was awful. I came out absolutely steaming.
>
> (C29)

Fourth, knowledge asymmetry in interactions with healthcare professionals made patients feel vulnerable, particularly if it was accompanied by inadequate information provision or explanations. In one instance, the patient was excluded from discussions about the decision-making process entirely:

> It was the person in charge on that ward her attitude was I'll decide what treatment my patients get not some old GP.
>
> (C35)

Finally, vulnerability was constituted by what patients considered to be incorrect assumptions made by healthcare professionals about patients based on their socio-economic status, which included gender, education, age or the circumstances that had led them to seek treatment:

> Maybe you should have . . . not just put me down as a fifty year old who was going round the bend! Which is what they did, they said you've got no children at home, your husband works away and I'm sorry I'm not that kind of person.
>
> (C29)

But he said what you do have to realise is that the paramedics are being called out . . . young man been drinking the night before . . . and I said yes but that's stereotyping and you shouldn't do that as an ambulance service.

(C35)

Feelings of vulnerability by patients often led family members or close friends to act as advocates, negotiating on their behalf with healthcare professionals and attempting to navigate unfamiliar institutional processes. The relationship to the patient was important as they knew them well, and had the opportunity to observe first-hand the difficulties they were encountering. These 'relational advocates' often performed a number of specific tasks, which included demanding more and better information about patients' treatment, critically questioning the treatment that was being provided, and pursuing a complaint when things went wrong:

So my sister she said can you not, just to ease his mind she said look at the state of him, he can hardly walk, just to ease our minds can you not give him an x-ray or something, send him down for an x-ray?

(C01)

It was my sister who is in the NHS itself . . . told me to write everything down while it was still fresh in my mind the following day really, write everything down she said because it shouldn't have happened. I was just going to accept what had happened but she said no, this shouldn't have happened you were here all those hours and they didn't do what they were supposed to do. So it was her that wrote everything down and said you need to look at taking this further and that's what kind of happened.

(C32)

On occasion, such advocacy also extended beyond immediate family and friends to encompass concerns about poor care being provided to third-party patients:

There were other men in the ward about obviously in their pyjamas but because they weren't aware of what they were doing their pyjamas were falling down and they didn't know that they were falling down and the nursing staff were walking past them and letting them walk about with no clothes on.

(C06)

Patients' feelings of vulnerability contributed greatly to their sense of disempowerment in healthcare settings. First and foremost, it was brought about by their own ill-health, as well as their fears and uncertainty over treatment and outcomes. Second, key aspects of their interactions with professional and institutional cultures made them feel vulnerable. This was experienced as knowledge asymmetry; paternalism in attitude and communication; a lack of dignity and respect for their bodies; and heuristic judgements being made about the reasons for patients' ill-health and levels of understanding.

Notwithstanding calls that have been made for healthcare professionals to adopt more effective communication strategies as part of addressing power asymmetries in interactions with patients,[33] the question remains as to whether such asymmetries are in fact embedded in (publicly funded) healthcare systems, as well as in the embedding of institutions of medicine in society more generally.[34] Patients' vulnerability made it much less likely that they would challenge the type and quality of care provided, or seek advice or redress about any problems that arose as a result of such care.[35] If there was a challenge, it was much more likely to have been brought by a relational advocate, such as a family member or close friend. Therefore, the activation of such advocacy was inextricably linked to patient vulnerability and designed to address disempowerment, albeit with mixed success.

Trust

Trust is a vital component of relationships between patients and those who treat them, both on a personal level and in terms of managing risks in relation to their treatment and care.[36] The findings from our study showed that there were a number of elements underpinning such trust for patients: information provision; being treated with dignity and respect; and being responsive to patient concerns, particularly when things went wrong. Patients valued communication exchanges with their treating healthcare professionals, as they provided opportunities to ask questions and receive information about their condition and treatment. When such information was not forthcoming, or was otherwise withheld from them, then patients felt frustrated, angry and undermined:

> When they operated on me they put a colostomy bag on and when I woke up in the morning I didn't know nothing about this so obviously it was a shock so I was pretty upset.
>
> (C01)

---

33 Hor et al. (n 25); see generally (n 29); General Medical Council, *Consent Guidance Partnership* [3–6] <www.gmc-uk.org> (accessed 25 March 2015).
34 Pilnick and Dingwall (n 22).
35 A Buck, P Pleasance and N Balmer, 'Do Citizens Know How to Deal with Legal Issues? Some Empirical Insights' (2008) 27(4) Journal of Social Policy 661, 671–3, 678; Healthwatch (n 18).
36 This has been well recognised in the relevant literature, see for example M Calnan and E Sanford, 'Public Trust in Health Care: The System or the Doctor?' (2004) 13 Quality and Safety in Health Care 92.

They came to see him but they didn't come while I was there they only came on morning rounds and you had to make an appointment if you wanted to see them.

(C06)

They just wouldn't listen and that's all it would have taken, for someone to have listened.

(C29)

When things went wrong, patients (and often their family members or close friends) actively sought out opportunities to express their concerns to treating healthcare professionals about the need for further information, explanations and even apologies for what had happened to them. We view this as an attempt to act responsibly in highlighting deficiencies in care so that they might be remedied. In our study, 23 of those interviewed attempted to make complaints about the treatment they received and the harm suffered. They did this prior to contacting a solicitor, with the majority raising concerns with their treating doctors during consultations. Several made a specific appointment with their doctor in order to complain, or wrote to the NHS Trust, and three made complaints through the Patient Advice and Liaison Service. What they encountered were a range of difficulties as they attempted to negotiate professional and institutional cultures that they experienced as defensive and largely unresponsive to their concerns about poor quality and unsafe healthcare:

[We attempted to make a complaint but] . . . we were finding that we were being blocked here there and everywhere because they were just closing ranks . . . Basically there was a lot of covering up going on they were saying this didn't happen that didn't happen and they'd not been told to do this and it turned out that it was all in the nursing notes that went with me to the other hospital so in the end they had to admit that they had been told.

(C24)

We felt that the [response to complaint to hospital] letter we got was sort of a grudging oh God keep them quiet and post them a letter . . . [As a result they contacted solicitors] . . . we felt that there wasn't a lesson being learned, that some other young lad could have gone in and been treated in exactly the same way.

(C35)

The difficulties patients encountered in engaging with complaints processes also served to undermine and erode their trust in previously valued relationships with healthcare professionals:

When you put them in hospital . . . when you take someone to hospital you put your trust in the medical team and it has lost all my trust in any sort of medical teams now, I always ask for a second opinion and I'm always very careful and aware if any of my family ever need to go into hospital I'm now very, very alert and make sure they receive the best care.

(C06)

The findings from our study revealed that trust provided a welcome counterbalance to feelings of vulnerability for patients. This accords with the findings from other published research in the field which has shown that patients invested (initial) trust in treating healthcare professionals in order to address fears and uncertainties about being in an unfamiliar environment,[37] as well as providing a strategy for managing risks associated with treatment and potential adverse outcomes.[38]

The difficulties experienced by patients in our study in relation to navigating NHS complaints processes are also well recognised within the academic and policy literature,[39] notwithstanding successive periods of reform.[40] Although outside the scope of this chapter, our study also revealed that the frustration and dissatisfaction experienced by patients (and their relational advocates) in navigating such processes operated as a strong catalyst for eventually seeking out independent legal advice with a view to bringing clinical negligence claims.[41] For present purposes, however, such difficulties only exacerbated patient disempowerment.

Blame

The construction and imposition of blame in social and institutional settings is a complex phenomenon.[42] In our study, blame was a pervasive theme running through patient interviews and was largely experienced as being imposed upon them by healthcare professionals and the institutions in which they received treatment and care. This occurred in a number of ways. First, patients were blamed for contributing to their poor health outcomes because they had failed to take appropriate responsibility for managing their body type, illness or condition:

> They said, they actually blamed my weight, how much I weighed at the time, I was really underweight obviously because I was poorly and they

---

37 S Halliday, S Kitzinger and J Kitzinger, 'Law in Everyday Life and Death: A Socio-Legal Study of Chronic Disorders of Consciousness' (2015) 35(1) LS 55, 61.
38 Hor et al. (n 25) 576–8.
39 For an historical overview, see L Mulcahy, *Disputing Doctors: The Socio-Legal Dynamics of Complaints About Medical Care* (Open University Press 2003).
40 See Healthwatch England (n 18); House of Commons (n 29).
41 It is a finding that has been confirmed elsewhere, see F Stephen, A Melville and T Krause, *A Study of Medical Negligence Claiming in Scotland*, Research Findings No. 113/2012, Government Social Research Scotland 1.
42 B Malle, S Guglielmo and A Monroe, 'A Theory of Blame' (2014) 25 Psychological Inquiry 147.

didn't give me a pressure mattress for me to go on which is how the burn actually got through my back.

(C04)

Patients (and their relational advocates) also felt blamed when they attempted to raise concerns or complain about healthcare quality and safety issues:

They were on the attack the whole time, on the attack the whole time but L started weeping and I wasn't expecting that and she wept, we were there an hour and a half and she wept the whole time, my poor daughter who is really strong, just wept the whole time. They were saying about my solicitor and bringing this law suit and I don't know what it's done to them and how many nights sleep, going on and on and on . . .

(C08)

On occasion, patients also experienced blame as being diffused through the healthcare system, which operated to shift responsibility away from treating healthcare professionals and institutions:

The letter did seem as though they were passing the buck, basically it came across as though they said we'll blame this nurse because she's no longer with us rather than somebody else.

(C09)

There are a number of well-known 'blame' tropes employed in healthcare settings. There are the 'difficult patients' who are considered by treating healthcare professionals to be overbearing; to have lifestyles that put them at risk of a range of health problems; or who are persistently non-compliant with treatment regimens.[43] It is these types of 'difficult patients' that have led to lively academic and policy debates about how we should conceptualise patient duties and responsibilities in ethical, legal and political terms.[44] In addition, patients who pursue legal action due to harm suffered as a result of poor or unsafe care are often depicted as fostering a 'blame culture'. This is depicted as anathema to the identification and analysis of individual and systemic errors in healthcare systems.[45] These tropes emanate largely from professional and/or institutional

---

43 J Abbott, 'Difficult Patients, Difficult Doctors: Can Consultants Interrupt the "Blame Game"?' (2012) 12(5) American Journal of Bioethics 18.
44 M Minkler, 'Personal Responsibility for Health? A Review of the Arguments and the Evidence at Century's End' (1999) 26(1) Health Education & Behavior 121; H Draper and T Sorell, 'Patients Responsibilities in Medical Ethics' (2002) 16(4) Bioethics 335; Brazier (n 1).
45 See for example *Learning from Bristol: The Report of the Public Inquiry into Children's Heart Surgery at the Bristol Royal Infirmary* 1984–1995 (Cm 5207) Final Report 16, 442.

perspectives on what constitutes the good and dutiful patient; such perspectives being particularly prevalent in publicly funded healthcare systems, such as the NHS.

In our study, patients who had suffered harm viewed blame as being imposed upon them by healthcare professionals and institutions in two main ways: first, through their failure to take responsibility for avoiding lifestyle risks thus resulting in their (diseased) bodies and poor health outcomes; and second, when patients challenged dominant professional and institutional narratives about the treatment they received through (in)formal complaints processes. Patients even found themselves buffeted by intra-institutional practices that were used to diffuse blame when things went wrong in treatment. When taken in the round, the imposition of such blame strategies served to disempower patients, hindering their attempts to address healthcare quality and safety issues.

Conclusion

In this chapter, we took up Brazier's challenge to re-think the moral and legal dimensions of patients' responsibilities. While we could not hope to resolve the complexities inherent in defining what is meant by responsibility on the part of patients, nor whether patient duties might take the form of legal or ethical obligations, we did critically reflect upon the notion of empowerment as a key variable structuring patient responsibility. Drawing on findings from empirical research into patients' experiences of healthcare when things go wrong, we found that a number of factors contributed to disempowerment in this context: first, *feelings of vulnerability* due to ill-health, knowledge asymmetry, and poor communication by healthcare professionals; second, *loss of trust* in healthcare professionals due to communication breakdown, a lack of dignity and respect, and defensive behaviours when challenged by patients about poor care; and finally, the *use of blaming strategies* by healthcare professionals and institutions in response to patients (and often family members or friends) challenging the treatment and care they had received which had resulted in harm. Unless supported in the form of appropriate cultural and procedural structures, these factors are likely to operate as barriers to patients' desire to play their part in improving healthcare quality and safety when things go wrong. In the circumstances, we respond to Brazier's challenge by suggesting that it is vital that factors contributing to patient (dis)empowerment are taken account of in ethical and legal analysis of patients' duties and responsibilities in healthcare settings.

10 Critical decisions for critically ill infants
Principles, processes, problems

Giles Birchley and Richard Huxtable

Introduction

Deciding what is best for a critically ill infant can be fraught, particularly if the question before the parent, healthcare professional or judge is 'to treat or not to treat?'. We explore the courts' dealings with cases in which this ethico-legal question has been posed, inspired by Margaret Brazier's work in this context with the Nuffield Council on Bioethics.[1] Specifically, we consider whether the clinical ethics committee (CEC) might improve the *principles* and *processes* by which resolution is achieved. The principle might appear straightforward: decisions must rest on the 'best interests' of the infant.[2] Yet this cardinal *legal* principle can have diverse *ethical* interpretations, such that the best interests of an infant are neither self-evident nor incontestable. When deciding, doctors should apparently engage in shared decision-making with parents, with the courts stepping in if agreement fails to materialise.[3] Yet, how – or whether – consensus is achieved is also open to question, as is the role that the courts play when consensus cannot be found.

These questions of principle and process inevitably introduce ethical questions, whose answers apparently require ethical sensitivity. Are the courts equipped to bear the moral load?[4] Perhaps CECs, increasingly available across the United Kingdom (UK), might have a role to play, since their functions include providing advice on ethically difficult situations.[5] In assessing this service, we will not only advance normative arguments, but also make reference to the views of those closest to the dilemmas that can arise on the paediatric intensive care unit (PICU). The findings we report indicate variation in the perceived effectiveness of CECs, obstacles to non-health professionals' access to CECs, and questions

---

1 Nuffield Council on Bioethics, *Critical Care Decisions in Fetal and Neonatal Medicine: Ethical Issues*, (NCB 2006).
2 'Best interests' can be considered synonymous with 'welfare': *Re B (a minor)(wardship: jurisdiction)* [1988] AC 199, 202 (Lord Hailsham LC).
3 *Re J (A Minor) (Wardship: Medical Treatment)* [1991] Fam 33; *Glass v UK* [2004] 1 FCR 553.
4 J Montgomery, 'Law and the Demoralisation of Medicine' (2006) 26 LS 185.
5 UK Clinical Ethics Network <www.ukcen.net> (accessed 17 October 2014).

about the expertise and authority of committee members. Such insights suggest that work identifying and disseminating best practice is needed, if CECs are to deliver on their apparent promise.

The data we report comes from the *Judging Best Interests in Paediatric Intensive Care* (BIPIC) study. BIPIC is a qualitative empirical ethics study funded by a Wellcome Trust fellowship in Society and Ethics. After gaining approval from an NHS research ethics committee, the first author (advised by the second, amongst others) conducted in-depth, semi-structured interviews in three clinical centres (here named Hospital A, B and C). The study recruited 14 parents, 10 doctors, 8 nurses and 7 CEC members through senior clinical collaborators. Interviews focused upon the process of making decisions about very sick infants and were subsequently analysed using thematic analysis.[6]

Intractable disputes?

Two recent cases involving infants with severe neurological conditions illustrate the dilemmas that can be confronted on PICU. In both cases, the parents sought treatment, which the doctors judged not to be in the infant's best interests. In *An NHS Foundation Trust v R (Child)* (hereafter *Reyhan*),[7] an infant, Reyhan, suffered from mitochondrial disease, which left him moribund and dependent on mechanical ventilation. His doctors sought to withdraw ventilation on the basis that continued treatment of his incurable and terminal disease would provide 'no benefit to him other than life itself'.[8] His parents opposed this, motivated inter alia, by a religious belief in the sanctity of his life. During the hearing, the court heard a second medical opinion which confirmed the terminal prognosis yet favoured treating Reyhan because of the deleterious effect that non-treatment would have on his family.

Having taken nine months to reach the courts, the case was rapidly decided in favour of the hospital. At this conclusive point, Jackson J ordered a break in proceedings of two months before he made the final order, to allow Reyhan's family time to come to terms with the verdict. Reyhan's family launched fresh proceedings in the interim, aimed at overturning the prospective order, and Reyhan died whilst still actively being treated, five months after the hearing had begun.

The next year, in *An NHS Trust v AB* (hereafter *AB*),[9] Theis J heard a similar case whose rapid passage through the courts contrasted sharply with that of

---

6 See further: G Birchley, 'Deciding Together? Best Interests and Shared Decision-Making in Paediatric Intensive Care' (2014) 22 Health Care Analysis 203; G Birchley, 'You Don't Need Proof When You've Got Instinct!: Gut Feelings and Some Limits to Parental Authority' in R Huxtable and R Meulen (eds), *The Voices and Rooms of European Bioethics* (Routledge 2015).
7 [2013] EWHC 2340 (Fam).
8 Ibid [20].
9 [2014] EWHC 1031 (Fam).

Reyhan. The infant, known as EF, had spent the sole year of his life in hospital with a degenerative neurological condition that manifested itself, among other serious symptoms, in worsening respiratory insufficiency. This had resulted in 11 episodes in which EF required mechanical ventilation, the most recent of which had led to court proceedings. EF's parents and doctors agreed that EF's decline was inexorable and that further aggressive measures should be withheld. However, EF's doctors felt that no treatment should be offered after ventilation was withdrawn, whereas EF's parents argued that withdrawal should be followed by a further 24-hour period in which supportive measures could be reinstituted. The parents' view was informed by the observation that such short-term support had proven efficacious in weaning EF from the ventilator in the past. On the basis that EF's doctors had no answer to this observation, Theis J decided on a compromise: EF was to be offered bag and mask resuscitation for 24 hours following withdrawal of his mechanical ventilation.

Problems of principle?

When seeking to resolve cases like *Reyhan* and *AB*, problems initially arise with regard to the principle(s) that purport to guide the resolution of parent–clinician conflict. Notwithstanding its familiarity and some statutory pointers,[10] the 'best interests' standard is notoriously difficult to define; as Brazier puts it, this can be 'an empty mantra'.[11] The principled basis of this standard is multi-faceted, which can make it unclear which values are actually influencing the resolution. We can understand best interests in (at least) three different ways: in *desire-fulfilment* theories, what individuals most desire conveys their best interests; in *hedonistic* theories, what makes individuals happiest is in their best interests; and in *objective-list* theories, best interests are independent of individual happiness or desire and align instead with objective accounts of the good.[12]

Of course, the theory that is chosen (whether overtly or otherwise) will affect the conclusions that are reached.[13] Each of these theories feature in the law. Desire-fulfilment features, for example, in the Children Act's instruction that reference be made to 'the ascertainable wishes and feelings of the child' whenever decisions are to be made in their best interests.[14] Hedonistic concerns surface when the courts favour the withholding or withdrawal of life-sustaining treatment in view of the infant's current or anticipated suffering, usually expressed in terms of his or her poor quality of life.[15] The courts also insist that life has an objective value, such that there is a presumption in favour of upholding the sanctity of life.[16]

---

10 Children Act 1989, s 1; cf. Mental Capacity Act 2005, s 4.
11 M Brazier, 'An Intractable Dispute: When Parents and Professionals Disagree' (2005) 13 Med L Rev 412, 415.
12 D Parfit, *Reasons and Persons* (OUP 1987) 493–502.
13 D Degrazia, 'Value Theory and the Best Interests Standard' (1995) 9 *Bioethics* 50.
14 Children Act 1989, s 1(3)(a).
15 See for example *Re J* (n 3).
16 See for example *Wyatt v Portsmouth Hospital NHS Trust* [2005] EWCA Civ 1181 [87].

Given its pluralistic inclination, the law inevitably encounters conflicts between the different values advanced in the name of best interests. We see this in *Reyhan*: the parents held 'conscientious beliefs about the sanctity of life',[17] whilst his doctors cited quality-of-life considerations, arguing that continued ventilation 'is delaying his death without significantly alleviating his suffering'.[18] Deciding which (if either) of these accounts should take priority is not only practically challenging, but also philosophically fraught. Each of the three rival theories outlined has its difficulties,[19] and there 'is no clear calculus' for determining best interests.[20] Identifying such a calculus will doubtless prove difficult, 'given the plurality of ethical world views that can and do exist'.[21]

Yet, even if one can give the best interests standard some substance, there is another difficulty to overcome: determining whether the best interests of the infant should be considered of *paramount* importance (and thus overriding) or of *primary* importance (and thus coequal with other primary – principally family – interests).[22] The Children Act favours the former approach,[23] but there is evidence of some inconsistency in the courts. In *Reyhan*, for example, Jackson J seemingly equivocates over whether the interests of those who are closest to the infant are relevant concerns for the court. He outwardly favours the paramountcy test, because he rejects the argument[24] that treatment should be continued in order to benefit the family.[25] Yet, he evidently considers parental interests to be a relevant consideration: despite having concluded that further treatment was against Reyhan's interests, he allows the parents time to come to terms with the verdict. The judge's reasoning thus indicates that the infant's interests were a primary, but not overriding, consideration for the court.

On some occasions (albeit controversially) judges have been particularly explicit in their regard for the parents' interests.[26] Whilst we can only speculate as to the exact situation in English law (at least, as it is applied), Seema Shah's survey of 101 judgments in the United States is revealing, since she found that courts were evenly divided between those which saw the child's interests as paramount and those which saw them as a primary consideration.[27]

---

17 *Reyhan* (n 7) [14].
18 Ibid [12].
19 DeGrazia (n 13).
20 P Baines, 'Death and Best Interests: A Response to the Legal Challenge' (2010) 5 Clinical Ethics 195, 197; cf. J Herring, 'Farewell Welfare?' (2005) 27 J Soc Wel & Fam L 159, 160.
21 R Huxtable, *Law, Ethics and Compromise at the Limits of Life: To Treat or not to Treat?* (Routledge 2012) 85.
22 S Parker, 'The Best Interests of the Child: Principles and Problems' (1994) 8 IJLPF 26.
23 Children Act 1989, s 1(1).
24 *Reyhan* (n 7) [34].
25 Ibid [60].
26 See for example *Re T (a minor)(wardship: medical treatment)* [1997] 1 All ER 906; see also *NHS Trust v A and others* [2007] EWHC 1696.
27 S Shah, 'Does Research with Children Violate the Best Interests Standard? An Empirical and Conceptual Analysis' (2013) 8 Northwestern Journal of Law and Social Policy 121.

The obverse of the apparent inconsistency of best interests is that it is a flexible standard.[28] Whether this flexibility is wielded (in)appropriately will turn not only on which principles we think should be determinative, but also on *who* does the wielding. Since every other actor will operate in the shadow of the courts, it is to judges we should look most closely. In the absence of a prescribed hierarchy of values, judges, whether knowingly or not, will probably favour one or other of the different theories outlined earlier. In short, we are likely to confront incommensurable accounts of a critically ill infant's best interests, and be left with a problem of indeterminacy.[29] The judges will also dictate the processes that must be followed. So what are these processes?

Problems of process?

Judicial rulings in this area reveal that a two-stage process for resolving conflicts in the paediatric setting is usually recommended: first, the parties in dispute should strive for consensus; and, second, if consensus ultimately cannot be reached, the matter should be referred to the court for a decision. Unfortunately, each of these stages present problems. The consensus-building stage can be captured by the phrase 'shared decision-making'. Successive rulings have emphasised the need for a partnership-based approach, such that the 'choice of treatment is in some measure a joint decision of the doctors and the court or parents'.[30] This idea commands some support in relation to adult patients, especially given its autonomy-respecting orientation.[31] However, it is open to question whether the idea translates easily to proxy decision-makers and thus to exercises of *parental* autonomy.[32] This translation must rest on the assumption that parents have *authority*, i.e. a right of say, over the lives of their offspring. Such authority might appear self-evident, but doubts about its basis arise,[33] for example, when the courts indicate that even estranged or incapacitated parents will retain some right of say.[34]

If, however, we ignore these doubts and thus recognise a need to respect parental authority, the next question is whether such authority is *actually* respected in (paediatric) practice. Empirical evidence suggests that practice varies.[35] As such,

---

28 G Douglas, *An Introduction to Family Law* (OUP 2004) 173.
29 R Heywood, 'Parents and Medical Professionals: Conflict, Cooperation, and Best Interests' (2012) 20 Med L Rev 29.
30 *Re J* (n 3) 41. See also e.g. *Glass* (n 3); *NHS Trust v B* [2006] EWHC 507; *NHS v A* (n 26); *AB* (n 9).
31 *Ms B v NHS Trust* [2002] EWHC 429 (Fam).
32 Birchley, 'Deciding Together?' (n 6).
33 Birchley, 'You Don't Need Proof When You've Got Instinct!' (n 6); M Freeman, 'Whose Life is it Anyway?' (2001) 9 Med L Rev 259.
34 See for example *An NHS Trust v H* [2013] 1 FLR 1471, [19] (Jackson J).
35 See for example T Moro et al., 'Parent Decision-Making for Life Support for Extremely Premature Infants: From the Prenatal Through End-of-Life Period' (2011) 25 J Perinat Neonatal Nurs 52; HE McHaffie, *Crucial Decisions at the Beginning of Life: Parents' Experiences of Treatment Withdrawal from Infants* (Radcliffe Medical Press 2001).

even in eligible cases,[36] we might doubt whether, at least with parents, there is always the 'true sharing of ethical authority and responsibility'" once envisaged by the supporters of this ideal.[37] Given the tenor of professional guidance (which necessarily follows the legal steer), this is unsurprising: for example, the General Medical Council instructs doctors that working in partnership with parents means that: 'You must *take account* of their views when identifying options that are clinically appropriate and likely to be in the child's best interests.'[38] On this view, sharing a decision might mean no more than being consulted about the decision.

The scope of parental influence therefore appears to be variable in practice and ill-defined in principle. These problems are then replicated (even accentuated) at the second stage of the process. The courts may say that doctors no longer know best,[39] but they still appear inclined to assign weight according not only to the content of the evidence, but also to the identity of the individual providing it. Theis J's ruling in *AB* exemplifies this, offering a compromise position between the doctors and parents, despite clearly concluding that the infant's doctors had overlooked crucial evidence. If (albeit only if)[40] 'the best interests test ought, logically, to give only one answer',[41] then surely the doctors' evidence in *AB* was either right or wrong, and, if it was wrong, it would only be correct to reject it. The courts, however, are not quite willing to do this, at least in the majority of such cases.[42]

These concerns with the process – and particularly with the authority that is accorded to the different parties therein – involve complicated questions of power, and we must always remember the least powerful party: the critically ill infant who is at the heart of the proceedings. Do current processes necessarily serve the infant's interests, particularly when negotiations are protracted? Lack of clarity on principles and processes may undermine this key aim of the law. In both *AB* and *Reyhan*, many months were devoted to finding a solution to apparently intractable dilemmas, yet it is unclear at what point attempts to reach agreement should be judged to have failed and the courts approached. In *AB*, continued communication had not yielded consensus, despite the relatively narrow basis of the disagreement (both parties, after all, favoured withdrawal), and this was so notwithstanding some apparently correctable misunderstandings (the parents' wishes were based on observations of their infant of which doctors were unaware). If, as in these cases, disagreement between parents and clinicians eventually leads to court action, then we might expect this to happen promptly

---

36 Assuming we can specify those cases.
37 R Veatch, 'Models for Ethical Medicine in a Revolutionary Age' (1972) 2 Hastings Center Report 5, 7.
38 General Medical Council, Treatment and Care Towards the End of Life: Good Practice in Decision Making (GMC 2010) 46, emphasis added; cf. Nuffield Council (n 1) 22.
39 See Brazier (n 11) 415.
40 See Parker (n 22); Huxtable (n 21).
41 *Re S (adult patient: sterilisation)* [2001] Fam 15, 27 (Butler-Sloss P).
42 cf. *Re T* (n 26).

and for the judge to decide without delay.[43] However, in *Reyhan*, we have noted the time which Jackson J felt it appropriate to allow, despite having already determined that continued treatment was not in the best interests of the infant.

The costs of courts?

Maybe Jackson J's decision in *Reyhan* shows commendable sensitivity to the parents – but it might also indicate that the courts are not always best placed to resolve the complicated clinical and ethical questions that come before them. The suspicion that the (legally-mandated) processes might not always be working is shared by the participants in BIPIC. Whilst few doubted the courts' capacity to make an authoritative decision, many questioned whether the courts are the ideal environment in which to resolve disputes like the one that arose in *Reyhan*.

Parents certainly viewed the courts' involvement with trepidation, and expressed little confidence in the court having adequate means to reach a satisfactory decision:

> Not a judge, no, 'cos they haven't even seen that child. . . . they have no attachment do they?
>
> (P59, parent)

Reservations were also expressed by doctors and nurses. One doctor had grave doubts about engaging with a process which imposed human and financial costs:

> It could go to court, it's very stressful, it's expensive, it risks more confrontation between the family and yourself, and we've still got to look after this child, therefore we're not going to, we won't get a judgement not to do this, this is usually a long-term ventilation thing, so we may as well just do it. So we've got children who I feel it's fundamentally wrong that we've ventilated.
>
> (D34, consultant intensivist)

Brazier has also long noted the limitations of the courts in settling conflicts in the clinic,[44] a critique that she pointedly applies in her commentary on the (prolonged and public) dispute between the parents and doctors of young Charlotte Wyatt.[45] Two of Brazier's observations are particularly pertinent here. First, by requiring that one party win and another lose, the courts encourage, rather than diffuse, conflict. Whilst a sensitive judge can do much to mediate between combatant parties, this role as a mediator is undermined by his or her status as a judge, since the judge's role is to *decide* – thereby typically signalling that

---

43 See Children Act 1989, s 1(2).
44 M Brazier, *Medicine, Patients and the Law* (1st edn, Viking Press 1987).
45 *Wyatt* (n 16); Brazier (n 11).

one party is 'right' and the other is 'wrong'. In such a context, principles may be obfuscated rather than openly discussed and misunderstandings incubated by the need of the parties to prepare a case in an adversarial spirit and of the judge to declare a winner and a loser. Second, Brazier notes that law *costs*. In addition to the undoubted emotional costs, recourse to the courts is financially costly.[46] Brazier has therefore urged consideration of alternative means of dispute resolution, such as no-fault compensation schemes[47] and mediation.[48] However, we want to explore a different mechanism, to which Brazier has also referred:[49] the clinical ethics committee.

From courts to committees?

Because judges have been asked to resolve the case (indeed, clinicians are compelled to consult the courts if consensus is unachievable),[50] the courts may by necessity depict cases in black-and-white. Of course, the courts are not entirely blind to the multiple ethical shades of grey in which these dilemmas are daubed. In *AB*, Theis J certainly seemed inclined towards accommodating both sides, rather than signalling that there was a 'winner' and a 'loser'.[51] However, we might question whether the compromise imposed in that case appropriately split the difference between the disputing parties. Quite what is an appropriate accommodation requires more transparent ethical assessment than (perhaps) the courts can provide in their role.[52] If they are wary of peering too closely at such matters, it would appear appropriate to turn the appraisal over to a group that is specifically tasked with such an ethical endeavour.

Whilst not (yet?) formalised in the manner of research ethics committees, the number of CECs are increasing in the UK.[53] These multidisciplinary groups, often containing legal and lay members as well as healthcare professionals, usually offer case consultation services that issue advice on individual dilemmas.[54] Notably many such cases involve the withdrawal or withholding of life-supporting treatment from young or incapacitated patients.[55] The enterprise has been challenged, not least by those who fear a 'due process wasteland',[56] but

---

46 These high costs could deter parties from seeking a legal resolution.
47 Brazier (n 44).
48 Nuffield Council (n 1) 145.
49 Indeed the second author was privileged to share a Manchester stage with Brazier at the second annual UK Clinical Ethics Network (UKCEN) conference in 2002.
50 *Glass* (n 3).
51 *AB* (n 9) [69–70].
52 Huxtable (n 21).
53 UKCEN (n 5).
54 A Slowther, L McClimans and C Price, 'Development of Clinical Ethics Services in the UK: A National Survey' (2012) 38 JME 210.
55 UKCEN (n 5).
56 S McLean, 'Clinical Ethics Committees: A Due Process Wasteland?' (2008) 3 Clinical Ethics 99.

it also commands some academic support.⁵⁷ But how is the process looked on by those with real experience of these dilemmas in PICU?

Interviews carried out in the BIPIC study revealed insights into both the opportunities for, and the barriers to, recourse to a CEC. Four themes emerged: the participants spoke positively of the possibility of *group decision-making*, but this was seen as reliant on *clinicians' engagement* with the process, and reservations were expressed about *referral* to the committee and the *identity* of its members. First, there was support for involving a group in deciding on these difficult cases, at least from parents and nurses. One parent commented:

> it needs to be different for every case really. Almost if there was some kind of team, if there can be a team that looks at every case, . . . and looks at the situation, and looks at the parents, and looks at the lifestyle, and talks with the medical team.
>
> (P62, parent)

Other parents felt that it would be less easy to avoid making a difficult decision if the situation had been scrutinised by a group of people. Some nurses, too, felt that a group decision would relieve the burden on individual parents and doctors, by ensuring that responsibility was shared. Notably, however, these nurses and parents had virtually no practical experience of a CEC, and they commented that the membership and processes of the committee were a mystery. N43, who nursed a patient who was subject to a CEC referral, commented:

> I haven't had any personal input from them. I obviously just hear that it's going to the clinical ethics committee and that's as much as you hear really.
>
> (N43, nurse)

Referrals at the interview locations took place only at the instigation of doctors. Notably, these gatekeepers had mixed views about the usefulness of CECs, and engagement with the local committee appeared to depend on location. In Hospital A, for instance, the doctors interviewed (all trainees), were supportive of the involvement of CECs. Reflecting on a referral with which they had been involved, one doctor said:

> I'm quite pro the clinical ethics committee. So I thought it was brilliant that the case was brought to be discussed, I thought that was really good.
>
> (D50, trainee intensivist)

Another doctor felt that the advice dispensed was more expert and objective than the decision of a court, which was seen to rely on:

> individual judges who have no clinical training – they hear evidence from clinical teams, but these are very much skewed to whichever purpose the

---

57 Huxtable (n 21).

legal teams want to drive things, and there are inherent interests maintained. Whereas a committee potentially could be more objective because it is a committee decision.

(D47, trainee intensivist)

However, in other study locations, participants were less positive. D30, a consultant intensivist at Hospital B with several decades of experience, was scathing of his local ethics committee, suggesting it was irresolute and inappropriately legally-focused in its advice:

They will give you a set of options, and they will not come back with anything that's of much help at all. Or they will withdraw into the legalistic arguments. It's been very disappointing. And, you know, we've gone to ethics committees several times, more than just me, and we've been highly disappointed with the response ... you've got too many views going round, and ultimately, if you have so many views, you do nothing. And that's what happens with the clinical ethics committee: they do nothing.

(D30, consultant intensivist)

This type of opinion seemed to depend on the location of the PICU, rather than the seniority of the staff. For example, D27, a trainee intensivist at Hospital B, appeared to view the ethics committee as moribund:

They didn't change the thoughts, they didn't really significantly change the process.

(D27, trainee intensivist)

At Hospital C, there was no engagement with the ethics committee at all. D46, a consultant intensivist, said the committee had no understanding of the types of issues they encountered in PICU, and so it had never been used:

Maybe if you're working in a standalone children's hospital where everyone on the ethics committee understands paediatric issues, it may be more useful. Um, as I say, we don't tend to use our own here so I can't comment on how useful it is or isn't in other places.

(D46, consultant intensivist)

This situation was confirmed by members of Hospital C's clinical ethics committee, who highlighted a lack of referrals. E53, a lay member, felt this was a widespread problem:

I think most other ethics committees, including ours, struggle to get more than a couple of cases a month, and you might not get a case in a month.

(E53, Lay member, clinical ethics committee)

A low level of referrals raised concerns among committee members that cases of real ethical difficulty may be missed. E36, a doctor, observed:

> People who bring ethics problems to an ethics committee have realised there is an ethical problem. . . . I think the areas where potentially unethical practice goes on is when it hasn't crossed anybody's mind that there is an ethical issue whatsoever.
>
> (E36, Doctor, clinical ethics committee)

At the same time, however, some committee members were wary of expanding the referral base by accepting referrals from non-clinicians. Whilst some parents expressed enthusiasm for committee advice, only one parent felt that they would have benefitted personally from this. However, although some ethics committee members were supportive of accepting referrals from patients or families, others were guarded:

> I think in certain cases it might be useful. I don't think in all cases, because often the reason that there is a referral [to the committee] is there is some sort of chaotic family life or there's some [other] reason why.
>
> (E53, Lay member, clinical ethics committee)

Other members felt that referral was proscribed, given the committee's occupancy of the hospital institution:

> with parents one has to bear in mind that they may end up in litigation against our employer institution, um and what we say might be used against us.
>
> (E39, lawyer, clinical ethics committee)

E39's concern introduces a new problem: the committee's ability to command the respect of the disputants. For clinicians, a recurring concern was the authoritativeness of the committee's opinion:

> I don't know that there is great buy-in to what it says, is the problem. You know, if they come up with a kind of opinion, and you've still got two groups that one group is not going to agree with the opinion.
>
> (D34, consultant intensivist)

Parents considered expertise to be an essential element in engendering the confidence of all the parties:

> As long as you felt confident, . . . that they had enough expertise in the areas that they were going to sort of discuss, and by expertise I mean, you know, they understood some of the repercussions medically, then

yeah I don't think that's a bad thing if things are becoming sort of at an impasse.

(P45, parent)

Whilst ethical and medical expertise would thus help to command the respect of parents and professionals alike, the issue of authoritativeness remained a vexed issue for many clinicians.

Analysis of the results from BIPIC gives us some cause for reflection upon the (current and future) role that a CEC might play in disputes over a child's best interests. Although some participants welcomed the involvement of ethics committees, the BIPIC study revealed variation in the perceived effectiveness of these groups, challenges in access, and questions about their identity and authority. If there is merit in providing such a service, then efforts will be needed to address these concerns. Variations in user perceptions mirror real variations in committee membership and procedure.[58] If some committees command the respect of clinicians, and some do not, then we must learn from those committees that are judged to be operating 'successfully'.

This could follow the model of identifying good practice that can be replicated elsewhere, or more radically, could point to a need for a national committee framework, with specially-convened sub-committees with subject-specific expertise. A low level of referrals could also signal a need to open up the referral system, so that (as indeed Brazier has suggested) we can hear the voices of those who might otherwise be missed – including not only the parents but also the nurses.[59] If power needs to be rebalanced, then there may even be a need to revisit the composition of committees, with a view to ensuring that there is appropriate medical expertise, but that this does not wholly dominate deliberations. Indeed, composition, training and the very notion of 'expertise' are likely to be particularly pressing concerns.

Of course, all of these proposals also raise questions. Organisationally, the current system is *ad hoc* and run on a voluntary basis, often by time-pressed chairpersons. Could the present structure cope with increased levels of referral? How is due process to be assured?[60] Should the system be formalised, along the lines of the research ethics committee? Issues of governance also need attention: non-medical referrals may challenge traditional hierarchies, and parental referrals need to be channelled in a way that differentiates the ethics consultation from the patient advice and liaison service. Finally, the vexed question of expertise will remain: judges may be self-evident experts in law, but what does an ethical expert look like?[61] Whilst we cannot resolve these questions here, we suspect

---

58 Slowther et al. (n 54).
59 Brazier (n 11) 416.
60 McLean (n 56).
61 Huxtable (n 21).

there ought to be an active search for answers, especially if there is a case for improving on the current processes, whilst also engaging effectively with what are not only legal, but also ethical principles.

Conclusion

In cases involving critically ill infants, as Brazier notes, it may be that '[t]here is no right answer'.[62] There may, however, be processes available that can engage appropriately with the principles (plural) and thus ensure that all of the relevant rights and wrongs are aired, in a timely fashion. Like Brazier, the BIPIC participants noted the costs imposed by recourse to the courts, not least because the adversarial process can exacerbate, rather than ameliorate, the dispute. Rightly or wrongly, the legal process – and even the prior process of consensus-building – would appear to be weighted against parents. Whether this is indeed right or wrong should be established: if, despite the ethically-laden nature of the best interests mantra, the courts are reluctant to peer too closely at these matters,[63] then we need a forum in which the exploration can occur.

CECs appear to offer the obvious location. From this point of view, the BIPIC results contain both positive and negative messages. CECs may be both desirable and appreciated, at least in some quarters. But, on a local level, relations between clinicians and committees apparently vary from good to non-existent, committees remain under-utilised and doubts remain over their authority and expertise. These challenges need to be overcome if the current service is to develop. Ideally, for parties to future cases akin to *Reyhan* and *AB*, we should be able devise a system that combines the best of both worlds, i.e. the decisive authority of the courts coupled with the sensitive ethical reflection of an appropriately composed and constituted ethics committee.

62 Brazier (n 11) 418.
63 Montgomery (n 4).

11 The role of the family in healthcare decisions
The dead and the dying

Monica Navarro-Michel

Introduction

The relationship between doctor and patient is a binary one, and yet the family projects its influence onto many healthcare decisions. Relatives are not part of the doctor–patient relationship, and healthcare professionals may feel they must protect the patient from their family, denying them access to medical information in order to preserve the patient's confidentiality, or even describing family participation as undue influence. Traditionally, relatives who question the professionals' decisions have been seen as a nuisance, and physicians have not been trained to engage families in a therapeutic alliance. Perhaps too often, perceptions of family involvement have been developed through the lens of judicial conflict. In order to get a complete picture of families in the healthcare context, it is misleading to focus only on the cases that have been taken to court, since this does not present an accurately representative picture of their involvement, which may often be positive. When families do participate in the decision-making process, they can shed light on the wishes of the patient faced with end-of-life decisions. Margaret Brazier has advocated for a cooperative partnership in healthcare decisions, between patient and healthcare professional,[1] and between parents and their child's physician.[2] Perhaps it is time we include in this list of partnerships one between families and healthcare professionals in end-of-life situations.

This chapter will focus on the family's role in decision-making when the adult patient is competent, when the adult patient becomes incompetent, and the family's role in end-of-life situations. Minors will not be included in this chapter, since a different set of principles may apply. Reference will also be made to the role families have in deceased organ donation.[3] The terms 'family' and 'relatives' are used here in a broad sense, to include persons who are close to the patient

---

1   M Brazier, 'Patient autonomy and consent to treatment: the role of the law?' (1987) 7 LS 169.
2   M Brazier, 'An intractable dispute: when parents and professional's disagree' (2005) 13 Med L Rev 412.
3   M Brazier, 'Retained organs: ethics and humanity' (2002) 22 LS 550.

even though they have no blood or marital ties with them. The chapter will end with some reflections on the role of the family in defining the patient's best interests, and whether it is sound practice to increase the voice of the family in end-of-life situations.

Competent adult patients' autonomy and family involvement

Informed consent aims to ensure the patient's right to make autonomous decisions, in particular being able to select the desired treatment option as well as to reject unfavourable ones. Before making a valid decision, certain requirements must be met: patients must be adequately informed, they must have capacity to make decisions, and these decisions must be made voluntarily and independently. If we focus on voluntary choice, emphasis is usually placed on the need to avoid undue pressure or coercion, exerted by either physicians[4] or the patient's family.

In theory, adults make decisions by themselves and relatives have no say in the matter. The doctrine of informed consent implies the notion of an independent, autonomous person who stands alone and is not subordinated to others' views. In practice, however, this is not the way medical decisions, or any other decisions, are made. Rather, relatives participate in all manner of decisions affecting the family (from buying a house to accepting a job offer, from having children to selecting a school for them), with family members' interests being weighed and taken into account in reaching decisions. In the 1990s, a number of scholars began to highlight the significance of family involvement in medical decision-making.[5] A social conception of autonomy takes into account the fact that relatives and significant others are actually involved in the decision-making process and have an influence on the decisions made by the patient.[6] Relational autonomy stems from the conviction that persons are socially embedded; it embraces the patient and his/her family, given that the patient–physician relationship does not occur in a hermetically sealed bubble.

Families' participation in medical decisions has traditionally been presented in the context of the doctrine of undue influence. The leading case of *Re T (Adult: Refusal of Medical Treatment)*[7] involved a pregnant woman who was

---

4　Undue influence by healthcare practitioners will not be examined in this chapter.
5　J Hardwig, 'What about the family?' (1990) 20 Hastings Center Report 5; J Lindemann-Nelson, 'Taking families seriously' (1992) 22 Hastings Center Report 6; J Blustein, 'The family in medical decisionmaking' (1993) 23 Hastings Center Report 6; H Lindemann-Nelson and J Lindemann-Nelson, *The Patient in the Family: an Ethics of Medicine and Families* (Routledge, 1995); M G Kuczewski, 'Reconceiving the Family: the process of consent in medical decision-making' (1996) 26 Hastings Center Report 30.
6　C Mackenzie and N Stoljar, 'Autonomy Refigured' in C Mackenzie and N Stoljar (eds), *Relational Autonomy: Feminist Perspectives on Autonomy, Agency and the Social Self* (OUP 2000) 23.
7　[1992] 4 All ER 649.

admitted to hospital after a car accident, where she refused a blood transfusion after a meeting with her Jehovah's Witness mother, even though she had previously stated that she was not a Jehovah's Witness herself. After a caesarean section, the patient became unconscious and in need of a blood transfusion. Her brother and boyfriend applied to the court for authorisation for a blood transfusion. Lord Donaldson, deciding that this refusal could not be taken into account since the patient's will had been overborne by her mother, stated:

> A special problem arises if at the time the decision is made the patient has been subjected to the influence of some third party. This is by no means to say that the patient is not entitled to receive and indeed invite advice and assistance from others in reaching a decision, particularly from members of the family. But the doctors have to consider whether the decision is really that of the patient. The real question in each such case is, 'does the patient really mean what he says or is he merely saying it for a quiet life, to satisfy someone else or because the advice and persuasion to which he has been subjected is such that he can no longer think and decide for himself?' In other words, is it a decision expressed in form only, not in reality?[8]

When considering the effects of outside influences several aspects need to be taken into account. Lord Donaldson highlighted two of them. First, the strength of will of the patient needs to be ascertained. If the patient is tired, suffering pain, depressed or on medication, he or she is less likely to resist the influence of others. Second, the patient's relationship with the persuading party needs to be established. The stronger the relationship, the greater the ability of the persuader to override the patient.[9] But these two factors would, in effect, make all family interventions subject to undue influence, because these factors are often typical of families of patients with a long-term illness.

The involvement of next of kin may be a cause for concern, particularly when religious beliefs are the reason for refusing treatment. But their participation may also be compatible with, or even enhance, a patient's autonomy, as several authors have maintained.[10] Individuals are not islands, acting in an isolated manner. In the context of healthcare, particularly long-term illness, when care is provided in an impersonal and fragmented manner by an array of different professionals, patients weakened by their disease or treatment understandably may turn to their families for comfort and guidance. The presence of relatives in the consultation may be beneficial to help the patient absorb and process

---

8 *In Re T* (n 7) 662.
9 C Stewart and A Lynch, 'Undue influence, consent and medical treatment' (2003) 96 Journal of the Royal Society of Medicine 599.
10 A Ho, 'Relational autonomy or undue pressure? Family's role in medical decision-making' (2008) 22 Scandinavian Journal of Caring Sciences 128; R Gilbar, 'Family involvement, independence, and patient autonomy in practice' (2011) 19 Med L Rev 192.

information, ask relevant questions and discuss options. Because family members generally care about the patient's wellbeing, they should be involved in the decision-making process.

In light of these arguments, physicians should not automatically presume that there is undue influence whenever relatives are involved in medical decisions. It is one thing to want to protect patients from their overpowering relatives (particularly when the family refuses life-saving treatment) and another to presume automatically that when relatives appear, coercion is not far away. There should not be a presumption that the family is in conflict with the patient and will take advantage of this situation to prevail over the patient. Relatives may help the patient make a choice. Physicians should welcome discussion with the family. However, it should be clear that the final decision will be that of the patient, not the family, and that the interests of the family may in certain circumstances be taken into account,[11] but should not prevail.[12]

There seems to be a bias against the family, in the sense that family involvement carries with it the suspicion of undue influence, of which physicians should be wary. But this bias only operates when relatives intervene to question a physician's judgement, not when they help professionals to convince (or coerce?) the patient into accepting treatment.[13] If relatives pressure the patient into accepting the proposed treatment, nobody will question the family's intervention. If, however, family members question the doctor's judgement, the accusation of coercive behaviour will fall on them.

Incompetent adults

When the patient is deemed incompetent and is unable to make medical decisions, physicians may turn to the chosen proxy with a lasting power of attorney to make medical decisions. In England, if no representative has been chosen, the Court of Protection (CP) may appoint someone as the deputy for the

---

11 Hardwig (n 5 at 7) argues that the theory of medical ethics should be built 'on the presumption of equality: the interests of patients and family members are morally to be weighed equally'. This leads him to conclude that the dying patient even has a moral duty to die, or a moral duty not to be a burden on the family. See J Hardwig, 'Is there a Duty to Die?' (1997) 27 Hastings Center Report 34.
12 But even this statement may, on occasion, be questioned. There seems to be a taboo in taking into account the interests of the family at the same level as those of the patient, which is a justified reaction against a long history of professional paternalism. However, we must admit that some decisions are made which expressly take into account the interests of others, such as saviour siblings and non-therapeutic sterilization of disabled adults.
13 T Grisso and P S Appelbaum, *Assessing competence to consent to treatment* (OUP 1998) 10: 'Clinicians need not refrain from initiating treatment because a patient has consented out of concern for the reaction of a loved one.' And the example they give is of a spouse who threatens to leave a patient unless he or she agrees to surgery. I think this is very close to undue pressure, and the only reason it is accepted is because the result may be medically advisable.

incompetent patient, although resort to the CP is not mandatory. Why not let families decide? Margaret Brazier and Emma Cave have argued that 'Laws granting automatic decision-making powers to "next of kin" would be fraught with difficulty and danger'.[14] The *difficulty* lies in identifying who the decision-maker should be, and the *danger* in that relatives might make decisions based on their own, rather than the patient's, interests. However, in countries such as Spain, Belgium and the Netherlands, families do play a role in making decisions as informal representatives, and regulations try to address these dangers specifically, adopting some safeguards. Even though these risks may persist, informal representation does have important advantages.[15]

The Spanish model of surrogate decision-making is set out in the State Law on patient autonomy,[16] which represented a milestone in the doctor–patient relationship. It states that when patients are unable to give informed consent, and in the absence of a court appointed representative (guardian) or a self-appointed proxy in an advance directive, 'consent by representation' may be sought from relatives or those with other *de facto* ties.[17] Apart from a general reference to the need for such decisions to be 'adequate to the circumstances and proportionate to the needs to be attended, always in favour of the patient and with respect for his/her personal dignity',[18] the law does not define how decisions are to be made, or how to limit the power of these informal representatives. The law does, however, stipulate that patients should be involved as far as possible in decision-making throughout the whole medical process. There is no provision in the event of conflict between physicians and surrogates, or between family members. When non-treatment would immediately and seriously put the patient's health at risk, 'physicians may carry out the indispensable clinical interventions in favour of the patient's health'.[19] Belgian and Dutch provisions are very similar, including the power of the doctor to disregard the decision of the surrogate in case of emergency.[20]

The arguments in favour of listening to informal representatives are the following. First, relatives know the patient and will be able act as advocates, making decisions in accordance with the patient's values, wishes and preferences. It is true that some relatives will be estranged from the patient and some next of kin will be callous, but this seems insufficient reason to close the door on all relatives. We do not know which family model is more prevalent: a loving family

---

14 M Brazier and E Cave, *Medicine, Patients and the Law* (5th edn, Penguin Books 2011) 160.
15 See also S Gevers, J Dute and H Nys, 'Surrogate decision-making for incompetent elderly patients: the role of informal representatives' (2012) 19 EJHL 65.
16 Law 41/2002, 14 November, on the regulation of patient autonomy and rights and obligations with regards to information and clinical documentation.
17 Article 9.3(a).
18 Article 9.5.
19 Article 9.2.
20 For details, see Gevers et al. (n 15) 62–4.

or an uncaring one. It seems unfair to presume that families will not look after the welfare of the patient, thus modelling the legal response to families based on the stereotype of an uncaring and selfish next of kin. Second, listening to relatives might avoid the burden of going to court. Finally, it is in accordance with article 6.3 of the Convention on Human Rights and Biomedicine (1997):

> Where, according to law, an adult does not have the capacity to consent to an intervention because of a mental disability, a disease or for similar reasons, the intervention may only be carried out with the authorization of his or her representative or an authority or a person or body provided for by law. The individual concerned shall as far as possible take part in the authorization procedure.[21]

Is it time we let families in the UK participate more significantly in the decision-making process,[22] as Spanish, Belgian and Dutch families do? This is particularly important in end-of-life situations, as I will argue.

Before we move on, however, there is another issue that needs to be mentioned, even though it cannot be dealt with in depth, namely, how there is an outcome-based approach to competence, by which if the patient agrees with the doctor he or she will be deemed competent, but if the patient disagrees, he or she will be deemed incompetent. Eccentric decisions raise the question of incompetence, albeit temporarily, yet English law maintains that however rational or irrational a decision is, it must be respected if the patient is competent.[23] Courts have stated that competent patients may refuse medical intervention for whatever reason or even for no reason at all.[24] However, because it goes against what doctors deem to be the right choice, courts may question the patient's capacity. Take, for example, the needle phobia case, where courts have said that refusal of injections based on fear or anxiety imply the patient is:

> at that moment suffering an impairment of her mental functioning which disabled her. She was temporarily incompetent. In the emergency the doctors would be free to administer the anaesthetic if that were in her best interests.[25]

This allows the concept of autonomy to be manipulated. In order to impose a medical intervention, there is no need to tamper with the principle of autonomy,

---

21 Similar terms are provided by principle 22.3 of the Recommendation R (1999) 4 by the Council of Europe on the legal protection of incapable adults.
22 This is not meant to imply that English families play no role in the decision making process, but it seems to be limited to a consulting capacity, as stated in section 4(7) of the Mental Capacity Act (MCA) 2005.
23 Section 1(4) MCA: 'A person is not to be treated as unable to make a decision merely because he makes an unwise decision.'
24 In *Re T (Adult: refusal of treatment)* [1993] Fam 95, 102.
25 In *Re MB (An adult: medical treatment)* [1997] 2 FLR 426, 438.

given that beneficence is also a guiding principle. But because autonomy seems to be the prevailing principle, and paternalism has become the new taboo, beneficence has to be hidden behind the respectable cloak of autonomy. Foster mentions the 'shrill totalitarianism of autonomy's rule that has for so long made bioethical debate uncomfortable'.[26] Perhaps it is time to re-focus on other principles, such as beneficence and dignity, and increase their importance.[27] As Foster says, 'autonomy might be unfit to be in sole charge of decision-making'.[28] If autonomy becomes the only justification for all decisions, then an outcome-based approach to competence seems justified. It would seem more consistent with the notion of autonomy to say that the person is autonomous but that the principle of beneficence justifies the decision to disregard the patient's refusal.

End-of-life situations, best interests, and futility

In England, the Mental Capacity Act (MCA) 2005 *Code of Practice* states that 'all reasonable steps which are in the person's best interests should be taken to prolong their life'. However, it also provides that in a limited number of cases it may be in the patient's best interests not to receive life-sustaining treatment 'where treatment is futile, overly burdensome to the patient or where there is no prospect of recovery',[29] even if this may result in the person's death.

The first case to reach the Supreme Court on these matters and apply the MCA was *Aintree University Hospital NHS Foundation Trust v James*.[30] In May 2012, Mr James was admitted to hospital because of a problem with a stoma fitted as part of a successful treatment for colon cancer. He was admitted to the critical care unit following complications after an infection, where he was put on artificial ventilation. Over the following months, he suffered a stroke, a cardiac arrest, recurring infections, septic shock and multiple organ failure. He later underwent a tracheostomy and received artificial nutrition and hydration. Two months after his admission to hospital, due to neurological deterioration he lost his capacity to make decisions about his medical treatment, although he still seemed to enjoy visits from his family and he was able to interact in a limited way. His prospects of leaving the hospital, however, were very slim. In September 2012, the Trust sought declarations from the CP to allow withholding treatment in the event of clinical deterioration. The family did not agree.

---

26 C Foster, *Choosing Life, Choosing Death: the Tyranny of Autonomy in Medical Ethics and Law* (Hart, 2009) 177–8.
27 Already in 1994, T L Beauchamp and J L Childress stated that 'autonomy rights have become so influential that it is today difficult to find affirmations of traditional models of medical beneficence': T L Beauchamp and J L Childress, *Principles of Biomedical Ethics* (4th edn, OUP 1994) 272.
28 C Foster, 'Autonomy in the medico-legal courtroom: a principle fit for purpose?' (2013) 22 Med L Rev 58.
29 *Code of Practice* 5.31.
30 [2013] UKSC 67.

The High Court Judge refused to grant the declarations for failing to meet the criteria established in the MCA's Code of Practice.[31] The judge took 'recovery' to mean return to a quality of life the patient would regard as worthwhile, rather than a return to full health, and found that Mr James' family life was close and meaningful. The hospital trust appealed. By then, Mr James' condition had deteriorated and he was comatose or semi-comatose and completely dependent on the ventilator. The Court of Appeal overturned the decision of the CP.[32]

On 31 December 2012, Mr James suffered a cardiac arrest and died. His widow appealed to the Supreme Court. Lady Hale gave the unanimous judgment of the Supreme Court:

> in considering the best interests of this particular patient at this particular time, decision-makers must look at his *welfare in the widest sense, not just medical but social and psychological*; they must consider the nature of the medical treatment in question, what it involves and its prospects of success; they must consider what the outcome of the treatment for the patient is likely to be; they must try and put themselves in the place of the individual patient and ask what his attitude to the treatment is or would be likely to be; and *they must consult others who are looking after him or interested in his welfare, in particular for their view of what his attitude would be*.[33]
>
> (Emphasis added)

She held that the first instance judge had been right in considering that a treatment is not futile if it brings some benefit to the patient, even if it has no effect upon the underlying disease or disability. Recovery does not mean a return to full health, but the resumption of a quality of life that the patient would regard as worthwhile. The Court of Appeal had been wrong to focus primarily on his medical condition. The Supreme Court took into account what Mr James's interests were during the period before he became desperately ill and that he appeared to be happy in spite of his medical condition. His medical condition may have been hopeless (objectively considered), but the enjoyment he got out of his life and its pleasures did not seem hopeless to him (subjectively considered). The patient's views were relevant here and his relationship with his wife, family and friends was an essential part of the decision-making process because it related to how he valued his life.

Perhaps the importance of *Aintree* is the weight placed on the role of patients' (or their family's) wishes in determining what constitutes futility, a worthwhile recovery and best interests. It highlights the importance of a patient-based understanding of best interests, which is not limited to best *medical* interests

---

31 *Aintree* [2012] EWHC 3524 COP.
32 *Aintree* [2013] EWCA Civ 65.
33 [39].

alone but should encompass the interests of the person as a whole. And it is not clear whether judicial intervention was really necessary. It seems the hospital sought judicial authorisation before it was actually needed. As Smith says, 'the situation should have been decided in the way all such conflicts are decided – either one side can change the mind of the other or the patient can seek the help of a different healthcare team'.[34]

There may be concern about uncaring relatives who would deny antibiotics to their demented but otherwise happy parent in order to hasten receipt of their inheritance, but surely not all families are like that. Caring relatives are sometimes afraid to accept Do Not Attempt Resuscitation Orders because they are under the impression that this would be tantamount to authorising or hastening their loved one's death. In this case, physicians and/or trusts should not be overly hasty in attempting to obtain judicial authorisation but should invest their time (and money) better in consultation with the family. Disagreements often stem from lack of open communication between physicians, patients and their families. If prevention is the best medicine, genuine communication with the family may well prevent judicial intervention, which drains all those involved (in cost, time, and emotional upheaval).

Physicians are expected to engage patients as partners in identifying the possible benefits and harms associated with medically appropriate treatment options, rather than simply dictating what treatments patients will and will not receive. This collaborative model needs to be extended to the family of patients in end-of-life situations. When the patient's medical condition deteriorates, if the time comes when he or she is expected to die unless treatment is provided, there may be a disagreement between relatives and professionals. The source of disagreement is often information imbalance, different appraisals of the risks and potential benefits of treatment. Doctors may be of the opinion that treatment is futile, while patients or surrogates may believe that any small chance of preventing the patient's (more or less imminent) death is sufficient to justify treatment. This does not mean that doctors should do what the family asks for, since there is no right to request treatment.[35] But this should also *not* mean that professionals need to obtain a judicial declaration to endorse their medical opinion. The first step in solving a dispute should be to engage with the family to find out the origin of disagreement. Most disagreements result from misunderstanding or lack of attention to the family's emotional reaction to the patient dying. Professionals need to be trained in communication skills and approach the family with compassion and empathy. Not all conflicts will be solved effectively; occasionally there will be a true conflict of values, but some conflicts may be resolved without seeking judicial help. Physicians may not have the time and willingness to support higher levels of patient, much

---

34 S W Smith, 'Aintree University Hospital NHS Foundation Trust v James, [2013] EWCA CIV 65' (2013) 21 Med L Rev 622, 630.
35 *R (on the Application of Burke) v General Medical Council* [2005] EWCA Civ 1003.

less, family, involvement.³⁶ Nonetheless, physicians should promote a decisional partnership with family members and provide on-going support throughout the end-of-life situation. This will generate trust toward professionals and the healthcare system, which would have the beneficial effect of avoiding, in most cases, a confrontational approach to decision-making.

Family members are at a clear disadvantage in this medical context: their experience with the dying process will be more limited than that of professionals. Physicians must ensure they communicate in a timely fashion any new change or development in the patient's condition, otherwise relatives may be making different assumptions, based on the information they have. The Report *One Chance to Get it Right* issued by the Leadership Alliance for the Care of Dying People³⁷ identifies as its second priority that 'sensitive communication takes place between staff and the dying person, and those identified as important to them'.³⁸ If communication flows in an honest manner, when the time comes, a long legal journey may be avoided.

Deceased organ donation

In the context of deceased organ donation, before any extraction takes place, bereaved relatives are approached, and their role will depend on whether the system works under presumed consent or informed consent norms. It is interesting to mention the Spanish system here, given that the law in theory and the law in practice differ as regards the role of the family.³⁹ Spain's legislation on deceased organ donation is based on presumed consent, and allows organ extraction to be carried out except when the deceased 'expressly opposed' organ donation.⁴⁰ This makes every dead person a potential organ donor. Legally, contacting the family would have the immediate aim of ensuring that the deceased had not expressed her or his opposition to organ donation. However, in practice, relatives are sought out to obtain their consent. And the family's wishes are always respected, even when the deceased carries an organ donor card.⁴¹ Consequently, the Spanish system works as an opt-in system, regardless

---

36 As illustrated by *Tracey v Cambridge University Hospital NHS Foundation Trust & others* [2014] EWCA Civ 822.
37 Report issued on 26 June 2014 in response to the recommendations made by the Liverpool Care Pathway Independent Review chaired by Baroness Neuberger published on 15 July 2013.
38 Ibid 19.
39 Turning to Spain seems useful as it has the highest deceased organ donor success rate in the world, at 35.3 per million population in 2013: see Newsletter Transplant 2014, <http://www.ont.es/publicaciones/Documents/NEWSLETTER%202014.pdf> (accessed 20 July 2015).
40 Article 5.2 of the Spanish Law 30/1979, October 27, on extraction and transplantation of organs.
41 R Matesanz and B Dominguez-Gil, 'Strategies to optimize deceased organ donation' (2007) 21 Transplantation Reviews 177, 181.

of its presumed consent legislation. Physicians yield to the decision made by the family, even though legally, in the absence of express opposition, they could proceed to graft the organs after the patient is declared dead. Why do physicians proceed like this? If the aim of organ procurement system is to obtain organs, and the law specifically allows extraction unless otherwise stated by the deceased, why do doctors choose to follow an opt-in system? The underpinning of this policy is the need to build and maintain trust in the organ procurement system.

We may assume that organ transplantation is a very specific sector within medical law, in which a number of organs may be lost in favour of keeping and promoting the necessary trust between physicians and society, which is at the core of the successful organ transplant system. And this takes us back to the idea of trust. Relatives did not claim to have this consent-giving role; physicians gave them this role. Perhaps with a hidden agenda, namely building trust, but it is an agenda that seems respectful of families and also works to reduce family refusal rates.[42]

Conclusion

When a person is bed-ridden, anguished and distressed by illness and/or medication, what they want most is to get help from someone with the relevant skills and knowledge. In the hospital setting, where care is fragmented, given the number of different professionals who intervene and do not know the patient, the patient may be in need of advocacy from someone who is aware of their values, wishes and preferences, who can seek information, ask relevant questions and discuss options with the medical team. The most obvious answer to the question of who should have this advocacy role is the family. The patient together with her or his family should be part and parcel of the 'unit of care'.

I have argued in this chapter that relatives do play an important role and so they should be able to shed the mistrust physicians seem to have for them, based on adversarial litigation. In end-of-life situations, families must be part of the therapeutic alliance, and professionals should promote genuine and sustained communication. Perhaps a lesson may be learned from *Aintree*, namely that before knocking on the court's door, physicians and healthcare trusts should try harder to reach an agreement with the family.

Could the experience of how the Spanish transplantation system works in practice have any bearing on family involvement when the patient is alive but incompetent? There are sound policy reasons to answer yes, in order to promote trust, which is an important value in the medical context. Onora O'Neill has pointed out that individual autonomy is not among patients' priorities; what they want most in their relationship with their doctor is to be able to trust

---

42 In Spain, family refusal rates are quite low, at 15.9% in 2013, as opposed to 41.4% in the UK. Newsletter Transplant 2014.

them.[43] This need to build trust should include families, who also want to be able to trust the professionals who treat their relatives. To ensure trust, families must be part of the therapeutic alliance in end-of-life situations.

Conflicts about medical treatment can usually be resolved through a process of effective communication and honest discussion, since disagreement is often caused by misunderstanding and information imbalance during the dying process. To avoid this, physicians should involve relatives in the decision-making process. This does not mean that physicians should do what the families say, especially if they request inappropriate life support. Doctors must retain their authority. There is no right to demand treatment that physicians consider futile. But when there is a debate about futility, physicians must take into account not only medical interests but also the patient's best (non-medical) interests, and relatives can help shape and define these. Healthcare professionals must remember that families do not always want to choose, but they do want to have a voice.

---

43 O O'Neill, *Autonomy and Trust in Bioethics* (CUP 2002) 38.

Part III
Law, ethics and the human body

12 Exploring the legacy of the Retained Organs Commission a decade on
Lessons learned and the dangers of lessons lost

Jean V McHale

Introduction

There are a few academics whose work defines a discipline and whose influence echoes through the decades. There are a few academics who go outside the doors of the academy and truly have a real and lasting impact upon law in practice and policy making. There are a few academics who kindly support and continuously and selflessly nurture students and colleagues throughout their careers. There are a few academics who are brilliant lecturers, illuminating the lecture hall with crystal clarity. And there are very, very few academics who could ever be said to fall into all four of these categories. Professor Margaret Brazier is one of those very, very few. Her brilliance, clarity and kindness have enriched colleagues, students and the broader academy over the last four decades. This chapter only looks at one aspect of Brazier's impact on health policy through her role as chair of the Retained Organs Commission (Commission), a demanding role which spanned some three challenging years from 2001 to 2004, but which left a legacy through the reform of the law in the area and by changing attitudes in practice. This chapter examines the backdrop to the Commission's establishment. It explores its role and some of the operational challenges it faced, together with its impact on subsequent law reform. Finally, it considers its legacy and the lessons learned. The paper draws also upon interviews with the following members of the Commission: Brazier, Professor Alastair Campbell (Campbell)[1] and Mr Hugh Whittall (Whittall).[2] The author gratefully acknowledges their generosity in giving time to enable the interviews to take place.

---

1 Vice-Chair, Retained Organs Commission. Professor Campbell was then Professor of Biomedical Ethics, University of Bristol. He is currently Professor in Medical Ethics, Centre for Biomedical Ethics at the National University of Singapore.
2 Mr Hugh Whittall was a senior civil servant at the Department of Health (DoH) during the Commission's latter period of operation. He is now Director of the Nuffield Council of Bioethics in the United Kingdom (UK).

Background

The organ retention scandal rocked the medical establishment and the public in the United Kingdom (UK). The revelations in relation to the retention of human bodily material (material), including children's hearts and other body parts, forced a major reconceptualisation of the use of such material in the UK.³ The reports of Michael Redfern QC into the Royal Liverpool Children's Hospital (Alder Hey) and the Bristol Infirmary Interim Inquiry Report by Professor Sir Ian Kennedy and his team uncovered the vast scale of unauthorised retention of body parts.⁴ On receipt of these reports, Mr Alan Milburn, then Secretary of State for Health, committed to implementation of the reports' recommendations, stating that:

> The existing law in this area has become outdated. The Human Tissue Act 1961 does not even contain penalties for breaches of its provisions. The law has ill served bereaved parents in our country and causes confusion for staff. It must be changed.⁵

However, the sheer scale of the retention nationally had yet to be revealed. Following these reports, Professor Sir Liam Donaldson, the then Chief Medical Officer (CMO), undertook a census reviewing the material retained in hospitals and medical schools. The census made for sober reading. It was found that there were over 105,000 body parts, stillbirths and fetuses stored in English hospitals and medical schools, nearly half of which were brains and one-sixth were eyes.⁶ In Alder Hey alone, 2,128 hearts were stored at the Institute of Child Health together with hundreds of stillbirths, fetuses, brains and other body parts, including what Michael Redfern QC described as 'perhaps the most disturbing specimen [which was] the head of a boy aged 11 years old'.⁷

It should also be noted that such retention was by no means confined to England and Wales; nor was it the case, despite some of the initial headlines, that it was concerned simply with children. This was indicative of an era in which clinical attitudes and responsiveness to questions of consent, lack of clear understanding of legal provisions, and at times also professional arrogance, led to practices which were appalling, insensitive but also fundamentally

---

3 See further D Price, 'From Cosmos and Damien to Van Velzen: The Human Tissue Saga Continues' (2003) 11 Med L Rev 1.
4 *Report of the Inquiry into the Royal Liverpool Children's Hospital* (Alder Hey) (2001) (The Redfern Report); Bristol Royal Infirmary Interim Report, *Removal and Retention of Human Material* (2000).
5 House of Commons Debates, 30 January 2001, vol 362, col 178.
6 Chief Medical Officer (CMO), *The Removal, Retention and Use of Human Organs and Tissue from Post Mortem Examination: Advice from the Chief Medical Officer*, 31 January 2001, 36.
7 Alder Hey (n 4) para 20.5.

outdated.⁸ The media coverage of the incidents raised long-held fears over use of the body after death, harkening back to the days of the body snatchers.⁹ Common to these media reports were the anger and distress expressed by parents and relatives of the deceased whose material had been retained, as well as concerns relating to the lack of respect and dignity which had been shown to them.¹⁰ It was inevitable that reform would be needed.

Following the CMO's census, he recommended to the Secretary of State for Health that the government establish an independent commission, which would have oversight of the return of retained organs and tissue to those families, where such requests were made. He further recommended that the commission address the issue of the existing historical and archived collections obtained consequent upon a post mortem. The commission was also to ensure that accurate records and catalogues were undertaken prior to material being returned to families. The aim here was to avoid the continuation of multiple funerals which had occurred in the wake of the return of materials to families by National Health Service (NHS) Trusts. In addition, NHS Trusts and universities were to work together to ensure there were complete records of retained organs which were identifiable. The CMO's recommendations emphasised the importance of engagement with affected families. He stated that the commission should ensure that the families were involved in reaching agreement with NHS Trusts regarding procedures for the dignified return and disposal of retained organs. It would also provide an advocacy service for families experiencing difficulties in obtaining information from local NHS Trusts. Finally, it was to provide advice to the government, the NHS and universities concerning the return, retention and further use of archival material, together with that held in museums.¹¹ It was a mammoth task.

The Retained Organs Commission: Role and challenges

In 2001, the Commission was established as a Special Health Authority.¹² This meant that it needed to work closely with its sponsoring department. While this could have operational advantages in relation to taking forward policy recommendations in this area, it also meant that it was not always seen as

---

8 Scottish Executive, *Final Report of the Independent Review on the Retention of Organs at Post Mortem* (Scottish Executive, 2002).
9 R Richardson, *Death, Dissection and the Destitute* (Penguin 1989).
10 See A Campbell and M Willis, '"They stole my baby's soul": narratives of embodiment and loss' in F Rapport and P Wainwright (eds), *The Self in Health and Illness: Patients, Professionals and Narrative Identity* (Radcliffe Publishing 2006); D Madden, '"Not Just Body Parts and Tissues" Organ Retention, Consent and the Role of Families' (2012) 1 Socio-Legal Studies Review 1.
11 CMO (n 6) 40.
12 National Health Service Act 1977, s 11.

independent; at times, this constrained its freedom of action.[13] There was considerable urgency to appoint the Commission. Civil servants from the Department of Health (DoH) approached Brazier to chair the Commission.[14] Brazier had previously been the Chair of the Surrogacy Review. Open advertisements were then placed for members of the Commission. Campbell, a leading bioethicist, had also been a member of the Surrogacy Review and he was appointed as Vice-Chair of the Commission. The Commission contained observers including Mr Jeremy Metters, Her Majesty's Inspector of Anatomy, and Sir James Underwood from the Royal College of Pathologists. In addition, there was representation from parents and families through the membership of Ms Helen Shaw from Inquest, as well as Ms Jan Robinson and Ms Michaela Willis (the latter being formerly Chair of the Bristol Children's Heart Action Group and also Chief Executive of the National Bereavement Partnership charity).

The Commission identified eight aims in relation to its work.[15] First, the NHS was able to, and would provide, comprehensive information concerning organs and tissue retained after post mortems. Second, arrangements concerning the return of organs and tissue, where requested by relatives, should be reflective of their needs and wishes. Third, such organs and tissues should be returned sufficiently promptly and with suitable sensitivity in a single comprehensive process in order to avoid the risk of multiple funerals. Fourth, future government policy and law regulating material should take 'full account of the needs of relatives and partners'. Fifth, steps should be introduced and promoted which would respond to the needs of families who were involved in the issue of organ retention. Sixth, the Commission should deal with the position of material where return was not requested and should address the question of respectful disposal. Seventh, the Commission should seek to restore public confidence in the system of post mortems and of public understanding of the need for retention of organs and tissue. Finally, after consultation, the Commission should ascertain what system should be adopted in relation to archives and collections of retained material.

What was the Commission? When reflecting on the role of Commission in 2014, Brazier observed that in many respects the Commission could be seen as a hybrid between regulatory bodies, but with very few powers: thus, a Hillsborough Panel type body.[16] The Commission did not have 'teeth'. If an NHS body did not comply with instructions, its only avenue was to advise the Secretary of State for Health to use directions; however, this did not arise during

---

13 The Retained Organs Commission (Commission), *Remembering the Past, Looking to the Future: The Final Report of the Retained Organs Commission Including the Summary Accountability Report for 2003/4*, March 2004, para 2.3.
14 Interview with Professor Brazier, Manchester, December 2014.
15 Retained Organs Commission, *Annual Report and Summary of Financial Statements* April 2002–August 2004, appendix 2, 36.
16 Ibid.

its time of operation.[17] That did not mean that all Trusts necessarily complied, as will be seen below. The Commission's remit was limited to the NHS (something which was problematic as many cases started with a coroner's post mortem); it excluded matters prior to the deceased's death and it was not involved in litigation.[18] It should be emphasised that while initial inquiries had arisen in relation to retention of children's organs, the Commission's work was not confined in this way and it also applied to adults' material.[19]

The Commission's public face was of great importance. It held meetings around the country every six weeks, which included 'open section' business where members of the public were able to attend.[20] Prior to the formal Board meeting itself, a public meeting was held in the evening so that families would have an opportunity to meet members of the Commission and participate in discussions.[21] In addition, arrangements were made for group meetings and discussions to be held during the day. Meetings with stakeholder representatives also included those from the DoH in England and in Wales. One of the backdrops to the work of the Commission was the running history of litigation, and therefore lawyers were also present at public meetings. Some families, understandably aggrieved at what had happened, brought legal proceedings against the hospitals involved in organ and tissue retention. Litigation on behalf of the Alder Hey families was eventually settled in 2003;[22] however, in 2004, in subsequent litigation concerning Leeds Royal Infirmary, Gage J held that the consent given by parents to post mortem without warning them that organs would be retained was a 'blanket practice'. This constituted negligence, which was actionable where harm was suffered.[23] The tension that this prospect of legal action created led to inevitable challenges for the Commission's work.

Behind the question of retention lay very different, indeed at times polarised, views as to the status of body parts.[24] One view, which has been strongly expressed in relation to tissue and organ retention, was that the dead have no autonomy interests, no rights requiring protection, and that consent could be seen as a mere 'courtesy' rather than a right.[25] Moreover, it was suggested that the interests and views of families should not be allowed to outweigh those of society where the latter may have a benefit from utilising such material for activities, such as research. The Commission itself repudiated this, reflecting

17 Commission (n 13) 7.
18 Ibid.
19 Ibid para 1.15.
20 Retained Organs Commission, *Annual Report April 2001–March 2002* (2002) 14.
21 Commission (n 13) 24.
22 Unknown Author, 'Alder Hey Families Accept £5 Million Settlement', (2013) *The Daily Telegraph*, 31 January.
23 *In Re Organs Retention Litigation* [2005] QB 506; see further R Hardcastle, *Law and the Human Body: Property Rights Ownership and Control* (Hart 2007).
24 See generally D Price, *Human Tissue in Transplantation and Research* (CUP 2009).
25 Commission (n 13); J Harris 'Law and Regulation of Retained Organs: The Ethical Issues' (2002) LS 527.

Brazier's own writings in this area.[26] It emphasised the hurt and anguish suffered by families. Moreover, many families noted that had they been asked to give consent to retention, they would have indeed provided it. In the circumstances, respect for the individual and their family should be the norm. The Commission also stressed that deeply held religious, cultural and personal views should be respected, unless there was an overwhelming public interest. [27] It was also the case that the true value of the physical remains to families had been underestimated. The Commission's work highlighted the underlying confusion in this area amongst professionals working in the area. Some pathologists were genuinely unaware of the real impact of the law in this area, while others knowingly and deliberately acted wrongfully. Attitudes towards families varied greatly, but it was clear that some pathologists had indeed exhibited contempt for the deceased and their relatives.[28]

One interpretation of the Commission's role was that it acted as a 'buffer' between the DoH and the key issues at stake. In many respects, the Commission could be seen as a 'brokering space' which enabled issues to be addressed and resolved and, indeed, avoided the prospect of running battles.[29] This role was not straightforward. Many parents were very angry, indeed. What was notable was that the reaction of family members transcended geography or social-economic background. There was a commonality of approach, which was largely one of anger.[30] There was also alienation and hurt from healthcare professionals, particularly those working in the pathology specialty. Many believed that they had been unjustifiably pilloried while undertaking their professional role with good intentions.[31] Some of this may have been reflective of the lack of understanding at the time of the existing law in the area. In addition, some pathologists were clearly motivated to not provide full information to parents and family members because of concerns about disclosing what might have been distressing details to them.[32] A particularly challenging role was that held by the parent representatives on the Commission, who faced considerable criticism from pressure groups.[33] As Campbell noted, 'huge credit' should be given to Brazier for the very effective and even-handed way in which she handled what were, on many occasions, very difficult public meetings.[34]

One of the Commission's key roles was to provide advocacy for the families. There were representatives from family support groups on the Commission itself

---

26 See M Brazier, 'Retained Organs: Ethics and Humanity' (2002) LS 551; M Brazier, 'Organ Retention and Return: Problems of Consent' (2003) JME 30.
27 Commission (n 13) 10.
28 Ibid para 1.23.
29 Interview with Mr Hugh Whittall (Whittall), phone interview, 22 January 2015.
30 Interview with Professor Alastair Campbell (Campbell) Skype interview, 29 January 2015.
31 Ibid.
32 Ibid.
33 Ibid.
34 Ibid.

and also frequent meetings between such groups and senior Commissioners.[35] The Commission also encouraged the development of nascent groups through suggesting that NHS Trusts provide support funding for them.[36] A project manager was appointed in 2002 to develop links between the Commission and the family support groups. In addition, the project manager's role was to manage aspects of casework.[37] At least 500 cases were taken up by the Commission.[38] For patients, this role was seen as invaluable, particularly as it provided an alternative outlet to dealing directly with hospitals at a time when many found such dealings acutely problematic. In addition, the DoH did not have the capacity at the time to both review the operation of the existing law and undertake the operational work that was needed to take things forward.[39] One of the difficulties the Commission also faced was that there was not necessarily uniformity in approach within family support groups.[40]

In the aftermath of the organ retention scandal, NHS Trusts had begun to return retained material. However, this process was frequently chaotic, with families being given material from their deceased relatives in batches as they were discovered. This was often a considerable time after an initial funeral had been held. Something needed to be done to stop the distress that this was causing and to create order. Initially, the Commission imposed a moratorium on the return of material in order that proper cataloguing and information systems were put into place. A period of just over six months elapsed before all except two NHS Trusts were authorised to release information.[41] This was not necessarily a straightforward process.[42] The Commission's role in liaising with hospitals in relation to the handing back of material was very important. In the first year alone, the Commission took up the cases of 300 families who were having problems getting material from NHS Trusts.[43] The Annual Report for 2002–2003 revealed that incidents arising out of unauthorised retention were still being uncovered.[44] Nonetheless, as the Commission noted, there were less than ten serious incidents, which had been identified in relation to 30,000 enquiries that NHS Trusts had dealt with in the period up until March 2003.[45] Members of the Commission experienced a range of different responses in relation to engaging with families and NHS Trusts concerning the return of material. These included differing levels of co-operation, as well as differing approaches taken by staff, including pathologists. Some of these variable responses may have been due to concerns relating to litigation.

---

35 Commission (n 13) para 4.9.
36 Ibid para 4.15.
37 Ibid 21.
38 Ibid para 4.5.
39 Interview with Whittall (n 29).
40 Interview with Brazier (n 14).
41 Commission (n 13) para 3.15.
42 Interview with Brazier (n 14).
43 Commission (n 13) 13.
44 Ibid 18.
45 Ibid.

Once the moratorium was lifted, material was returned to families. This also raised a number of challenges, as there were different teams involved in this exercise across the country. There was also suspicion and concern from the relatives' groups in relation to the moratorium itself. One major debate was the question of the retention of very small quantities of material which were held on slides. The CMO had stated that time limits should be specified for the retention of tissue blocks and slides.[46] Attitudes concerning retention and returning this type of material varied considerably. The Redfern Report had stated that: 'A more liberal attitude should be considered with regard to the retention and use of tissue, particularly in the form of wax blocks and slides.'[47]

On the one hand, these could be seen as very tiny amounts of excised material which were very much divorced from the individual; for some, this is where a line could be drawn.[48] The sample size might be small, and the quantity was virtually insignificant in clinical terms.[49] Yet for the family, its importance might be immense, particularly if retention of such material was part of a much broader retention. In the circumstances, this remaining sample might have been all that was left to the family of a deceased relative. In other cases, material that was uncovered was left unclaimed and/or was unidentifiable. This led to difficult questions about whether the material should be retained or respectfully disposed of. This was subsequently the subject of consultations by the Commission,[50] with views sought in particular from family support groups, leaders of religious and ethnic communities and researchers.[51] This also led to the provision of advice to the DoH by the Commission.[52]

Law reform

The Redfern Report had recommended that criminal penalties be introduced to enable enforcement of the relevant provisions of the Human Tissue Act 1961 (1961 Act). In his report, the CMO had recommended that there should be an immediate amendment to the 1961 Act to clarify that consent was required for further retention of tissue and organs after a post mortem, where not necessary to establish the cause of death, along with a broader process of law reform concerning material from the living and the dead and providing regulation.[53]

---

46 CMO (n 6) rec 9.
47 The Redfern Report (n 4) para 3.3.
48 Interview with Campbell (n 30).
49 Ibid.
50 Retained Organs Commission, *A Consultation Document on Unclaimed and Unidentified Organs and Tissue and a Possible Regulatory Framework* (February 2002).
51 Retained Organs Commission, *Annual Report and Summary of Financial Statements*, April 2002–March 2003.
52 Retained Organs Commission, *Advice to the Department of Health on the Use and Disposal of Unclaimed and Unidentifiable Human Organs and Tissue*, June 2003.
53 CMO (n 6).

The emphasis would move 'from 'retention' to 'donation' to signal a new relationship with the public and bereaved families'.[54] In fact, legislative change took much longer, and it was five more years before the Human Tissue Act 2004 (2004 Act) finally came into force in 2006. Although Brazier had initially perceived that a primary role for the Commission would be to engage in legal reform in the area, in fact its role was much more subsidiary. The reform process was further complicated by other related inquiries, including into the operation of the coronial system[55] and the ongoing Inquiry in relation to the deaths caused by the serial murderer Dr Harold Shipman.[56]

In 2002, the UK government published the consultative report *Human Bodies Human Choices*.[57] The Commission contributed to the response, drawing upon the personal reflections of its members who had suffered the retention of organs of close relatives and also drawing upon the impact of the Commission's work in meeting with affected families. Its contribution underlined the consequences resulting from a lack of understanding of communication and a lack of trust, and it emphasised the importance of obtaining consent.[58] As the Commission noted: 'Effective new laws will help to ensure that the breaches of trust and failures to inform families which happened in the past will not be repeated.'[59] The majority of the Commission's recommendations are now reflected in the 2004 Act, though not in relation to tissue from living persons.

Members of the Commission were of the view that there were two essential conditions for the success of the 2004 Act. First, reform of the coroners system should 'continue apace'.[60] This proved to be a much longer process and, in fact, reforms were still being implemented as late as 2010. Second, it noted the need for effective implementation of the 2004 Act by coroners. This was based on the reasoning that even if NHS practices were excellent, this would prove worthless if coroners' own practices were not up to standard. Retention of material following coroners' post-mortems remained a vexed issue. In a situation in which a sudden or unexplained death occurred, the coroner had jurisdiction to order a post mortem. After the post mortem, the body would be released. During the post mortem, samples may have been taken and retained. At times, it would be necessary to retain these for some time – even going beyond the period of the funeral itself.

---

54 CMO (n 6) rec 38.
55 T Luce, *Death Certification in England, Wales and Northern Ireland. Report of a Fundamental Review* (2003), Cm 5831.
56 Dame Janet Smith, *The Shipman Inquiry, third report: Death Certification and the Investigation of Deaths by Coroners* (14 July 2003) Cm 5854.
57 *Human Bodies: Human Choices, The Law on Human Organs and Tissue in England and Wales: A Consultation Report*, July 2002, published jointly by the Department of Health and the Welsh Assembly Government.
58 Commission (n 51) 14.
59 Ibid 15.
60 Commission (n 13) para 5.27.

Previously, the practice had been that such material was considered to be waste and was disposed of as such. In 2001, the Commission produced guidelines which recommended that relatives were to be informed about the likelihood of retention by the coroner, as this might impact upon whether they wished to postpone the funeral or not. This remained an issue up to and including when the Human Tissue Bill was being debated in Parliament. [61] At this point, Baroness Finlay and a group of pathologists expressed their wish to retain material in situations where the police and the coroner had determined that there was no need for further retention for criminal justice purposes, but the pathologists themselves were concerned that this material might have utility in relation to new tests becoming available, or for a subsequent criminal investigation. This latter case was particularly sensitive, given that in situations of unexplained or cot deaths, suspicion tended to fall on the parents.

The Commission engaged with a wide range of the issues, which were addressed in *Human Bodies and Human Choices* and ultimately in the 2004 Act. Some of these questions also related to ongoing enquiries and reports in other areas such as museums and archives. This could give rise to a greater detachment. Nonetheless, this exercise brought its own challenges, and the Commission had to engage with a very diverse group of stakeholders. One major controversy was caused by the Bodyworlds exhibition by Gunther von Hagens. This was a commercial enterprise which enabled the public to view plasticated human bodies placed in life-like postures. It was claimed that this practice was justifiable as the corpses had been donated by consent; however, that was disputed in relation to certain corpses.[62] The exhibition caused a furore. The Commission advised the government that commercial exhibitions involving human bodies, body parts, organs and tissue should be prohibited.[63] However, this recommendation was not taken forward. Instead, under the 2004 Act, exhibitions involving the use of dead bodies are permitted where there is written consent from the deceased which is witnessed and the exhibition is licenced by the Human Tissue Authority.[64] Von Hagens' exhibition proved popular, indicative perhaps of a morbid fascination with dead bodies and a worrying fundamental lack of engagement with questions of dignity relating to the dead.[65] Such exhibitions can indeed be seen as having more in common with the 'freak shows' of the late 1800s and early 1900s than engagement with scientific knowledge and understanding. There is a strong argument to be made for regulation in this area to be revisited in the future.

---

61 Baroness Finlay 'The Human Tissue Bill', (2004) *The Parliamentary Monitor*, December.
62 L Harding, 'Von Hagens forced to return controversial corpses to China', (2004) *The Guardian*, 23 January <http://www.theguardian.com/world/2004/jan/23/arts.china> (accessed 2 April 2015).
63 Commission (n 51) 11.
64 Human Tissue Authority, *Code of Practice 7 Public Display* (HTA 2014).
65 Bodyworlds exhibited at a range of venues in the UK, including the Manchester Museum of Science and Industry.

The 2004 Act established the regulatory body the Human Tissue Authority (HTA). This body was not modelled on the Commission. Instead, it is similar to the Human Fertilisation and Embryology Authority, the statutory regulator established under the Human Fertilisation and Embryology Act 1990 (HFE Act 1990). As Brazier stated in her foreword to the final report of the Commission in March 2004, the HTA 'will succeed to some of the responsibilities which once were ours. That Authority will be able to do more than we were. It will enjoy powers we never had and an independence we could not enjoy.'[66] There are a number of notable similarities between the HFE Act 1990 and the 2004 Act. Both are consent-based pieces of legislation. Both have a regulator with oversight which is concerned with the production of Codes of Practice and the licensing of various activities regulated under their respective governing legislation. Both have prohibitory and permissible activities, clearly stated. While the HTA was not quite the successor of the Commission, the DoH was nonetheless concerned not to lose continuity between the work of the Commission and the HTA.[67] As a result, three members of the Commission joined the HTA from the outset: Sir James Underwood, Helen Shaw and Michaela Willis (see earlier).

Lessons learned and the dangers of lessons lost

What was notable about the investigations and reports that led to the establishment of the Commission and the conduct of its work was the lack of information provision and general comprehension deficit. There was a lack of information provided to parents and relatives and a lack of comprehension of matters, such as the difference between coroners' post mortems required by law and post mortems undertaken by hospitals with consent but not mandated by the justice process. There was also a lack of general understanding amongst healthcare professionals and, at times, an empathy deficit too. The legacy of the Commission from Brazier's perspective was in relation to education and information. As Brazier noted in her foreword to the Commission's final report, what was critical was the implementation of law reform through what would become the 2004 Act:

> Professionals must be enabled to understand the framework which will govern their practice. The public needs to know much more about post mortem examinations and the uses to which our bodies can be put.[68]

This is a continuing legacy of the Commission. The work of the HTA concerning the provision of information and engagement with healthcare

---

66 Commission (n 13) 1.
67 Interview with Whittall (n 29).
68 Commission (n 13).

professionals and other stakeholders has also resulted in further change in the past decade. During the time period in which the Commission operated, and in the preceding period, attitudes amongst some leading pathologists and the Royal College of Pathologists had begun to change. Past problems were being recognised and new approaches were being adopted.[69] As the final report of the Commission acknowledged, however, it was also clear that by no means all healthcare professionals welcomed change, as the controversy in relation to the 2004 Act ultimately demonstrated.[70] The Commission stressed that work was still required in relation to bereavement services, which needed to be family-centred rather than being what the NHS thought families would want. True engagement requires cultural change, as well as time and resources. In an era of straightened NHS resources, it is vital that we do not lose sight of these critical lessons. Communication and education, openness and real empathy can facilitate trust, respect and ultimately better research, treatment and patient care. It can be a truly virtuous circle; but equally in a time- and financially-pressured NHS, there is the danger of the 'race to the bottom'.

A further practical lesson for the future for regulatory bodies, such as the Commission, is in facilitating enhanced independence from their sponsoring department. This was because on occasion the Commission was perceived as not being sufficiently independent of the DoH.[71] Challenges were also faced by the broad cross-departmental aspect of the work. The retention of organs had implications for a range of government departments including the Home Office, Department of Culture, Media and Sport and the Department of Education.[72] The Commission's work also highlights the fact that there can be very different religious and cultural perspectives concerning organ and tissue donation. The Commission did not perceive that the decision of certain groups not to participate would necessarily be problematic; if 'others in the community remain ready to donate body parts no argument about harm to medical care or scientific research [could] be sustained'.[73] Perhaps, however, if by not consenting, a whole sector is excluded from, for example, certain types of research, this might be seen as a problem, not least if they benefit from research which others have been involved in.[74] Moreover, there is a question here of the balance to be struck between respect for fundamental rights to faith and belief and the delivery of healthcare more generally, which goes beyond the scope of this chapter.

The question of organ retention has sadly not disappeared. In May 2012, an audit of retained organs which had been ordered in relation to police forces in England, Wales and Northern Ireland revealed that there were 492 body parts

---

69 Ibid para 1.24.
70 Ibid para 1.25.
71 Ibid para 2.3.
72 Ibid para 2.5.
73 Ibid para 2.6.
74 J McHale, 'Faith, Belief, Fundamental Rights and Delivering Health Care in a Modern NHS: An Unrealistic Aspiration' (2013) 21(3) Health Care Analysis 224–6.

which had been 'unnecessarily retained'.[75] In addition, allegations have also recently been made in relation to organ retention by a hospital in Birmingham, with the mother of a deceased child only being informed in 2014 that material had been retained for a period of 15 years in relation to the child.[76] It is to be hoped that such discoveries remain historic and that the 2004 Act and the creation of criminal penalties for unconsented-to organ and tissue retention remain unused for many years to come. The legacy of the Commission lies in the emphasis it placed upon communication, dignity, empathy and stakeholder engagement. Most importantly, it underlined the importance of respect and the need for consent, which is apparent in the 2004 Act and in the day-to-day work of the HTA. It is critical that healthcare professionals and other stakeholders continue to engage with these principles and ensure that lessons learned never become lessons lost.

---

75 'Almost 500 Body Parts Kept Without Justification', (2012) *Channel 4 News*, 21 May <www.channel4.com/news/almost-500-body-parts-kept-without-justification> (accessed 29 March 2015).
76 'Expert Lawyers Call For Public Inquiry into Birmingham Baby Organ Retention "Scandal"' <www.irwinmitchell.com/newsandmedia/2014/january/expert-lawyers-call-for-public-inquiry-into-birmingham-baby-organ-retention-scandal> (accessed 29 March 2015).

13 Property interests in human tissue

Is the law still an ass?

Muireann Quigley and Loane Skene

Introduction

Until recently, in England and other common law jurisdictions, separated human bodily materials could not legally be the property of the person from whom they were removed. However, third parties could acquire property rights in these materials through the application of work or skill – the so-called work or skill exception ('work/skill' exception). Although there were no generalisable principles about the types of activities which could trigger the exception, the effect of this common law principle was, as Margaret Brazier has explained, that 'body parts become, as if by magic, property, but property owned by persons unknown, for purposes unforeseen'.[1] To this, she added, 'If that represents the law, the law is an ass.'[2]

In this chapter, we ask whether the law is still 'an ass' when it comes to its treatment of human bodily materials. We start with an historical snapshot of the law in the United Kingdom (UK) in 2002 when Brazier made this observation. Her comments at the time must be understood within the wider context of the then lack of clarity in the law generally regarding bodily materials, whether from the living or deceased. We then examine subsequent developments in the jurisprudence relating to property and bodily materials to see how the legal landscape has changed, focusing on the recent shift towards the recognition of limited 'source' property rights which has occurred. Our analysis draws, in particular, on the judgments in four recent cases: one in England, *Jonathan Yearworth and Others v North Bristol NHS Trust*;[3] and three from Australia: *Bazley v Wesley Monash IVF Pty Ltd*;[4] *Jocelyn Edwards: Re the estate of the late Mark Edwards*;[5] and *Re H, AE*.[6] In examining these cases, we demonstrate how the work/skill exception has been criticised in the English case and subject to a novel repurposing in the Australian ones.

---

1 M Brazier, 'Retained Organs: Ethics and Humanity' (2002) 22 LS 551, 563.
2 Ibid.
3 [2009] EWCA Civ 37.
4 [2010] QSC 118.
5 [2011] NSWSC 478.
6 [2012] SASC 177, (No 3) [2013] SASC 196.

Toothless tigers, no property, and nebulous exceptions

Much of the current law in the UK regarding human bodily materials is governed by the Human Tissue Act 2004 (England and Wales) and the Human Tissue Act (Scotland) 2006. The English Act regulates the removal, use and storage of materials from a deceased person, including the use of deceased bodies themselves, as well as the use and storage of materials removed from the living, whereas the Scottish Act only covers activities regarding the deceased and bodily materials from the deceased.[7] The Acts are inextricably linked to, and are the direct result of, organ retention scandals in the UK, the details of which came to light in the 1990s.[8] Following investigations into the deaths of children who had undergone heart surgery at the Bristol Royal Infirmary, it was found that organs and tissues from these children had been retained after post-mortem examination, without the knowledge of their parents or guardians. Subsequently, it was discovered that such retention was happening on a large scale at hospitals around the country in the case of both adults and children.

Part of the problem lay in the vague and inadequate law regulating the use of human tissue and deceased bodies, which was then governed by six different pieces of legislation and the common law.[9] The key piece of legislation was the Human Tissue Act 1961. According to the Final Report of Retained Organs Commission, which Brazier chaired from 2001 to 2003, the '[1961] Act itself was obscure and unhelpful', as well as 'unsatisfactory'.[10] A pathologist or researcher who asked whether it was lawful to retain organs or tissues for teaching, display, research or other purposes would have found little to suggest that they could not do so. The Act allowed a person, orally or in writing, to 'request that his body or any specified part of his body be used after his death for therapeutic purposes or for medical purposes of medical education or research'.[11] The 1961 Act also provided that the 'person lawfully in possession of the body' could also authorise the removal of organs and tissues,[12] so long as 'having made such reasonable enquiry as may be practicable' the person believed that neither the deceased nor the relatives would have objected.[13] In

---

7 Living transplantation is covered by the Act, but materials removed from the living for other purposes are not.
8 See *The Royal Liverpool Children's Inquiry Report* (HC 12–11, 30 January 2001); Department of Health, *Learning from Bristol: The Report of the Public Inquiry into Children's Heart Surgery at the Bristol Royal Infirmary 1984–1995* (Cm 5207 (1), 2001); and Department of Health, *Human Bodies, Human Choices: The Law on Human Organs and Tissues in England and Wales* (2002).
9 Human Tissue Act 1961; Anatomy Act 1984; Corneal Tissue Act 1986; Coroner's Act 1988; Human Organs Transplant Act 1989; Human Fertilisation and Embryology Act 1990.
10 Retained Organs Commission, *Remembering the Past, Looking to the Future: The Final Report of the Retained Organs Commission, including the Summary Accountability Report for 2003/2004* (Department of Health 2004), 1.23 and 5.2.
11 Human Tissue Act 1961, s 1(1).
12 Ibid s 1(2).
13 Ibid ss 1(2)(a) and 1(2)(b).

many cases, it may have been that reasonable enquiries were not in fact made. But what could have been done about this under the Act? Since the 1961 Act did not provide any specific penalties for its breach, the answer is nothing much.[14] As Brazier stated, it was 'a toothless tiger'.[15]

To a certain extent, the two new Human Tissue Acts in the UK remedied existing gaps in the law. The English Act in particular, in being applicable to bodily materials from both the deceased and the living, goes some way to protecting the potential interests that individuals might have in their materials. 'Appropriate consent' is required for all scheduled activities under the Act, including, for example, transplantation, research, anatomical examination and public display.[16] Penalties are also attached to breaches of the Act's provisions. The shortcomings of the 1961 Act, however, were not the whole story, nor the only problems, when it came to the regulation of the use of human tissue. It was coupled with the questionable and uncertain common law position regarding property in human bodily materials.

The longstanding baseline position regarding excised human bodily materials can be captured by the 'no property' rule. This principle was stated more than a century ago by the High Court of Australia in *Doodeward v Spence*.[17] The central issue in this case was whether actions in detinue or trover could lie.[18] The body of a two-headed fetus, which was preserved in a jar, had been confiscated by a police inspector from the appellant who was using it as an exhibit. This had previously been in the possession of a doctor who had preserved it following a stillborn birth. It was sold as part of the doctor's estate upon his death, which is how the appellant obtained it.[19] In his dissenting judgment, Higgins J's fundamental finding was that, apart from the right to possession of a body for burial, the corpse was not subject to property rights. He considered this principle to be supported by a number of cases.[20] A stillborn birth, where the baby had not lived independently of the mother, fell into the same category in his view. He said that he was 'unable to see how we can ignore such definite judgments and pronouncements as to the law'.[21]

14 M Brazier, 'Human Tissue Retention' (2004) 72 Medico Legal Journal 39, 43.
15 Ibid.
16 Human Tissue Act 2004, Schedule 1.
17 *Doodeward v Spence* [1908] HCA 45; (1908) 6 CLR 406.
18 Actions in detinue and trover could be brought when it was alleged that personal property (in this case, the fetus and the jar and liquid in which it was stored) had been wrongfully taken. The former allowed recovery of damages as well as the item itself, whereas the latter allowed for recovery of damages only.
19 *Doodeward* (n 17) 407.
20 Ibid 420–422.
21 Ibid 422.

Despite Higgins J's contention, the origins of the 'no property' rule are opaque, as commentators have noted.[22] For example, *Haynes' case* is cited as support for the proposition that there is no property in a corpse, but the ruling in the case was likely to have been that a corpse could not own property.[23] The case of *Handyside* is also cited as support for the contention that 'there can be no property in the human body, either living or dead'.[24] However, the reporting texts were published long after the case itself and there could not have been any 'personal knowledge of the case'.[25] Nevertheless, whatever the rule's origins, by the mid to late 19th century we find cases which state that there is no property in a (whole) *corpse*.[26] Moreover, in contemporary cases the rule has been taken as applying to *materials removed* from the living body, as well as from a corpse.[27]

The 'no property' rule may have gained legal acceptance, but difficulties remained as to how this would apply in practice. This was illustrated in the more recent case of *R v Kelly and Lindsay*.[28] Lindsay (a technician) had at the behest of Kelly (a sculptor) removed numerous body parts from the Royal College of Surgeons, including heads, arms, legs, feet and torsos.[29] The parts were subsequently discovered in Kelly's attic, a field and a friend's flat. The question before the Court of Appeal was whether the men could be prosecuted for theft. That would have required the body parts to be considered property for the purposes of the Theft Act 1968.[30] Counsel for the appellants argued that since there could be no property in body parts, a prosecution in theft could not succeed. The court rejected this argument and held that 'parts of a corpse are capable of being property within section 4 of the Theft Act, if they have acquired different attributes by virtue of the application of skill, such as dissection or preservation techniques, for exhibition or teaching purposes'.[31] In this case, use was made of an exception to the general 'no property' rule. This had also been stated in *Doodeward*:

> [W]hen a person has by the lawful exercise of work or skill so dealt with a human body or part of a human body in his lawful possession that it has

---

22 See for example P Matthews, 'Whose Body? People as Property' (1983) 36 CLP 193; JK Mason and G Laurie, 'Consent or Property? Dealing with the Body and its Parts in the Shadow of Bristol and Alder Hey' (2001) 64 MLR 710, 713–715; and PDG Skegg, 'Human Corpses, Medical Specimens and the Law of Property' (1976) 4 Anglo-Am L R 412.
23 (1614) 12 Co Rep 113.
24 *Hawkins Pleas of the Crown* (vol. 1, 8th edn, 1824) 148.
25 Skegg (n 23) 413. Skegg states this of *East's Pleas of the Crown* (E.H. East, 2 Pleas of the Crown (1803) 652), but it must also be true of *Hawkins Pleas of the Crown* (see n 25), which is another source given in *Doodeward*.
26 *R v Sharpe* (1857) Dears & Bell 160, [163]; *R v Price* (1884) 12 QBD 247; *Williams v Williams* (1881–5) All ER 840, 1881 W. 247.
27 See for example *Dobson v North Tyneside Health Authority* [1997] 1 WLR 596 (CA), 600.
28 *R v Kelly and Lindsay* [1999] Q.B. 621.
29 Ibid 623.
30 Theft Act 1968, ss 1(1) and 4(1).
31 *Kelly* (n 29) 631.

acquired some attributes differentiating it from a mere corpse awaiting burial, he acquires a right to retain possession of it, at least as against any person not entitled to have it delivered to him for the purpose of burial.[32]

This part of the Australian case is widely quoted. Although it has been utilised in only a few contemporary cases involving human bodily materials, it became for a time the 'predominant rationale' for the normative transformation of bodily materials into things capable of being property.[33] This can be seen in cases like *Kelly*, as well as in the Human Tissue Act 2004. This Act codifies the exception in the transplantation context: 'material which is the subject of property because of an application of human skill' is exempt from the prohibition on commercial dealings.[34] Although this provision does not cover research and other contexts, it is an indication of the acceptance that the work/skill exception had gained when the drafting of the legislation took place. It is interesting that it did gain such contemporary acceptance, because, as we are about to see, the original judgment in *Doodeward* may not have required an appeal to work or skill at all.

Questioning old rules

In *Doodeward*, although Higgins J was satisfied that the preserved fetus was not property, he did admit that:

> If this corpse can be the property of any one, it is the property of the plaintiff as against the defendant. It is enough that the plaintiff was in possession of the corpse, and that the defendant took it having no better title to it than the plaintiff.[35]

Such an admission would not have helped the appellant, since he added that 'there can be no rights to recover in trover or in detinue in respect of a thing which is *incapable of being property*'.[36] The other two judges took a different view. In considering whether a thing could be the subject of detinue if it was taken, Griffiths CJ noted that 'it does not follow from the fact that an object is at one time *nullius in rebus* that it is incapable of becoming the subject of ownership'.[37] For example, the 'dead body of an animal . . . is not at death the property of anyone, but it may be appropriated by the finder'.[38] There was, he

---

32 *Doodeward* (n 17) 414.
33 M Quigley, 'Property in Human Biomaterials: Separating Persons and Things?' (2012) OJLS 659, 661.
34 Human Tissue Act 2004, s 32(9)(c).
35 *Doodeward* (n 17) 417.
36 Ibid 417 [emphasis added].
37 Ibid 411.
38 Ibid 412.

concluded, no general rule on these matters and, even if there were, there must be exceptions. The court, he noted, was 'free to regard it as a case of first instance arising in the 20th century, and to decide it in accordance with general principles of law, which are usually in accord with reason and common sense'.[39]

The matter of whether or not remedies would be available turned on whether the appellant was in lawful possession of the body. Griffiths CJ considered that there could not be a general principle that the possession of the preserved body was unlawful. If such a principle existed, then it would be on the grounds of 'religion or public health or public decency'.[40] He rejected the idea that such grounds would always obtain, remarking that, if possession was always unlawful, then 'the many valuable collections of anatomical and pathological specimens or preparations formed and maintained by scientific bodies, were formed and are maintained in violation of the law'.[41] Thus, he concluded that 'a human body, or a portion of a human body, is capable by law of becoming the subject of property', which a person may lawfully possess. Moreover, a person who lawfully possesses it may transfer the possession to another person. The effect of this determination was that, in such cases, 'the law will by appropriate remedies redress any . . . disturbance [with that lawful possession]'.[42] He concluded that the doctor initially acquired the malformed body lawfully and that 'some – perhaps not much – work and skill had been bestowed by him upon it, and that it had acquired an actual pecuniary value'.[43] This value was presumably inferred from the fact that it was later sold after his death. Hence it was held that an action would 'lie for an interference with the right of possession'.[44]

Barton J stated that he 'entirely agree[d]' with Griffiths CJ's reasoning.[45] His focus, however, was not on the process of preservation, but on whether there was a duty to bury the body. His concern was whether retaining it without burial would be a misdemeanour and, thus, make the initial possession of the body unlawful. He said that, although cases and textbooks referred to a duty to bury a human corpse, a 'well-preserved specimen of nature's freaks' could not fall within 'the meaning conveyed by the term "unburied corpse"'.[46] Through the period of its preservation, it had acquired a material value not because it was a human body, but rather because it was not. As such, not being an unburied corpse in the relevant sense, it would not be captured by the general

---

39 Ibid. Griffiths CJ also drew attention to the fidelity of using old law to decide these matters: 'I do not, myself, accept the dogma of the verbal inerrancy of ancient text writers. Indeed, equally respectable authority, and of equal antiquity, may be cited for establishing as a matter of law the reality of witchcraft.'
40 Ibid 413.
41 Ibid 413.
42 Ibid 412.
43 Ibid 414–415.
44 Ibid 414.
45 Ibid 417.
46 Ibid 416.

'no property' rule.[47] Taken in conjunction with Griffiths CJ's admission that not much work or skill had in fact been applied (only some), we may well wonder how the exception applied in this case. The same question is prompted by another of Griffith CJ's comments. He said: '[i]t is not necessary to give an exhaustive enumeration of the circumstances under which such a [property] right may be acquired.'[48] This can reasonably be seen as an acceptance that other circumstances, not involving the application of work or skill, could give rise to property rights over a (deceased and unburied) human body. Given all of this, it is possible that the doctor who originally preserved the fetus could still have had a right to lawful possession on other grounds, even if he had expended no work or skill and its 'attributes' were unchanged.

If we return to the situation in *Kelly*, we can see that the employing the work/skill exception allowed the court in this case to find a way to remedy the wrong done; that is, the removal of the body parts from the College. Without it the accused may, as the saying goes, have 'got off on a technicality'. The wider consequence, however, of both the general 'no property' rule and the exception, is that third parties can gain property rights in bodily materials, while the person from whom the materials have been removed cannot. Yet, since it was, and indeed still is, unclear exactly what is required for the exception to apply, some difficult questions present themselves. What does it mean for separated bodily materials to acquire 'different attributes'? How much or what type of work or skill brings about the requisite transformation? Furthermore, on what basis does a person gain a legal right to work on the bodily material in the first place?[49]

One would assume, for instance, that if the person had stolen the material or obtained it by deception, then any work or skill that was undertaken could not, in and of itself, give the person a right that would override the interest of someone who had acquired the material legally. Recent cases suggest that the source of human bodily materials can be deemed to have more control over them either without the need to employ the work/skill exception, or via a repurposing of it. Moreover, these cases serve to remind us of the broad scope for interpretation that is evident in *Doodeward*.

Legal (r)evolutions: England and Australia

In 2009, the English Court of Appeal decided the case of *Yearworth*. It became the first case in which individuals were explicitly deemed to have property rights in their separated bodily materials. Specifically, the case was about sperm samples.

---

47 Ibid 416 [this is possibly suggested here].
48 Ibid 414.
49 One possibility is that those undertaking 'work or skill' on the bodily material should be rewarded for their efforts. They thus acquire property rights on a Lockean–type labour theory basis. As other commentators have noted, this potential philosophical basis is problematic in a number of respects, see D Price, *Human Tissue in Transplantation and Research* (CUP 2010) 256.

Six men (one of whom had subsequently died) had stored sperm samples for later use before undergoing chemotherapy. Due to a combination of a malfunctioning storage unit and a failure to manually top up the liquid nitrogen, the samples perished. Arguments were heard regarding claims in personal injury, property and bailment. The first failed, but the other two succeeded. In relation to the property claim, it was held that 'the men had ownership of the sperm for the purposes of their present claims'.[50]

In reaching this conclusion, it was accepted that the 'work/skill' exception could have been employed.[51] However, their Lordships were of the view that the principle stated in *Doodeward* is problematic, referring to the exception as 'not entirely logical'.[52] They said that they were 'not content to see the common law in this area founded upon [a] principle . . . which was devised as an exception to a principle, itself of exceptional character, relating to the ownership of a human corpse'.[53] Given this, what generated the men's rights in respect of their samples? This is not a straightforward question because the court did not substantively analyse the basis of the men's original 'ownership' of the sperm, something that gave them the right to bail it to the trust and have it returned to them, or destroyed, on request. What we can say is that use and control are taken as the locus of property in the case, with the Court of Appeal accepting that the men should be able to use and control their own sperm.

As the case involved gametes, the operative legislation was the Human Fertilisation and Embryology Act 1990. Lord Judge CJ stated that: 'the Act assiduously preserves the ability of the men to direct that the sperm be not used in a certain way: their negative control over its use remains absolute.'[54] Preceding this, it was also noted that '[b]y their bodies, they alone generated and ejaculated the sperm'.[55] The court was not dissuaded by the limitations which existed on the positive use to which the men could put their sperm.[56] Further, their Lordships also considered that the men could bring a claim in bailment: 'the men had ownership of [the sperm samples] for the purposes of their claims in tort . . . from that conclusion it follows *a fortiori* that the men had sufficient rights in relation to it as to render them capable of having been bailors of it.'[57] This conclusion follows because a bailment minimally requires that individuals have rights of immediate possession. In summary, the court accepted that the men were entitled to use and control their sperm and they could not do that when the sperm had been negligently destroyed. The men were therefore entitled to be compensated for their loss.

50 *Yearworth* (n 3) [45(f)(v)].
51 Ibid [45(c)].
52 Ibid [45(d)].
53 Ibid.
54 Ibid [45(f)(ii)].
55 Ibid [45(f)(i)].
56 Ibid.
57 Ibid [47].

Not long after the judgment in *Yearworth*, a series of Australian cases also addressed the question of property interests in sperm samples.[58] The first of these, *Bazley*, involved an application by a widow requesting that an *in-vitro* fertilisation (IVF) unit continue to store her deceased husband's sperm samples. These had been collected and stored prior to his death. The application was granted on the basis that the samples were the property of the deceased prior to his death (the judgment in *Yearworth* was influential here) and, thus, also the property of his personal representatives after his death.[59] The second Australian case is *Edwards*. Like *Bazley*, this case involved an application by a widow, but unlike the earlier case, no sperm samples were stored prior to the deceased's death. However, a previous application by Ms Edwards had been granted, which had permitted samples to be extracted and stored. The question was then whether she had a right to possess the samples for the purposes of IVF treatment. Hulme J was persuaded by the reasoning in *Yearworth* and *Bazley* and said that 'the law should recognise the possibility of sperm being regarded as property, in certain circumstances'.[60] He also said that 'Ms Edwards is the only person in whom an entitlement to property in the deceased's sperm would lie.'[61] The final case is *Re H, AE*. Again, this case involved an application by a widow for possession of her deceased husband's sperm samples. As in *Edwards*, there had been no samples stored prior to death and so a separate application had already been made for their extraction and storage. The Court followed the judgment in *Edwards* and said that the applicant was entitled to possess the sperm for the purposes of IVF.[62]

In outlining these judgments, it may be noted that the 'work/skill' exception was not invoked in *Bazley*, while it was in *Edwards* and *Re H, AE*. The reason for this is that, in *Bazley*, the Court concluded, following *Yearworth*, that the stored sperm was the property of the deceased before his death. The normative transformation of the sperm from *res nullius* to *res* had already taken place, and therefore extra steps were not required for a determination of property.[63] In the later cases, however, there was no extraction and storage prior to death. Hulme J in *Edwards* held that the judgment could be made with due regard to the law stated in *Doodeward* (which, as a judgment of the High Court of Australia, was binding on the state court). Hence, the sperm samples were property by virtue of the application of work/skill during the storage and

---

58 For a fuller examination of some of the details see L Skene, 'Proprietary Interests in Human Bodily Material: *Yearworth*, Recent Australian Cases on Stored Sperm and Their Implications' (2012) 20 Med L Rev 227.
59 *Bazley* (n 4) [33].
60 *Edwards* (n 5) [84].
61 Ibid [91].
62 *Re H, AE* (n 6) [69].
63 Although we are unable to deal with this fully in this chapter, we note that this approach raises other problematic questions, including: What exactly is required for the requisite normative transformation to take place? Is it mere separation from the person? Or is something else required? Does this apply to all tissues or simply gametes, or specifically just sperm?

preservation process.⁶⁴ This alone was not enough, since, as one of us has noted elsewhere, 'even if the application of the "*Doodeward* exception" could give stored bodily material the status of property, it would not, in itself, give rise to property rights for the *originator* [or their next of kin]. On the contrary, those rights would ordinarily vest in the person or entity that undertook the work and skill.'⁶⁵

Indeed, up until this point, that was exactly how the exception had operated (and been presumed to operate), a recognition of which was absent when it was noted in *Yearworth* that the exception could be applied.⁶⁶ In order for it to apply, an extra explicit step would have been required. Such a step was taken in *Edwards* where it was stated that the technicians and doctors who preserved the samples 'were acting as [Ms Edwards'] *agents* and so did not acquire any proprietary rights for their own sake'.⁶⁷ This reasoning was subsequently followed in *Re H, AE*: the staff 'who exercised work and skill did so not for their own purposes, but performed these functions as a consequence of the orders of the Court. They were acting as agents and did not acquire any entitlement to the sperm in their own right.'⁶⁸

The judgments in these cases represent an interesting new direction with regard to property and bodily materials. They indicate an initial judicial willingness to vest property rights in separated materials in either their source or the source's representatives. These judgments also serve to remind us that that neither *Doodeward* itself nor later cases such as *Kelly* ever ruled out alternative bases for property rights in bodily materials. However, the Australian cases raise, as yet, unanswered questions. The court in *Bazley* accepted that the man who generated the sperm was a bailor of his stored sperm, so implicitly accepted that he had property rights in his sperm (and thus obviating any need to employ the 'work/ skill' exception). However, the basis of the deceased's property rights was not explained. A 'condition precedent' to a bailment is that the bailor must have a property interest in the thing to be bailed – minimally, a right to possession – but that matter was not explicitly discussed in *Bazley*. Instead, the judgment in *Yearworth* was cited positively. On this basis, one presumes that the reasoning *qua* ownership set out in *Yearworth* was accepted; that the property rights were assumed from the fact that the man generated the sperm solely for his later use.

No such bailment existed in the later two Australian cases, hence the apparent need to employ the exception. We say apparent, however, because like the original judgment in *Doodeward*, it is not obvious that the exception is doing all the normative work. Consider, for example, Hulme J's words in *Edwards*. He said that Ms Edwards' right to the sperm samples arose because they were

64 *Edwards* (n 5) [82].
65 Skene (n 61) 236.
66 *Yearworth* (n 3) [45(c)].
67 *Edwards* (n 5) [88] [emphasis added].
68 *Re H, AE* (n 6) [60].

'removed on her behalf and for her purposes. No-one else has any interest in them.'[69] The work or skill involved in freezing a sperm sample seems relatively small, so to say that the exception is doing the work, rather than some possible pre-existing entitlement, is to set a low standard for establishing a property right by undertaking work or skill. Yet a stand-alone principle that one can lawfully remove tissue from a corpse, for one's own purposes, provided the corpse is in one's lawful possession, is surely too wide.

There are also other questions which arise from regarding excised bodily material *ipso facto* as subject to a property right that can found a bailment. Would people whose bodily materials are removed for imminent treatment (such as gametes for use in assisted reproductive technology, or an organ for transplant), rather than stored for later use, also have a property right in the excised material? The Court of Appeal in *Yearworth*, albeit via a seemingly rhetorical question, suggested that an amputated finger about to be reattached could be property. It was implied that a negligent surgeon ought not to 'be able to escape liability' merely because work and skill has not been carried out. In this situation, would the finger be regarded as bailed, albeit briefly? These examples suggest that principles other than bailment and the 'work/skill' exception may need to be explored for the establishment of property rights in human bodily materials, and we await further judicial pronouncements on these issues with interest.

Conclusion

At the beginning of this chapter, the brief review of both legislation and case law regarding property and bodily materials illustrates why Brazier previously commented that 'the law is an ass'. We have examined the various legislative and judicial developments which have since attempted to grapple with this difficult area, drawing attention to gaps and inconsistencies. With the codification of the 'work/skill' exception in the Human Tissue Act 2004, it looked for a while as if it would continue to enable parties other than the source to acquire property rights in bodily materials. As Brazier and Cave have noted, this is a significant issue, because '[w]hat is beyond doubt is that our human body parts have value to others'.[70] The work/skill exception essentially makes it possible for control over the fate of bodily materials to pass out of the hands of the source, something which is out of kilter with the (supposed) underlying purpose of the 2004 Act. In this respect, the recent cases examined in this chapter represent a welcome evolution in the law. Vesting the source with recognised property rights sends the message that this is where control regarding the use of bodily materials ought to lie. This was done in *Yearworth* through a rejection

---

69 *Edwards* (n 5) [91].
70 M Brazier and E Cave, *Medicine, Patients, and the Law* (5th edn, Penguin Books 2011) 529.

of the 'work/skill' exception and in two of the Australian cases by a novel repurposing of it with the concept of agency.

Despite this, we perhaps should remain circumspect about the judgments and their potential impact. In at least two respects, it is as yet unclear what the impact and scope of the recent cases will be. First, the cases concern the use and storage of sperm samples and are thus extremely narrow in scope. This suggests judicial reticence in stating broad principles of wider application without undertaking the detailed research that accompanies a thorough law reform process. The potential application of the findings to bodily materials more generally, therefore, remains to be seen. Second, we do not know if later cases will follow *Yearworth* in rejecting work/skill or will utilise the 'acting as agent' reasoning of the Australian ones. As one of us has noted elsewhere, even though '[a]gency was not mentioned in *Yearworth* or *Bazley* . . . such an arrangement might have been presumed from the parties' intention that the sperm should be available for later use by those men'.[71] All of this prompts us to conclude that while the law in relation to the use of human bodily materials still requires development and clarification, it is not quite as asinine as it was (or could be). One thing which has not changed, however, is that '[t]he "property" debate cannot be shirked'.[72] Although Brazier said this before the introduction of the current legislation and the recent cases, developments in biotechnology will continue to raise new questions for the law regarding the use of human bodily materials and we must be ready to answer them.

---

71 Skene (n 61) 236.
72 M Brazier, 'Organ Retention and Return: Problems of Consent' (2003) 29 JME 30, 32.

14 Law and humanity

Exploring organ donation using the Brazier method

Marleen Eijkholt and Ruth Stirton

Introduction

Margaret Brazier has been described as one whose work 'light[s] the way'[1] for those that follow, the 'paradigmatic female role model for young academics'[2], and as a 'lawyer, whose heart is in the law'.[3] We agree and argue that Brazier has a distinctive way of both analysing legal issues and evaluating legal problems. This chapter identifies and examines the distinctive elements of the Brazier method. Drawing on this method, and a case study, we argue that she has made a fundamental contribution to the development of healthcare law. Brazier has highlighted the importance of recognising the humanity of different stakeholders in the healthcare enterprise. Particularly important is her recognition of the fallibility and vulnerability of healthcare professionals alongside patients. Where previously medical law was a tool for confrontation between human patients and machine-like doctors, Brazier has facilitated its evolution into a new role as mediator between fallible and vulnerable players.

Methodology

In legal scholarship there is a tradition of reading and interpreting eminent jurists to explore their contribution to the development of the law. Law libraries are full of books about Ronald Dworkin's contribution to jurisprudence.[4] Stanford University Press publishes the 'Jurists: Profiles in Legal Theory' series which is recognised as a leading work identifying 'major thinkers who have significantly

---

1 J Montgomery, 'The Compleat Lawyer- Medical Law As Practical Reasoning: Doctrine, Empiricism, And Engagement' (2012) 20 Med L Rev 8, 28.
2 L Gostin, 'Foreword in Honour of a Pioneer of Medical Law: Professor Margaret Brazier OBE QC FMEDSCI' (2012) 20 Med L Rev 1, 4.
3 J Mason, 'Autonomous Humanity? In Tribute to Margaret Brazier' (2012) 20 Med L Rev 150, 151.
4 A Ripstein, *Ronald Dworkin* (CUP 2007); M Cohen, *Ronald Dworkin and Contemporary Jurisprudence* (Duckworth 1984); S Hershovitz, *Exploring Law's Empire: The Jurisprudence of Ronald Dworkin* (OUP 2008).

influenced the development and practical application of legal theory'.[5] This has not been done in healthcare law and we think that this is a significant gap. Brazier's particular jurisprudence is as worthy of attention as the more general jurisprudential theory.

We have adopted William Twining's method of analysing our jurist from three perspectives, 'the historical, the analytical and the applied'.[6] Our historical analysis involves a brief consideration of the state of medical law research in the 1980s and attempts to situate Brazier in that tradition. For the analytical part we have read Brazier's published work on the use of human tissue[7] and undertaken a qualitative thematic analysis to identify the implicit and explicit ideas within Brazier's work. We coded her work and extracted various themes, which together highlight the Brazier method. Finally, we explored the Brazier method by applying it to the issues on organ use that arise in the *Murnaghan* case.[8]

Medical law: The pre-Brazier era

The state of medical law research prior to Brazier's first major book, *Medicine, Patients and the Law*,[9] is best illustrated by two works. In 1983, Ken Mason and Alexander McCall Smith's *Law and Medical Ethics*[10] and Sheila McLean and Gerry Mayer's *Medicine, Morals and the Law*[11] were first published. Both books explored the appropriate role for law in relation to medicine.

Mason and McCall Smith argued that the function of medical jurisprudence was to find a 'middle way, based on respect and trust'[12] to reconcile the polarised general views that first, society should regulate medical practice, and second, that doctors should be left alone to practise their art in their own way. The problems were largely caused by the public's distrust of the medical profession, which was due to the public's ignorance about the practice of medicine. Addressing this would only be possible if the medical and legal professions dropped their 'essentially paternalistic seclusion'[13] and attempted to educate the public about the concerns of medicine.

McLean and Mayer took a similar starting point – that medical law's purpose was to provide a practical solution to a difficult situation.[14] They referred to Ian

---

5 See 'Jurists' at <http://www.sup.org/browse.cgi?x=series&y=Jurists:%20Profiles%20in%20 Legal%20Theory> (accessed 2 October 2014).
6 W Twining, 'Reading Law' (1988) 23 Val U L Rev 1, 20.
7 The scope for consideration of Brazier's full publication history is limited by space. In addition to the pieces cited, we read the final report of the Retained Organs Commission: Retained Organs Commission, *Remembering the Past, Looking to the Future: The Final Report of the Retained Organs Commission* (29 March 2004).
8 *Murnaghan v HHS* 13–3083 US District Court, Eastern District of Pennsylvania 6.5.13.
9 M Brazier, *Medicine, Patients and the Law* (Penguin 1987).
10 J Mason and A McCall Smith, *Law and Medical Ethics* (Butterworths 1983).
11 S McLean and G Mayer, *Medicine, Morals and the Law* (Gower Publishing 1983).
12 Mason and McCall Smith (n 10) 13.
13 Ibid 14.
14 McLean and Mayer (n 11) vii.

Kennedy's *The Unmasking of Medicine*[15] and Ivan Illich's *Limits to Medicine*[16] and argued that the problems of medical law came from the medical profession's annexation of non-medical ideas and concerns. They argued that many medical questions 'inevitably involve considerations beyond the purely technically medical',[17] specifically social and moral considerations. They wanted doctors to loosen their hold on medicine because 'it is too central a social institution to be entrusted solely to medical practitioners'.[18]

These works focused on the deficiencies of the medical profession, its power and control over illness. Both sought to break the barriers between the medical profession and the public, using different methods. Mason and McCall Smith advocated for doctors to educate the public, and McLean and Mayer sought laypersons' involvement in medical decision-making. Ultimately, both agreed that the fault lay with the medical profession for its insularity.

Brazier saw things differently. She argued[19] that the public had set medical professionals on a pedestal. Public outcries about poor performance were caused by a failure to see doctors as human beings. She argued that the law should encourage collaboration between relevant stakeholders in healthcare. In order to do this, law needed to regulate medical practice, offer doctors guidance on ethical dilemmas, and provide appropriate mechanisms for compensation in the event of failure.[20] She argued that the law failed on all counts to meet these needs, ultimately recommending wholesale reform of medical law, including a no-fault compensation scheme for medical accidents or radical reform of medical litigation procedure.

Brazier's arguments in the first edition of her textbook show an alternative approach from that of other academics in the emerging field of medical law. She emphasised doctors' humanity and how they had been let down by the law. She argued that it was essential to recognise and give appropriate weight to the vulnerability of all involved in the healthcare setting rather than perpetuating the 'doctor is god' myth. The law's success was dependent on proper collaboration between relevant stakeholders.

The Brazier method

Through our qualitative thematic analysis we identified several recurring themes in Brazier's work on human tissue. We have categorised them as (i) commitment to the role of law, (ii) recognising humanity and (iii) law and life: embracing complexity. Taken together, these themes highlight the innovative way that Brazier approached legal scholarship, emphasising the humanity of all involved in healthcare. We argue that her work shows that the existence of stable legal

---

15 I Kennedy, *The Unmasking of Medicine* (George Allen and Unwin 1981).
16 I Illich, *Limits to Medicine. Medical Nemesis: The Expropriation of Health* (Penguin 1977).
17 McLean and Mayer (n 11) 202.
18 Ibid 204.
19 Brazier (n 9).
20 Ibid 8.

Commitment to the role of law

The first theme to emerge from our reading of Brazier's work is her commitment to the role of law in regulating medicine. In her inaugural editorial as editor of the *Medical Law Review*, she instructed future authors that 'the technical niceties of legal analysis must not be neglected'.[21] Brazier has high expectations of the law:

> The law should reflect the expectations of the community, should act as an incentive to effective and co-operative health care, should safeguard the patient's autonomy and provide a clear and certain framework for the discharge of professional obligations.[22]

Her concern about the presence of a well-constructed legal framework is not just an academic concern. It is grounded in her understanding of the essential interactions between law and medicine, and a recognition that medical practice is difficult to regulate, especially in the area of human tissue: 'one of the most challenging questions in relation to law reform is how can any law accommodate the broad spectrum of questions relating to our bodily materials?'[23]

The organ retention crisis of the early 2000s highlighted the inadequacy of the Human Tissue Act 1961 and how far medical practice had diverged from the law's expectations. Brazier argued that 'it is crucial to look at the inadequacy of the law, because doctors, primarily pathologists, have been blamed, not just for their own failures, but for failures of the law'.[24] Failings in the law should not be blamed on the stakeholders, but rather should fall with those responsible for reform, such as the judiciary or Parliament. Brazier offered a note of caution to those responsible, to avoid overturning accepted legal principles too rapidly in response to the single hard case, if that will undo the rest of the law's good work:

> Whenever an attempt is made to establish general legal principles to govern human affairs as emotive as infertility treatment or regulating birth itself, those principles will yield some harsh individual results. . . . Changing the law in haste, stretching the law to accommodate the hard case is not the answer.[25]

---

21 M Brazier, 'Times of Change' (2005) 13 Med L Rev 1, 16.
22 M Brazier, 'Patient Autonomy and Consent to Treatment: The Role of the Law' (1987) 7 Legal Stud 169, 192.
23 M Brazier, 'Human Tissue Retention' (2004) 72 Med Leg J 39, 40.
24 Ibid.
25 M Brazier, 'Hard Cases Make Bad Law?' (1997) 23 JME 341, 342.

This commitment to law includes her recognition of the role that medical ethics and moral philosophy have in developing stable legal frameworks. However, since the two disciplines have different aims, they may not lead to the same conclusions. Brazier and John Harris point out that:

> The essence of our disagreement is not what is morally right but what should be legally enforceable. Brazier would agree that a person should be prepared to donate their organs after death, but unlike Harris she would not wish to introduce laws to make them do so.[26]

Law and morality will not necessarily agree, because the law is concerned with the practicalities of making something happen, whereas ethics and moral philosophy are not constrained in that way. They offer an opportunity to explore the implications of a particular approach free from practical considerations. While the law cannot work without ethics, ultimately the law must provide a solution for the real world. Brazier asks 'whether the process of adversarial litigation alone can ever provide satisfactory answers to the difficult questions of ethics and law raised in the debate on informed consent'.[27]

Recognising humanity

A second theme emerging from Brazier's work is her strong belief in the value of recognising the vulnerability, fallibility and emotions of stakeholders in the healthcare setting in order to reach successful legal solutions. While we might wish that healthcare delivery could function as a well-oiled-machine, that machine is made up of fallible human beings.

Brazier's concern for humanity is evidenced at a conceptual level in her argument that 'rationality alone cannot offer solutions for ethical dilemmas that touch on the most intimate parts of human existence'.[28] It is also seen at a practical level through her contributions on the Retained Organs Commission, recognising the rawness of the impact on families:

> Nearly two years of meeting families whose relatives' organs were taken without any genuine consent on their part has offered me an insight into the impact of organ retention which radically affects the arguments I pursue.[29]

Brazier emphasises the impact of human narratives in any legal problem. Her descriptions of cases illustrate her empathy and understanding that the law is not distant from the individuals involved. Instead, her approach considers that

---

26 M Brazier and J Harris, 'Does Ethical Controversy Cost Lives?' in A Farrell, D Price and M Quigley (eds), *Organ Shortage, Ethics, Law and Pragmatism* (CUP 2011) 20.
27 Brazier (n 22) 170.
28 Brazier (n 21) 6.
29 M Brazier, 'Retained Organs: Ethics and Humanity' (2002) 22 LS 550, 551.

the two are necessarily intertwined. She does not anonymise legal questions. The parties are 'Diane'[30] and the parents of 'Thomas', 'Stephen', and 'Kathryn'[31] – whose suffering is real, and should be considered fully in any legal analysis.

Focusing on patients, Brazier insists that the law should protect autonomous individuals' rights to make decisions according to their own values, irrespective of rationality. Her co-authored paper with Harris shows an ongoing commitment to the importance of consent, even in the face of Harris' strong advocacy favouring organ conscription from deceased donors.[32] Further, she emphasises the inherent gaps in an approach which ignores different views of the role of consent:

> The reasonable relative would rejoice if some part of his lost relative would benefit others. We do not live by reason alone. Organ retention demonstrated with acute clarity the chasm between many lay people and both many scientists and the rationalist school of ethics.[33]

Not living by reason alone is significant in Brazier's understanding of humanity. For Brazier, it is clear that autonomy is not properly protected unless that protection recognises that while some decisions might be objectively wrong, the individuals who made those decisions deserve respect as emotional beings. She argues that 'the right to self-determination includes the right to take decisions based on factors other than pure reason' and the decision-maker 'must be the judge of' the rightness or wrongness of her or his decisions.[34]

In 1987, Brazier entreated us not to ignore the humanity of healthcare professionals charged with caring for patients. She argued that giving proper weight to their role and motivations was a key aspect to analytical approaches underpinning healthcare law. This concern is evident in her later work:

> The ethical dilemma faced by the doctors in the pain clinic is more readily mirrored in clinical practice where real life ethical dilemmas are that much more demanding, because what some regard as ethical, others will categorise as unethical.[35]

Healthcare professionals are often put in impossibly difficult situations, forced to weigh and arbitrate upon numerous conflicting views on the ethically appropriate solution. Our interpretation of Brazier's work suggests that legal analysis should acknowledge the humanity – vulnerability and fallibility – of doctors, rather than treating them as non-emotional beings.

---

30 Brazier (n 25) 341.
31 Brazier (n 23) 41.
32 Brazier and Harris (n 26).
33 M Brazier, 'Where the Law and Ethics Conflict?' (2005) 1 Res Eth Rev 97, 99.
34 Brazier (n 22) 175.
35 Brazier (n 33) 97.

Finally, it is important to consider the humanity concerns of the wider public. It is through her own thought experiments that Brazier seeks to uncover these. After arguing that it is 'ludicrous' that 'consent is required for using an excised lump or bump in educating Manchester's medical students' she shows that this is not the real concern. The issues are more starkly illustrated with the experiment's development where she argued that to 'ask whether a research team should be allowed (without consent) to retain and use the whole of an excised ovary for research into reproductive cloning and the ethical equation may look very different'.[36]

We argue that Brazier has a rich conception of humanity, which encompasses the fallibilities and vulnerabilities of the individual alongside concerns that are revealed through broader ethical analysis. Understanding Brazier's conception of humanity is central to understanding the significance of her contribution to the development of healthcare law scholarship.

Law and life: Embracing complexity

The richness of Brazier's work is in bringing together her commitment to the role of law in regulating healthcare practice with her conception of humanity. The messiness of life does not neatly match up with the law's expectations. For example, while there could be a clear formulation of the amount of information necessary to ensure consent to a post-mortem is valid, the practical issues associated with doing so might undermine the law's usefulness:

> Graphic descriptions of the post-mortem process and the possible uses to which their child's heart or brain may be put could be seen as risking harm to the parents. Some families may not want explicit comprehensive information, yet still be prepared to make a personal sacrifice for the benefit of others.[37]

In relation to human tissue, the law's most significant challenge is regulating the complex family relationships that only become apparent after someone's death: 'No rules can legislate for happy families. No law can impose a mandatory obligation to talk sensitively and sensibly to your family.'[38] What is needed is a cultural shift towards open discussion about death and organ donation amongst families and healthcare professionals. But, as Brazier suggests, while 'the law can outlaw theft. It can do little to promote a genuine culture of donation, which is what society needs.'[39] Brazier cautions those who think that changing the law is the first step to cultural change, 'changing the law surrounding donation so that it may in turn change these beliefs is a little naïve

---

36 Brazier (n 33).
37 Brazier (n 29) 568.
38 Brazier (n 23) 46.
39 Brazier (n 23) 47.

at best and at worst will make martyrs of many whose beliefs will not be changed'.⁴⁰ Bringing humanity to the forefront of legal analysis might lead to solutions which limit the negative impact on humanity, and improve the efficacy of the law.

It is difficult for legal scholars to avoid considering the interaction between law and humanity. This is especially so in healthcare law where questions attract significant media interest. Medical law is practised in a 'glare of publicity' from a media seeking 'drama' and a simple polarisation of views: 'right to life vs "euthanasia" – parental love vs medical paternalism.'⁴¹ This is inevitably in conflict with legal scholarship, which seeks balance and thoughtfully constructed arguments. The challenge is even greater for the law reformer, or the academic suggesting policy changes. The media is one important forum for the public to contribute to debates on issues relevant to medical lawyers. Brazier emphasises the importance to legal scholarship of engagement with the media and the views it portrays.⁴²

The conjunction of law and humanity, and the consequent argument that law can be of limited usefulness when faced with emotionally laden issues, highlights an important contribution from Brazier's work. Since law and humanity cannot be unlinked, we should not try to do so. Instead, where the law's usefulness is limited, we should look beyond the law for solutions. For example, since a law cannot compel sensible discussion between families, we should look to 'the actual process of communication'⁴³ and seek to make changes to practice to facilitate the legal change sought.

The Brazier method

Our analysis of key themes in Brazier's work suggests that there is something uniquely valuable about her approach to legal dilemmas in the healthcare context. We propose that these amount to a distinctive method of analysis – the Brazier method – which highlights the importance of recognising the humanity of all those involved with the healthcare setting. This method offers a systematic framework for evaluating and analysing legal questions and proffered solutions. We summarise the method as follows:

1) Identify and outline the legal problem at stake. Suitable cases are those where the law adversely affects the humanity of the individuals involved, or that of the wider public;
2) Explore the legal problem identifying the humanity concerns of all stakeholders, including patients, their relatives, healthcare professionals, the broader public, the media as an entity and concerns of politics;

---

40 S McGuinness and M Brazier, 'Respecting the Living Means Respecting the Dead too' (2008) 28 OJLS 297, 316.
41 Brazier (n 21) 4.
42 Brazier (n 22) 7.
43 Brazier (n 22) 178.

3) Interrogate whether the legal solution posed addresses the original problem and accommodates the human concerns of stakeholders. A successful solution is one that creates a legal framework by forging a compromise that accommodates and offers some balance between the concerns of all stakeholders, and which is stable in the face of media outcry.

Academic scholars, law reformers and policymakers could all use the Brazier method to reveal the human issues of concern to healthcare law. They can use it to evaluate the success and stability of legal and policy solutions, and to raise broader concerns about the interface between humanity and law. While we have only considered the Brazier method in the context of healthcare law, because its core theme is the accommodation of human narratives in the legal or policy solution, it may also be applicable to wider legal scholarship.

The *Murnaghan* case study: Human tissue and the role of law

In this section we use the Brazier method to explore issues relating to human tissue use arising in the *Murnaghan* case.[44] Sarah Murnaghan's battle to receive a lung transplant in the United States concerned a policy that amounted to a blanket ban on lung transplants for those under 12 years of age.

Sarah's problem

Sarah Murnaghan was a 10-year-old girl with cystic fibrosis, who urgently needed a lung transplant or she would die within weeks. The scarcity of paediatric lung donations meant that Sarah could not rely on organ availability on the paediatric or adolescent transplant list. Further, she had no real chance of being allocated a suitable organ on the adult transplant list, which was about 50 times larger than the other lists. The 'under 12 rule' meant that Sarah would be last on the adult waiting list. Children under 12 were placed on the waiting list according to time waited, whereas older candidates were assigned a place based on the urgency of their condition.

Sarah's parents mounted a legal challenge to the organ allocation criteria as it applied in their daughter's case, arguing that the 'under 12 rule' was arbitrary and discriminatory. The judge agreed and temporarily suspended the rule. Sarah was placed into the adult pool on the basis of her medical need, rather than remaining at the back of the queue. Following the ruling, the main policymaking body – the Organ Procurement and Transplantation Network and United Network for Organ Sharing (OPTN/UNOS) – stated that it would apply a temporary policy for one year, allowing children under 12 to be classified as adolescents, allowing them to access the adult waiting list. In early 2014, the

---

44 *Murnaghan v HHS* 13–3083 US District Court, Eastern District of Pennsylvania 6.5.13.

OPTN/UNOS published a proposal to adopt the 'adolescent classification exception' as a permanent feature of their organ allocation criteria policy.[45]

Applying the Brazier method, we see first that the legal problem is the blanket application of the under 12 rule. It fails to accommodate the human concerns of those who might be suitable for an adult donation despite their age. Second, by ignoring the input of healthcare professionals, the court's ruling fails to accommodate other interests. It focuses on one ethical concern – waiting list mortality – and does not take account of other interests in the chain of organ distribution. Finally, scrutinising the OPTN/UNOS' eventual policy shows a stable framework that is more effective in accommodating the interests of different stakeholders.

The legal problem

The under 12 rule amounted to a blanket ban on offering adult lungs to this group. The rule relied on the inability to validate the Lung Allocation Score (LAS) for under 12s. The LAS is a standard measuring score for allocation, which has been validated for use in adults. It was not validated for use in children because of prevalent co-morbidities and the likely need to resize the lung to fit the child's body. Without a LAS, under 12s could not be compared to adolescents or adults, and consequently could not be placed on the list using the same criteria as adults. This approach disregarded both the impact on the individual and the professional judgement of those involved in their care. There was no scope for appealing against the effect of the under 12 rule.

Humanity in the Murnaghan case

The vulnerability and fallibility of the different actors were central to the *Murnaghan* case. Media headlines such as 'Dying girl intubated as she awaits lung transplant',[46] and 'Lung transplant gives Sarah Murnaghan chance to live her dreams'[47] called for attention to and sympathy for Sarah's cause. They emphasised Sarah's story as a battle between life, death, bureaucratic policies and antagonistic regulators, and portrayed the medical professionals as cold and inhumane.

---

45 OPTN/UNOS, 'Proposal for Adolescent Classification Exception for Pediatric Lung Candidates' <http://optn.transplant.hrsa.gov/PublicComment/pubcommentPropSub_345.pdf> (accessed 5 November 2014).
46 'Dying girl intubated as she awaits lung transplant', (2013) *Fox News*, 10 June <http://www.foxnews.com/health/2013/06/10/parents-file-lawsuit-in-girl-lung-transplant-case/> (accessed 20 November 2014).
47 C Welch and J Carroll, 'Lung transplant gives Sarah Murnaghan chance to live her dreams', (2013) *CNN*, 26 August <http://www.cnn.com/2013/08/26/health/sarah-murnaghan-update/> (accessed 20 November 2014).

This focus on Sarah's narrative was met with both approval and hesitation.[48] Those who approved suggested that the media offered a platform for a story not otherwise heard.[49] Murnaghan's lawyer argued that the media was the only route to raise awareness about Sarah's story and to highlight the stories of other such transplant candidates.[50] The media attention could remove barriers to fighting a policy since legal avenues are often restricted to a financially equipped elite.[51] Hesitant advocates were concerned about the media impact and the disproportionate response to a single media outrage:[52] 'it is important that people understand that money, visibility, being photogenic . . . are factors that have to be kept to a minimum if we're going to get the best use out of the scarce supply of donated cadaver organs.'[53]

Brazier's red flag: Failure to recognise the different stakeholders

The court's response and the OPTN/UNOS's subsequent policy change revealed the power of Sarah's narrative and the difficulty of recognising the humanity of all stakeholders. The court relied on emotive justifications to suspend the under 12 rule, stating that:

> Their 10-year-old daughter Sarah may soon die if she does not receive new lungs and that every hour that she can participate in the OPTN's system for allocating lungs without being forced to stand at the back of the line for the much larger pool of lungs donated from adults . . . could save her life.[54]

Sarah's story featured explicitly in the initial OPTN/UNOS response: 'We must use the power of the story that brought us here today to ensure that each person imploring us to make the system better also makes a personal

---

48 A Caplan, 'Ethicists: Bureaucrats, politicians shouldn't decide if Sarah get lungs', (2013) *BBC News*, 13 June <http://www.bbc.com/news/world-us-canada-22882614> (accessed 20 November 2014); M Henderson and J Chevinsky, 'Medical Ethics and the Media: The Value of a Story' (2014) 16 Virtual Mentor 642.
49 J deSante, A Caplan, B Hippen, G Testa and J Lantos, 'Was Sarah Murnaghan Treated Justly?' (2014) 134 Pediatrics 1; Henderson and Chevinsky, ibid; K Ladin and D Hanto, 'Rationing Lung Transplants – Procedural Fairness in Allocation and Appeals' (2013) 369 New Eng J Med 599; J Snyder, N Salkowski, M Skeans, T Leighton, M Valapour, A Israni, M Hertz and B Kasiske, 'The equitable allocation of deceased donor lungs for transplant in children in the United States' (2014) American Journal of Transplantation 178; Henderson and Chevinksy, ibid.
50 S Harvey, 'Statement of Stephen G Harvey to the organ procurement and transplantation network executive committee' (Pepper Hamilton LLP) <http://www.pepperlaw.com/news.aspx?AnnouncementKey=1881> (accessed 20 November 2014).
51 See deSante et al. (n 49) and Harvey (n 50).
52 Henderson and Chevinsky (n 48).
53 Caplan (n 48).
54 *Murnaghan* (n 44).

commitment to organ donation.'[55] References to a single case changing the legal direction should raise a red flag for the Brazierian analyst. Brazier cautions against changing legal principle to accommodate the hard individual case because it may create injustice more widely. It is therefore necessary to consider whether that is the effect of this change.

Arguably, the court's decision in *Murnaghan* did create injustice more widely. It disregarded the concerns of other stakeholders and prioritised one individual. First, it ignored the interests of other potential recipients higher up the list. Adults on the list had been assigned a position using the LAS, which took account of concerns around size of the lungs and graft survival as well as the urgency of the case.[56] The court's decision, which placed Sarah on the list according to the severity of her condition only and assigned her priority without concern for others on the list, ignored other stakeholder interests. Second, the judgment ignored the contribution of healthcare professionals. The court ordered that Sarah be placed on the list according to the medical numbers attached to her condition, setting aside most of the healthcare professionals' concerns about other interests. As such, the court seemed to suggest it was better equipped than healthcare professionals to make allocation decisions.[57] This was more egregious given the uncertainty about the evidence of transplant success in children aged under 12.

The court focused on a single concern: how to get Sarah a lung transplant. It ignored interests such as efficacy and efficiency in using the organ pool, which underpin organ donation policy. The court prioritised concerns about waiting list mortality: if Sarah could get a lung, she would not die on the list, regardless of how long she survived post-transplant.

The revised policy as a mediating solution

The finalised adolescent classification exception policy does not make the ruling in *Murnaghan* permanent. Children under 12 will not be automatically transferred to the adult waiting list. They must apply to the Lung Review Board who will consider medical criteria to decide whether the adolescent exception classification is relevant. If it is, then an LAS assessment is provided.[58]

The policy takes account of professional judgement, other stakeholder interests and the importance of collaboration. The new rule requires the decision to take

---

55 OPTN/UNOS Executive Committee, 'Executive Committee Meeting Materials 06–10–13' <http://optn.transplant.hrsa.gov/ContentDocuments/OPTN_Exec_Comm_mtng_materials_06–10–13.pdf> (accessed 20 November 2014, 142).
56 OPTN/UNOS, *Proposal for Adolescent Classification Exception for Pediatric Lung Candidates* <http://optn.transplant.hrsa.gov/PublicComment/pubcommentPropSub_345.pdf> (accessed 24 November 2014).
57 M Russo, A Iribarne, K Hong, R Davies, S Xydas, H Takayama, A Ibrahimiye et al., 'High lung allocation score is associated with increased morbidity and mortality following transplantation' (2010) 137 CHEST Journal 651; T Liou and B Cahill, 'Mini Review on Pediatric Lung Transplantation for Cystic Fibrosis' (2008) 86(5) Transplantation 636.
58 OPTN/UNOS, *Lung Allocation* <http://www.unos.org/docs/Lung_Patient.pdf> (accessed 5 November 2014).

account of the individual's interests in a wider context.[59] Doctors will not be forced to transplant adult lungs into unsuitable paediatric recipients. Children under 12 are to be considered on a case-by-case basis. Had the *Murnaghan* ruling been adopted permanently, it would have justified a greater limitation on professional judgement, because all paediatric patients would have been automatically placed on the adult list, regardless of concerns about their size and success of the graft.

Despite our concerns about this being a hard case, it has highlighted a real legal injustice to many potential stakeholders. The blanket ban failed to take account of individual narratives. However, regardless of the range of different interests at stake, it is unjust to ignore the rule's impact on the individual. The paediatric/adolescent boundary is difficult to identify precisely, but using an arbitrary measure such as chronological age masks the real issue in the context of lung transplant, namely physical maturity.

Using the Brazier method to analyse the *Murnaghan* case allows us to see the legal dimensions of the problem amidst the human concerns. A blanket ban on transplants for children under 12 does not fit with traditional approaches to medical practice, which focuses on the individual patient's needs. Similarly, this concern does not imply favouritism for the individual who appeals to the court. Allowing some individuals to be placed on the transplant list without reference to their chronological age does not undermine the integrity of the general principle that children get paediatric lungs and adults get adult lungs. The Brazier method allows us to argue that the eventual solution takes account of the variety of relevant stakeholder interests and, as a result, it offers a framework which is more likely to succeed.

Conclusion

We think that jurisprudential analysis can make a significant contribution to our understanding of the intellectual history of healthcare law and can help us to see the path for its future development. This general point is illustrated here by our qualitative thematic analysis of Brazier's work on human tissue, which highlights her role in the development of medical law. The Brazier method shows a fundamental shift in the focus of medical law scholarship, to one where the stability of law depends on it embracing the messiness of human interactions and the humanity of different actors. The requirements of humanity may also dictate that law cannot provide a complete solution, which means we must look for assistance outside the law to create a successful framework. Brazier's recognition that law cannot and should not try to impose order on the complexity of everyday life is an important one, which is valuable to all those involved in academic endeavours and law reform. The future development of healthcare law as a discipline remains to be seen, but we predict a further embedding of the Brazier method and a greater recognition of the importance of recognising the fallibility and vulnerability of stakeholders in the framework of healthcare regulation.

---

59 S Sweet and M Barr, 'Pediatric Lung Allocation: The Rest of the Story' (2014) 14 American Journal of Transplantation 11.

15 Sex change surgery for transgender minors
Should doctors speak out?

Simona Giordano, César Palacios-González and John Harris

Introduction

Margaret Brazier is deservedly famous worldwide for many reasons: one is her continued commitment to the defence of the bodily integrity of all people, alive or dead. Her work has always been inspired not only by a robust ethical and legal analysis, but also by an engaged, compassionate understanding of the predicaments and needs of the people involved. Drawing inspiration from some of her work, we discuss the issue of genital surgery involving transgender minors. In her seminal work *Medicine Patients and the Law*, Brazier discussed moral and legal issues involved in one particular type of genital surgery, namely infant male circumcision. In certain circumstances, this may be deemed lawful in England[1] and is widely accepted in some communities, but its moral legitimacy remains contested.[2]

Of course, circumcision is not comparable with the type of genital surgery we are discussing here: sex change surgery involves major mutilation (e.g. mastectomy and gonadectomy) and constructive surgeries (e.g. vaginoplasty and phalloplasty). It culminates in the amendment of the *identity* of the person. Yet Brazier's discussion of circumcision invites us to reflect upon the moral complexities surrounding body modification, especially those involving genitalia. This is because they often carry high symbolic meaning: they may indicate the belonging to a certain community; the acceptance of certain values; or they may involve belonging to certain (female or male) groups and the acquisition of roles that such belonging may entail within a certain society.

More recently, Brazier has considered the case of female genital surgery.[3] In England, female genital mutilation is a criminal offence.[4] No offence is

---

1 Non-therapeutic circumcision must be in the child's 'best interests'. If those with parental responsibility are in disagreement as to whether their child should be circumcised, a court order should be sought before the procedure is carried out: *Re J (Child's Religious Upbringing and Circumcision)* [2000] 1 FRC 307.
2 M Brazier, *Medicine, Patients and the Law* (2nd edn, Penguin 1992) 350.
3 M Brazier and S Ost, *Bioethics, Medicine and the Criminal Law Volume 3: Medicine and Bioethics in the Theatre of the Criminal Process* (CUP 2013) 49–53.
4 Female Genital Mutilation Act 2003, c 31, s 1(1).

committed, however, where such surgery is considered, inter alia, 'necessary for [the woman's] physical or mental health' and was performed by a 'registered medical practitioner'.[5] An examination of this legislation is outside the scope of this chapter. Instead, we explore the more fundamental questions raised by Brazier's work: how much discretion do we have to make decisions – whether radical or not – to alter our own body? What restrictions can justifiably be placed on what we can do to our bodies,[6] such as organ transfer and sale, and even to post-mortem decisions to donate our body parts? In this chapter, in order to examine these questions in detail, we focus on the case of sex change surgery in minors.[7]

Sex change surgery in transgender minors

Transgenderism, also known as Gender Dysphoria, or Gender Identity Disorder, refers to a *mismatch* between the person's perceived gender and the person's chromosomal and genital makeup (natal sex). This mismatch can manifest itself very early in the life of a child, with differing consequences. Some gender dysphoric children become homosexual adults, while others become heterosexual adults; there are yet others who transition to other more 'complex' gender identities.[8] Most transgender people require some kind of medical intervention in order to live in their perceived gender. The interventions needed vary in different individuals, and may include partial surgery, such as mastectomy or breast implants with no genital surgery, or may encompass comprehensive surgery, which may include vaginoplasty or phalloplasty.

Important international guidelines for clinicians in the treatment of transgender patients include the World Professional Association for Transgender Health's Standards of Care (WPATH guidelines) and the Clinical Practice Guideline issued by the Endocrine Treatment of Transsexual Persons (ETTP guidelines). Both sets of guidelines advise that sex change surgery should be deferred until adulthood, with the ETTP setting the threshold at 18 years old.[9] The WPATH guidelines, which are the most recent and detailed, state that in order to have *any type of surgery*, the patient must present with persistent and

---

5   Ibid s 1(2)(a).
6   Brazier and Ost (n 3) 52.
7   In this chapter, we employ the commonly used terms: 'sex change surgery' and 'transgender', although we note that other terms may be more appropriate. On the problems with the use of terminology in this area, see S Giordano, *Children with Gender Identity Disorder* (Routledge 2012) ch 1.
8   D Thomas, D Steensma, R Biemond et al., 'Desisting and Persisting Gender Dysphoria after Childhood: A Qualitative Follow-up Study' (2011) 16(4) Clinical Child Psychology and Psychiatry 499.
9   W Hembree, H Cohen-Kettenis et al., 'Endocrine Treatment of Transsexual Persons: An Endocrine Society Clinical Practice Guideline' (2009) 94(9) Journal of Clinical Endocrinology and Metabolism 3133; E Coleman, W Bockting, M Botzer et al., 'Standards of Care for the Health of Transsexual, Transgender, and Gender-Nonconforming People, Version 7' (2012) 13(4) International Journal of Transgenderism 178.

well-documented Gender Dysphoria; show capacity to make a fully informed decision; consent to treatment; and be of the *legal age of majority in a given country*.[10] We shall return briefly to this final point in the next section.

The guidelines caution both doctors and patients against rushing into a series of highly invasive surgical procedures, which are not only inherently risky but also life-changing. It would be rather invidious to begin a process of surgical transition to then find out that either the expectations of the patient have not been met or, in the worst case scenario, that the transition is not what the patient truly wanted or needed. Both WPATH and the ETTP guidelines emphasise that attainment of the legal age of majority should not be taken as a guarantee that the patient is competent to give informed consent. Instead, it should be regarded as a *minimum criterion*.[11] Neither set of guidelines is legally binding. The WPATH guidelines are intended to be flexible, although it is stated that any departure from them should be clearly documented, as should the reasons for doing so.[12] However, there is a strong presumption in the transgender healthcare professional community that these guidelines should be strictly adhered to, especially when it comes to irreversible interventions.

Deferring sex change surgery in minors until adulthood

Although our focus is on the ethical issues surrounding sex change surgery in minors, there may be legal reasons for advising patients to wait until adulthood before having such surgery. In some countries, such as Italy for example, a minor is not recognised as having legal capacity until the age of 18 years. They are therefore unable to consent to any form of medical treatment before that age. In these circumstances, those with parental/guardian responsibility must provide consent on the minor's behalf. As a result, sex change surgery has traditionally been denied to minors under Italian law on the grounds that changing gender is a strictly personal choice. There can be no consent to such change on behalf of the individual concerned in 'very personal matters'.[13]

---

10 Coleman et al. (n 9) 227.
11 Ibid 178; Hembree et al. (n 9) 3143.
12 Ibid 166; Hembree et al. (n 9) 3132.
13 Sex change in minors has traditionally *not* been regarded as lawful. For example, an Italian court made a declaration in 2005 that a minor was incapable of giving consent for sex change surgery. It was also found that such consent could not be given by the minor's parents/guardians. This was because of the very personal nature of the surgery, see Tribunale di Catania, 12 March 2004, in *Giust. civ.* 2005, 4, I, 1107. More recently, sex change surgery was authorised on the grounds of preservation of the health and gender identity of the minor, see Tribunale di Milano, 11 March 2011 and Tribunale di Santa Maria Capua Vetere, Sentenza, 9 January 2012, n 28.

Having a legal age of majority may facilitate the process of obtaining consent in various countries. Under English law, individuals aged 16 years and over have a *prima facie* right to consent to medical treatment:

> The consent of a minor who has attained the age of 16 years to any surgical, medical or dental treatment which, in the absence of consent, would constitute a trespass to his person shall be as effective as it would be if he were of full age: and where a minor has by virtue of this section given an effective consent it shall not be necessary to obtain any consent for it from his parent or guardian.[14]

In addition, a 'mature minor' who is under 16 years of age can be considered capable of consenting to treatment if they have 'sufficient understanding and intelligence to be capable of making up [their] own mind on the matter requiring decision'.[15] As noted previously, the ETTP guidelines advise that surgery should only be offered to people who have reached the age of 18.[16] In contrast, the WPATH guidelines appear to offer more flexibility, as they suggest that it should be postponed until the 'age of majority in any given country'.[17] This may of course be relevant to specialists operating in countries such as England, where minors acquire the right to consent to medical treatment before the age of 18.

Perhaps more important than the legal reasons for deferring sex change surgery to adulthood are the *clinical* reasons for doing so. For example, in male-to-female transgender adolescents,[18] there may not yet be enough genital tissue for the creation of a sensitive vagina of a size which is adequate for sexual intercourse. This problem can be overcome with additional surgery: the tissue for the creation of the vagina can be taken from other body parts, such as the radius, the abdomen or the inner thigh, but the scars will be significant and permanent, and sensitivity can also be reduced. Phalloplasty in female-to-male patients is an even more complex procedure. Different techniques may be used and sometimes several surgical procedures are required to increase the dimensions of the neophallus, for example. Results are not always reliable. For example, urination while standing is not always achieved. Both appearance and function depend not only on the technique used but also on the amount of sensitive tissue that can be utilised to create the phallus. In addition, permanent scars

---

14 Family Law Reform Act 1969, s 8(1).
15 *Gillick v West Norfolk and Wisbech Area Health Authority* (1985) 3 All ER 402, 422. Of course, even where a minor is incapable of providing consent, a procedure can be authorised by those with parental responsibility or by the courts if the procedure is in the minor's best interests. For present purposes, this is not relevant because typically sex change surgery is requested by the minor, and not by third parties on their behalf.
16 Hembree et al. (n 9) 3133.
17 Coleman et al. (n 9) 178.
18 For the purposes of this chapter, we use the term 'male-to-female'. However, we acknowledge the preferred use of other descriptors such as 'female' or 'transwomen' in such cases.

will remain at the sites from which the flap for the creation of the phallus has been removed. However, there are counterbalancing considerations.

Offering sex change surgery to minors

It could be argued that sex change surgery may still be appropriate or even necessary in some cases. This surgery could, for example, reduce the mental distress of dysphoric adolescents and facilitate healthy psycho-social and psycho-sexual development. Having appropriate genitalia may be crucial to such development. Romantic relationships for some adolescents may be essential to their immediate and long-term welfare. Natal genitalia may render the natural progression of those relationships impossible. The secrecy, isolation, sense of marginalisation and deviance that are caused by such developments may cause psychological disintegration in the adolescent.[19]

It must also be noted that waiting until adulthood does not necessarily resolve the problems relating to tissue availability. The first stage of the therapy for transgender minors involves suppression of puberty, with analogues similar to those used in cases of precocious puberty.[20] These analogues may be prescribed at the start or soon after the start of pubertal development (known as Tanner Stage 2 or 3),[21] and they temporarily suspend the endogenous production of testosterone and oestrogens. This means that virilisation and feminisation are temporarily suspended. In male-to-female adolescents whose puberty has been suppressed, for example, testes' descent and penile growth are inhibited. The phallus remains smaller than it would have been if puberty had been allowed to progress.

Therefore, waiting until adulthood does not necessarily guarantee that enough tissue will be available. In order to have sufficient genital tissue for the creation of the vagina, the minor would have to suspend the therapy with the analogues and let the body 'grow' until more tissue is available. The same would have to be done if male-to-female adolescents wanted to store sperm for future reproductive purposes. In these cases, they would also have to cease treatment with analogues for long enough for spermatogenesis to occur. This would ensure that they would have gametes for future reproductive purposes, but this would mean they would have to deal with the consequences of 'natural' progression of puberty.

A balancing exercise

This long sequence of sex change interventions may be some way from what the patient would ideally want. Thus, a balance needs to be struck between the patient's expectations and the side effects and/or consequences of the requested

---

19 C Milrod, 'How Young Is Too Young: Ethical Concerns in Genital Surgery of the Transgender MTF Adolescent' (2014) 11(2) Journal of Sexual Medicine 338.
20 C Roth, 'Therapeutic Potential of GnRH Antagonists in the Treatment of Precocious Puberty' (2002) 11 Expert Opin Investig Drugs 125.
21 Hembree et al. (n 9) 3140.

interventions. This balancing exercise is necessarily speculative to some extent, because the side effects may be experienced differently to those the individual had anticipated. For example, a patient may experience the permanent scars left on her body as more (or less) frustrating than she anticipated. The same can be said about most, if not all, surgical and non-surgical interventions meant to change the body and the identity of the person. As the results will be unique to the individual person, and as each individual comes with their own unique set of expectations, it may not be possible to foresee exactly what the final outcome will be. It is also probably because of this uncertainty that most doctors ordinarily adhere strictly to the WPATH and ETTP guidelines. This gives them a clear path to follow and serves to avoid potential future complaints by professional peers or patients.

Sex change surgeries 'in the shadows'

Although sex change surgery is typically only offered to adults, there is anecdotal evidence[22] that such surgery on minors does take place.[23] However, doctors who have performed sex change surgery on minors tend to be secretive about it for fear of professional repercussions, because they have not followed leading clinical guidelines.[24] Indeed, in the area of transgender care, there have been at least two precedent-setting cases involving doctors who have been suspended from practice and subjected to professional investigation for these very reasons. In the United Kingdom (UK), Dr Richard Curtis was subject to investigation for failing 'to follow accepted standards of care'[25] by the peer professional body, the General Medical Council (GMC). The investigation into Dr Curtis' conduct began in 2013 following a number of allegations. A woman complained that she regretted treatment; moreover, Dr Curtis was accused of prescribing sex change hormones to patients, and to patients under 18, though the Tavistock and Portman Clinic in London (the main NHS clinic) held that these drugs should not be provided to patients under the age of 18. During the investigation for failing 'to follow accepted standards of care',[26] restrictions were imposed on his practice. Two years after investigations had started, the case was dismissed,

---

22 Personal communication by first named author with a number of international specialists during the WPATH International Conference in Bangkok, February 2014.
23 Apart from a few Italian cases, including those described above (n 13), courts in most Anglo-Saxon countries do not authorise these kinds of treatments and/or surgery unless a dispute arises between relevant parties.
24 See above (n 22).
25 M Evans and A Hough, 'Dr Richard Curtis: Transsexual Doctor Faces Investigation', (2013) *The Telegraph*, 7 January <www.telegraph.co.uk/health/healthnews/9784545/Dr-Richard-Curtis-transsexual-doctor-facesinvestigation.html> (accessed 10 October 2014).
26 D Batty, 'Doctor under fire for alleged errors prescribing sex-change hormones', (2013) *The Guardian*, 6 January, <http://www.theguardian.com/society/2013/jan/06/transexualism-gender-reassignment-richard-curtis> (accessed 10 October 2014).

with no Fitness to Practice hearing and no sanctions.[27] The Curtis case echoed the earlier case of Dr Russell Reid, a psychiatrist who treated patients privately. He was found guilty of serious professional misconduct by the GMC in 2007, for breaching international guidance in relation to the treatment of patients during the period 1988 to 2003.[28]

These cases did not involve sex change in minors, but they are relevant here because they highlight the risks that doctors may face if they decide not to follow clinical guidelines accepted as authoritative by their peer group at the time treatment is provided. The cases are also important because they illustrate the risks that *other patients* face if some doctors who are willing to offer individualised treatment are suspended from practice. In the case of Dr Curtis, for example, some patients have complained that these investigations have resulted in them being denied an alternative route than having to accept treatment through the publicly funded National Health Service, which they view as unbearably slow and unsupportive.[29]

The way in which some doctors have attempted to escape the problem has been to offer sex change surgery while trying to keep it as secret as possible. This choice is understandable in the current situation, but it has important disadvantages. Given the complexities of these surgical procedures, especially on minors, it is crucial that data relating to such procedures are published in the relevant peer-reviewed literature. Sharing information is necessary to refine the techniques used and thus enhance existing treatments for transgender persons. Such information could include data relating to the amount of tissue used, the resulting function of the genitalia, the post-operative level of body satisfaction and patient satisfaction. This could be hugely beneficial to other clinicians in the field and, as a consequence, to the other patients. Such data could eventually also foster evidence-based amendments to existing clinical guidelines. For example, it might provide evidence for the amendment of the age-based criterion for accessing surgery. This could in turn have a knock-on effect on the age of access to cross-sex hormone therapy. Transparency is arguably the only way in which good evidence-based clinical care can, and should, be provided.

Of course we are not suggesting that adolescents should be used to collect data. What we are suggesting is that in cases in which it is argued that it would be worse for a patient not to receive an operation, or that an operation is in the patient's best interests, then doctors should not automatically be at risk of

---

27 Statement by Dr Curtis, received by one of the authors (SG) on 26 February 2015.
28 The international guidelines in question were those devised by the Harry Benjamin International Gender Dysphoria Association (HBIGDA): see P Tatchell, 'Listening Is Not A Crime', (2006) *The Guardian*, 6 October, <www.theguardian.com/commentisfree/2006/oct/06/drrussellreidunjustlyaccus> (accessed 10 October 2014).
29 Transgender Zone Team, 'Dr. Richard Curtis Under Fire – It is Dr Russell Reid Again!' (Transgenderzone, 06 January 2013) <http://forum.transgenderzone.com/viewtopic.php?t=3459#.VN3PZrvOPas> (accessed 01 February 2015).

professional censure. Instead, they should be able, and indeed encouraged by the governing bodies, to share the data they collect. If doctors consider that what they are doing is in their patients' best interests, then what they should do is seek the approval of their professional bodies, such as the GMC (or perhaps even seek a judicial declaration from the courts). This should be done in order to show how and why this is the best course of action and, in doing so, they would be challenging the current guidelines in an appropriate way.

Conclusion

The WPATH and ETTP guidelines represent current best practice in the field of the care and treatment of transgender persons: they are not legally binding and are intended to be flexible. However, there is a strong presumption in the transgender healthcare professional community that these guidelines should be followed strictly. In this chapter, we have shown that doctors can instead have good reasons for performing sex change surgery on minors in particular cases. In the circumstances, it is paramount that data relating to such surgery be made publicly available, preferably in relevant peer-reviewed literature. This is to be supported primarily on the grounds that other doctors may learn from, and other patients may also become aware of, the advantages and disadvantages of such surgery.

There is thus a strong moral reason to make the results of such surgery publicly known, on the basis that it is in the interests of patient protection. This, in turn, means that doctors should not be put in the position of having to conceal the fact that such surgery is being performed for fear of adverse legal and/or professional consequences. If doctors operate in good conscience, with appropriate consent in place, and in the belief that surgery is likely to minimise harm and promote patients' best interests after careful assessment, then they should be able to do so without fear. In the current climate, we cannot suggest that doctors have a *moral obligation* to publish their data, but we do suggest that there is a moral obligation on the part of the clinical community to enable doctors to do so.

16 The lawyer's prestige

Iain Brassington and Imogen Jones

Introduction

Law is surprisingly amenable to flights of fancy. Imaginary situations help us test the implications of policies and statutes, and good legislation may require a kind of science-fictional thinking, since one might hope that laws governing technology would anticipate, rather than attempt to keep up with, innovation. Good lawmakers will speculate about possible worlds as well as this one, and the future as well as the present, and some of that speculation may appear fantastical. Good researchers and good teachers will do something similar: by tweaking reality, a scholar – let's call her Margaret Brazier – might hope to gain insight into what the law means in practice or what it should be, and provide similar insight to students. But thinking about merely possible worlds isn't simply legislatively and academically valuable. Sometimes it's just fun.

Arthur C Clarke once suggested that any sufficiently advanced technology would be indistinguishable from magic.[1] The plot of Christopher Priest's novel *The Prestige* involves a device that allows a magician, Rupert Angier, apparently to transport himself instantly from the stage to another part of the theatre in a trick that he calls IN A FLASH.[2] There is no magic – only technology: the device creates a perfect facsimile of the user in the desired location; the original itself is reduced to 'the half-dead, half-alive condition I called "prestigious". The prestige is the source body in the transportation, left behind in the apparatus, "as if dead".'[3]

When the trick is performed, the 'prestigious' source body falls into a compartment built into the base of the device, to be got rid of after the show. The persistence of the prestigious body is an apparently unavoidable part of the procedure, and a part that Angier[4] would rather be without, admitting that '[c]oncealing

---

1 A Clarke, *Profiles of the Future* (eBook edn, Gollancz 2013) loc3744.
2 C Priest, *The Prestige* (Gollancz 2011).
3 Ibid 330.
4 Since the device creates a succession of Angiers, we shall use the name to refer to whichever iteration happens to serve as narrator at a given point in the novel.

and disposing of these prestigious bodies was the single greatest problem I had had to solve before I could present the illusion to the public'.[5]

Great as it may be, it is a problem to which Angier has a convenient solution, thanks to his access to a large vault at his family home that has been used as a crypt for centuries, and staff – stage hands and retainers – loyal enough to turn a blind eye to, or to assist with, the prestiges being deposited there. Angier never has to explain himself and his prestiges to the Victorian authorities.

A piece of technology like Angier's would appear magical to a Victorian audience, but no less magical now. If, though, a modern-day Angier existed and happened to come to the authorities' attention, what would – and should – they say? A machine like Angier's raises many ethico-legal questions. We might wonder about the legal status of the prestiges, and whether a crime takes place upon each use of the machine. Other questions concern the retention and disposal of body parts, self-ownership, cloning, eternal life and successive selves, and so on. We cannot consider all these lines in depth, and so will concentrate on only a couple – although in doing so we touch on others.

Asking the right question

We shall begin with a very important question: are the prestiges dead? Angier's turn of phrase – '*as if* dead' – suggests that he thinks they might not be; and the glimmer of a hint towards the end of the novel that one of them may have been reanimated suggests that he may be correct. The prestiges do seem to be immune to decay ('It was as if each one had been frozen in life, made inert without being made dead'[6]), and that might tempt us to class them as lifeless rather than dead. On the other hand, something that was once alive but is now lifeless – in the sense of having been but no longer being the subject of a life – seems to have been killed under any normal understanding of the word; and it is reasonable to assume that the law would think along these lines also.[7] So, for the sake of the argument, let's assume that whatever the existential status of the prestiges, they would have been killed in the eyes of the law. When a human is killed in 'unnatural' or unexpected circumstances,[8] it is inevitable that we will consider whether any crime has been committed. What might that crime be?

---

5   Priest (n 2) 262.
6   Priest (n 2) 354.
7   The term 'subject of a life' is borrowed from Tom Regan (see T Regan, 'The Case for Animal Rights' in P Singer (ed), *In Defence of Animals* (Blackwell 1985) 22), and indicates here the kind of being whose own existence matters to it. PVS patients present a tricky borderline and possible counterfactual: it is tempting not to think that they have been killed, although *qua* subject, they might have been. We do not have time here to follow this line fully.
8   These refer to the circumstances under which a coronial investigation into the cause of death is required under Coroners and Justice Act 2009, s 2. We expand on the significance of the need for coronial inquiries below.

On the understanding that the prestiges were killed, it would seem that as long as the *ur*-Angier stepped into the device deliberately, knowing what would happen to him, he would be treating it as a suicide machine. Suicide may have been a crime in Victorian England, but it is not today, and neither is attempting it. This would make Angier's actions considerably less (legally) serious for him.

Those who assisted Angier, however, would not be exempt from liability.[9] Yet any charge relating to assisting suicide would be faced with an enormous evidential difficulty: someone with all the physical and mental characteristics of the supposed suicide would demonstrably be still alive at the end of the performance. A great deal would hinge on whether the court knew and accepted how the machine worked. If we assume not – either because of the courts' own scepticism, or because Angier is unwilling to reveal his secret – the courts would presumably have to accept that the living person was *not* an impostor: after all, every conceivable test would suggest as much; and if the law cannot show someone to be an impostor, then it must allow that they are who they say they are. It is possible that the living putative Angier could be a twin, but that hypothesis has only a minimal power: although Angier has a whole vault of bodies, there would be no plausible way that they could all be twins without industrial-scale surrogacy, for which there would be no evidence. Hence charges relating to assisted suicide are unlikely to stick.

Still: the authorities would be left with several lifeless human bodies, corresponding in number to the number of uses of the machine, which would have to be accounted for. There would be a lingering mystery about whose they are, given that the most likely candidate would be walking around, but that headache ought not to deter a serious investigation of the situation: persons unknown are still entitled to justice. It would be tempting for the authorities to conclude that they were dealing with a case of homicide of some sort. That the mystery person appeared to enter the contraption willingly would be irrelevant. But how could any kind of homicide offence possibly be argued?

One possibility might be to suggest that those who worked with Angier had committed manslaughter. In using a device that they presumably knew from the beginning would present a substantial risk of the unknown participant losing his life, a jury might well be persuaded that Angier and his crew were reckless as to the consequences of their acts. A court could plausibly find that Angier and his crew had committed gross negligence manslaughter on the basis that the recklessness displayed by Angier *et al.* was so bad that it was criminal.[10] In

---

9 Suicide Act 1961, s 2.
10 In *A-G's Reference (No.2 of 1999)* [2000] 3 All ER 182, Rose LJ concluded that indifference to risks to life could amount to gross negligence in criminal law. This is essentially the test developed in the leading case of *R v Adomako* [1995] 1AC 171. Should the *ur*-Angier have been placed in fear of the apprehension of a force when he stepped into the machine, there could have been an assault and, thus, constructive manslaughter too. However, it is possible that his consent would be seen to negate the existence of an assault with the result of there being no initial unlawful act from which to construct the manslaughter. (See the kind of reasoning in *R v Slingsby* [1995] CLR 570.)

such circumstances, the liability would not just be for one death; they would consider each body to represent a different person.

But why stop at manslaughter? It might be risky to try the trick once or twice, but any good lawyer would argue that there must have been virtual certainty of its deathly consequences after that.[11] This reasoning suggests an intention that goes beyond reckless indifference or negligence: it implies that there was intent to kill the person to whom it was applied, thus justifying a charge of murder. (Attempts to invoke a double-effect defence here would probably founder; it's one thing to say that ending *ur*-Angier's life was a foreseen but unintended consequence of flicking the switch when flicking it is necessary to achieve some greater end – but flicking the switch served no purpose except to instigate a process that would bring about the *ur*-Angier's death: and though an impressive spectacle may be *a* good, it's not *that* good.)

All this potentially casts the net of liability very wide. As we noted, the trick was only possible because of the complicity of a range of assistants. Assuming that it is established that the trick and its consequences amounted to a crime, it seems that they all embarked upon a common purpose to commit that crime. That they all do not actually flick the switch together is immaterial: the doctrine of joint enterprise assigns the same liability to assisting accessories as to the principle actor.[12]

In response to either of these charges, Angier and friends might wish to argue that the mystery person knew the risk he or she was taking and consented to participation in the trick nevertheless. However, unless they were willing to expose their methods, our fact-finders would be none the wiser that the supposedly dead person entered the machine in the belief that he or she would materialise in a different part of the theatre, not significantly the worse for wear. In any event, even if evidence of consent could be produced, it would provide no defence to a homicide charge.

Sharing the secret

All this assumes that Angier would not defend himself and his crew by making public his secret in court. If he were to do that, and the courts were to accept that and how the machine worked, what difference would that make?

It would certainly provide an account of where the bodies came from, and it might make questionable the basis for any suggestion of homicide: though the number of lifeless bodies in the world would have increased by one, the number of living people would not have fallen correspondingly. It might still be insisted that the *ur*-Angier was killed in the process of becoming prestigious. But that would mean having to admit that the Angier in the dock could not

---

11 This test of oblique intention was affirmed in *R v Woolin* [1999] 1 AC 82.
12 See *R v Clarkson* [1971] 1 WLR 1402; *R v Jones and Mirrless* [1977] 65 Cr App R 250 CA.

possibly be culpable, because he would be a new creation that did not exist at the point when the machine was activated and could not exist except with its activation. More: presumably, legal systems prohibit homicide because of a moral claim about there being something worth protecting that it destroys; but if the new Angier is indistinguishable from the old, it becomes hard to see what has been lost.

With the secret of the trick revealed, the crew members could defend themselves against a homicide charge by drawing attention to a claim that Angier the person is irreducible to his body. The prestiges may have been the biological vessels of a former version of him, but because of his re-appearance, they would in no way consider themselves to be complicit in Angier the person dying. (If this had not been the case they might have been less willing to be complicit in the whole affair.) Indeed, the law is quite clear that for homicide to be made out a 'human being' needs to have been killed;[13] but it is not clear what the relationship between that human being and her or his body should be. One might suppose that having a human body is a necessary condition of being a human being. But Angier's assistants' defence could then rest on the claim that this leaves aside the question of whether one must be confined to just one body – it might be that one must have *at least* one. Since the revelation of the trick's secret would show that one could reasonably believe it possible to have more than one body, the law probably ought to take the defence seriously. Thus it is possible that the law could recognise that Angier the person lived on (or at least a good-faith belief that he would and did), irrespective of what has happened to the particular body that had once housed him.[14]

Bodies and things

This brings us to another question: what kind of thing is the prestige, and what does that tell us about what can be done with it? One possible response, which rides on accepting that Angier is a duplicate, would be to accept that the prestige is the corpse of the *ur*-Angier. Another possibility would be to insist that Angier really is transported (by means unknown), and that the prestige is a new creation – an industrial by-product, as it were, that never had legal personality.

In the latter case, the legal position would be fairly straightforward. As an artefact of what is at root a technological process, the prestiges could quite possibly count as Angier's property, to dispose of as he wished. The dogma that human tissue is *res nullius* – nobody's property – might be expected to render

---

13 This is the first element of the common law offence of murder (and indeed is a requirement for all homicides).
14 A peculiarity of this interpretation of the law is that it might mean that we only ever hold inherited property provisionally, for as long as the ghosts of our ancestors do not bring a claim to get it back.

this move hard to make, but it probably does not hold as a general rule.[15] Hence the move may not be all that difficult for him and his lawyer after all: there is a lot of tissue here, but its ontology would be the same as that of any smaller tissue sample for as long as it is accepted that Angier was transported. Since we've already suggested that the authorities would have to accept that the current Angier is the Angier who got into the machine, accepting that does not seem like too much of a stretch. The potential complication is that, granted Angier's indication that one prestige may be reanimated, there is the outside chance that we ought treat the prestiges – or, at least, one of them – rather as cloned embryos: that is, as organic matter that will later become a person in the legal and moral sense. If Angier's device is a cloning machine, then it may draw the attention of the Human Fertilisation and Embryology Authority, and he may not be able to do with the prestiges entirely as he wishes after all. But even here, it is not clear what the Authority would say: while English law outlaws human cloning by specifying which embryos may or may not be implanted in a woman,[16] it is (quite understandably) very quiet about clones that are produced in other ways – say, by using an artificial womb, or in the course of a theatrical performance.

What if the prestige is deemed to be a corpse? Given criminal justice officials' tendency to want to reflect the general societal attachment to dead bodies, it seems likely that they would be keen to consider them such. Even in the event that homicide charges failed, they would want some sort of criminal liability to be attached to the creation of so many human corpses. One way of achieving this would be to focus on Angier's method of disposing of the prestiges. Two issues arise here.

The first is that, in concealing the prestigious bodies during his show and then sneaking them into the vast family vault, Angier and colleagues have subverted both the normal procedures for investigating deaths and accepted methods of disposal.

There are rules and regulations about the notification of deaths and disposal of bodies. The authorities would, at minimum, want the deaths to be registered. It is obvious why Angier would prefer to avoid this – it would court unwanted attention, risk exposing his methods and, doubtless, deter audiences. Moreover, given that the deaths were neither 'natural' nor 'expected', it is likely that discovery of the bodies would trigger a coronial inquiry into their circumstances. Again, this could risk the involvement of the criminal justice system – and even if that system were to struggle to convict, it would be understandable for Angier to prefer to avoid it altogether. Yet the public interest in such investigations is underpinned by the existence of the offence of 'obstructing a coroner's inquest'.[17]

---

15 M Quigley, 'Property in Human Biomaterials – Separating Persons and Things?' (2012) 32(4) OJLS 659, 660–662.
16 See Human Fertilisation and Embryology Act 2008, s 3.
17 This is a common law offence, see for example, *R v Skinner and Skinner* [1993] 14 Cr App R (S) 115.

The intention to do this, inferred from the deception involved, would be relatively easily made out.

Alternatively, English and Welsh law recognises a criminal offence in preventing the lawful and decent burial of a body.[18] Is it possible that Angier's method of storing the prestiges falls foul of that? There is no burial ceremony; but it doesn't follow from that that their disposal would be considered legally unacceptable. And the fact that there's a family vault, the tenants of which presumably took up their occupancy with at least tacit legal approval, suggests that there is nothing particularly untoward about disposing of lifeless bodies there. The bodies are not causing any public health concern;[19] nor are there any family members left in a state of inconsolable distress, wondering what has happened to their loved one;[20] nor are any religious needs being ignored. Those closest to Angier are aware of what he is doing, and they never experience loss of the person they know as Angier.

Moreover, Angier carefully tags each of the bodies with the date and place of their creation. This suggests an element of sentimentality towards them – rather than just being 'prestige materials', they are a version of him. As such, maybe he wants to treat them with respect and decency, ensuring that they had the burial he considers fitting. Even for an offence without an intention requirement, it seems difficult to conclude on the facts that a lawful and decent burial has been prevented here.

All of this indicates that Angier thinks his lifeless prestiges to be dead; but we know that the most he is willing to admit is that the prestigious state renders them 'as if dead'. Therefore the second, and more likely, explanation for the way that he tends to the bodies is that he does not think that they are really corpses. This possibility would potentially transform any potential criminal liability arising from the trick – if they are not dead, there can be no homicide, and Angier and his crew could not be indicted for offences that depend on the presence of a dead body.

But in that case, we'd naturally wonder why, if Angier doesn't think the prestiges dead, he thinks fit to leave them in a vault. Putting them there may be explicable as a way of avoiding hard questions, but Angier appears to abandon them altogether. Though he believes them inert, the possibility that they require

---

18 This common law offence, and that it can exist in conspiratorial form, was confirmed in *R v Hunter, MacKinder and Atkinson* [1974] 1 QB 95, [1973] 3 All E.R. 286, CA.

19 The need to regulate the disposal of human remains as a way to protect public health as industrialisation led to greater urban populations certainly prompted many provisions (see D Davies, *A Brief History of Death* (Blackwell, 2005) 138), but that is clearly not the case here.

20 The distress caused to others by acts done to, or the delay in the disposal of, corpses has been commonly cited as a reason to justify legal interference with the treatment of the dead. This was also a major theme of Margaret Brazier's findings regarding the retained organs scandals: see M Brazier, 'Retained Organs: Ethics and Humanity' (2002) 22(4) LS 550.

some kind of care cannot be dismissed: they may be in a kind of minimally-conscious or vegetative state. If the prestiges *are* treated as being vegetative, they would have legal personality. Having said that, it wouldn't follow that they would have any interests that Angier might have neglected: as Lord Mustill argued in *Bland*, some legal persons cannot be treated in their best interests because they have no interests at all.[21]

What remains would be a wholly moral case: it may be that he is morally, if not legally, negligent for not arranging such care, and further culpable for creating more and more prestiges. Moral duties are frequently held to apply only to persons or the sentient, but they need not be so restricted. A Kantian, for example, might insist that Angier had indirect duties not to treat the prestiges arbitrarily; these duties would match duties that Kant describes in *The Doctrine of Virtue* in respect of 'brute nature':

> A propensity to wanton destruction of what is *beautiful* in inanimate nature (*spiritus destructionis*) is opposed to a human being's duty to himself; for it weakens or uproots that feeling in him which, though not of itself moral, is still a disposition of sensibility that greatly promotes morality or at least prepares the way for it: the disposition, namely, to love something (e.g., beautiful crystal formations, the indescribable beauty of plants) even apart from any intention to use it.[22]

Neither is it clear that rule-utilitarian ethicists concerned with sentience rather than personhood would have no concerns about arbitrarily damaging the non-sentient – arbitrary action might be suboptimal by their lights. But we know from the care Angier takes of the prestiges that his treatment is not arbitrary, and so even if moral duties translated easily into legal ones, it is not a given that there is anything much to say.

Problem cases

The Prestige has a number of narrators. One seems not to be certain of his own identity; another – Angier – seems to be much more sure of *his*, even though he might well have died several times. We are confident that a modern-day Angier would be of interest to the authorities, but their main puzzle would be how to articulate why this should be so. Any lawyer attached to the case could expect to be dizzied by it. But the case would doubtless attract commentary for years afterwards – and so such lawyer could also hope to earn an impressive reputation.

Prestige, even.

---

21 'The distressing truth which must not be shirked is that the proposed conduct is not in the best interests of Anthony Bland, for he has no best interests of any kind.' *Airedale N.H.S. Trust Respondents v Bland* [1993] AC 798 at 897, *per* Mustill LJ.
22 Immanuel Kant, *The Metaphysics of Morals* (Mary Gregor tr, CUP 1996) 6:443.

Part IV
Regulating reproduction

17 The science of muddling through

Categorising embryos

Marie Fox and Sheelagh McGuinness

Introduction

In a 1988 paper, Margaret Brazier stated: '[t]he trouble with the embryo is that . . . we cannot resolve [its] disputed nature.'[1] Brazier has spent almost 30 years puzzling over, amongst other things, the nature of embryos and 'muddled' social and regulatory responses to them in the United Kingdom (UK).[2] Here, we draw on her work to address law's muddled position on embryos. Wisely, Brazier suggests that we need to 'move beyond the scientific disciplines of medicine, law and philosophy and into more human social sciences particularly social anthropology'.[3] We heed this suggestion by drawing on scholarship which understands embryos as 'socially, culturally and politically' constructed entities.[4] We add that embryos are also *legally* constructed. Human fertilisation and embryology legislation has characterised embryos in various ways, and we suggest that these statutes form part of the general process by which we make sense of our world by sorting things into categories. As Minnow notes, we need to attend to this sorting process because 'when we identify one thing as like the others, we are not merely classifying the world; we are investing particular classifications with consequences and positioning ourselves in relation to those meanings'.[5]

Taking up Brazier's analysis of the relationship between embryology and abortion law, which is part of law's sorting process, we examine the permitted/non-permitted dichotomy. We argue that distinctions are now drawn between different *in vitro* embryos, with the legal distinction between 'permitted' and 'non-permitted' categories, mapping onto distinctions between 'reproductive' and 'research' embryos. In turn, this reflects boundaries drawn between the

---

1 M Brazier, 'Embryos' Rights: Abortion and Research' in M Freeman (ed), *Current Legal Problems* (Stevens & Sons 1988) 15.
2 M Brazier, 'Regulating the Reproduction Business?' (1999) 7 Med L Rev 188.
3 Ibid.
4 M Mulkay, *The Embryo Research Debate* (CUP 1997).
5 M Minnow, *Making All the Difference: Inclusion, Exclusion and American Law* (Cornell UP 1990) 3.

human embryo, which can be used for reproductive purposes, and the human/animal hybrid embryo, which cannot. Drawing on Brazier's early identification of the differential protections offered to embryos *in utero* and *in vitro*, we track how English law has drawn boundaries around what it is permissible to do to embryos.[6] We further argue that legislation has effectively categorised embryos to ensure that they do not trouble foundational legal categories, such as 'person' and 'property'. Thus, the original Human Fertilisation and Embryology (HFE) Act 1990 (1990 Act) sought to govern the human embryo *in vitro*. In contrast, legislative reforms in 2008 (2008 Act) introduced two specific legal constructions of the embryo: the 'permitted' and 'non-permitted' embryo. In so doing, law has limited the potential of embryos to complicate what it means to be human – a theme which has been central to Brazier's work.

Embryonic constructions

As we shall outline below, we understand the embryo as occupying a liminal space between the foundational legal categories of human and non-human, personhood and property. The embryo is constituted privately as 'a human being', a 'potential person', 'an unborn child' or specifically 'my child', 'research material' or 'stuff'. In its more public incarnations, it acts as 'a boundary object', 'a life saving tool', 'a moral work object', 'a politically contested entity', 'a highly regulated legal entity' or 'a legal artefact'.[7] Underpinning these constructions are distinct concepts of the person and views of what can legitimately be done to persons. For those who attach special and universal value to human life, the embryo should receive special protection, just as born humans do.[8] Consequently, research on embryos ought to be very limited, even if it promises untold benefits 'to humanity': it is as wrong to experiment

---

6   Brazier (n 1).
7   Ibid. See also Z Szawarski, 'Talking About Embryos' in D Evans (ed), *Conceiving the Embryo: Ethics, Law, and Practice in Human Embryology* (Nijhoff 1996); M Fox, 'Pre-Persons, Commodities or Cyborgs: The Legal Construction and Representation of the Embryo' (2000) 8 Health Care Analysis 171; M Sandel, 'Embryo Ethics – The Moral Logic of Stem-Cell Research' (2004) 351 NEJM 207; R George and P Lee, 'Embryos and Acorns' (2004/2005) 7 The New Atlantis 90; E Haimes et al., '"So What Is An Embryo?" A Comparative Study of the Views of Those Asked to Donate Embryos for hESC Research in the UK and Switzerland' (2008) 27 New Genetics and Society 113; K Ehrich, C Williams and B Farsides, 'The Embryo as Moral Work Object: PGD/IVF Staff Views and Experiences' (2008) 30 Sociology of Health and Illness 772; M Fox, 'Legislating Interspecies Embryos' in S Smith and R Deazley (eds), *The Legal, Medical and Cultural Regulation of the Body* (Ashgate 2009); S McGuinness, 'The Construction of the Embryo and Implications for Law' in M Quigley, S Chan and J Harris (eds), *Stem Cells: New Frontiers in Science and Ethics* (World Scientific Publishing 2012); S Franklin, *Biological Relatives: IVF, Stem Cells, and the Future of Kinship* (Duke UP 2013) 69.
8   M Brazier, 'Can English Law Accommodate Moral Controversy in Medicine?' in A Alghrani, R Bennett and S Ost (eds), *The Criminal Law and Bioethical Conflict: Walking the Tightrope* (CUP 2012).

on an embryo as it would be to experiment on a child or unconsenting adult.[9] Similarly, restrictions would be imposed on what is permissible for embryos generated for reproductive purposes. For those with opposing views – that the embryo is 'just a bundle of cells', for example – any limitation on embryonic stem cell research is perverse and harmful. Such differing constructions reflect different moral perspectives but also different background conditions or institutional frameworks against which, and within which, the embryo is addressed.

With the ability to create extra-corporeal embryos, the nature of the debate changed. Prior to 1978 and the birth of Louise Brown, embryos formed part of the broader category of the 'unborn':

> There is a 'thing' that counts for something, but little consensus about why, or how, or when. So from the mists of history to today, law has turned to medical science to attempt to find that missing certainty.[10]

Yet, rather than offering certainty, science frequently serves to question what certainty existed in legal categorisations, given that '"medical facts" rarely stand still, nor are they as clear as lawyers might like'.[11] In a pluralistic society, lawmakers must also navigate a seemingly impossible path between competing and incommensurable views.[12] As Franklin observes:

> [O]ver-attachment to an idealized and singular invocation of 'the' human embryo is both partisan and illogical . . . human embryos, in their enormous diversity, by definition exceed and overflow. Scientifically, 'embryo' is a basket category – like 'clone', it is famously imprecise. Legally, it is an equally indeterminate appellation, and philosophically it has been the subject of debate for more than two millennia.[13]

Legal controversies

Given this indeterminacy, we argue that law engages in boundary work[14] to contain the radical potential of embryos. Inhabiting the frontiers of the human, embryos exist in a liminal position, literally on a threshold 'betwixt-and-between the moral, day-to-day, cultural and social stages and processes of getting and

---

9 Brazier examines these issues further in M Brazier, 'Exploitation and Enrichment: The Paradox of Medical Experimentation' (2007) 34 JME 180.
10 Brazier (n 8) 198.
11 Brazier (n 2).
12 This is a theme in much of Brazier's writing in this area. See for example Brazier (n 2; n 8).
13 S Franklin, 'Response to Marie Fox and Thérèse Murphy' (2010) 19 Social & Legal Studies 505.
14 D Haraway, *Modest Witness@Second Millennium. Female Man MeetsOncoMouse: Feminism and Technoscience* (Routledge 1997) 67.

spending, preserving law and order and registering social status'.[15] Such liminality carries the power to destabilise or disrupt and, as such, demands a regulatory response to shore up legal categories. In these situations, functionality underpins social construction.[16] Functionalist definitions often depend on our intention towards the embryo.[17] Legally, the move from reproductive function to research function aligns with the desire to preserve important legal principles (e.g. sanctity of life), with the legal facilitation of research and with the advancement of science. As Brazier observed, legitimising embryo research was a key driver for regulation:

> Unregulated embryo research was simply not an option, paradoxically because Warnock and ultimately the majority of Parliament favoured permitting such research. Regulation was the price for ensuring the 'legitimacy' of such research. Thus to ensure those opposed to embryo research could not undermine that 'legitimacy', any procedure which involved creating an embryo must fall within the jurisdiction of the 'legitimating' authority.[18]

This legal work – legitimising embryos' use (and destruction) – means that embryos can be understood as legal artefacts. They come to mark a starting point in the attribution of a particular legal categorisation, such as legal personhood or property. In this sense, they are legal tools, as much as 'life saving tools'.[19]

Legal controversies pertaining to the embryo reflect two main areas of contestation that are distinct yet intertwined. The first concerns the embryo's contested moral status and the legal implications of such status. As Brazier demonstrated, a preoccupation with status characterised legal debates around abortion, where the embryo was deemed part of the broader category of the unborn – a preoccupation that carried over to early debates on embryo research. However, as she recognised:

> [T]he status which should be accorded to the embryo . . . is a circular debate. The central thesis of whether or not humanity is simply a rational animal whose rationality alone commands respect or a unique, divinely created species is unprovable either way.[20]

---

15 V Turner, 'Frame, Flow and Reflection: Ritual and Drama as Public Liminality' in M Benamou and C Caramello (eds), *Postmodern Culture* (Coda Press 1977) 33; S Squier, *Liminal Lives: Imagining the Human at the Frontiers of Biomedicine* (Duke UP 2004) ch 1.
16 J Searle, *The Social Construction of Reality* (Free Press 1995).
17 M Mulkay, 'The Triumph of the Pre-Embryo: Interpretations of the Human Embryo in Parliamentary Debate over Embryo Research' (1994) 24 Social Studies of Science 634.
18 Brazier (n 2).
19 Franklin (n 7).
20 Brazier (n 1) 14.

Since both embryos and their moral status are contested,[21] reliance on arguments about moral status to guide regulation of the embryo is not helpful.[22] Not only is moral status something that is not fixed, obvious or demonstrable; the criteria for granting moral status differ from those for granting legal status.[23] Recognising this, there is a discernible shift from the notion that moral status can be legally determined, with judges, committees of inquiry and legislators deeming that the crucial question for law is when life acquires legal protection.[24] This is not to claim that law never faces moral questions, but rather to recognise that at the margins of legal personhood, moral status is inconclusive.[25]

In consequence, as Brazier notes, law in this area is not underpinned by any particular philosophical position but rather has evolved pragmatically. Since the 1984 Warnock Report, which paved the way for the 1990 Act,[26] the pragmatic legal response to uncertainty generated by the 'murky status of the "unborn"',[27] has been the attribution of 'special status' to the embryo. This requires that embryos be treated 'with respect', although disagreement surrounds what this means.[28] While clearly not a legal person with the strong protection that entails, varying levels of statutory protection have been accorded to the unborn, at least since Lord Ellenborough's Act in 1803.[29] Yet, as Brazier notes, it would be mistaken to presume that moral status was the primary basis for law,[30] since other factors, such as concern for maternal health, concealment of sin, and a concern with the 'life of the unborn',[31] have also underpinned laws governing abortion and miscarriage.

The second broad area of legal controversy is procedural and concerns the scope of the Human Fertilisation and Embryology Authority (HFEA). It was

---

21 McGuinness (n 7); S Uí Chonnachtaigh, 'The Monopoly of Moral Status in Debates on Embryonic Stem Cell Research' in Quigley et al. (n 7); Franklin (n 13).
22 J English 'Abortion and the Concept of a Person' (1975) 5 Canadian Journal of Philosophy 236.
23 HLA Hart, *The Concept of Law* (2nd edn, Clarendon Press 1994).
24 *Robert M. Byrn, as Guardian ad Litem for an Infant 'Roe', an Unborn Child, and All Similarly Unborn Infants, Appellant, v. New York City Health & Hospitals Corporation et al., Respondents* 286 N.E.2d 887, 889 (N.Y. 1972); M Warnock, *A Question of Life: The Warnock Report on Human Fertilisation and Embryology*, (Blackwell 1985); *MR v. TR & Ors* [2006] IEHC 359.
25 M Little, 'Abortion and the Margins of Personhood' (2008) 39 Rutgers LJ 331.
26 *Report of the Committee of Inquiry into Human Fertilisation and Embryology* (The Stationary Office 1988).
27 Which can be contrasted with 'the more certain world of being a person': see J Herring, 'The Loneliness of Status: The Legal and Moral Significance of Birth' in F Ebtehaj et al. (eds), *Birth Rites and Rights* (Hart 2011) 97.
28 Mary Warnock herself has questioned the utility of this approach, see E Jackson, *Regulating Reproduction: Law, Technology and Autonomy* (Hart 2001) 226–36; E Jackson, 'Fraudulent Stem Cell Research and Respect for the Embryo' (2006) 1 BioSocieties 349.
29 Brazier (n 9) 198.
30 M Brazier and S Ost, *Bioethics and Medicine in the Theatre of the Criminal Process* (CUP 2013) ch 4.
31 Ibid; Brazier (n 8) 195–8.

tasked with licensing assisted reproduction and embryo research following enactment of the 1990 Act.[32] The 1990 Act contained the following precise definition: '[a]n embryo means a live human embryo where fertilisation is complete.'[33] However, this left the HFEA's ambit open to challenge as new ways to create embryos, such as cell nuclear replacement, emerged.[34] Consequently, it was decided that amendments to the 1990 Act would offer an open-ended definition better equipped to accommodate scientific advances in embryology to 'future-proof' the Authority's remit[35] against litigation.[36] To avoid legal ambiguity about the HFEA's remit, the House of Commons Science and Technology Committee[37] proposed to define the embryo in a negative way: deploying a strict definition of the type of embryo that could legitimately be implanted into a woman (a 'permitted embryo') but leaving vague and open-ended its definition in other contexts where it will be used for research rather than reproductive purposes ('non-permitted'). Thus, the 2008 Act enshrines a distinction between permitted and non-permitted embryos.[38] This legislative framing aimed to address the criticisms of academic commentators, such as Herring and Chau, who have argued that 'it is the potential of an embryo to develop into a human being, rather than the process by which the embryo was created', which gives it special significance.[39]

Simultaneously, allowing a category of embryo beyond 'permitted embryos' safeguards the Authority's remit by allowing it to respond to technological advances, thereby performing its 'legitimating' function, as noted by Brazier.[40] Significantly, this new definition clearly delineates the 'permitted' embryo destined for procreation and birth, while also guaranteeing its human nature, since the reproductive embryo can only be the product of 'permitted' or human gametes. The 'permitted' embryo is thereby distinguished from so-called human admixed embryos, whose creation in a variety of forms is now permitted, but only for research purposes and provided they are destroyed by 14 days.[41] The removal of the ban on creating animal/human hybrid embryos was necessitated

---

32 Human Fertilisation and Embryology Act 1990, s 5.
33 Ibid s 1.
34 For an overview of the litigation, see M Johnson, 'Escaping the Tyranny of the Embryo? A New Approach to ART Regulation based on UK and Australian Experiences' (2006) 11 Human Reproduction 2756.
35 The litigation questioned whether embryos created by cell nuclear replacement counted as embryos under the original legislative definition.
36 *Government Response to the Report from the House of Commons Science and Technology Committee: Human Reproductive Technologies and the Law* (Department of Health 2007) para 53 <www.gov.uk/government/uploads/system/uploads/attachment_data/file/243182/7209.pdf> (accessed 16 March 2015).
37 House of Commons Science and Technology Committee, Fifth Report of Session 2004–5, *Human Reproductive Technologies and the Law*.
38 HFE Act 1990 (as amended), schedule 3ZA.
39 J Herring and P-L Chau, 'Are Cloned Embryos Embryos? (2002) 14(3) CFLQ 318.
40 Brazier (n 2).
41 HFEA Act 1990 (as amended), s 4(6).

by the shortage of human gametes and embryos donated for research purposes.[42] Scientists advocated using animal eggs to create hybrid embryos to address this shortage. This provides another instance of how law has pragmatically accommodated scientific developments and conflicting accounts of the embryo. It exemplifies Brazier's demonstration of how pragmatism can be understood as a virtue of the common law.[43]

The politics of muddling through

Law's pragmatic approach has, however, entailed a lack of theoretical depth in our regulatory frameworks, meaning that 'again and again, as new medical developments emerge, we debate the same issues in different disguises'.[44] Thus, objections to embryo research prior to the adoption of the 1990 Act resurfaced in debates about hybrid embryos in the run up to reforms to the 1990 Act in 2008.[45] Yet the problem with pragmatically deploying law to legitimate certain scientific enterprises, such as embryo research or the creation of hybrid embryos, is not primarily a failure to resolve the issues in a principled way (we doubt that this is possible). Rather it is that little attention is devoted to the productive power of law and the boundary work in which it is implicated.

In this regard, we argue that shifting legal constructions of embryos are generated not just to accommodate conflicting perceptions of the embryo, or to protect the territory of regulatory bodies, but to preserve existing legal categories, like that of person or property. In what follows we suggest that since embryos are intimately connected to future legal persons, the legal definition and redefinition of the embryo can be seen as a starting point in law's process of creating and defining legal persons.[46] As has been noted previously, by strictly defining what sort of embryo can be implanted for human reproductive purposes and leaving the definition of the embryo otherwise open-ended, law facilitates what Hennette-Vauche describes as a 'conceptual severance' of the activities of reproduction and research.[47] This conceptual severance and the categorisation of embryos into 'permitted' and 'non-permitted' are invoked as a legal response to fears that all hybrid embryos are potential hybrid persons.

---

42 N Brown, 'Beasting the Embryo: The Metrics of Humanness in the Transpecies Embryo Debate' (2009) 4 Biosocieties 147.
43 See for example Brazier (n 2; n 8).
44 Brazier (n 2) 167.
45 Fox (n 7); U Ogbogu, T Caulfield and S Green, 'From Human Embryos to Interspecies Creations: Ethical and Legal Uncertainties Surrounding the Creation of Cytoplasmic Hybrids for Research' (2008) 9 Med Law Int 227.
46 N Naffine, 'Who Are Law's Persons? From Cheshire Cats to Responsible Subjects' (2003) 66 MLR 346.
47 S Hennette-Vauchez, 'Words Count: How Interest in Stem Cells Has made the Embryo Available – A Look at the French Law on Bioethics' (2009) 17 Med L R 54.

In distinguishing various types of *in vitro* embryos, fertilisation and embryology law treads a fine line between the activities of reproduction and research.[48] Our thinking about permitted reproductive embryos is shaped by certain characteristics that mark them off from mere research embryos, which are more akin to legal property. A key characteristic is *visibility*. The ability to create *in vitro* embryos and keep them alive for research purposes prompted the first attempts to settle questions about the legal status of the embryo as an entity which in itself is distinct from the broader category of 'the unborn'. In the United States context, Morgan describes the significance of the embryo becoming visible:

> The earliest embryos were overlooked by pathologists because they were literally too small to see. The embryo collectors were part of an immense social transformation that changed all that, turning embryos from entities that were socially and scientifically insignificant into tangible, material objects of enormous cultural importance.[49]

In debates preceding the 1990 Act, a similar (legal) transformation occurs in how we conceive of embryos. Older arguments do not fade completely, but new ways of thinking about embryos emerged, with Franklin singling out the central positioning of the human embryo and consequent displacement of women's roles, as the most significant feature.[50]

Linked to the increasing visibility of the embryo is the notion of *individuality*, as embryos were ontologically separated from their progenitors, which as Jackson notes is key to debates about their status.[51] The emergence of the primitive streak was deployed to mark the start of an individual something that is qualitatively different than that which has gone before it,[52] simultaneously disqualifying the embryo prior to 14 days from legal protection. In turn, the '*humanness*' of embryos is related to individuation. Thus, for *in utero* embryos, a presumption exists that such entities are human; hence much discussion about regulating them turns on balancing the interests of potential legal persons (human embryos) against existing legal persons (pregnant women).[53] In contrast, the individuality and humanity of extra-corporeal embryos are more contested, and the legal construction of different types of embryo is a response to this.

---

48 Brazier (n 1); Fox (n 7)
49 L Morgan, *Icons of Life: A Cultural History of Human Embryos* (University of California Press 2009) 5.
50 S Franklin, 'Making Representations: The Parliamentary Debate on the Human Fertilisation and Embryology Act 1990' in J Edwards et al. (eds), *Technologies of Procreation: Kinship in the Age of Assisted Conception* (Manchester UP 1993).
51 Jackson (n 28) 226–7.
52 N Richardt, 'A Comparative Analysis of the Embryological Research Debate in Great Britain and Germany' (2003) 10 Social Politics 108.
53 M Strathern, *Reproducing the Future: Anthropology, Kinship, and the New Reproductive Technologies* (Manchester UP 1992).

The upshot is the exclusion of a broad range of embryos from the category of potential legal person, because they fail to meet the most basic criteria of legal personhood.[54] For instance, in debates preceding the 1990 Act, the construct of the 'pre-embryo' versus embryo proper played a prominent role.[55] This is illustrated in the following quote from Kenneth Clarke (then Secretary of State for Health):

> I am influenced by the tiny size of the embryo . . . and by the fact that on rare occasions it could develop into *more than one person* if it developed at all . . . I cannot see that this is a very important stage of human development to which we should give the absolute *protection as a citizen*.[56]

Similar distinctions between 'proper' embryos and entities designated as 'early-stage embryos' or 'blastocysts' were evident in public and political debates around the amendments to guidance on embryonic stem cell research (ESCR) in 2000.[57]

The classification of the embryo not just as a being, but specifically as a *human* being, was evident in debates around the 2008 legislative reforms to the 1990 Act, when the creation of interspecies embryos challenged this categorisation.[58] Accounts of legal persons have typically displayed an anthropomorphic bias to date.[59] Entities falling outside the parameters of the human have attracted less protection, regardless of generalisable features like sentience.[60] Legally, a correlation exists between 'human' person and 'legal' person.[61] Therefore, designating an embryo as 'human' carries important legal implications; indeed, *humanness* has been integral to what it is to be a legal person. Karpin describes how certain embryonic forms, notably interspecies embryos, challenge this anthropomorphic orthodoxy:

> What does it mean to be a human person, in a world where these transformations are possible? . . . The legal response to such transformative possibilities has so far been to ensure their prohibition at the earliest

---

54 Fox (n 7).
55 Mulkay (n 17); S Kettell, 'Rites of Passage: Discursive Strategies in the 2008 Human Fertilisation and Embryology Debate' (2010) 58 Pol Stud 789.
56 K Clarke, House of Commons, 23 April 1990, col 31.
57 C Williams et al., 'Envisaging the Embryo in Stem Cell Research: Rhetorical Strategies and Media Reporting of Ethical Debate' (2003) 25 Sociology of Health and Illness 800.
58 Brazier (n 8).
59 P French, 'The Corporation As a Moral Person' (1979) 16 Am Phil Q 207.
60 For criticisms see L Bortolotti, 'Moral Rights and Human Culture' (2006) 13 Ethics Perspectives 603; T Bryant, 'Sacrificing the Sacrifice of Animals: Legal Personhood for Animals, the Status of Animals as Property, and the Presumed Primacy of Humans' (2008) 39 Rutgers L J 247.
61 Indeed accounts of corporate personality often rely on anthropomorphised accounts of the corporation, see M Hildebrandt, 'Criminal Liability and 'Smart' Environments' in R Duff and S Green (eds), *Philosophical Foundations of Criminal Law* (OUP 2011).

stage – the embryonic stage . . . ensuring at least for now that such *persons* cannot be born.⁶²

Law responds to such challenges by redefining and excluding certain entities from being brought into existence, thus aiming to ensure that the dilemma cannot arise. *Human*ness thus becomes an important feature of whether an embryo is to be regarded as potentially *someone* as opposed to *something*.⁶³ In earlier debates, Enoch Powell played on this characteristic to garner support for his Private Members' Bill, known as The Unborn Children (Protection) Bill, which would have banned ESCR entirely back in 1985. He emphasised that the embryo was one of us and should thus be protected: 'This is the recognition by a *human* society of its obligations to itself, to future generations and to *human* nature.'⁶⁴ In framing this argument, Powell implicitly relied on an acceptance of humanity as foundational in the attribution of legal protection. Indeed, it was the response to his Bill which prompted the coining of the term 'pre-embryo'.⁶⁵

Potentiality has had mixed success in debates over how crucial this feature is for the purposes of moral status.⁶⁶ However, for the attribution of legal personhood, and hence legal status, potentiality is important, because embryos are precursors to future people. Certain embryonic forms are thus intrinsically related to future full legal persons. The institutional fact⁶⁷ of legal personhood thereby sets the parameters for certain embryonic constructions, and entities that challenge these parameters are, as noted by Karpin, excluded from the status function of legal person. In legal terms, intentionality towards the embryo carries particular consequences, not just in terms of what activities are permissible, but also regarding what gets to count (or be ascribed a particular function) in the

---

62 I Karpin, 'The Uncanny Embryos: Legal Limits to the Human and Reproduction Without Women' (2006) 28 Sydney L Rev 611.
63 Fox (n 7).
64 E Powell, House of Commons, 15 February 1985, vol 73 col 641.
65 S Franklin and C Roberts, *Born and Made: An Ethnography of Preimplantation Genetic Diagnosis* (Princeton UP 2006) 65.
66 See the debate between M Lockwood, 'Warnock versus Powell (and Harradine): When Does Potentiality Count?' (1988) 2 Bioethics 187; and R Hare, 'When Does Potentiality Count? A Comment on Lockwood' (1988) 2 Bioethics 214; see further J Harris, 'The Concept of the Person and the Value of Life' (1999) 9 Kennedy Institute of Ethics Journal 297.
67 Searle summarises the existence of institutional facts in the following way: 'An institution is a system of constitutive rules, and such a system automatically creates the possibility of institutional facts. Thus the fact that Obama is President or the fact that I am a licensed driver or the fact that a chess match was won by a certain person and lost by a certain other person are all institutional facts because they exist within systems of constitutive rules', see J Searle, *Making the Social World: The Structure of Human Civilization* (OUP 2010) 10–11.

first place. Clarke affirmed the former point when he claimed in debates prior to the adoption of the 1990 Act:

> I think that the researchers all say that it would be irresponsible for doctors to replace in the womb fertilized human eggs that had been subjected to novel procedures or tests, for these might themselves lead to abnormality.[68]

It seems obvious that particular concerns apply to entities that may one day become full legal persons.[69] However, the circularity of the process of legal categorisation is less apparent.

The move from reproductive function to research function aligns with the desire to preserve important legal principles that underpin research in this area; the principle of the sanctity of life in this instance conflicts with law's role in facilitating research or advancing science.[70] The decision to 'discard' or 'donate' an embryo follows a process of re-imagining the sort of thing it is: this transformation is not just personal but also legal.[71] In relation to decisions to donate 'spare' embryos for research, Charis Thompson observes that: '[m]aking an embryo into waste is an outcome and not a by-product'.[72] This statement also rings true in law. A functional approach to constructions of the embryo is now enshrined in the HFE Act 2008 as regards those embryos that may legitimately be gestated and those that may not. Reproductive embryos after 14 days are thus cast as belonging to the much broader legal category of 'the unborn' or of the potential future legal person. Embryos in a research context are not so constructed, and consequently are afforded a reduced level of legal protection.

Conclusion

In this chapter, we have analysed the contested nature of the embryo in the hope of providing a less muddled account of the legal framework which categorises and regulates them. Drawing on Brazier's work, we have highlighted how

---

68 Clarke (n 56) col 31.
69 See further Congenital Disabilities (Civil Liability) Act 1976, s 1A; Human Fertilisation and Embryology Act 1990 (as amended), s 13(5).
70 Richardt (n 52).
71 K Ehrich, C Williams and B Farsides, 'Classifying 'Spare' Embryos for Donation to hESC Research' (2010) 71 Social Science & Medicine 2204; B Farsides and R Scott, 'No Small Matter for Some: Practitioners' Views on the Moral Status and Treatment of Human Embryos' (2010) 20 Med L Rev 90.
72 C Thompson, *Making Parents: The Ontological Choreography of Reproductive Technologies* (MIT Press 2005) 264.

regulation of the embryo fits within the broader legal framework that assigns this entity to particular legal categorisations in seemingly arbitrary ways. Jacob and Prainsack summarise the rationale for such an approach as the 'need to analyse embryos in the context of networks of social and biological relations they are embedded in'.[73] We have suggested that legal responses in the UK to these different contexts have variously either attempted or eschewed engagement with questions of moral status.

However, we have also highlighted how this engagement has been motivated by a need to defend the regulatory territory statutorily accorded to the HFEA. At a more fundamental level, law has striven to assign different types of embryos to either side of the fundamental division of legal entities into persons or things. Since 1990, embryos destined for human reproduction effectively count as human individuals once they are implanted and are entitled to greater legal protection than the pre 14 day embryo. More recently, certain sorts of embryo (hybrid or artificial) can be created under licence for research purposes, but are 'not permitted' to be implanted in the uterus for reproductive purposes. Utilising such categorisations, law has effectively contained the subversive challenge of the embryo by classifying some as potential legal persons and others as mere research material. In so doing, law not only contains the liminality of the embryo but reifies the pre-existing legal categories to which it is assigned.

In her paper 'Embryo "Rights": Abortion and Research', Brazier suggests that research on embryos must be preferable to destruction of what *may* be human life.[74] In practice, the current law strips away protections that 'non-permitted' embryos may otherwise be accorded by virtue of their humanity. Yet, the way regulation has developed in this area does accord with Brazier's view about the value of human bodies:

> I would want to contest the view that only some bodies have value and argue that the human organism has itself a value from conception to decay. But that does not mean that embryos are necessarily sacrosanct or that no uses may be made of bodies of the dead or parts of the living.[75]

In summary, Brazier's body of work on embryos and the unborn prompts reflection on why we should care about embryos – whether we see them as symbols of life, as corporeal beings enmeshed in a network of relations, or as research tools. However we conceptualise their existence, Brazier's work causes us to reflect upon what we mean by being human and how it matters, as well as how legal constructions influence the ways in which we answer these questions.

---

73 MA Jacob and B Prainsack, 'Embryonic Hopes: Controversy, Alliance, and Reproductive Entities in Law and the Social Sciences' (2010) 19 Social & Legal Studies 497.
74 Brazier (n 1).
75 M Brazier, 'Introduction: Being Human: Of Liberty and Privilege' in S Smith and R Deazley (eds), *The Legal, Medical and Cultural Regulation of the Body: Transformation and Transgression* (Ashgate 2009) 11.

18 Revisiting the regulation of the reproduction business

Danielle Griffiths and Amel Alghrani

> 'There is little conceptual depth underpinning British law. The result is that, again and again, as new medical technologies emerge, we debate the same issues in different guises.'[1]

Introduction

In 1999, Margaret Brazier wrote a paper exploring 'some of the issues arising out of the way in which the United Kingdom has tackled developments in reproductive medicine'.[2] The paper discussed how the Human Fertilisation and Embryology Act 1990 (HFE Act 1990) worked to regulate selected issues relating to reproductive medicine in the UK. Since Brazier's seminal piece, the law in this area has been updated by the Human Fertilisation and Embryology Act 2008 (HFE Act 2008) to reflect the fact that science has once again moved on. Some of the questions in Brazier's paper continue to challenge us. For example, why do we interfere in the reproductive choices of infertile people; who does such interference discriminate against; and what status does the embryo have? Other issues, however, have changed significantly. Science and society has marched on over the past 15 years and regulation has had to grapple with new reproductive technologies and their implications for familiar concepts such as parenthood and family.

In this chapter we will revisit some of Brazier's discussions in order to explore the workings of the legislation over the past 15 years. We will first look at the implementation of the HFE Act 1990 and why reproductive medicine is singled out to be in need of specialist regulation, Brazier having noted that neither the science nor the infrastructure which then underpinned the 'reproductive business' was well developed.[3] Brazier was proved correct, and we will outline how the legislation was updated with the creation of the HFE Act 2008 to respond to developments in science. However, we will show that regulation of the

---

1 M Brazier 'Regulating the Reproduction Business' (1999) 167 Med L Rev 167.
2 Ibid 166.
3 Ibid 173.

'reproductive business' remains insufficiently developed to respond to the challenging questions that reproductive medicine raise. We will then place Brazier's arguments into context with recent developments in reproductive technologies. New technologies such as mitochondria replacement techniques as well as existing techniques such as surrogacy are testing the boundaries of UK law and how it defines familiar yet contested understandings of genetics, gestation and parenthood. While some developments in reproductive technologies are new, we will suggest that the responses are familiar and are underpinned by a failure to properly conceptualise or reconsider definitions of family and parenthood in the context of new reproductive technologies. In revisiting Brazier's paper and examining the regulatory and scientific changes that have taken place since its publication, we will show that she was indeed correct when she stated that due to the fact there is little conceptual depth underpinning British law, 'we debate the same issues in different guises'.[4]

Regulation: The Human Fertilisation and Embryology Act 2008

Reproductive medicine is regulated in the UK by statute (The Human Fertilisation and Embryology Acts (HFE Acts)), with oversight by a powerful statutory regulator, the Human Fertilisation and Embryology Authority (HFEA). The creation of the HFEA was described as representing 'a milestone in biomedical regulation'.[5] The HFEA is responsible for licensing and monitoring centres carrying out *in-vitro* fertilisation (IVF), donor insemination and human embryo research and providing a range of detailed information for patients, professionals and government.[6] Noting the strengths of the British model of regulating fertility treatment and embryo research, Brazier stated:

> It ensures a degree of public accountability in the development and delivery both of new treatments and research procedures. It promotes high standards of medical practice and offers those lucky enough to benefit from advances made in reproductive medicine assurances that their treatment is not likely to be marred by gross misadventure delivered by maverick doctors, or rank 'amateurs' because the British system is built on consensus, regulators clinicians and scientists work well together.[7]

---

4 Ibid 167.
5 J Montgomery, 'Rights, Restraints and Pragmatism: The Human Fertilisation and Embryology Act 1990' (1991) 54 MLR 524, 524.
6 Department of Health, *Impact Assessment on the Human Fertilisation and Embryology Bill* (2008) (8 November 2007) [14] and [15] <http://www.dh.gov.uk/en/Publicationsandstatistics/Legislation/Regulatoryimpactassessment/DH_080209> (accessed 25 March 2015).
7 Brazier (n 1) 167.

As Brazier notes in her paper, 'reproductive medicine is singled out as special, a part of medicine of such particular social concern and significance that the state should have a direct stake in its evolution'.[8] A decade later when updating the legislation in this field, the government retained its position that this area should remain subject to specialist regulation:

> Ultimately, the Government believes that the force of law remains justified in the distribution of permissions, rights, responsibilities and prohibitions for the development and use of human reproductive technologies. Law and active regulation are necessary to set out and monitor a system of public oversight and accountability, taking account of the principles of good regulation.[9]

It was decided in 2008 to update the legislation. Legal challenges on numerous issues ranging from disputes over frozen embryos[10] the creation of saviour siblings[11] and the controversy surrounding reproductive cloning[12] highlighted the weaknesses of the HFE Act 1990. As pointed out by Brazier:

> Warnock deliberated at a very early stage of the 'reproductive revolution'. Neither the science, nor the infrastructure which now underpins the 'reproductive business' was well developed.[13]

Since its inception in 1990, the legal landscape within which the HFE Act 1990 was operating had altered greatly; The Human Rights Act 1998, The Gender Recognition Act 2004, The Human Tissue Act 2004 and The Civil Partnerships Act 2004 had all come into force. Numerous legislative initiatives and amendments had been introduced to consolidate the HFE Act 1990, often on an *ad hoc* basis. Such amendments included information disclosure in 1992;[14] in 2001 the purposes for which embryo research could be licensed were extended to allow for therapeutic stem cell research;[15] in the same year the Human Reproductive Cloning Act 2001 was passed; and in 2004, Parliament agreed that donor-conceived children would be able to access the identity of their

---

8 Brazier (n 1) 167
9 Department of Health (n 6) [7].
10 *Natalie Evans v Amicus Healthcare Ltd and Others; Lorraine Hadley v Midland Fertility Services Ltd and Others* [2003] EWCH 2161, [2004] 1 FLR 67 (Fam); *Natalie Evans v Amicus Healthcare Ltd and Others* [2004] EWCA (Civ) 72, [2004] 2 FLR 766, CA; *Case of Evans v The United Kingdom* (Application 6339/2005), [2006] 1 FCR 585 (ECtHR); *Evans v United Kingdom* (Application no 6339/05); [2007] 22 BHRC 190 [54] (ECtHR).
11 *R (on the application of Quintavalle) v HFEA* [2003] 3 ALL ER 257, [2005] 2 ALL ER 555.
12 *R v Secretary of State for Health, Ex P Quintavalle* [2003] 2 WLR 692.
13 Brazier (n 1) 173.
14 Human Fertilisation and Embryology (Disclosure of Information) Act 1992.
15 Human Fertilisation and Embryology (Research Purposes) Regulations 2001.

gamete donor on reaching the age of 18.[16] As these initiatives demonstrated, and as the government conceded, 'time, particularly in this field does not stand still'.[17] The HFEA acknowledged:

> the regulatory landscape has changed considerably over the last decade and human reproductive technologies have developed into both a mainstream and a complex, cutting-edge area of healthcare. Regulation of this field should adapt to these changes by trying to avoid overlap and by becoming more proportionate, efficient, targeted, flexible and able to accommodate new developments.[18]

It was fair to assert that the law in this area was 'marching with medicine, but in the rear and limping a little'.[19] Against this background the government belatedly accepted that if the legislative framework was not to be superseded by technology, it was time to redraft the 1990 legislation:

> The Government thought a review into existing legislation was timely and desirable in light of the development of new procedures and technologies in assisted reproduction, possible changes in public perceptions and attitudes on complex ethical issues, and the continuing need to ensure effective regulation in this area to reduce uncertainty and the scope for legal challenge.[20]

Following much activity in this area,[21] the HFE Act 2008 received Royal Assent on 13 November 2008. The majority of the HFE Act 2008's

---

16 Human Fertilisation and Embryology Authority (Disclosure of Donor Information) Regulations 2004.
17 Human Tissue and Embryos (Draft) Bill, (Cm 7087) foreword by Caroline Flint, Minister of State for Public Health, May 2007.
18 Human Fertilisation & Embryology Authority, *Response by the Human Fertilisation & Embryology Authority to the Department of Health's Consultation on the Review of the Human Fertilisation and Embryology Act* (24 November 2005) 2 <http://www.hfea.gov.uk/docs/ReviewoftheActResponse.pdf> (accessed 25 March 2015).
19 *Mount Isa Mines v Pusey* (1970) 125 CLR 383.
20 Department of Health (n 6) Evidence Base, Background [3].
21 The government announced a review of the HFE Act 1990 in January 2004 citing developments in reproductive medicine since the enactment of the 1990 legislation, and conducted a public consultation in 2005. In December 2006 the government published the policy proposals in the White Paper: *Review of the Human Fertilisation and Embryology Act: Proposals for Revised Legislation (including establishment of the Regulatory Authority for Tissue and Embryos)* (Cm 6989). The Human Tissue and Embryos (Draft) Bill (Cm 7087) followed in May 2007. This was scrutinised by the Joint Committee of both Houses: see the House of Lords and the House of Commons, *Joint Committee on the Human Tissue and Embryos (Draft) Bill*, July 2007 (HL Paper 169-I, HC Paper 630-I). Policy proposals from the White Paper and pre-legislative scrutiny were then incorporated into the Human Fertilisation and Embryology Bill which was introduced into Parliament on 8 November 2007.

The regulation of the reproduction business 215

amendments came into force in October 2009, with the exception of the provisions pertaining to parenthood, which commenced in April 2009. Welcoming Royal Assent, Professor Lisa Jardine, Chair of the HFEA, stated:

> This is a momentous day for the HFEA and for those with fertility problems. The regulatory system that has served us so well has been renewed. Parliament has provided a clear framework for the future and a solid base on which to regulate 21st century practice within 21st century law.[22]

Jardine was perhaps overly optimistic about the achievements of the new legislation. This chapter will demonstrate that in certain areas the HFE Act 2008 has failed to overcome some of the weaknesses and inconsistencies of the HFE Act 1990.

Surrogacy: Still a special case?

A significant part of Brazier's paper discussed the 'special' case of surrogacy. At that time, surrogacy was one of the most controversial infertility techniques available but had escaped the reach of the HFEA and the professionalisation which characterised other fertility services.[23] Official rates of surrogacy have increased significantly over the intervening years. Since 2007, numbers of UK Parental Orders (PO) (which transfer legal parentage from a surrogate to the commissioning couple) have increased from 50 per year in 1995 to around 203 in 2013.[24]

Surrogacy separates motherhood from gestation and in so doing challenges traditional understandings of how we define who a mother is. The law has, however, resisted revising our notions of these roles in line with surrogacy, deeming it too disruptive and troublesome to do so.[25] For example, consultations in advance of the drafting of the HFE Act 2008 failed to consider changing provisions defining parenthood following surrogacy from those based on gestation to ones taking account of pre-conception intentions to care.[26] More than other forms of assisted reproduction, surrogacy also challenges our understanding of fertility services as essentially a medical endeavour; issues of recompense for reproductive labour – whether through expenses or through payment – leave

---

22 Human Fertilisation and Embryology Authority, Press Release, 'HFEA Chair Welcomes Royal Assent for HFE Act', 13 November 2008 <http://www.hfea.gov.uk/en/1746.html> (accessed 25 March 2015).
23 Brazier (n 1) 167.
24 E Blyth, M Crawshaw and O van den Akker, 'What are the best interests of the child in international surrogacy?' (2014) 742 Bionews.
25 See K Horsey 'Challenging presumptions: legal parenthood and surrogacy arrangements' (2010) 22 CFLQ 440.
26 Ibid 453.

many deeply uncomfortable. For example, the Warnock report stated that surrogacy 'is inconsistent with human dignity that a woman should use her uterus for financial profit and use it as an incubator for someone else's child'.[27] Surrogacy also resists professionalisation due to the lack of medical intervention required in some forms of surrogacy, in particular partial surrogacy established via self-insemination where a surrogate uses her own egg. As Brazier put it, in the context of assisted reproduction, 'legislators and judges perceive surrogacy as both special and especially problematic'.[28]

There was a hope among the Warnock Committee that surrogacy arrangements would fade away; the Committee feared that regulation and professionalisation would be counterproductive by actually encouraging arrangements.[29] Yet lack of regulation is perhaps not the best solution to this practice where risk, confusion and fears of harm to both child and surrogate are high. Drawing on the Surrogacy Review she chaired in 1998, Brazier proposed that surrogacy legislation should be reviewed and a new regulatory system be implemented.[30] She argued that all agencies involved in assisting surrogacy be registered with the Department of Health and subject to a Code of Practice. Following Warnock, she also rejected advocating overt payment for a surrogate's services. Brazier described such reforms as offering a 'policy of containment'[31] which would better regulate the practice in a way that would be unlikely to encourage it. The proposals she suggested in the Review were never acted upon.

In 2015 the 'special' and 'problematic' practice of surrogacy is even more challenging, and it has been argued that the 'law governing surrogacy remains confused, incoherent and poorly adapted to the specific realities of the practice of surrogacy'.[32] With her usual prescience, Brazier had foreseen many of the current problems. Discussing the efforts to restrict the role of commerce in reproductive medicine in the UK, she wrote that 'those wealthy enough to participate in reproduction markets can readily evade their domestic constraints'[33] and foresaw that the effects of reproductive tourism may be a bigger test of British law than all other dilemmas. This is indeed true of surrogacy. The ban on commercialisation of surrogacy in the UK[34] has led to a shortage of surrogates here. A ready supply of surrogates as well as enforceable contracts in

---

27 *Report of the Committee of Inquiry into Human Fertilisation and Embryology* (Cmnd. 9314 1984) 345.
28 Brazier (n 1) 179.
29 (n 27).
30 The proposals were taken from the government commissioned review which Brazier chaired. See *Review for Health Ministers of Current Arrangements for Payments and Regulation*, (Cm. 4068) (1998).
31 Brazier (n 1) 183.
32 K Horsey and S Sheldon 'Still Hazy after All These Years: The Law Regulating Surrogacy' (2012) 20 Med L Rev 67.
33 Brazier (n 1) 193.
34 The Surrogacy Arrangements Act 1985.

other countries provides incentives for increasing numbers of intending parents from the UK to travel abroad in order to found their family. Yet such foreign arrangements continue to generate problems for and test the current boundaries of British law. For instance, due to conflicting laws on surrogacy in different jurisdictions, children born through foreign surrogacy have been refused entry to the UK on the basis that the person the UK recognises as the legal mother is the foreign surrogate, regardless of whether the genetic mother is a UK citizen. Children are thus being left 'marooned stateless and parentless', as in the case of *X v Y*.[35] This is exacerbated by the lack of accurate information that the voluntary and unaccredited surrogacy agencies sometimes provide to intending parents.[36]

Furthermore, the law is not only being tested but is also proving ineffective. While there is a ban on anything other than the payment of 'reasonable expenses' to surrogates in the UK,[37] excessive payments have been made. While the courts can refuse to issue a PO on the grounds of paying over what is deemed to be reasonable expenses, such denial of legal parenthood to a child would conflict with the Human Fertilisation and Embryology (Parental Orders) Regulations 2010 which provide that the child's welfare must now be the court's paramount consideration when granting a PO. As a result, payments made which have exceeded 'reasonable expenses' have been retrospectively authorised by the courts in at least seven cases in the last five years, and the courts have made it clear that a PO would only be withheld in cases of the most blatant abuse of public policy.[38] The law in this context clearly is not working. In those cases where medical intervention is not required, such as where self-insemination is undertaken, current regulation is also compounding problems. Restrictive legislation and lack of surrogates may be driving some to use such informal routes to establishing surrogacy arrangements, such as in the case of *CW v NT*,[39] which leaves all parties subject to physical, economic and emotional risks.[40]

Calls for more effective regulation and professionalisation of surrogacy are becoming stronger.[41] This includes proposals Brazier advocated over ten years ago such as accreditation of surrogacy agencies.[42] Many, including Brazier, have argued that it is also time to reconsider the ban on payments to surrogate

---

35 *X v Y (Foreign surrogacy)* [2008] EWCH 3030 [Fam].
36 A Alghrani, D Griffiths and M Brazier 'Surrogacy Law: From Piecemeal Tweaks to Sustained Review and Reform' in A Diduck, N Peleg and H Reece (eds), *Law and Michael Freeman* (Brill Publishers 2015).
37 Ibid.
38 Ibid.
39 [2011] EWHC 33 (Fam).
40 Brazier (n 1) 181.
41 Horsey and Sheldon (n 32). See also N Gamble and H Prosser, 'The "Brilliant Beginnings" of Surrogacy Reform in the UK' (2013) 27 Bionews.
42 *Review for Health Ministers of Current Arrangements for Payments and Regulation* (Cm. 4068) (1998).

mothers.[43] This would make the law more coherent by ensuring there is no conflict between ensuring a child's best interests and not exceeding reasonable expenses. Offering payment may also perhaps increase the supply of surrogates in the UK, thereby reducing the demand for foreign surrogates. Brazier's previous work highlighted the potential risks of such a regulated market in motherhood including the potential for exploitation of vulnerable women. There is rich debate on the meaning of exploitation in the context of surrogacy.[44] Regardless of the extent to which we consider it exploitative, intending parents are already founding a family through commercial foreign surrogacy and paying women who may be more vulnerable to exploitation than women in the UK. The climate in which surrogacy is operating has altered dramatically since Brazier's paper, something she forecast. We live in an age where the use of the internet to facilitate private arrangements or international surrogacy is a fingertip away. Brazier's 'policy of containment' is now perhaps unfeasible. Furthermore, UK surrogates are currently performing a crucial and valued job for many infertile people; perhaps it is time that they are recompensed properly for such labour. Thus, as well as the need to be better equipped to deal with new advances in reproductive technologies, there is an urgency for current regulation to be better equipped to deal with old ones such as surrogacy.

Despite such significant changes in surrogacy arrangements in the UK, at a governmental level, there has been a familiar response characterised by the hope the practice will fade away. Despite increasing pressure to change legislation over the past ten years, the Department of Health and other relevant agencies have remained relatively resistant to any change in the law. In consultations on the amendments to the HFE Act 1990, ministers indicated that surrogacy was a sensitive issue which would be looked at separately. In section 7 of the consultation, it was stated that 'the government ha[d] agreed to consider the need to review surrogacy arrangements and . . . gauge public and professional opinions on what, if any, changes [might] be needed to the law and regulation as it relate[d] to surrogacy'.[45] Yet, ten years later no firm commitment for this review, or a date, has ever been set.[46] It seems that for the government, the issue of surrogacy is still as special and problematic as it was 15 years ago, and the lack of reform in this area is still related to a desire that the practice will fade away. The result of this is that there is a failure properly to re-conceptualise or accept what family and parenthood are in the context of surrogacy. Fears of public backlash mean that it will be a brave political party which will take on the issue and push for law reform. While there may be a similar level of institutional

---

43 See Alghrani, Griffiths and Brazier (n 36).
44 S Wilkinson 'The Exploitation Argument against Commerical Surrogacy' (2003) 17 Bioethics 169.
45 Department of Health, *Review of the Human Fertilisation and Embryology Act: A Public Consultation* (August 2005) [7.14].
46 N Gamble and L Ghevaert 'Moving Surrogacy Law Forward? The Department of Health's Consultation on Parental Orders' (2009) 532 Bionews.

silence on the issue of surrogacy as there was when Brazier wrote her paper, rates of surrogacy are increasing along with the concomitant problems it raises in the courts and in families due to outdated legalisation. As these problems become ever more prevalent, the government may be forced to commit to the review they promised over ten years ago, bringing an end to them *avoiding* 'the same issues in different guises' in the context of surrogacy.[47]

'What's the fuss about donor gametes?':[48] Mitochondria replacement

In the context of gamete donation in the UK, Brazier noted that much of the 'fuss' has revolved around control of one's own genetic heritage and how tightly an individual should retain command over their own genes.[49] Schedule 3 of the HFE Act 1990 establishes high standards of consent for gamete donors and requires anyone storing gametes or embryos to decide on what may be done with those materials before any treatment begins. Brazier interpreted schedule 3 as being designed to protect the donor's genetic heritage. This is certainly true when we look at cases where there has been conflict between the donors of genetic material such as in the cases of Diane Blood and Natalie Evans. Here, the donor's interests in control over their genes have taken precedence over those of the infertile individual.[50] In the case involving Ms Evans, after she had found out that she had to have both ovaries removed due to pre-cancerous growths, she and her partner underwent IVF and signed the relevant consent forms to store the resulting embryos for future use. After the relationship broke down, Ms Evans' partner withdrew consent for the use of the stored embryos. Evans took her case through the UK courts[51] and on to the European Court of Human Rights,[52] where she lost her five-year battle to use the stored embryos. The judges stated they did not consider her right to become a parent in the genetic sense deserved greater respect than her former fiancé's right not to have a child with her. For Brazier, it seems that the law has favoured the donor's interests in their genes over those of the infertile individual.

Adding consistency to this principle in a very different way, at the time of Brazier's paper, gamete donors were anonymous and no identifying information could be given to their genetic offspring. As Brazier notes, this framework appears to centre on protecting the interests of donors above their 'offspring's interest in their genetic heritage'.[53] While these donors consented to their gametes being used, there is a well-known interest in wanting to donate but remain

---

47 Brazier (n 1) 166.
48 Ibid 18.
49 Ibid 83.
50 *R v Human Fertilisation and Embryology Authority Ex P Blood* [1997] 2 All ER 687, CA; *Evans v Amicus Healthcare Ltd* [2003] EWHC 2161 (Fam).
51 *Evans v Amicus Healthcare Ltd* [2004] EWCA Civ 727.
52 *Evans v United Kingdom* (6339/05) [2007] 2 FCR 5.
53 Brazier (n 1) 186.

anonymous.⁵⁴ Typically the donor does not donate in order to become a parent and presumably wishes to remain unknown to resulting children. Relatedly, such protection of donors is also strategic; it ensures the continuing supply of gametes. However, it is not just protection of donors at issue here; there is another factor at play.

Kirsty Horsey has pointed out that many areas of the HFE Act 2008 are a reflection of what 'lawmakers think that a family should "look like"'.⁵⁵ That is, the law reflects cultural and political norms. While disclosure of genetic origins has been established for some time in cases of adoption, such disclosure in donor conception families has raised much more sensitivity giving rise to secrets in family and kin networks.⁵⁶ Families who have used gamete donors have most often kept it a secret in order to pass as a 'normal' genetically related family.⁵⁷ Donor anonymity enshrined in law could be said to support this notion, aiding families to keep 'their secret' and pass as a genetic family.

Since Brazier's paper, the law has been changed, and the Human Fertilisation and Embryology Authority (Disclosure of Donor Information) Regulations 2004 abolished anonymous donation. Donor-conceived children are considered to have the 'right to know' about their genetic origins, and family secrets are seen as harmful.⁵⁸ This growing impetus reflects a general policy shift towards the idea that openness about genetic history is in the best interests of children.⁵⁹ This is related to what is known as the 'geneticisation of everyday', the growing and socially constructed tendency to see familiar relationships as being determined in the most part by genetics.⁶⁰ Here, then, it seems that the interests of donors have been trumped; the importance of a donor-conceived adult's knowledge of their genetic heritage is deemed more important.⁶¹ Yet studies focusing on donor insemination have found that since the change in law, a high proportion of parents still state an intention never to reveal the genetically 'true'

---

54 L Frith, 'Donor conception and mandatory paternity testing: the right to know and the right to be told' (2013) 13 American Journal of Bioethics 50.
55 K Horsey, 'Challenging Presumptions: legal parenthood and surrogacy arrangements' (2010) 22 CFLQ 453.
56 P Nordqvist and C Smart, *Relative Strangers. Family and Intimate Life* (Palgrave Macmillan 2014).
57 Ibid. This applies of course only to heterosexual families, in same-sex couples it is more obvious that a gamete donor would have been used.
58 Nuffield Council on Bioethics, 'Donor Conception: Ethical Aspects of Information Sharing' (2013) <http://nuffieldbioethics.org/wp-content/uploads/2014/06/Donor_conception_report_2013.pdf> (accessed 25 March 2015).
59 T Freeman et al. 'Gamete Donation: Parents' Experiences of Searching for their Child's Donor Siblings and Donor' (2009) 24 Human Reproduction 505.
60 J Edwards, *Born and Bred: Idioms of Kinship and New Reproductive Technologies in England* (OUP 2000).
61 As Brazier predicted, the shift to non-anonymity has been linked to a shortage of gamete donors in the UK. See A Pacey, 'Sperm donor recruitment in the UK' (2010) 12 The Obstetrician & Gynaecologist 43.

background of their children.[62] Due to the importance of genetics, there is a fear among many parents that telling a child their 'real' genetic heritage will undermine the non-genetic parental relationship they have built. Thus the law may now reflect a new cultural norm, the imperative to reveal genetic heritage, but this is at odds with the existing norm of the 'the genetic family'[63] and the imperative to pass as a biologically related family.

Techniques of mitochondria replacement have recently added a new dimension to debates on the donation of gametes. In February 2015, MPs voted to approve the draft Human Fertilisation and Embryology (Mitochondrial Donation) Regulations which will allow for mitochondrial donation techniques to be used as part of IVF treatment to prevent the transmission of serious mitochondrial disease from a mother to her child. Although the techniques differ, they all involve the donation of an egg in which the nucleus is discarded and the mitochondria are used to replace the faulty mitochondria of the intending mother. This has led to descriptions of the practice creating 'three parent babies'. However, refuting such a three parent tag and contrasting with current regulations on gamete donation, mitochondria donors will be anonymous and treated more like organ donors.[64] Such anonymity is said to be due to the fact that mitochondria DNA (mtDNA) accounts for a mere 0.054% of our overall DNA and it does not have any impact on the physical characteristics and personality traits of any resulting child, which come solely from nuclear DNA.

However, the impact of mitochondria on identity is contested.[65] For example, mtDNA is a validated technique for the identification of skeletons in forensics and can be used in genealogy.[66] MtDNA clearly has some effect on identity in these circumstances, and, while it is indisputably different from nuclear DNA, it is still genetic material and so somewhat different to donating a kidney. The HFEA conducted public consultations on mtDNA replacement techniques, and while they found broad support for the technique, the three parent tag, regardless of how accurate or not that tag is, was deemed too controversial and potentially harmful to the resulting children and acceptance of the technique itself. Thus the links between genetic parenthood and mtDNA were deliberately detached and played down. For example, in policy consultations, mtDNA was stressed to be just a battery with no significance for a resulting child's identity. While this is to an extent true, mtDNA are still genes and we know that genes

---

62 C Smart, 'Family Secrets: Law and Understandings of Openness in Everyday Relationships' (2009) 38(4) Journal of Social Policy 551–567.
63 M Strathern, *Kinship, Law and the Unexpected: Relatives are Always a Surprise* (CUP 2005).
64 The Human Fertilisation and Embryology (Mitochondrial Donation) Regulations 2015.
65 A Bredenoord, W Dondorp, G Pennings et al., 'Ethics of Modifying the Mitochondrial Genome' (2011) 37 *JME* 97.
66 C Jones and I Holme, 'Relatively (Im)material: mtDNA and Genetic Relatedness in Law and Policy' (2013) 9 Life Sciences, Society and Policy 1.

matter to people.⁶⁷ The provision of anonymity for mtDNA donors cannot be wholly related to the quantities of genes they provide. Rather, it also relates to the prevailing cultural and political constructs engendered in legalisation surrounding reproductive technologies. While the primacy of genetic heritage now rules in one area, in another it is deemed too disruptive of current norms. As Brazier noted, 'British law displays contradictions, no single, coherent philosophy underpins the law's response to reproductive medicine.'⁶⁸ Instead, and as seen in the regulation of gamete donation and mtDNA donation, the law's response is often underpinned by prevailing cultural norms and a failure to reassess what parenthood means in the context of reproductive technologies. This failure results in the contradictory versions of parenthood that are currently recognised in legislation: for example, the prominence of the genetic parent in one context and not another and the significance of gestational links in one area of law but not another.

Conclusion

There have been many developments in reproductive medicine since Brazier wrote her seminal piece on its regulation over 15 years ago. The HFE Act 2008 was a regulatory attempt to keep pace with them, but as we have shown, this has failed in a number of areas. Regulation continues to lack 'conceptual depth',⁶⁹ illustrated in inconsistent definitions of parenthood and motherhood, and in the unwillingness to introduce changes that would be disruptive of traditional understandings of these roles. A reason underpinning such inconsistencies is the fact that law in this sphere 'is really only a reflection of what lawmakers think that a family should look like'.⁷⁰ In one area it is emphasised that genetic ties should be revealed regardless of any care and intention to parent (as in the case of donor conception); in another, genetic ties are downplayed and excluded when they are deemed to rupture the traditional family too much (as in the case of mtDNA replacement techniques). In other areas such as surrogacy the law reflects a hope that certain techniques will disappear rather than a recognition of the realities of incidence and practice which raise uncomfortable questions about reproduction and parenthood. Despite such inconsistencies, Brazier noted in 1999 that 'a regulatory system is in place and perhaps suggests that pragmatism has its advantages'.⁷¹ As Britain is to become the first country in the world to allow the use of mitochondria replacement techniques in humans, giving light to many families afflicted by this disease, and as surrogacy is blossoming in the UK, albeit with numerous problems, perhaps such pragmatic inconsistencies have their advantages.

67 Strathern (n 63).
68 Brazier (n 1) 167.
69 Ibid.
70 Horsey (n 55) 453.
71 Brazier (n 1) 167.

19 Regulating responsible reproduction

David Archard

Margaret Brazier writes with a rare combination of great legal knowledge, robust common sense, a refusal to accept anything on trust or on account of its possibly distinguished provenance, a willingness to make her own personal views known without an intolerant disregard for the contrary views, and a welcome sensitivity to the real life tragedies and difficult personal circumstances that must necessarily lie behind and be affected by legal judgments. At bottom, medical law concerns people who are (or who are not but should be) receiving medical treatment or who have suffered in their attempt to be treated. The practice of medicine makes a real difference to how well people's lives go. The practice of medical law should reflect this basic fact. Brazier's writing has always been alive to this requirement and it consequently displays real practical wisdom, informed by judgements of what is right that do not derive from the rigid observance of rules and that is also conjoined with a sense of why what is right matters to real flesh and blood human beings.

Nowhere is this wisdom more evident than in her writing on the regulation of reproduction. I want to consider what she says in two pieces: 'Liberty, Responsibility, Maternity' and 'Regulating the Reproduction Business?'.[1] I want to offer some critical thoughts about her views, albeit in a spirit of sympathetic engagement with a position that I find congenial.

In the first piece, Brazier insists upon the need for 'procreative responsibility'. Her insistence is refreshing. However, it does go against the grain both of orthodox bioethics and, apparently, of a feminist view that women alone should be left free to determine whether and how to reproduce.[2] Her overall position is, I think, consonant with common sense. However, it is hard to defend. I want to spell out why and then, since her concern is with the regulation of procreation, to say something about what difference her stance on these matters ought to make.

---

1 'Liberty, Responsibility, Maternity' (1999) 51(1) CLP 359–391; 'Regulating the Reproduction Business?' (1999) 7 Med L Rev 166–193.
2 For excellent guides to the philosophical literature see E Brake and J Millum, 'Procreation and Parenthood', and D Satz, 'Feminist Perspectives on Reproduction and the Family', both in *The Stanford Encyclopedia of Philosophy* <http://plato.stanford.edu/> (accessed 23 January 2015).

What I have termed the bioethics orthodoxy subscribes to the view that all individuals have a strong presumptive liberty of procreation constrained only by the requirement to avoid harm. In the case of procreation, the key relevant harm is to the offspring, and under the influence of two assumptions it would be rare indeed if a procreator caused harm to his or her future child.

The two assumptions are as follows: first, that a life is worth living if, on balance and overall, it is better than non-existence (often, although not always, this is taken as being of the same negative value as death); and, second, that procreators who procreate at a different time or under different circumstances so as to create a child with better (or worse) life prospects do not thereby create a better (or worse) version of the same child, but an entirely different child. This second assumption is the influential 'non-identity' condition due to the work of Derek Parfit.[3]

The upshot of the two assumptions is this: procreating a child with what are known in advance to be terrible life prospects does not harm that child if and insofar as its life is still better (even if only just) than non-existence, and inasmuch as the only alternatives to creating this child are creating no child at all or creating an entirely different child. This means that a couple who deliberately have a child that they know will inherit an awful condition do not harm that child if its life is at least marginally better than not being born at all.

Common sense will surely insist that the couple act wrongly. Common sense is, it seems to me, right to do so. But here is the problem. We cannot explain their wrongfulness in terms of a harm done to the child – for the reasons sketched above. And any attempt to explain the wrongfulness of their procreative acts in ways that do not make essential reference to what is done to the child would seem to fail to capture what in such cases is wrongful. It is not that, somehow, the couple do wrong in some impersonal sense of making the *world* worse; they do wrong by wronging *this* child.[4]

One way forward is to maintain that there is no simple liberty to procreate constrained only by an avoidance of external harm to third parties. Rather, there is a freedom to procreate internally constrained by a duty to do so with proper regard for the child created. Thus, Onora O'Neill has argued for a right to beget or bear that is 'contingent upon begetters and bearers having or making some feasible plan for their child to be adequately reared'.[5] And I have argued that procreators wrong a future child if they cannot reasonably assure the child the enjoyment of its basic rights.[6]

---

3 D Parfit, *Reasons and Persons* (Clarendon Press 1987) 357–366.
4 For a critical review of the philosophical literature on this topic see my 'Procreating' in S. Luper (ed), *The Cambridge Companion to Life and Death* (CUP 2014).
5 O O'Neill, 'Begetting, Bearing and Rearing' in O O'Neill and W Ruddick (eds), *Having Children: Philosophical and Legal Reflections on Parenthood* (OUP 1979) 25–38.
6 D Archard, 'Wrongful Life' (2004) 3 Philosophy 403–420. I have discussed what I take to be some of the problems of O'Neill's approach in my 'Procreative rights and procreative duties' in D Archard, M Deveaux, N Manson and D Weinstock (eds), *Reading Onora O'Neill* (Routledge 2013) 157–171.

I think Brazier's defence of responsible procreation is in this same spirit, and she understands responsibility precisely in terms of the welfare of the future child. Now there are various problems with this approach, one of which is that of the threshold. On the orthodox view, one may procreate so long as one creates a life that is better than non-existence. Some of course think that one cannot make the comparison – including the judge in the celebrated English wrongful life case *McKay v Essex Health Authority* who asserted that '[n]o comparison is possible' since the court 'can know nothing' of non-existence.[7] But so long as one *can* make such a comparison, then the compared terms – this particular life and the 'death' suffered by not coming into existence – readily allow a judgement as to which is better. Life, even a terrible one, wins out.

Brazier's preferred threshold is different. Although in 'Liberty, Responsibility, Maternity' she initially talks about responsible procreation in terms of a more general obligation simply to 'to seek to avoid causing suffering to other people',[8] she is later clear about her disagreement with the orthodoxy:

> a threshold turning either on whether harm to the child is avoidable or on a 'better not to live at all' test, is set too low. If as a society we recognize that every human being is entitled to protection of those basic interests which constitute a decent life, the children we plan to bear or beget enjoy just the same entitlements. If potential disability or disadvantage significantly impairs a child's prospects of enjoying a life free from degrading treatment, free from acute pain and suffering of mind or body, endowed with dignity and protected by security of his person, a choice to bring him into the world regardless is morally questionable.[9]

I think this fits with the child's 'birthright' approach that I have defended and that is indebted to important work by Joel Feinberg:

> if you cannot have that to which you have a birthright then you are wronged if you are brought to birth. Thus, if the conditions for the eventual fulfilment of the child's future interests are destroyed before he is born, the child can claim, after he has been born, that his *rights* (his present rights) have been violated.[10]

Bonnie Steinbock, also indebted to Feinberg, talks about a child's entitlement to a 'minimally decent existence'.[11]

---

7 *McKay v Essex Health Authority* [1982] 2 All ER 771, 787 and 790.
8 'Liberty, Responsibility, Maternity' (n 1) 369.
9 Ibid 373.
10 J Feinberg, *Harm to Others*, vol 1 of his *The Moral Limits of the Criminal Law* (OUP 1984) 99.
11 B Steinbock, 'The Logical Case for "Wrongful Life"' (1986) 16 Hastings Center Report 19.

I have no quarrel with the substantive content of the child's putative birthright. My difficulties – and they afflict my own account as much as Brazier's – are in two areas. First, it needs to be clear what motivates the specification of this threshold. At least the orthodoxy can rest the defence of its threshold on the key notion of harm and the comparison it implies between living and not living. What motivates the adoption of the more stringent threshold? It is not enough to say that it fits with common sense, as philosophers will remind us that the task of critical normative reflection is to subject common sense to robust review and reject what will not withstand such scrutiny.

It will not do, either, to invite a comparison with how we ought responsibly to treat those who are already alive: because we might be required to do no more than not harm others, and because defenders of the orthodoxy will insist upon the radical difference between what we owe to those already in existence and what we owe to those we might bring into existence.

The second difficulty with Brazier's preferred threshold of 'responsible' procreation is how it might guide the regulation of procreation. The orthodoxy's advice to the regulator is relatively straightforward: 'You can allow individuals to procreate so long as they do not harm the resultant offspring in doing so.' This provides a relatively clear line between permissible and impermissible procreation, and also gives the procreator considerable latitude. Indeed, one defender of the orthodoxy, Stephen Wilkinson, spells it out in the following terms and in respect of deliberately choosing a disabled future child: 'the upshot of this is that while a handful of selecting for disability cases can be condemned because the resultant child would be "better off not existing", the majority cannot be criticized on this ground.'[12] Note that Wilkinson does not just say that most cases are permitted, but that they are not even open to criticism!

By contrast, a threshold that talks in terms of a 'decent' life is open to enormous difficulties of interpretation, and consequently of difficulties in regulatory implementation. Brazier is clear, however, that she is not demanding that responsible procreation as she understands it be enforced by regulatory measures. Indeed, I read her as wishing the law to stay out of reproductive choices even where these are to have children whose lives would be worse than non-existence.

There are at least two reasons why one would not wish to use the law to enforce responsible procreation. These are not mutually exclusive and might both apply in some circumstances. The first is that the bar for the warranted use of legal coercion should be set reasonably high – to prevent or deter egregious wrongful actions – and irresponsible procreation falls below that bar. The second is that the use of the law is not feasible: the harms are not ones that the law can prevent or are those that it can prevent only at an unreasonably high cost. John Stuart Mill's harm principle is the background normative precept,

---

12 S Wilkinson, *Choosing Tomorrow's Children: The ethics of selective reproduction* (Clarendon Press 2010) 97.

and he understood the avoidance of harm to be the necessary but not sufficient ground for the legal proscription of an act.[13] In other words, he thought that the law could in principle prevent some instances of harm but would only be able to do so in a manner that overall and on balance caused greater harms than those that would be prevented. On his view, the law should not proscribe these harmful acts.

I think Brazier believes that the second reason applies in the case of responsible procreation. She speaks thus of 'unthinkably draconian restrictions'[14] on a woman's choice to conceive and of the 'practicalities of defying a legal norm of behaviour'.[15] She also, consistent with her feminist commitments and with her sympathies for those who make very difficult personal choices, believes that it is an impossible task for the law to determine exactly what might motivate someone to reproduce in a putatively irresponsible manner.

This seems fair. However, I am less persuaded that the case for not legally regulating the irresponsible choices of the *infertile* can be made in the same way. Brazier believes that it is appropriate to grant to clinicians a right to determine that they will not assist in realizing the morally irresponsible procreative choices of the infertile. Nevertheless, she is clear that '*legal* constraints on access to assisted conception mandating consideration of the impact of a couple's reproductive choice on their future offspring are unjustified'. And she thinks this is 'because no similar legal constraints fetter the reproductive freedom of the fertile'.[16]

Here, as her citation indicates, she is impressed by John Harris's view that the entitlements of the fertile and of the infertile to procreate are equally well grounded. Hence there should be no moral asymmetry: if restrictions of the fertile are unwarranted, then so too are those of the infertile.[17] Again citing Harris in 'Regulating the Reproduction Business?', she asks, rhetorically one presumes, 'The law does not interfere with the reproductive choices of the naturally fertile. What justification is there for interference with the choices of the unfortunately infertile?'[18]

However, the response to her rhetorical question is simple. There *is* a morally relevant difference between restricting the fertile and the infertile, namely that the moral costs of doing so in the former case are unconscionable, whereas they are not in the case of the latter. A refusal of treatment on the grounds of the welfare of the future child is not of the same order as compelling a woman to abort her fetus, sterilizing her or pursuing a criminal prosecution of her after the birth of the child.

---

13 JS Mill, *On Liberty* (1859) <https://ebooks.adelaide.edu.au/m/mill/john_stuart/m645o/>.
14 'Liberty, Responsibility, Maternity' (n 1) 385.
15 Ibid 380.
16 Ibid 388.
17 J Harris, *The Value of Life* (Routledge and Kegan Paul 1985) 150–155.
18 'Regulating the Reproduction Business?' (n 1) 175.

Moreover, exposing the moral difference between the two kinds of case brings into sharper focus the strength of the obligation to reproduce responsibly. For the costs of legally preventing the fertile from being irresponsible procreators are at least *prima facie* so great as to outweigh the harm done to the prospective children. By contrast, the costs of legally preventing the infertile from being irresponsible procreators are *not* so great as to outweigh the harms they might otherwise cause to the future child.

Thus one might assert that the first ground for not legally proscribing irresponsible procreation – the threshold extent of the harm – is met, but that the second ground – the costs of doing so – is met only in the case of the fertile. In short, Brazier might grant the moral asymmetry between the cases of the infertile and the fertile, and thereby give real regulatory teeth to her ideal of procreative responsibility. She would thus avoid the charge she makes against herself of 'cowardice' by not 'clothing' the obligation to reproduce responsibly with 'the force of law'.[19]

Brazier is suspicious of regulating reproduction yet equally clear about the importance of recognizing that reproduction should be responsible. The problem lies in knowing how a society can acknowledge that obligation without enforcing it. This problem is compounded by Brazier's entirely warranted claim, in 'Regulating the Reproduction Business?', that Britain's approach to the regulation of artificial reproduction, consequent upon the enactment of the Warnock Committee Report, is both generally permissive and essentially pragmatic.[20]

The charge of conceptual fudging made by many philosophical and legal commentators is entirely fair. Indeed, Warnock herself is very clear in her own account of how the Committee Report was drafted that she abandoned any attempt to use the 'inflammatory' language of 'right' and 'wrong'. Instead, she affirms, 'the very best one could hope for was to find something roughly "acceptable"'.[21] Pragmatism reigned over moral principle.

Yet the problem of regulation is even worse. First, however well Britain might choose to regulate artificial reproduction, the choice is still open to infertile couples to travel abroad. We can stop someone from providing unlicensed fertility treatment in the United Kingdom (UK). We can even stop someone from importing gametes for use in a licensed UK clinic if the procurement and use of those gametes would not be legal in the UK – if, for instance, the gamete donor was to remain anonymous or be paid a sum significantly in excess of that permitted in the UK. In the same fashion, we can prevent someone from exporting gametes obtained in a licensed UK clinic if they would be used in a foreign clinic in a manner that would be forbidden in the UK. What we cannot

---

19 'Liberty, Responsibility, Maternity' (n 1) 390.
20 'Regulating the Reproduction Business?' (n 1) 174.
21 M Warnock, *Nature and Mortality: Reflections of a philosopher in public life* (Continuum Press 2003) 98.

do is prevent anyone from simply travelling abroad and securing treatment there that would not be permitted in the UK.

All of this means that the more robust the regulation of artificial reproduction in the UK, the more likely it is that the infertile here will simply evade that regulation and travel abroad. Such is the nature of 'reproductive tourism'.

To the possibility of travel we should add a further feature of modern fertility treatment. It can be bought and sold. Brazier is thus absolutely right to state that, 'The most profound change in regulating reproductive medicine since Warnock is ... the dramatically increased role of commerce'.[22] Those with money, and desperate to have children, will pay to increase their chances of having them. They will pay for what they can obtain abroad, especially if they believe that it is denied to them or made more difficult in the UK.

John Stuart Mill thought that trade – producing and selling goods and services – is a 'social act' and thereby subject to the constraints of the harm principle. However, he also thought that, on balance and consistent with a laissez-faire principle, the harms of intervention into a free market outweighed those other-regarding harms one might prevent.[23] He further thought that consumers should be free to use their income in whatever way they wished to do, so long as their purchased goods and services harmed no-one else. Thus there might be *some* reasons to intervene in the market, but not, he was inclined to judge, ones sufficiently strong to warrant preventing people from buying fertility services. Moreover, Mill was talking about regulating the market of *a* liberal society. The harm principle does not warrant any state in attempting to regulate what its citizens might choose to purchase outside its jurisdiction. In a global market anything can be bought and sold.

Brazier is right in consequence to say, in a concluding sentence of her 'Regulating the Reproduction Business?', that, 'The international ramifications of the reproductive business may prove to be a more stringent test of the strength of British law than all the difficult ethical dilemmas that have gone before.'[24] Indeed, for no-one seriously suggests that those seeking to have babies should be legally prevented from leaving the country to have treatment elsewhere.

The question mark in her article title indicates a clear doubt about the point of regulation. She does not doubt that reproduction is now a business. And, if the reach and effectiveness of national regulation is uncertain, the ethical dilemmas of which she speaks may only be academic (in the worst sense of that word). The Human Fertilisation and Embryology Authority (HFEA) might set an excellent example of addressing those dilemmas but still only be able to give limited practical effect – within the UK alone – to those principles that, after consideration of the 'difficult ethical dilemmas', it has come to think critical.

---

22 'Regulating the Reproduction Business?' (n 1) 191.
23 Mill (n 13) ch V, para 4.
24 'Regulating the Reproduction Business?' (n 1) 193.

The irony of Brazier's two pieces taken together is this. She thinks that the law should not enforce responsible reproduction, but also that any attempt to do so would be somewhat beside the point given what prospectively irresponsible procreators can do to evade the short arm reach of the regulator.

That of course does not make her wrong to insist on the importance of responsible reproduction, or to worry about the consistency of the principles that underlie the regulation of reproduction, or to be sceptical about how effective any regulatory machinery can be in a global market where individuals are only too willing to travel and pay a lot of money to have children. In all of this she is characteristically thoughtful, compassionate, and unafraid to say what others do not and will not say.

20 Donor conception and information disclosure

Welfare or consent?

*Rosamund Scott**

Introduction

In relation to the regulation of assisted reproduction in the United Kingdom (UK), Margaret Brazier has very insightfully observed that 'all too often crucial issues of individual rights, the balance between rights and public policy, and issues of conflicting rights are skated over'.[1] This might well be thought to be true of the construction of the welfare of the child clause of the Human Fertilisation and Embryology (HFE) Act 1990 (as amended by the HFE Act 2008), which stipulates that '[a] woman shall not be provided with treatment services unless account has been taken of the welfare of any child who may be born as a result (including the need of that child for supportive parenting)'.[2] Despite being amended, the clause retains a controversial and contested status in the regulation of assisted reproduction treatment.[3]

The law was also amended in an important way relevant to the welfare of future children in 2005, such that donor conception treatment could no longer proceed on an anonymous basis. Thus, a donor-conceived person conceived after this legal change now has the legal right to find out at the age of 18 the identity of their donor (as well as non-identifying information at 16).[4] However, the ability to exercise this right turns, crucially, on whether their parents tell

---

* I am very grateful to Stephen Wilkinson for very helpful comments on an earlier draft.
1 M Brazier, 'Regulating the Reproduction Business' (1999) 7 Med L Rev 166, 167.
2 HFE Act (as amended), s 13(5). See further discussion in M Brazier (n 1) 173, where she emphasises the Warnock Report's focus on '*public* policy' (emphasis in original) rather than 'private rights', and see also 174–8; *Report of the Committee of Inquiry into Fertilisation and Embryology* (Warnock Report, Cm 9314).
3 See for example E Jackson, 'Conception and the Irrelevance of the Welfare Principle' (2002) 65 MLR 176. For a critique of the operation of the revised clause, see S Sheldon, E Lee and J Macvarish, "Supportive Parenting', Responsibility and Regulation: The Welfare Assessment under the Reformed Human Fertilisation and Embryology Act 1990' (2015) MLR (in press). The amendment substituted 'supportive parenting' for 'father'.
4 HFE Act (as amended), s 31ZA. The change was preceded by The Human Fertilisation and Embryology Authority (Disclosure of Donor Information) Regulations 2004, SI 2004/1511.

them about the fact of donor conception. Mindful of this, the amended Act also requires, as a licence condition, that clinics must give prospective parents 'such information as is proper about . . . the importance of informing any resulting child at an early age that the child results from the gametes of a person who is not a parent of the child'.[5] Given that parents 'hold the key' to their offspring's ability to exercise the right to establish their donor's identity, the question this chapter considers is whether the possible interests of donor-conceived people in knowing about their genetic origins should be relevant to the operation of the welfare clause itself. For instance, should the clause be used in such a way as to decline treatment to prospective parents who are not, or may not appear, committed to the idea of disclosure to their future child?

I argue that the question of a donor-conceived person's possible interest in knowing about their genetic origins should *not* be considered with reference to the operation of the welfare clause. Rather, this issue should be seen as relevant to the question of prospective parents' *consent* to donor-assisted treatment. Within this, and so far as the welfare of the future child is concerned, a donor-conceived person's possible interest in knowing their genetic origins is pertinent to prospective parents' contemplation of the *prima facie* moral obligation to disclose that they take on in creating a donor-conceived child. The chapter considers the Human Fertilisation and Embryology Authority (HFEA) *Code of Practice*'s interpretation of the standard of harm at stake in the welfare clause and draws on relevant ethical analysis of the Non-Identity Problem to consider aspects of the relationship between harm and non-disclosure.[6] It also draws on both person-affecting and non-person-affecting analyses of reproductive ethics in order to explore a range of possible scenarios in which parents may act in relation to the issue of information disclosure, relating these to the question of the potential for harm to their future child. The analysis raises questions about – and attempts to analyse – some of the relevant links between ethics, policy and the law in relation to this issue in the HFE Act. The important implication of the analysis is that prospective parents' duty to disclose the fact of donor conception can at best be a *moral*, rather than a *legal*, one.

Information disclosure and the welfare of the child clause

The important question of whether information disclosure issues could be relevant to the operation of the welfare clause was also considered by the UK Nuffield Council on Bioethics (Nuffield Council) in its 2013 report, *Donor Conception: Ethical Issues in Information Sharing*, relevant findings of which are noted below.[7] In this section, I turn first to the HFEA's interpretation of the clause.

---

5 HFE Act (as amended), s 13(6C).
6 D Parfit, *Reasons and Persons* (OUP 1984) ch 16.
7 Nuffield Council on Bioethics, *Donor Conception: Ethical Aspects of Information Sharing* (Nuffield Council 2013). I was a member of this Working Party but write on this occasion in my own capacity.

The HFEA's interpretation of the clause

Section 13(5) of the HFE Act is particularly important because it is a licence condition of clinics. As such, it has been described as one of the 'twin pillars' of the HFE Act; the other is the requirement of consent.[8] In considering this section of the HFE Act, we might first ask what 'take account of' means or requires? The section states: '[a] woman shall not be provided with treatment services unless account has been taken of'; the implication is that, on some occasions, treatment should not be provided on the grounds of the welfare of the future child. This possibility, either generally in the *in vitro* fertilisation (IVF) context or particularly in that of reproductive donation, implies a concern with possible harm to the future child. However, the ethical question regarding under what conditions a child can be harmed by being born is not straightforward.

With reference to a clinic's assessment of a given couple, the HFEA *Code of Practice* states: 'The centre should assess each patient and their partner (if they have one) before providing any treatment, and should use this assessment to decide whether there is a *risk of significant harm or neglect* to any child.'[9] It also states: 'The centre should consider factors that are likely to cause a risk of significant harm or neglect to any child who may be born or to any existing child of the family.'[10] Thus, the *Code* interprets the clause as being concerned with '*significant* harm or neglect'. It also uses the phrase '*serious* harm'.[11] As for the question of the degree of *risk* of such harm, as can be seen, the *Code* refers to 'a risk'; it also uses the phrase 'likely to cause a risk'.[12] This is perhaps a somewhat curious formulation. On the one hand, it might be interpreted as meaning that there must be a *likelihood* of serious harm or neglect, but it is also possible that this overstates what is intended. On the other hand, if taken literally, 'likely to cause *a* risk' could encompass risks of a very small magnitude and it seems doubtful that that is what is intended either.

With regard to the factors that are 'likely to cause a risk of significant harm or neglect to any child who may be born', none of those mentioned in the *Code* could be of relevance to the question of a couple's attitude to the issue of disclosure of information regarding genetic parenthood. However, the list is indicative rather than exhaustive. Further, as we have seen, the amended Act itself highlights, in the form of licence condition section 13(6C), 'the importance of informing any resulting child at an early age that the child results from the

---

8 'The twin pillars of the Act are effective consent to treatment and the welfare of the unborn child': Wall J, *Evans v Amicus Healthcare Ltd and Others (Secretary of State for Health and Another intervening); Hadley v Midland Fertility Services Ltd and Others (Secretary of State for Health and Another intervening)* [2003] EWHC 2161 (Fam) 148. See also Thorpe and Sedley LJJ, on appeal, para 23. For the relevant facts, see n 19.
9 HFEA, *Code of Practice* (8th edn, 2009, updated 2011), in force October 2011, para 8.3 (my emphasis).
10 Ibid para 8.1.
11 Ibid para 8.10(b)(iv) (my emphasis).
12 Ibid para 8.10.

gametes of a person who is not a parent of the child'. Adding to this, paragraph 20.7 of the *Code* observes that '[t]here is evidence that finding out suddenly, later in life, about donor origins can be emotionally damaging to children and to family relations'.

Suppose a given prospective parent presents as reluctant to, or nervous about, disclosing the use of donor gametes to a future child. Could or should a clinician's decision as to whether to treat a given couple using (in part or in whole) donor gametes be affected by issues relating to the disclosure of information regarding genetic parenthood? Under what conditions can a concern with harm to a future child influence the question of whether that child should be brought into existence?

Reproductive ethics, harm and the Non-Identity Problem

Questions about the welfare of future, as yet unborn, children are particularly ethically complex because, if it were not for a particular procreative attempt (the union of an egg and sperm) successfully giving rise to the birth of a child, the child in question would have no chance of existence. So the life of that child is the only life that the union of two gametes (after the possibility of twinning) could come to have. Accordingly, philosophically speaking, reproductive decisions regarding the welfare of the future child, including in the context of reproductive donation, raise familiar but controversial problems relating to the Non-Identity Problem.[13] This concerns the idea that a child cannot be wronged or harmed by being born unless the child has a 'wrongful life': one that is not worth living.[14]

The Non-Identity Problem necessarily, and arguably rightly, establishes a rather demanding threshold for the assessment of when, if at all, a given person can be said to be harmed by being born. It is supported, for instance, by Allen Buchanan et al., who focus – with regard to the notion of a 'wrongful life' – on the question of the degree of burdens that may come with, or soon after, birth, and on the lack of sufficiently compensating benefits or goods.[15] Stephen Wilkinson has also employed this threshold of harm, for instance in his analysis of reproductive selection practices, thus endorsing the implications of the Non-Identity Problem.[16]

To what extent can questions about the timing, manner of disclosure or withholding of information regarding genetic parentage affect the quality of life of a donor-conceived individual? As we have seen, the HFEA notes in its *Code* that '[t]here is evidence that finding out suddenly, later in life, about donor

---

13 Parfit (n 6).
14 On the notion of a life not worth living, see for example A Buchanan et al., *From Chance to Choice: Genetics and Justice* (CUP 2000) 235.
15 Ibid.
16 S Wilkinson, *Choosing Tomorrow's Children: The Ethics of Selective Reproduction* (OUP 2010).

origins can be emotionally damaging to children and to family relations'. In the course of its review of both written and oral evidence, the Nuffield Council observed: 'We note that some donor-conceived individuals have indeed asserted that it would be better for prospective parents not to have children at all, than to use donated gametes to conceive.'[17] The question, however, as the Nuffield Council points out, is whether it is plausible to argue that if a clinician were concerned about the possibility that a given couple might not wish to tell their future child about their genetic origins either at all or in a timely fashion, treatment should therefore not be provided, and a possible child should not be born.

To argue in favour of this position would entail the claim that not being born would be preferable to being born and at risk of emotional harm of some kind, such as that which may be caused by accidental disclosure. This seems implausible. Indeed, following a review of the evidence submitted to it, the Nuffield Council concluded that this 'does not bear out . . . [the claim that it would be better for prospective parents not to have children at all, than to use donated gametes to conceive], notwithstanding the distress and difficulties that some individuals have undoubtedly experienced'.[18] In any event, a possible concern could only be with a *risk*, and not necessarily more than a minor one, of serious emotional damage ensuing. Accordingly, it would not be ethically justifiable to withhold treatment from prospective parents, for example, on the grounds of a concern about whether they planned to tell their future child about the fact that one or both (rarely) were not their genetic parents. This means, in effect, that the HFE Act's statement of the importance of parents disclosing information about genetic parenthood could not reasonably be said to be relevant to the welfare clause of the HFE Act, since that clause is concerned with treatment or non-treatment.

Prospective parents' right to respect for private life

Nor would it be a proportionate interference with prospective parents' Article 8 rights under the Human Rights Act 1998. Article 8(1) of the European Convention of Human Rights (ECHR) states: 'Everyone has the right to respect for his private and family life, his home and his correspondence.'[19] Although Article 8 cannot by itself guarantee the provision of reproductive treatment, the

---

17 Nuffield Council (n 7) para 5.58, stating in n. 446: 'See, for example, TangledWebsUK (2013) Why We Believe Donor Conception is Harmful, available at: http://www.tangledwebs.org.uk/tw/WhyWrong/.'
18 Ibid para 5.62.
19 In *Evans v United Kingdom*, the European Court of Human Rights held that 'the right to respect for the decision to become a parent in the genetic sense, also falls within the scope of Article 8': see *Evans v United Kingdom* App no 6339/05 (ECHR, 10 April 2007), para 72. The case concerned an unsuccessful challenge to the consent provisions of the HFE Act 1990.

Grand Chamber of the European Court of Human Rights has held that the decision to have a child by means of donor conception is one which falls within the domain of private life,[20] such that any interference with that decision will need to be justified under Article 8(2). This states (in part):

> There shall be no interference by a public authority with this right except such as is in accordance with the law and is necessary in a democratic society in the interests of . . . the protection of morals, or for the protection of the rights and freedoms of others.

The interests of the future child could well count under the last section of the limiting provision. However, the test to justify interference is a stringent one, requiring that it is in accordance with law, has a legitimate aim and is necessary in a democratic society. The last condition hinges on the notion of proportionality. The *Sunday Times v United Kingdom* case established a commonly used three-fold test interpreting the notion of necessity. The test asks whether the interference corresponds to a 'pressing social need', whether it is 'proportionate to the legitimate aim pursued', and whether the reasons offered to justify the interference are 'relevant and sufficient'.[21] Arguably, a decision not to provide donor conception treatment to a given couple because of concerns about their attitude to disclosure would not pass the necessity test.[22]

Information disclosure and the consent of the prospective parents

On the argument so far, treatment of prospective parents could not be legitimately withheld on the basis of a concern about their attitude to disclosure; in other words, the question of information disclosure cannot be relevant to the welfare clause. This means that we need to think further about the 'location' of the HFE Act's concern with the importance of information disclosure within the framework of the HFE Act as a whole. While irrelevant to the welfare clause, I argue that it is very relevant to the second of the twin pillars – consent.

The question of consent in assisted reproduction treatment is governed by both common law and statute. In addition to the common law elements of

---

20 *S.H. and Others v Austria* App no 57813/00 (ECHR, 3 November 2011), para 82. The case concerned an unsuccessful challenge to Austria's prohibition on the use of egg donation, as well as sperm donation for IVF treatment.
21 (1979) 2 EHRR 245, para 59. For relevant discussion, see for example J Wadham et al., *Blackstone's Guide to the Human Rights Act 1998* (6th edn, OUP 2011) paras 2.57–2.68.
22 The question of the state mandating disclosure by birth certificates would be similarly problematic: see further Nuffield Council (n 7) para 9.

valid consent (capacity, information as to nature and purpose, and voluntariness),[23] the HFE Act requires a higher standard of information disclosure. The statutory provisions are contained in Schedule 3 of the HFE Act, compliance with which is a condition of a clinic's licence under section 12(1). Paragraph 3(1) states:

> Before a person gives consent under this Schedule – (a) he must be given a suitable opportunity to receive proper counselling about the implications of taking the proposed steps, and (b) he must be provided with such relevant information as is proper.

As we have seen earlier, the HFE Act explicitly requires that clinics give 'such information as is proper about . . . the importance of informing any resulting child at an early age that the child results from the gametes of a person who is not a parent of the child'. Understood in relation to the issue of consent, to advise prospective parents that the law holds that it is considered important to tell a child that they are donor-conceived is to give the prospective parents information that is relevant to their decision as to whether to proceed with donor conception. This is because it requires them to think about their future child's possible interest in knowing about their genetic origins. Given evidence, for example, of possible harm through accidental disclosure, it might be said that parents have at least a *prima facie* moral obligation to tell a future child in a timely fashion about their conception (although this may be defeasible if the obligation is particularly difficult for them to fulfil, for instance, for religious reasons). Indeed, having reviewed the evidence submitted to it, the Nuffield Council concluded that:[24]

> [. . . although w]e argued above that the possibility of harm arising from inadvertent disclosure or discovery is not sufficient to justify the conclusion that parents act wrongly if they use donor gametes without committing to openness in advance . . . there *is* sufficient evidence to point to the conclusion that, **other things being equal, it will usually be better for children to be told, by their parents and at any early age, that they are donor-conceived**.

Accordingly, reflecting on a child's possible interest in knowing their genetic origins in advance of an attempted conception will be to reflect on the *prima facie* obligations that one takes on by conceiving in this way. Thus, while the HFE Act's concern with the importance of information disclosure cannot

---

23 See respectively *Re M.B.* [1997] 8 Med L Rev 217, *Chatterton v Gerson* [1981] 1 All ER 257, *Re T (Adult: Refusal of Treatment)* [1992] 4 All ER 649.
24 Nuffield Council (n 7) para 5.46, referring to evidence discussed in para 4.61, emphasis in original.

justifiably be relevant to the *legal* question of whether to provide treatment in the light of the welfare clause, it is instead very relevant to parents' contemplation of the *moral* question of their *prima facie* obligations to their future child. So far as the HFE Act is concerned, this occurs as part of the process of giving legal consent to treatment. Significantly, the implication is that the notion of an obligation to tell a future child about their donor conception is *at best a moral one, and not a legal one*. Further, as we shall see, it is at best a *prima facie* moral obligation.

Viewed as part of the informational duties relevant to consent, a concern with the importance of information disclosure could also be seen as focused on the interrelated nature of parents' and offspring's interests in flourishing, trusting relationships.[25] In this regard, the Nuffield Council noted that '[a] number of values embedded in those relationships, in particular trust and honesty, are widely regarded as playing a central part in promoting wellbeing within families'.[26] Such an understanding is more sympathetic to the relationship between parents and children than a focus on the importance of information disclosure as an interest (or even a right) that is just held by the child, and potentially in opposition to prospective parents' interests in becoming parents. This would be the case if the child's interests in information disclosure were, for instance, conceived in opposition to parents' interests. This could potentially bar them from receiving treatment by means of the welfare clause, unjustifiably so, as my argument in relation to the Non-Identity Problem shows.

Prospective parents, treatment options and family implications

When prospective parents contemplate a child's possible interest in knowing about their donor conception and their legal right to find out at the age of 18 the identity of the donor (as well as non-identifying information at 16), there are a number of different possible courses of action they might take, with a range of possible outcomes. A few are discussed below.

Scenarios 1 and 2: Deciding to tell or not to tell

In Scenario 1, having thought about their *prima facie* moral duty to tell a child that he or she has a genetic parent outside their social and legal family unit, they may proceed with treatment using donated gametes and plan to tell their (hopefully) subsequently born child about their donor origins. Alternatively, in Scenario 2, having taken note of a clinic's advice – in accordance with the HFE Act – of the importance of telling a future child about his or her donor origins,

---

25 For thoughts on the interwoven nature of parents' and children's interests, see T Murray, *The Worth of a Child* (University of California Press 1996) 138.
26 Nuffield Council (n 7) para 29.

they may proceed with treatment, at the same time deciding not to tell their child. With reference to the relevant evidence as to non-disclosure, the Nuffield Council stated:[27]

> [F]amilies in which parents choose not to disclose to their offspring that they are donor-conceived have been found to function well into early adolescence although much less is known about families with older offspring . . . Harms may potentially arise if donor-conceived people find out late, or inadvertently, although from the limited survey data available it would appear that in many cases initial negative reactions will fade over time.

Thus, in either of these scenarios, the child would have a life that he or she would think was worth living, although the child in Scenario 2 may be at risk of harm compatible with this (for instance, accidental disclosure as an adult). Of course, scenarios such as these are necessarily highly speculative: it is possible that the donor-conceived person in Scenario 1 will regret having been advised of their donor conception, or that the one in Scenario 2 will either never accidentally discover their donor origins, or, alternatively, that accidental disclosure will not cause significant harm. In either case, the parents may also change their minds about disclosure.

Scenario 3: Deciding not to have treatment

In Scenario 3, perhaps feeling very doubtful of their ability to tell a child about their donor-assisted conception, the prospective parents decide not to proceed with treatment. Thus, instead of attempting to have a donor-conceived child with a life worth living, they decide to have no child at all. Is it morally preferable that, instead of trying to have a donor-conceived child with a life worth living, but without the knowledge of their donor conception, or the accompanying ability to assert their legal right at the age of 18 to establish the donor's identity, the prospective parents have decided not to have a child at all?

Of note, this course of action cannot be viewed as 'better' for the future child who will not now be born, since that child would have had a life worth living. This is the case even if he or she would (most likely) never have found out about their donor conception. Further, as has been discussed by others, making ethical comparisons between the resulting outcomes is complex and contested because this has in fact become a 'different number' case: that is, it involves comparing an outcome with one child with an outcome with no child.[28] In two further variants of possible reproductive decisions and actions in this

---

27 Ibid para 5.43, referring to paras 4.29–4.32 and 4.14.
28 Such choices are noted by Parfit (n 6) 356. Their complexity is acknowledged and discussed by Buchanan et al. (n 14) 254–5.

Scenario 4: Deciding to have treatment that will give the child further legal rights

In order to explore the first of these scenarios, we have to go back in time in the UK to the cusp of the legal change from anonymous to non-anonymous donation. Just before the removal of donor anonymity in 2005, a couple contemplating treatment before the change to the law could well have been advised by a clinic that a child born after April 2005 would have access to identifying information regarding their donor at the age of 18, but not before. If they wished, such a couple could wait a few months to have their donor-assisted treatment and, if successful, give birth to a donor-conceived child with the legal right to access the relevant identifying information. In fact, exactly such a couple gave evidence to the Nuffield Council Working Party, saying that they wished 'their child' to be able to establish their donor's identity.[29] In such a case, if they had not waited, Child A – born before the legal change – would have had a life worth living but no such right; by contrast, Child B – born after the change to the law took effect – would (other things being equal) likewise have a life worth living, but would *also* have the legal right to access potentially valuable information about their donor's identity.

Was it morally preferable that this couple waited and chose to have Child B? Arguably it was, since Child B would have something of potential value relevant to their quality of life that Child A could not have had. The case is analogous to Allen Buchanan et al.'s example of delaying conception by a few months (and taking medication) so that a child with a health problem compatible with a life worth living is not born but one without that problem, and a life worth living, is born instead.[30] This analysis turns on the use of 'non-person-affecting' principles, which consider states of the world or states of affairs, rather than 'person-affecting' principles, which look at the effect(s) of decisions or actions on persons themselves. Here the comparison is between the same number of children – one (in each case) – who have lives worth living but with a qualitative difference between them. However, the extent of any moral duty on the part of prospective parents to wait for such a change in the law would turn on the length of the possible delay to their plans to start, or add to, their family. Facts about the prospective parents' lives would be relevant to the moral balance here, particularly relating to their reproductive history to date.

---

29 Nuffield Council (n 7) para 5.43, n. 438, citing 'Fact finding meetings with people with person experience of donor conception, 27 April 2012'.
30 A Buchanan et al. (n 14) 244, adapting an example of Parfit (n 6).

Scenario 5: Deciding to have treatment in a jurisdiction with anonymous donation

Alternatively, a couple might consider seeking treatment abroad, resulting in the birth of a donor-conceived child who has fewer legal rights than he or she would have under UK law. Although (as noted above), the UK abolished anonymous donation in 2005, there is a mixture of approaches to this issue in Europe. In Scenario 5, a couple seeks treatment in a country that maintains anonymous donation because of a shortage of donor eggs in the UK.[31] In light of the clear UK legal position regarding non-anonymous donation, coupled with the law's explicit endorsement of the importance of telling donor-conceived children of their donor-conceived origins, how might such a course of action be viewed?

Given that a future child conceived by anonymous donation cannot be said to be at risk of having a life that is not worth living, arguably these prospective parents would be morally justified in seeking such treatment, *assuming* there were little or no chance of treatment in the UK. For instance, there may be a shortage of eggs of a particular ethnicity and little likelihood of these becoming available soon. In this scenario, the alternative could mean that the couple were unable to have donor-assisted treatment, and they would thus lose the opportunity to create a child. The comparison in this case would then be between treatment abroad resulting in the birth of a child (born from an anonymous donor) who has a life worth living, and no treatment in the UK and thus no child. As noted above, the ethical assessment of reproductive decisions in cases where different numbers of people with lives worth living would be created are complex and controversial. I cannot resolve these difficulties here.

However, in this scenario there is also a highly relevant person-affecting factor at stake, namely the effect on the parents of having, or not having, a child. If they want a child very much, the loss and suffering to them of not being able to have one (by means of treatment with donor eggs in the UK) is highly morally relevant. Arguably, it would not be justifiable for a UK clinician who has no gametes to offer within a reasonable time frame to attempt to dissuade prospective parents from seeking treatment in a country with an anonymous donation regime. Rather, more constructively, the focus might be on the care of the prospective parents in other ways, such as by providing them with the best available information about treatment options abroad (in conjunction with the HFEA, which includes relevant information on its website).[32]

---

31 HFEA, 'Considering Fertility Treatment Abroad: Issues and Risks' <www.hfea.gov.uk/fertility-clinics-treatment-abroad.html> (accessed 16 March 2015).
32 Ibid.

Conclusion

As Brazier's analysis of the HFE Act shows, beneath its seemingly pragmatic framework lie complex questions regarding moral and legal interests, rights and duties, and the formulation of appropriate guidance and policy in relation to them. In an era in which human rights analyses are ever more required, these have increasingly to be 'unpacked' and considered. They can no longer be 'skated over'. In the context of decisions that affect information disclosure in the area of reproductive donation, it has been argued that a concern with the welfare of the future child cannot justifiably be relevant to the welfare clause under section 13(5) of the HFE Act. In this light, it would not be helpful to understand the HFE Act's concern with the importance of the disclosure of information regarding genetic parentage to donor-conceived individuals as potentially relevant to the *legal* question, under the welfare clause, of whether treatment should be provided to prospective parents. Rather, it is best understood as being relevant to the legal question of prospective parents' consent to donor-assisted treatment. Within this, and insofar as the welfare of the future child is concerned, it is very relevant to the *moral* question of the *prima facie* obligations that they would take on as parents in creating a donor-conceived child. The highly significant implication is that the obligation to tell children about their donor conception is, at best, a moral rather than a legal one. The HFE Act should be interpreted accordingly and, as the Nuffield Council has likewise emphasised, relevant policies should aim sympathetically to support parents in this potentially difficult task.[33]

---

33 The recommendations of the Nuffield Council (n 7) are notable in this regard. See for example para 43: '[I]t is the professional duty of the counsellor, and other relevant professionals, to ensure that they provide information and support in a non-judgmental and understandable manner that encourages prospective parents to engage with the issues of disclosure and nondisclosure. It is crucial that prospective parents are able to feel confident about expressing their own anxieties, views or concerns about disclosure, to seek advice and guidance without fear of being judged, and to own their ultimate decisions about disclosure or non-disclosure with regard to the well-being of their future family.'

21 Are we still 'policing pregnancy'?

Sara Fovargue and José Miola

Introduction

During the 1990s, seven cases were heard concerning the ability of women in the later stages of pregnancy to choose their method of delivery.[1] In every case, for various reasons, it was declared lawful to perform a caesarean section against the woman's wishes. These cases caused some commentators, including Margaret Brazier and ourselves, to consider the moral and legal responsibilities of pregnant women for foetal health when the decision to continue the pregnancy to term had been made.[2] While some questioned whether the decision of the Court of Appeal in *St George's Healthcare NHS Trust v S*[3] was the end of the story,[4] Brazier presciently cautioned that 'the conclusion, or news of a conclusion, to the story is premature . . . in terms of legal analysis because other issues where liberty and procreative responsibility conflict remain to be resolved'.[5] Only one case involving a court-ordered caesarean was reported between 1998 and 2003,[6] but since 2013 at least five

---

1 *Re S (Adult: Refusal of Medical Treatment)* [1992] 4 All ER 671; *Rochdale Healthcare (NHS) Trust v C* [1997] 1 FCR 274; *Norfolk and Norwich (NHS) Trust v W* [1996] 2 FLR 613; *Re L (An Adult: Non Consensual Treatment)* [1997] 1 FLR 837; *Tameside and Glossop Acute Services Trust v CS* [1996] 1 FCR 753; *Re MB (Caesarean Section)* [1997] 2 FLR 426, CA; *St George's Healthcare NHS Trust v S, R v Collins, ex parte S* [1998] 3 WLR 936, CA.
2 E.g. M Brazier, 'Liberty, responsibility, maternity' (1999) 52 CLP 359; S Fovargue and J Miola, 'Policing Pregnancy: Implications of the *Attorney-General's Reference (No 3 of 1994)* (1998) 6 Med L Rev 265; M Brazier, 'Parental responsibilities, foetal welfare and children's health' in C Bridge (ed), *Family Law Towards the Millennium: Essays for PM Bromley* (Butterworths 1997); H Draper, 'Women, forced caesareans and antenatal responsibilities' (1996) 22 JME 327.
3 *St George's* (n 1).
4 See e.g. S Michalowski, 'Court ordered caesareans – the end of a trend?' (1999) 62 MLR 1157.
5 Brazier (1999) (n 2) 359–360.
6 *Bolton NHS Trust v O* [2003] 1 FLR 824.

have been heard,[7] all involving women under the protection of the Mental Health Act 1983 (MHA). When these cases are read alongside the decisions relating to *CP (A Child) v First-tier Tribunal (Criminal Injuries Compensation)*,[8] discussed by Emma Cave and Catherine Stanton in this collection,[9] we see that the issue of maternal responsibility during pregnancy is again in the spotlight.

In this chapter we consider the role of the law in determining maternal responsibility for foetal welfare in relation to decisions regarding delivery, note identifiable trends in the older cases, and examine four recent reported decisions. We suggest that, as Brazier said, such cases will continue to be brought to court until 'other issues where liberty and procreative responsibility conflict' are resolved.

Moral and/or legal maternal responsibility for foetal health in the 1990s

When considering the legal and ethical issues raised by maternal and parental responsibility for foetal health, Brazier argued that:

> mothers-to-be have especial responsibility to their children *in utero*. The absolute dependency of the future child on its mother increases, not diminishes her *moral* responsibility for its welfare. She can no more morally justify causing injury to that child than to any of her born children, or any other woman's children.[10]

Nevertheless, moral responsibility should not result in *legal* responsibility, which '[w]omen rightly fear . . . not out of a lack of concern for their future child but because of the potential impact on their liberty and privacy during and prior to a pregnancy'.[11] The lack of tortious liability for maternal behaviour affecting foetal welfare, and the family courts' refusal to extend wardship to a

---

7 *Re AA* [2012] EWHC 4378 (COP); *In the matter of P* [2013] EWHC 4581 (COP); *Great Western Hospitals NHS Foundation Trust v AA* [2014] EWHC 132 (Fam); *NHS Trust 1, NHS Trust 2 v FG* [2014] EWCOP 30. The fifth case involved the Royal Free London NHS Trust and is unreported, but it is discussed in, e.g. Press Association, 'Judge gives permission for a caesarean section on mentally ill woman', (2014) *The Guardian*, 31 January <http://www.theguardian.com/society/2014/jan/31/judge-caesarean-section-mentally-ill>; Patrick Sawer, 'Judge orders mentally ill woman to have forced caesarean', (2014) *Daily Telegraph*, 1 February <http://www.telegraph.co.uk/health/healthnews/10611575/Judge-orders-mentally-ill-woman-to-have-forced-caesarean.html>;'Judge approves forced Caesarean for mentally-ill woman', (2014) *BBC News*, 1 February <http://www.bbc.co.uk/news/uk-england-london-25996231> (all accessed 16 January 2015).
8 [2014] EWCA Civ 1554. See previously *CICA v First-Tier Tribunal and CP (CIC)* [2013] UKUT 638 (AAC).
9 'Maternal responsibility to the child not yet born', chapter 24.
10 Brazier (1997) (n 2) 272, emphasis in original.
11 Ibid 273.

foetus, or to authorise the non-consensual treatment of pregnant women with capacity, was not due to women owing no moral duty to have regard to the welfare of the child-to-be, but because the price of legally enforcing that duty was too high.[12] Law's limited involvement in foetal welfare was thus a pragmatic recognition of three realities. First, legal intervention was unlikely to be effective unless it entailed 'intrusive policing of . . . pregnancies', setting women apart from all others in society and 'subject to medically dictated codes of pregnancy practice'.[13] Second, because even pre-conception acts can affect a child, if the law were to enforce any responsibility for foetal welfare this would mean that fertile women *and* men must 'prioritise the health of their future children over all other competing interests'.[14] Finally:

> [f]oetal welfare is most likely to be maximised if society concentrates, not on using the law to pursue the occasional 'bad' mother-to-be, but on ensuring that all those who may become parents grow up themselves and reproduce in a society which ensures that parental health maximises foetal health.[15]

Thus, '[w]e need to rediscover means of support and encouraging responsible choice without inevitably allowing the heavy boots of the law to trample over private choice'.[16] We suggest that the recent caesarean cases highlight the continuing deficiencies in this regard, but that they were somewhat unexpected for three reasons. First, the decisions in *Re MB* and *St George's* made it clear that cases involving refusals of consent from women with capacity should be rejected because such women *are* able to make decisions concerning their medical treatment.[17] Indeed, Andrew Grubb cautiously welcomed the decision in *St George's* as being a potential watershed, with its influence to be determined in later judgments.[18] Although the Court heard that case *after* the caesarean had been performed, it provided guidelines to ensure that labouring, or near-to-labouring, women were not automatically deemed to lack capacity if they refused to consent to a proposed form of delivery.[19] These included the need to identify concerns about capacity as early as possible, that the hearing should be *inter partes*, the woman represented, and relevant and accurate information provided to the court.

---

12 Ibid 281.
13 Ibid 293.
14 Ibid.
15 Ibid.
16 Brazier (1999) (n 2) 391.
17 *St George's* (n 1); *Re MB* (n 1).
18 A Grubb, 'Competent adult (pregnant woman): Forced treatment and Mental Health Act' (1998) 6 Med L Rev 356.
19 *St George's* (n 1) 968–970.

Second, the law on capacity, formalised in the Mental Capacity Act 2005 (MCA), now presumes that those aged 16 and over have the capacity to make decisions for themselves.[20] A lack of capacity must be proved by those alleging otherwise on the balance of probabilities,[21] by applying the tests set out in sections 2(1) and 3(1). A least restrictive alternative approach is endorsed,[22] and anything done in or on behalf of the person must be in their best interests.[23] Factors to be considered when determining a patient's best interests are set out, building on and drawing from common law developments prior to the MCA, which emphasised a less medically focused definition.[24] Thus, under section 4, there is a duty to consult the patient and certain other people, including those caring for the patient, so that their views can be taken into account in a best interests assessment.[25] This assessment includes a consideration of what the patient would have wanted (their 'past and present wishes and feelings' and their 'beliefs and values' likely to influence any decision if they had capacity),[26] and the person determining whether a patient has capacity 'must, so far as reasonably practicable, permit and encourage the person to participate, or to improve his ability to participate, as fully as possible in any act done for him and any decision affecting him'.[27] The (easy) assumption, identifiable in the 1990s cases, that a woman's best interests were her best *medical* interests should now thus be rare,[28] and serious regard should be given to what the pregnant woman wants and/or wanted.

Finally, the landscape of medical law has changed dramatically since the 1990s. When the first caesarean case, *Re S*, was decided in 1992, medical law was dominated by *Bolam*.[29] The answer to most medical law questions, including what was in a patient's best interests, was determined by whether there was a body of medical opinion that would do as the doctors proposed to do. Medical interests and expertise dominated. Times have changed, and the courts have acknowledged their ability to examine health professionals' decisions, albeit that it will be rare to go against them.[30] The prime consideration is now *balancing* the patient's autonomy with her welfare and best interests, rather than purely welfare considerations dominating.[31] This exercise should result in the woman's

---

20 s 1(2).
21 s 2(4).
22 s 1(6).
23 s 1(5).
24 See e.g. *Re A (Medical Treatment: Male Sterilisation)* [2000] 1 FCR 193, CA; *Re S (Adult Patient: Sterilisation)* [2001] Fam 15, CA.
25 ss 4(6) and 4(7), respectively.
26 s 4 (6)(a) and (b).
27 s 4(4).
28 *Tameside* (n 1).
29 *Bolam v Friern Hospital Management Committee* [1957] 2 All ER 118.
30 See *Bolitho v City and Hackney Health Authority* [1998] AC 232 and *Montgomery v Lanarkshire Health Board* [2015] UKSC 11.
31 See *Chester v Afshar* [2004] UKHL 41.

voice being heard in decisions about delivery, minimising the possibility that decisions are made *about* her but *without* her, as occurred in some of the 1990s cases.[32] Rather, the broader definition of best interests should introduce balance where previously there was none.

It might therefore be imagined that the law has accepted that while women have a *moral* responsibility to their foetuses, this does not extend to a *legal* duty. Brazier's view thus seems to accord with the law's development since the 1990s caesarean cases. However, we suggest that the newer cases indicate a continued scope for and desire to create the sort of legal framework that she warned against, at least with regards to a specific category of pregnant woman.

The backdrop to the recent cases: Criminal responsibility for (maternal) conduct during pregnancy?

Just as the 1990s cases were heard while the criminal responsibility of a third party for harm caused to a foetus *in utero* was being considered by the House of Lords,[33] during 2013 and 2014 the courts were asked to consider whether maternal conduct (drinking alcohol) which harmed the foetus *in utero* could be viewed as a crime (for the purposes of awarding the child compensation under the Criminal Injuries Compensation Scheme) if it results in a child being born injured.[34] In 1998, the House of Lords held that a man who stabbed his pregnant girlfriend in the abdomen, causing the baby to be born alive but subsequently dying from the injuries sustained in the attack, could be charged with unlawful act manslaughter.[35] At the time we argued, as did Brazier, that this decision was dangerous for pregnant women because if one sort of manslaughter was appropriate, then why not another, such as gross negligence manslaughter? And if a third party might be liable for foetal injuries, what was to stop maternal liability?[36] We all concluded that when the philosophies of the caesarean cases and the *Attorney-General's Reference* were considered together, there was a danger that the desire to protect the foetus might develop into maternal liability for foetal health. Our concerns have, in some ways, been vindicated by the arguments presented in the recent criminal injuries case and media reports of it,[37] but our focus here is on the themes evident in the recent caesarean cases and what they tell us about law's policing of pregnancy today.

---

32 *Norfolk* (n 1); *Rochdale* (n 1).
33 *Attorney-General's Reference (No 3 of 1994)* [1998] AC 245, HL.
34 *CP (A Child)* (n 8); *CICA* (n 8).
35 *Attorney-General's Reference* (n 33).
36 Fovargue and Miola (n 2); Brazier (1999) (n 2).
37 See e.g. O Bowcott, 'Foetal damage caused by alcohol "equivalent to manslaughter"', (2014) *The Guardian*, 5 November; L-M Elefthriou-Smith, 'Drinking while pregnant is a "crime of violence" court hears', (2014) *The Independent*, 6 November.

The newer caesarean cases

Re AA[38]

AA was 39 weeks pregnant and compulsorily detained under the section 3 of the MHA with 'a schizophrenic disorder, which [was] psychotic in nature'.[39] It was determined that she lacked the capacity to make decisions for herself. She had already had two caesarean sections. An NHS Trust made an urgent application for a declaration that it would be in AA's 'medical best interests' to deliver by caesarean section.[40] This was supported by a consultant obstetrician and the consultant psychiatrist treating her. Because of her previous caesareans there was a 'significant risk' of a ruptured womb if AA delivered vaginally, and this would endanger both her and the foetus' health.[41] Mostyn J held that AA's 'mental health best interests' would be best served by the birth of a healthy baby,[42] and authorised a planned elective caesarean delivery the following day.[43]

Prima facie the case was straightforward, but an examination of the detail highlights the complexities and our concerns. For example, as the 'significant risk' of uterine rupture was actually only 1%, 'it was 99 per cent likely that the patient's uterus would not rupture'.[44] Given the size of this risk, we suggest that had this been a risk-disclosure case the risk would not have been deemed 'material', and so would not require disclosure.[45] As well as relying on this risk, Mostyn J appears to have equated best interests with *medical* best interests in the form of AA's '*mental health* best interests'.[46] This is not necessarily problematic, because mental health well-being is so fundamental to our well-being as individuals, and when we are mentally well we are able to function properly and express our genuine wishes. Thus, mental health best interests may weigh more heavily than other *purely medical* best interests.[47] Nevertheless, wider best interests considerations, required by the MCA, were only minimally attended to.

The health of the foetus was, however, noted, and the Trust argued that a planned caesarean was required because if AA were 'dissembling' because of her mental state 'or otherwise being uncooperative, [the Trust] would not be able to monitor the baby's heartbeat to see whether there were potential uterine rupture complications emerging'.[48] Given this, the least restrictive option,

---

38 *Re AA* (n 7).
39 Ibid proceedings.
40 Ibid note by Mostyn J.
41 Ibid [4].
42 Ibid [5].
43 Ibid proposed proceedings.
44 E Walmsley, '*Mama Mia!* Serious shortcomings with another "(en)forced" caesarean case *Re AA* [2012] EWHC 4378 (COP)' (2015) 23 Med L Rev 135, 138.
45 *Pearce v United Bristol Healthcare NHS Trust* [1999] PIQR 53, CA; see also *Montgomery* (n 30).
46 *Re AA* (n 7) [5], emphasis added.
47 We thank Catherine Stanton for this point.
48 *Re AA* (n 7) proceedings.

which under the MCA and it's *Code of Practice* is required for the treatment to be in the patient's best interests,[49] may have been to authorise foetal heart monitoring using reasonable restraint, and if signs of uterine rupture presented then the caesarean could be authorised.[50] Instead, the move to caesarean was swift and medically supported.

Speed was also evident in the urgent nature of the application, which resulted in AA only being represented by the Official Solicitor. It is unclear whether AA was aware of the Trust's application and/or contributed to the proceedings at all. Was she lacking capacity at all times, or were there lucid periods when she was able to express an opinion? It is also unclear from the case report and transcript whether any attempts were made to treat AA's mental health condition and explore the delivery plans with her. AA was detained under section 3 of the MHA on 13 June 2012, and the Trust's application was made on 23 August when she was 39 weeks pregnant and, presumably, known to midwives and obstetricians. So why was the management of her labour seemingly not considered until so late? Furthermore, it was surely known that AA had already had two caesareans and that this might influence the delivery method for subsequent pregnancies.

These are precisely the sorts of issues that the *Collins* guidelines were supposed to address, along with the provisions of the MCA.[51] Yet the factors to be considered in the MCA's best interests assessment are conspicuous by their absence. Rather, the medical evidence was seemingly determinative, with the best outcome for AA deemed to be the delivery of a healthy baby. While this may have been true, the decision appears to have been taken without AA, and her voice, as in some of the 1990s cases, is lacking. Additionally, there is no evidence in the judgment as to if or how the MCA's tests for capacity were applied. However, if AA was being treated under section 3 of the MHA, then her schizophrenia would not necessarily eliminate her capacity to make decisions.[52] Thus, if we ask whether the 'heavy boots of the law' trampled over AA's private choice,[53] the answer here is 'yes'.

In the matter of P[54]

The boots are, we suggest, also evident here. P was 36, in the final stages of her fourth pregnancy, and was compulsorily admitted to a psychiatric hospital in November 2013. Her first two children were delivered vaginally and

---

49 Section 1(6); Department of Constitutional Affairs (DCA), *Mental Capacity Act Code of Practice* (TSO 2007) 27.
50 Walmsley (n 44) 139.
51 DCA (n 49) 20–24.
52 See e.g. *Re C (Adult: Refusal of Treatment)* [1994] 1 WLR 290.
53 We leave aside here the question of whether she could, in fact, make a private choice, given that we do not know how her capacity was assessed and on what evidence.
54 *P* (n 7).

subsequently taken into care, and her third was delivered via caesarean and did not live with P. P was thought to suffer from paranoid schizophrenia and was, at times, psychotic. Due to her diabetes, P was carrying a large baby and an excessive amount of amniotic fluid. P did not always co-operate with her doctors or reliably take her medication for schizophrenia, and four senior psychiatrists agreed that she lacked the capacity to make decisions about her obstetric care. The Trust sought a declaration that it would be lawful to induce P's labour and, if necessary, perform a caesarean. The declaration was granted, with Jackson J deciding that P lacked capacity to make decisions relating to delivery and that it was in her best interests to safely deliver her baby as it would have 'extremely adverse effects' on her if 'the child was not born safely or was born with some avoidable disability as a result of a lack of obstetric care'.[55]

P was in hospital and was 'relatively calm and accepting of the idea of being induced'[56] by having her waters broken and 'instrumental delivery'.[57] Nevertheless, the Trust sought a declaration in anticipation of any problems during delivery, and wanted authorisation to induce P's labour and perform a caesarean if this was required to 'avoid significant bleeding', particularly from her existing section scar, or to 'avoid foetal distress'.[58] The risk of bleeding was said to be 'small, but not insignificant'.[59] In contrast to *Re AA* this was not an emergency, but Jackson J only 'heard from the parties' advocates, . . . three consultant doctors by telephone link, and . . . the Official Solicitor's case manager'.[60] Even though sections 4(6) and (7) of the MCA require that the views of the patient and those close to her regarding her ascertainable past and present wishes and feelings are considered as part of the best interests assessment, it is noticeable that neither P nor her relatives were heard by the judge. The requirements of section 4 were, however, noted, and Jackson J stated that P was 'very opposed' to a caesarean, which 'conflicts with her strong views'.[61] It is unclear how this information was obtained, and there is no discussion of the effect on P of ignoring her wishes. Jackson J merely stated that he had given 'full weight to what she feels and believes' but that the declaration sought would give P 'a good chance of having a normal labour' and 'provide her with safety if it were to be necessary'.[62] He did not mention the views of her family or other carers, and it is not clear whether those who would be responsible for caring for her during labour were in favour of the proposed course of action. Indeed, in his evidence, Mr B, a consultant obstetrician, merely set out the options available.[63]

55 Ibid [17].
56 Ibid [4].
57 Ibid [3].
58 Ibid [3].
59 Ibid [16].
60 Ibid [6].
61 Ibid [15].
62 Ibid [18].
63 Ibid [12].

As with *Re AA*, minimal account was taken of P's views, and those of her relatives or friends do not appear at all. The focus was on medical best interests relating to P's physical health and her mental health if 'the unborn child' was adversely affected.[64] A wider consideration of best interests was, again, absent. It is thus easy to see how the law can slip, almost blindly, into policing delivery options at the end of a pregnancy. P was found to lack capacity to decide for herself, and her objections to the caesarean were overruled with a minimum of fuss. The law, in this case at least, did not refrain from interfering in delivery decisions and thereby policing pregnancy.

Great Western Hospitals Foundation Trust v AA[65]

AA was 25 years old and 38 weeks pregnant with her first child. She had a history of bipolar disorder, substance and alcohol abuse, and had been prescribed a 'battery of antipsychotic medication'.[66] She and her partner (BB) welcomed the pregnancy and complied with the antenatal care provided. At the time of the application, AA's father described her as being in the worst state that he had seen her in, and when she arrived at hospital on 26 January 2014 she was 'confused and disoriented', and her membranes had ruptured though she was not in labour.[67] On 27 January she was detained under section 5(2) of the MHA,[68] and was 'highly agitated and . . . largely uncooperative with almost every aspect of her care'.[69] The concern was that, because of her pregnancy, AA had not been able to receive appropriate antipsychotic medication. Because her waters had already broken there was an increased risk of maternal and foetal infection until delivery was complete. Standard practice was to induce labour via an IV drip, but there was unanimity that AA would not co-operate with this, and she had previously removed IV lines.[70]

On 27 January 2014, Moor J made an interim order, because AA was unrepresented, authorising a caesarean section if AA went into labour or began to show signs of infection before the full hearing on 28 January.[71] She did not go into labour, and at the full hearing Hayden J heard that AA had become more distressed and had 'run at the window and tried to get out', stating that she 'wanted to go to heaven'.[72] There were two alternatives available: medically

---

64 Ibid [17].
65 *Great Western* (n 7).
66 Ibid [3].
67 Ibid [6].
68 Section 5 provides for the admission to hospital of patients who are already in-patients at a hospital (for example, where a patient is detained for assessment but the clinicians want to detain for treatment) and s 5(2) provides a doctor with a 72-hour period in which to detain the patient while a report is prepared in support of the application.
69 *Great Western* (n 7) [6].
70 Ibid [7].
71 *Great Western Hospitals NHS Foundation Trust v AA* [2014] EWHC 166 (Fam).
72 *Great Western* (n 7) [9].

inducing labour or a planned caesarean. As already noted, there were concerns about induction, and the court heard that in a quarter to a third of cases where labour is induced an emergency caesarean is still required.[73] This would be particularly dangerous in this case and could result in infection and sepsis leading to the foetus dying or being brain damaged, and there were risks of shock or haemorrhage to AA. The Trust thus concluded that a planned caesarean under general anaesthetic was the best option.[74]

AA appeared to lack capacity at the time the decision needed to be made. The decision was relatively urgent and she, seemingly, wanted a healthy baby but was acting in a way contrary to this. It is thus understandable why a court might support performing a caesarean, regardless of AA's consent. But it is notable that a different approach is identifiable here from the outset. While Hayden J said that it was 'self-evident' that AA did not have the capacity to make the decision about delivery for herself, he still spent time explaining *how* he reached that conclusion.[75] He explored the MCA's requirements in the context of the medical evidence available to him, and so this was more than a mere declaration that AA had been assessed and declared to lack capacity. Rather, Hayden J engaged with the evidence, including from her father, and Hayden J's conclusion that AA's level of agitation meant that she was unable to absorb, retain or process information mirrored the opinions of the doctors and her father.[76] Furthermore, a caesarean was not the only option considered by the court, but it was, ultimately, determined to be the best one.

On the face of it, the case for a caesarean seems stronger here than in *Re AA and P*, but the court approached the issue in a very different way. In relation to best interests, Hayden J stated that '[w]hen I consider the best interests of AA here, I do so by evaluating the clinical alternatives keeping her medical interests in focus. *But a best interests decision requires a broader survey of the available material.*'[77] He heard from BB *and* AA's father, and interpreted their evidence as meaning that if AA were lucid she would follow the medical advice and have a caesarean.[78] Although sections 4(6) and (7) of the MCA were not explicitly mentioned, it is clear that Hayden J was cognisant of them and so he gave weight to what AA would have wanted if she had capacity. His reasoning, therefore, is an example of best practice as there was a serious and successful attempt to give weight to AA's views and to engage with those of her family. It is, of course, easier to do this when these seem to accord with the recommendations of the doctors, but the law was correctly and appropriately applied, and the decision and the reasoning should thus be welcomed. It would, of course, be interesting to know if the same approach would have been adopted if, for

---

73 Ibid [10].
74 Ibid [11].
75 Ibid [18]. Capacity is discussed at [18]–[20].
76 Ibid [20].
77 Ibid [16], emphasis added.
78 Ibid.

example, AA's father had not supported the medically recommended course of action. Nevertheless, in this case the heavy boots of the law did not trample on AA. Rather, the law supported her and the 'police' were, for once, on her side.

NHS Trust 1, NHS Trust 2 v FG[79]

Finally, FG was 24, in the later stages of her first pregnancy, and was detained under section 3 of the MHA with a schizoaffective disorder. The Trust sought a declaration that she lacked the capacity to make decisions about her medical treatment and that it was in her best interests for a number of medical procedures to be undertaken, if necessary, when she went into labour. These included taking blood, inserting needles for IV access, and 'instrumental or operative delivery'.[80] Keehan J held that FG lacked the capacity to make decisions about medical treatment, and, having set out sections 1 and 4(1)–(4) and (6) of the MCA,[81] concluded that the orders sought by the Trust were in FG's best interests.[82] Although this is a lengthy judgment, 130 paragraphs in total and 24 paragraphs of guidance in an annex, there is nothing to explain how Keehan J reached his conclusions, beyond the simple acceptance of all of the medical evidence. Indeed, there was no input from other voices, as required by section 4(7) of the MCA.

Nevertheless, this case is notable because of the guidance which Keehan J set out for cases 'where a pregnant woman who lacks, or may lack, the capacity to make decisions about her obstetric health . . . resulting from a diagnosed psychiatric illness, falls within one of four categories of cases'.[83] These are where the proposed interventions 'probably amount to serious medical treatment' in the meaning of COP Practice Direction 9E,[84] there is 'a real risk that [the patient] will be subject to more than transient forcible restraint', there is a 'serious dispute as to what obstetric care is in [the patient's] best interests' or there is 'a real risk that [the patient] will suffer a deprivation of her liberty'.[85] There are nineteen points made relating to assessment and application, including that once an individual is identified as being the possible subject of an application to the court, the Acute and Mental Health Trusts should liaise to arrange an assessment of her capacity and best interests.[86] If capacity is likely to fluctuate, it should be 'kept under review',[87] and once a decision to go to court has been made, the application should be made 'at the earliest opportunity',[88] if possible 'no later than' 4 weeks before

---

79 *FG* (n 7).
80 Ibid [17].
81 Ibid [30] and [32], respectively.
82 Ibid [54].
83 Ibid guidance [2].
84 Court of Protection, Practice Direction 9E Applications relating to serious medical treatment (15 May 2014).
85 *FG* (n 7) guidance [3].
86 Ibid guidance [7].
87 Ibid guidance [9].
88 Ibid guidance[18].

the baby is due,[89] to give the Official Solicitor as much time as possible to 'undertake any necessary investigations'.[90] And 'emergency' applications should only be made if there is a 'genuine medical emergency'.[91] Some of these are similar to the *St George's* guidelines, but it is notable that the *FG* guidelines do not require attempts to be made to involve the patient in the process, only that her ascertainable wishes are to be provided to the court for consideration.[92] Thus, while the guidelines may be read as building on the lessons from the other more recent cases, the reasoning of Hayden J in *Great Western* does not, unfortunately, appear to have been recognised and developed.

Conclusion

So, where are we now with policing pregnancy? In some ways we are experiencing déjà vu. A case concerning liability for foetal injury has recently been heard by the courts, as has a series of cases involving the delivery options of women under the auspices of the MHA who are judged to lack the capacity to decide for themselves. In some of these cases, despite the requirements of the MCA, the capacity of the women was minimally considered[93] and their voices absent in the decision-making process.[94] Yet the reasoning in *Great Western Hospitals* stands out and is to be praised, and the *FG* guidelines may help to minimise the number of cases reaching court that involve women under the MHA. Indeed, the *St George's* guidelines appear to have helped to stop the policing of pregnancies of women with capacity, and the same may be the result of the FG guidelines for women under the MHA. We can but hope that this occurs, because it appears that law's gaze has shifted to this category of pregnant women. This is concerning, as is the misapplication of the MCA in some of the recent cases.

We suggest that Brazier's diagnosis of why the decision in *St George's* was unlikely to be the last forced caesarean case, because we had yet to resolve issues where procreative responsibility and liberty come into conflict, is still valid today. The question of *how* we address moral duties to the foetus without seeing them leak into legal ones remains unanswered. This has not gone unnoticed by others, and Ken Mason and Graeme Laurie, for example, have commented that the MCA was 'silent on the challenges thrown up by the pregnant woman' and that 'reinforcement of the pregnant woman's absolute right to refuse through the *Code of Practice* may have been welcomed on a number of fronts'.[95] We agree and suggest that without such, law's heavy boots may continue to be in evidence in the policing of some pregnancies.

---

89 Ibid guidance [19].
90 Ibid.
91 Ibid guidance [19].
92 *FG* (n 7) annex para 23(f).
93 *Re AA* (n 7); *FG* (n 7).
94 *P* (n 7); *FG* (n 7); *Re AA* (n 7).
95 JK Mason and G Laurie, *Mason and McCall Smith's Law and Medical Ethics* (9th edn, OUP 2013) 92.

Part V
The criminal law and the healthcare process

22 Vulnerability and the criminal law

The implications of Brazier's research for safeguarding people at risk

Kirsty Keywood and Zuzanna Sawicka

Introduction

In the 1980s the medico-legal landscape looked rather different. Whilst ethical notions of patient autonomy were beginning to seep into the courtroom, the courts' preoccupation remained rather firmly focussed on supporting doctors to do what would be in the patient's interests, whether in the context of reproductive decision-making,[1] the withdrawal of treatment from children and infants,[2] or the framing of medical malpractice liability.[3] Notions of patient autonomy had not yet gained dominance in judicial discourse, there was no clearly articulated legal test of mental (in)capacity,[4] the legal basis for decision-making in relation to adults lacking capacity had yet to be articulated by the appellate jurisdictions,[5] and the prospect of looking to what reasonable patients might want to know in order to shape the legal obligations of clinicians seemed an oddly exotic practice carried out in foreign lands.[6]

At that time, Margaret Brazier began to interrogate legal and ethical conceptions of autonomy and the impact that these had on individuals – a theme to which she has returned on numerous occasions. Some of those subject to the medico-legal gaze were individuals who were considered by the courts to be vulnerable by virtue of disability,[7] illness[8] or youth.[9] Others were rendered

---

1 *Re B (a minor) (wardship: sterilisation)* [1988] AC 199.
2 *Re B a minor) (wardship: medical treatment)* [1981] 1 WLR 1421 CA.
3 *Maynard v West Midlands Regional Health Authority* [1984] 1 WLR 634 HL.
4 The threshold of legal competence being discerned, by implication, from the ruling in *Chatterton v Gerson* [1981] QB 432.
5 *Re F (mental patient: sterilisation)* [1990] 2 AC 1.
6 *Sidaway v Bethlem Royal Hospital and the Maudsley Hospital Health Authority and Others* [1985] AC 871.
7 M Brazier 'Competence, Consent and Proxy Consent' in Margaret Brazier and Mary Lobjoit (eds), *Protecting the Vulnerable: Autonomy and Consent and Health Care* (Routledge 1991) ch 4.
8 M Brazier 'Do No Harm: Do Patients Have Responsibilities Too?' (2006) 65(2) CLJ 397.
9 M Brazier and C Bridge 'Coercion or Caring: Analysing Adolescent Autonomy' (1996) 16(1) LS 84.

vulnerable because of the court's framing of the limits of autonomy and the judicial preoccupation with according significant deference to the medical profession.[10]

Brazier's engagement with questions pertinent to the theme of vulnerability continued in the Arts and Humanities Research Council (AHRC) funded project, *The Impact of the Criminal Process on Health Care Ethics and Practice*, a major four-year research grant for which she acted as Principal Investigator. One of the strands of that project involved exploring possible criminal justice responses to adults who had experienced significant neglect or ill-treatment in hospital. This chapter seeks to review the significance of Brazier's research in the context of emerging theoretical work on vulnerability, shifting policy responses and legal developments. In so doing, we highlight that portion of Brazier's early writing that exposed some of the mechanisms through which law renders people vulnerable. We move on to explore, in brief, contemporary accounts of vulnerability and highlight the ongoing relevance of those critiques to Brazier's recent work on the role of the criminal law in healthcare. Brazier's work, we suggest, constitutes one of the important antecedents to vulnerability scholarship and continues to engage with themes that are central to that theoretical work today.

Protecting the vulnerable – Brazier's critique of autonomy and consent

In 1988, the Centre for Social Ethics and Policy (CSEP) at the University of Manchester hosted a series of public lectures which sought to tease out some of the challenges of recognising the legal and ethical significance of patient consent, whilst at the same time responding to the needs of those considered to be vulnerable. This series was subsequently published as *Protecting the Vulnerable: Autonomy and Consent and Health Care* which was edited by Brazier and her then colleague Mary Lobjoit.[11] In the book, Brazier challenged the framing of the patient as an object of professional beneficence and questioned what it means to be vulnerable and considered how the law should respond to vulnerability.[12] In what has become a hallmark of Brazier's writing, she interrogated a series of assumptions that underpin prevailing legal and ethical norms, through a sensitive and detailed reflection on the impact of the law on the lives of those subject to it. This included an acknowledgement that our vulnerability cannot always be explained solely by virtue of a person's inherent features.

In the late 1980s, such a perspective was at odds with prevailing judicial pronouncements on disability, articulated primarily in the context of cases

---

10 M Brazier 'Sterilisation: Down the Slippery Slope?' (1990) 6 Prof Neg 25.
11 M Brazier and M Lobjoit, *Protecting the Vulnerable: Autonomy and Consent and Health Care* (Routledge 1991).
12 Brazier (n 7).

concerning the proposed sterilisation of young women with learning disabilities.[13] Those cases construed vulnerability as an innate feature of a learning disability. This construction was secured through judicial adherence to a medical model of deficiency, which relied upon references to cognitive and physical impediments arising from the disability, allied with a framing of female, learning-disabled sexuality as volatile and dangerous. For Brazier and Lobjoit, vulnerability is, at least in part, socially situated. Their conceptualisation identifies individuals as vulnerable: 'by virtue of their youth, or nature, or position in society.'[14] At first glance, this does not seem to offer much by way of challenge to essentialising notions of disability and frailty which have limited the potential of the courts and policymakers to provide responses that acknowledge the potential for social transformation. Brazier's research goes on to acknowledge, however, that the presence of external factors, such as poverty, may impact greatly on a person's ability to shape and execute healthcare decisions.[15] In this way, her research resonates with the body of scholarship on the social model of disability and the principle of normalisation that was emerging at the time.[16]

Equally importantly, she exposes the extent to which the law is complicit in the production of this essentialising notion of vulnerability as attaching to particular individuals by reason of their physical or mental deficiencies. In critiquing the law's response to autonomy and consent, she unravels the arbitrary impacts of distinguishing between those considered to be vulnerable by virtue of their 'nature' and those who are not. Writing about the notion of mental capacity, at that time still grossly underdeveloped by the courts, she observed that:

> [T]housands of patients whose competence is never questioned stay away from dentists out of 'irrational' fear to the detriment of their dental, and sometimes their general, health. Yet it is only patients labelled mentally handicapped or demented who will find their 'irrational' treatment refusals overridden.[17]

In this way, her work fits neatly within the taxonomy of vulnerability developed by MacKenzie, Rogers and Dodds, which identifies such individuals as pathogenically vulnerable.[18] Pathogenic vulnerability is said to be arise when

---

13 See e.g. K Keywood, '"People Like us Don't have Babies": Learning Disability, Prospective Parenthood and Legal Transformations' in J Herring and J Wall (eds), *Landmark Cases in Medical Law* (Hart 2015) ch 3.
14 Brazier (n 7) 2.
15 Brazier (n 7) 40.
16 See e.g. J Goodall, 'Living Options for Physically Disabled Adults: A Review' (1988) 3(2) Disability, Handicap & Society 173; W Wolfensberger, *Normalization: The Principle of Normalization in Human Services* (National Institute of Mental Retardation 1972).
17 Brazier (n 7) 40.
18 C MacKenzie, W Rogers and S Dodds, 'Introduction: What is Vulnerability and Why does it Matter to Moral Theory' in MacKenzie, Rogers and Dodds (eds), *Vulnerability: New Essays in Ethics and Feminist Philosophy* (OUP 2014) 9.

individuals are subject to legal interventions and social practices which compromise a person's autonomy and security. These interventions, paradoxically, may themselves have been triggered to safeguard a person who was considered inherently vulnerable.

Brazier and Bridge's critique of the law involving consent in respect of 'mature' adolescents provides a useful illustration of this pathogenic vulnerability. Young people have historically been regarded as inherently vulnerable in law and social policy, deserving of protection because their immaturity renders them incapable of safeguarding their own interests.[19] In their article, the authors question the appropriateness of the use of the inherent jurisdiction to make best interests decisions in respect of young people deemed competent to make a decision to refuse medical treatment. In exploring those judicial rulings that acknowledge the right of the capacitous minor to consent to medical treatment but not to refuse it, Brazier and Bridge posit the question: 'should chronological age alone be the criterion by which capacity to refuse medical treatment should be judged? Can coercion be justified on grounds of age?'[20] They also challenge the converse position, questioning whether adult age alone provides sufficient justification for failing to protect those lacking the means to make meaningful choices about their lives. Their critique of adolescent autonomy suggests that the judiciary's adoption of a conceptually thin version of autonomy precluded a meaningful interrogation of the circumstances in which it may be appropriate to accede to, or decline, the wishes of the mature minor.

What is significant about Brazier's work during this time is that vulnerabilty is acknowledged but its scope and foundations are not fully articulated. Rather, Brazier engages with the increasingly familiar concepts of competence, maturity and autonomy. This is not to suggest, however, that Brazier's work can be readily dismissed by contemporary scholars of vulnerability. Indeed, in terms of legal scholarship, we suggest that Brazier's work provides an important foundation for the flourishing of that later work. The challenging of assumptions about the source of disability and incapacity, the problematisation of the connection between capacity and autonomy, and her critique of the law's response to adolescence suggests an intellectual affinity with vulnerability scholarship. In our next section, we demonstrate that affinity through an overview of contemporary vulnerability research.

Autonomy, liberty, vulnerability

The value of exploring relationships and obligations through the lens of vulnerability is that it enables us to begin to ground our ethical framework upon a commonality of human experience. Vulnerable at birth and entirely dependent

---

19 F Sherwood-Johnson, 'Constructions of "Vulnerability" in Comparative Perspective: Scottish Protection Policies and the Trouble with "Adults at Risk"' (2013) 28(7) Disability & Society 908, 914.
20 Brazier and Bridge (n 9) 87.

upon others for our survival and development, we are at risk of future vulnerability. How that vulnerability will be experienced depends on our environment and the necessary interplay of social and economic structural arrangements with our health, gender, disabilities, ethnicity. At some point, in some way, we are all vulnerable. For some, vulnerability matters morally because vulnerability becomes the moral principle that grounds a series of ethical obligations;[21] for others it serves as a useful analytical device that will trigger the application of other principles.[22]

Vulnerability has been described as 'antithetical to the ethos of individualism that pervades and dominates the moralities of Western societies',[23] requiring attention to the issues of dependency rather than independence, interconnection rather than separateness from others and the value of care rather than non-interference. Liberal values of liberty and autonomy are perceived as underpinning capacity for social advancement and prosperity. Those who fail to thrive according to current measures of success are considered vulnerable or 'at risk' populations, segmented according to their shared (internal) characteristics. For Fineman, these processes of categorisation are damaging for a number of reasons. First, they serve to obscure the differences that exist between individuals who are clustered together for the purposes of policy formation or legal regulation because of a perceived, internal vulnerability. Second, they fail to attend to an examination of the social, economic and political structuring that is necessarily implicated in the generation of a person's vulnerability. Finally, they obscure from consideration the fact that those who are perceived as being autonomous, active participants in the social contract may experience ongoing and significant challenges that render them vulnerable during their lifetime.[24]

Attention to vulnerability, then, enables us to challenge the foundational status of the liberal subject in healthcare law. The primacy afforded to patient autonomy in the law on consent to treatment underscores the notion that the legal order respects the right of individuals to shape for themselves their own destiny, free from state intervention or the illegitimate actions of others. But the general expectation – indeed a presumption under the Mental Capacity Act 2005 (MCA) – that most of us are capable of self-determination entails also the implication that those unable to exercise autonomy are precluded because

---

21 See e.g. M Albertson Fineman, 'Equality, Autonomy and the Vulnerable Subject in Law and Politics' in M Fineman and A Greer (eds), *Vulnerability: Reflections on a New Ethical Foundation for Law and Politics* (Ashgate 2013) ch 1.
22 L Pritchard-Jones, 'Ageism and Autonomy in Health Care: Explorations Through a Relational Lens' (2014) Health Care Anal 13; C MacKenzie, 'The Importance of Relational Autonomy and Capabilities for an Ethics of Vulnerability' in MacKenzie, Rogers and Dodds (n 18) ch 1.
23 B Hoffmaster, 'What Does Vulnerability Mean?' (2006) 36(2) Hastings Center Report 38, 42.
24 M Fineman (n 21) 16–17.

of their own psychological or age-related limitations.[25] The ethical premise of the MCA does not yet admit sufficient space to accommodate an analysis of power;[26] consideration of systematic oppression and social disadvantage currently reside at the margins of the courts' health and social care decision-making.[27]

Since Brazier's early writing on mental incapacity, the High Court has developed its jurisdiction to safeguard decision-making in respect of 'vulnerable adults'. The jurisdiction has focussed its attention on giving effect to the best interests of those individuals whose decision-making abilities have been compromised by the coercive or abusive influence of third parties. Those interests may be met through the imposition of injunctions to restrain assaulting or threatening behaviour,[28] best interests declarations to regulate contact,[29] or through the imposition of orders intended to secure assistance for and advice to the 'vulnerable' person.[30] To date, the exclusive application to those experiencing particular challenges associated with infirmity or mental disability serves to reinforce rather than undermine the liberal, legal order. The implication that risks being drawn here is that a healthy, non-disabled, psychologically robust individual would be able to withstand oppression and not require the assistance of the law. Here too, autonomy may be seen as compromised because of features inherent in the individual (e.g. they were exploited 'because they were old' or 'because they were disabled').[31]

Both Brazier's early work on vulnerable people and the emerging literature on vulnerability provide a powerful reminder that those presumed to be autonomous may in fact be vulnerable to a range of structural factors and social practices that may preclude their ability to lead a life of their choosing. Barry Hoffmaster's reflections on the circumstances surrounding his parents are particularly pertinent here.[32] His elderly father's vulnerability arises from an interplay of his health circumstances and the environment which does not always attend effectively to his needs and wants. His mother's vulnerability is a product of individual failings to inform her of key events in her husband's care, organisational practices that

---

25 Mental Capacity Act 2005 s 1(2). Note, however, recent developments in the Court of Protection to acknowledge the autonomy of those who are deemed to lack capacity under the MCA as part of the Court's evaluation of P's best interests: Nell Munro, 'Taking Wishes and Feelings Seriously: The Views of People Lacking Capacity in Court of Protection Decision-Making' (2014) 36(1) JSWFL 59.
26 See, on this point, John Harrington, 'Privileging the Medical Norm: Liberalism, Self-Determination and Refusal of Treatment' (1996) 16(3) Legal Studies 348.
27 For a notable exception to our general proposition, see Lady Hale's dissenting opinion in *McDonald v Royal Borough of Kensington and Chelsea* (2011) UKSC 33 at [78].
28 E.g. *DL v A Local Authority and Others* [2012] EWCA Civ 253; *The London Borough of Redbridge v G, AC, FC* [2014] EWCOP 17.
29 *G (an adult) (mental capacity: court's jurisdiction)* [2004] EWHC 2222.
30 E.g. the granting of access to a solicitor: *Re SA; FA v Mr A* (2010) EWCA Civ 1128.
31 B Clough, '"People Like That": Realising the Social Model in Mental Capacity Jurisprudence' (2015) 23(1) Med L Rev 53.
32 Hoffmaster (n 23).

shape the care her husband receives which results in increased emotional stress, and (unmet) cultural expectations that medicine can and should be able to do more to assist. To this, we may wish to note that the intersection of her status as carer with her gender would also have compounded her experience of vulnerability.[33]

Moreover, Brazier's work also highlights that a sensitive and contextual appraisal of the processes that render us vulnerable may not always be replicated by the law, even when our legal institutions purport to intervene explicitly on the grounds of vulnerability. For example, safeguarding frameworks anticipate state interventions which are predicated upon a desire to protect all children and those adults 'affected by disability, mental disorder, illness or physical or mental infirmity' in Scotland, or adults who have 'needs for care and support' in England.[34] Structural arrangements and social practices that impact on the lives of many children, adults and their families in such a way as to render them poor, disadvantaged, and without effective opportunities and supports to access to basic social goods are simply not acknowledged as representing factors that may be complicit in generating the sorts of risks of personal harm that provide the legal platform for intervention.[35]

The assumption that some people are more vulnerable than others is evidenced further in the criminal law. The statutory offences of ill-treatment and wilful neglect that apply to children[36] and to adults who either lack capacity[37] or who have a mental disorder[38] underscores the unarticulated legal and policy intuitions that there is something different about these populations and that this requires that they are accorded an enhanced degree of protection. Brazier and colleagues' research on the criminal law argued compellingly for a new offence which would criminalise ill-treatment and neglect of all in receipt of hospital care. Not only

---

33 See also G Boyle, 'Facilitating Decision-Making by People with Dementia: is Spousal Support Gendered?' (2013) 35(2) JSWFL 227.
34 Adult Support and Protection (Scotland) Act 2007, s 3; Care Act 2014, s 42.
35 In the context of child protection law, the threshold required is of a risk of 'significant harm': Children Act 1989, s 31. From April 2015, s 42(1) of the Care Act 2014 creates a duty to undertake investigations in respect of adults who have 'needs for care and support and are experiencing, or are at risk of, abuse or neglect'. In Scotland, the Adult Support and Protection (Scotland) Act 2007 triggers interventions if the adult is 'at risk of harm': s 3(2).
36 The Children and Young Persons Act 1933, s 1(1) is much broader in scope than its adult counterparts and extends to wilful assault, abandonment or exposure to unnecessary suffering or injury to health.
37 Mental Capacity Act 2005, s 44. The offences apply where the defendant reasonably believes P to lack capacity. Furthermore, in cases where an individual has committed an act of ill-treatment or wilful neglect when they believed a patient lacked capacity, but it later becomes apparent that the victim had capacity, then the offence can still apply.
38 Mental Health Act 1983, s 127. An offence arises where the person with a mental disorder is accessing treatment for their disorder on the premises of a hospital or home, or where the person is subject to guardianship, custody or care by the abuser.

were the current statutory offences doctrinally unsound for their lack of precision[39] and infrequently used with any success,[40] they also failed to attend to the very real vulnerabilities that any person may experience when accommodated in an environment which pays scant attention to their basic needs.

Brazier, vulnerability and the criminal law

Reviewing the dismal care standards at Staffordshire NHS Trust, in which 400–1200 more deaths were reported in a four-year period than was expected, Brazier and colleagues observed that 'patients who cannot get themselves to the lavatory and/or eat without help are of necessity vulnerable'.[41] Whether it is our dependency on others, the 'totalising effect'[42] of the institution in which that dependency arises, or an interplay of these, is an important question, albeit one beyond the scope of this chapter. Significantly, however, Brazier and colleagues eschew any confidence that any liabilities imposed by the criminal law should arise from the possession of a mental disorder or a lack of mental capacity. In calling for new offences of ill-treatment and wilful neglect that apply to all individuals in any healthcare setting, they acknowledge the commonality of vulnerability which is experienced by individuals in hospital. Indeed, it is now recognised that hospitalisation and, indeed, recurrent healthcare episodes can be associated with frailty and lead to an increased vulnerability.[43] This vulnerability can often lead them to be at increased risk of all forms of abuse, but especially neglect.[44]

In 2013, the Francis Report made clear recommendations including the need for openness, transparency and candour throughout the healthcare system (including a statutory duty of candour) and the establishment and maintenance

---

39 N Allen, 'Psychiatric Care and Criminal Prosecution' in A Alghrani, S Ost and R Bennett (eds), *The Criminal Law and Bioethical Conflict: Walking The Tightrope* (CUP 2013).
40 The lack of prosecutions under these Acts suggests that the current system is ineffective. In 2011–2012, local authorities in England completed 84,000 investigations into alleged abuse of neglect of a vulnerable adult. Of these, 42% of the cases assessed were fully or partly upheld. The Serious Case Review into events at Winterbourne View revealed hundreds of previous incidents of abuse at the hospital, yet only 11 people pleaded guilty to criminal offences of wilful neglect and ill-treatment: C Tozer and J Plomin, 'The abuse of vulnerable adults at Winterbourne View Hospital: the lessons to be learned' (2013) 15(4) Journal of Adult Protection 182.
41 A Alghrani, M Brazier, A M Farrell, D Griffiths and N Allen, 'Healthcare Scandals in the NHS: Crime and Punishment' (2011) 37 Journal of Medical Ethics 230.
42 E Goffmann, *Asylums: Essays on the Social Situation of Patients and Other Inmates* (Anchor Books 1961).
43 H Ming Ma, R Yu and J Woo, 'Recurrent hospitalisation with pneumonia is associated with a higher 1-year mortality in frail older people' (2013) 11 Internal Medicine Journal 1210.
44 See S Wood and M Stephens, 'Vulnerability to Elder Abuse and Neglect in Assisted Living Facilities' (2003) 43(5) The Gerontologist 753.

of fundamental standards for healthcare providers.[45] Following the publication of the Francis Report, the Prime Minister commissioned Professor Don Berwick, an expert in patient safety, to look at what needs to be done 'to make zero harm a reality in our NHS' and ensure that effective mechanisms were put in place to safeguard individuals from such abuse and neglect.[46] The Berwick Report recommended the creation of a new statutory offence of 'wilful or reckless neglect or mistreatment of patients' that could be used to prosecute individuals or organisations. The United Kingdom (UK) government acknowledged that everyone should expect 'safe, compassionate care'[47] and that the creation of a new offence would ensure 'ultimate accountability for those guilty of the most extreme types of poor care'.[48]

The proposed offences of ill-treatment or neglect by care workers or care providers was inserted into the Criminal Justice and Courts Act 2015 and came into force on 13 April 2015.[49] The new offences apply to all formal health and social care settings, including all NHS hospitals and ambulance services, independent hospitals, community health and care services, primary care services, all nursing and adult care homes, all domiciliary care and day care services. The criminal law holds individuals who are care workers (which includes healthcare professionals as well as social care professionals working in the field of adult social care),[50] as well as organisations who provide care, to account.[51] The latter

---

45 *Report of the Mid Staffordshire NHS Foundation Trust Public Inquiry* HC 898-I (The Stationery Office 2013)
46 National Advisory Group on the Safety of Patients in England, *A Promise to Learn – a Commitment to Act: Improving the Safety of Patients in England* (National Advisory Group 2013).
47 Department of Health, *Hard Truths, the Journey to Putting Patients First* (CM 87771 2014).
48 Ibid para 1.41.
49 The Criminal Justice and Courts Act (Commencement No.1: Saving and Transitional Provisions) Order 2015, SI 2015/778.
50 The UK economy thrives on the provision of informal and family care arrangements. In 2011, it was estimated that carers of all ages save the United Kingdom economy £119 billion a year: Age UK, *Later Life in the United Kingdom* (Age UK 2014). The potential reduction in this resource as a result of a new loss of such a resource could significantly reduce the amount of informal care that is provided and place increased strain on the current pressurised social care system. This in turn would lead to further delays in discharges from NHS hospitals which are already significant: M Bauer, L Fitzgerald, E Haesler and M Manfrin, 'Hospital discharge planning for frail older people and their family. Are we delivering best practice? A review of the evidence' 2009 18(18) Journal of Clinical Nursing 2539.
51 Criminal Justice and Court Act (CJCA), s 21(1). Although note that the notion of a 'gross' breach seems at odds with that developed by the common law in framing the offence of gross negligence manslaughter. Under this Act, a breach will be gross 'if the conduct alleged to amount to the breach falls far below what can reasonably be expected of the care provider in the circumstances': s 21(6). The aim of the new offence to organisations is to ensure that there is collective responsibility to prevent wilful neglect occurring in the first instance.

offences are triggered when the ill-treatment or neglect has resulted from, or is more likely to have resulted from, a 'gross' breach in the duty of care by the service provider in their organisation or management of their activities.[52]

Under the new offences, penalties for care workers include imprisonment, a fine, or both.[53] Additionally, however, they can be made subject to a remedial order, a publicity order, or both.[54] A remedial order would require the person/organisation to take specified steps to remedy any or all of a breach in the duty of care; deficiencies in policies, systems or practices are resolved, to prevent the breach or any concerns which may be connected to the episode of wilful neglect or ill-treatment reoccurring. We anticipate that such orders often further throw individuals and organisations into the media spotlight and may act as a considerable deterrent to mistreatment and neglect in a care setting.

Concerns were raised that the introduction of the new offence may lead to unintended negative consequences, such as under-reporting of incidents.[55] There was also significant fear that individual employees may become scapegoats for what is in fact a direct failure in managerial or organisational practice. For example, the National Institute for Health and Care Excellence (NICE) has produced guidance on safe staffing levels in hospitals.[56] If individuals rather than managers or the organisation are held accountable for situations where staffing is inadequate, the latter may be ill-equipped to take responsibility for failure of managerial or organisational practices, and staff morale will significantly suffer.[57] Recruitment and retention may plummet, leading to increasing staff shortages and further strain on the healthcare system. Finally, the overlay of the new offences onto the pre-existing offences under the MCA and Mental Health Act (MHA) may produce a patchwork of legal provision that becomes so complex that it proves unworkable in practice. To this end, Brazier and colleagues recommended in their response to the public consultation on the proposed offences[58] that the offences under the MHA and MCA should be abolished and a new offence created which is applicable to all, irrespective of their health circumstances, age or impairing conditions. This would have prevented statutory

---

52 CJCA, s 21(1). The Act excludes informal care provision, prompted perhaps in part by a desire to maintain the valuable resource provided by informal carers, which, as indicated above (n 50) are so important.
53 CJCA, s 23(1).
54 CJCA, s 23(2).
55 R Griffith 'Extending the scope of wilful neglect will result in paternalistic nursing care' (2013) 22(20) British Journal of Nursing 1190.
56 National Institute of Health and Care Excellence, *Safe Staffing for Nursing in Adult Inpatient Wards in Acute Hospitals* (National Institute of Health and Care Excellence 2014); Royal College of Nursing, *Safe Staffing for Older People's Wards* (Royal College of Nursing 2012).
57 'Have you lost faith in the NHS', (2001) *BBC News*, 23 February <http://news.bbc.co.uk/1/hi/talking_point/1171867.stm> (accessed 15 December 2014).
58 N Allen, M Brazier, S Devaney, D Griffiths, K Keywood and H Quirk, *New Criminal Offence of Ill-treatment or Wilful Neglect. Response to Consultation* (University of Manchester, 21 March 2014).

duplication, clarified the application of the criminal law and promoted adherence to the law by streamlining prosecution processes.

Conclusion

Brazier's ongoing concern with those who are vulnerable in their encounters with medicine and social care invites us to reflect on how we might best, as a society, attend to the needs of those who depend on us. She rightly cautions that the criminal law will not effectively and neatly resolve matters of significant bioethical conflict.[59] The criminal law, at different points in time and in different domains of the discipline, accommodates a mosaic of ethical considerations, political claims and philosophical positions. Will the criminalisation of conduct which purports to be 'care' escape the controversies attached to other forms of criminalisation which, according to Brazier and Ost, may render the medical profession vulnerable?[60] We suggest that in large part it will. Cases of ill-treatment and wilful neglect do not routinely engage the same bioethical controversies as those at stake in the criminal law of abortion or assisted dying where, for Brazier and Ost, clinicians have 'acted for the highest of motives'.[61] The definitions of ill-treatment and wilful neglect, borrowed as they are from existing offences under the MHA and MCA, offer some comfort to those concerned that the legislation will punish professionals for 'innocent' lapses in care.

Oversights in care by health and social care professionals have not generally attracted the attention of the criminal courts, for it is the wrongfulness of conduct rather than the harm sustained that warrants criminal sanction under these offences. Negligent errors in organisation or management may well attract criminal sanction, albeit these are likely to be financial in nature. Such regulatory offences are not uncommon in the criminal law and provide necessary recognition that organisations have a responsibility to secure minimum standards of safety and wellbeing. Perhaps more importantly for the purposes of this chapter, the new offences may also safeguard against the systemic threats to vulnerability that are beyond the available means of care workers and care recipients to avoid. Our focus latterly on the criminal law must not, however, obscure the importance of other legal domains acting to foster resilience in the structures, environments and circumstances of those who are rendered vulnerable in their health and social care encounters.[62] The light that Brazier shone on the question of vulnerability 25 years ago shines ever brighter today. It is still too early to call off the search.

---

59 M Brazier and S Ost, *Bioethics, Medicine and the Criminal Law: Medicine and Bioethics in the Theatre of the Criminal Process* (CUP 2013).
60 Ibid 6.
61 M Brazier, 'Can English Law Accommodate Moral Controversy in Medicine? Lessons from Abortion' in Alghrani, Ost and Bennett (n 41), ch 12; Brazier and Ost (n 59) 1.
62 For an excellent illustration of this approach, see B Clough, 'Vulnerability and Capacity to Consent to Sex – Asking the Right Questions?' (2014) 16(4) CFLQ 371.

23 Revisiting the criminal law on the transmission of disease

David Gurnham and Andrew Ashworth

Introduction

In her 2006 article 'Do no harm – do patients have responsibilities too?'[1] Margaret Brazier offers a characteristically thoughtful critique of what she describes as the 'overselling' of a 'facile' understanding of patient autonomy as individuated, unfettered and atomised. Approving Onora O'Neill's richer formulation, Brazier insists that autonomy entails 'self-mastery' and 'self-control', possibly even 'self-sacrifice';[2] we live in a social world of mutual and reciprocal obligations in which patients (as persons) as well as doctors owe a duty to 'do no harm'[3] as well as to 'take responsibility for [their] own actions'.[4] Patients' responsibilities 'do not disappear simply because they are ill',[5] and that this should convert into 'some kind of legal responsibility' for infecting others with a serious disease, Brazier argues is 'self-evident'.[6] Such remarks might well be taken as an uncompromising rejection of the arguments of those who call for the decriminalisation of disease transmission. However, as we shall see, we disagree with commentators who have read Brazier as straightforwardly endorsing a pro-criminalisation agenda.[7]

An opportunity to revisit this question of the appropriate legal consequences of a failure by a patient to avoid doing harm to others, as well as the implications to be drawn from Brazier's arguments, now arises. While the transmission of HIV was criminalised a decade ago,[8] the Law Commission has issued a scoping paper on offences against the person in November 2014,[9] and the Court of Appeal has ruled on the reckless transmission of STIs in *R v Golding*.[10]

---

1 M Brazier, 'Do no harm – do patients have responsibilities too?' (2006) 65 Cam LJ 397.
2 Ibid 400.
3 Ibid 402.
4 Ibid 403.
5 Ibid 399.
6 Ibid 408–9.
7 G R Mawhinney, 'COMMENT – To Be Ill or to Kill: The Criminality of Contagion' (2013) 77 J Crim L 202.
8 *Dica* [2004] EWCA Crim 1103.
9 Law Commission Consultation Paper No. 217, *Reform of Offences against the Person: a Scoping Consultation Paper* (2014).
10 [2014] EWCA Crim 889.

In this judgment, the Court upheld the conviction of David Golding for maliciously inflicting grievous bodily harm[11] in the form of genital herpes (Herpes Simplex type 2, or HSV-2), which he transmitted to his girlfriend (CS) through unprotected sexual intercourse. He had known that he was infected with genital herpes but had not disclosed his infection to her. She subsequently suffered many of the unpleasant symptoms often associated with herpes, including excruciating pain during urination. Golding had pleaded guilty on what would otherwise have been the first day of his trial and was sentenced to 14 months' imprisonment. The Crown Prosecution Service (CPS) then belatedly commissioned expert reports, and a delay of two years occurred, followed by another delay of 6 months before the case could be re-listed for hearing. Without finding fault with either the conviction or the sentence, the Court of Appeal nonetheless 'exceptionally' allowed him to be released after serving just three months (time served), on the basis that he had suffered enough through the delays.[12]

The appeal raises important issues both about criminal procedure and about the application and meaning of substantive criminal law concepts. However, constraints on space here dictate that we can only examine the substantive issues. We first make some brief remarks about the Court of Appeal's approach, before trying to identify the fundamental policy issues raised by the *Golding* case. We then pass to more detailed policy issues that remain to be dealt with, either within or outwith the criminal law.

The Court of Appeal's approach

In its judgment the Court devotes far more space to personal assessments of the parties themselves[13] than to a properly detailed consideration of the appropriate reach of criminalisation and substantive criminal law concepts. We find it to be problematic that the judgment – an opportunity after all to consider important and controversial implications of the criminalisation of disease – places as much weight as it does on these personal matters and upon general impressions of Golding and CS as witnesses. As Brazier rightly observes, the 'full ramifications of criminalisation of disease transmission are endless'[14] but you would not know that from the *Golding* appeal. The problem with the Court of Appeal's approach is that, in placing such a heavy emphasis on the personal integrity and truthfulness of the parties involved, the judgment fails to grapple with key principles of *general* importance such as harm, fault and causation, which are crucial to this sphere of the criminal law. Given the fact that this is a judgment that confirms the CPS's effective extension of the net of criminal law further into the sexual lives of individuals, we submit that whether such an extension is right or wrong, there is a strong argument either for a Supreme

---

11 Offences Against the Person Act 1861, s 20; in practice 'maliciously' means 'recklessly'.
12 *Golding* (n 10) [93]; see further K Laird, 'Commentary on *R v. Golding*' [2014] Crim LR 686.
13 Ibid [4]–[5], [26], [36], [60]–[61], [78].
14 Brazier (n 1) 409.

Court ruling on this case that takes account of the wider policy issues or for a detailed examination of the issues by the Law Commission.

Fundamental policy issues

The questions that have required full discussion since *Clarence*[15] are whether the sexual transmission of disease ought to be criminalised, or whether it ought to be dealt with as a matter of public health law. If it is contended that the knowing or risky transmission of disease to another does pass the threshold for criminalisation – a massive issue, in the context of a burgeoning criminalisation debate,[16] and one that depends to a large extent on the harmful consequences of particular diseases – then there are questions about countervailing considerations. If we focus on the transmission of disease through sexual activity rather than the general transmission of disease to another (such as tuberculosis or Ebola), does that not raise questions about the private sphere? Should the criminal law intervene in the private sphere of sexual activity, or is there a sufficient public interest in intervention here (as in the case of domestic violence, where references to the private sphere are subordinated to the importance of protecting people from violence)?

The arguments against any form of disease criminalisation are now well-known, but worth noting briefly here. A number of commentators have in various ways sought to distinguish disease transmission from, for instance, domestic violence and sexual assault, not on the basis that 'law should stay out of the bedroom', but rather by challenging the view that disease transmission is necessarily a victimising act as those crimes are.[17] In the contexts in which disease is transmitted, those roles may not be quite as clear or distinct as they are in other, less contentious offences. For example, the infector may be just as much a 'victim' (of HIV/AIDS, of problems of access to healthcare resources or information on safer practices, of societal stigma, etc.) and the infectee as 'responsible' for the spread of infection, by failing to take her or his own precautions, ask questions, etc. And while there may well of course be reasons that explain an infectee's failure to insist on safer practices that would have protected her or him (such as the fear of domestic violence), there may also be reasons other than callousness about another's health explaining the infector's failure to disclose.[18] For some commentators, the idea that disease is something that is 'inflicted'

---

15 (1888) 22 QBD 23.
16 See A P Simester and A von Hirsch, *Crimes, Harms and Wrongs: on the Principles of Criminalisation* (Hart 2011), and D Husak, *Overcriminalization: The Limits of the Criminal Law* (OUP 2008) for general analysis.
17 See M Weait, *Intimacy and Responsibility: The Criminalization of HIV Transmission* (Routledge-Cavendish 2007); A Houlihan, 'When "No" means "Yes" and "Yes" means harm: HIV risk, consent and sadomasochism case law' (2011) Law & Sexuality: A Review of Lesbian, Gay, Bisexual and Transgender Legal Issues 20, 31–59; D Gurnham, *Crime, Desire and Law's Unconscious: Law, literature and culture* (Routledge 2014).
18 Weait (ibid).

upon another artificially individuates responsibility for its spread, when such responsibility is arguably the responsibility of everyone. Looked at more broadly than the individual relationship between infector and infectee, disease spreads because people in general fail to take the precautions that would prevent it.[19] The focus on the responsibility only of those infected (namely, to disclose that they are infected) is a perspective particular to the punitive function of criminal justice, and it is not necessarily in concert with the larger aim of stopping the global spread. For this reason primarily, criminal justice imperatives frequently find themselves in conflict with the values and priorities of public health and sexual health professionals and clinicians.[20]

However, the appeal decision in the case of *Golding* confirms that the criminalisation of disease communication in England and Wales, far from being beaten back, is well established. Critical engagements with the topic that acknowledge this fact must focus their attention, not on whether disease communication is *to be* criminalised, but how this might be done in ways that are as fair to individuals, as helpful for public health initiatives and cause as little harm to vulnerable and stigmatised populations as possible. Returning to the issues in *Clarence*, another major question is whether the wrong here is intrinsically one of deception as well as one of infection. People can pick up harmful infectious diseases from many sources. The big difference here is that the transferee consented to a communicative act (sexual intercourse) on a mistaken premise, because the transferor knowingly engaged in that act without informing the transferee. The latter was wronged as a result of being deceived, or at least not being informed of a consideration that was obviously highly material to her decision to consent.[21] Of course, part of the wrong also resides in the harmful consequences of the disease to which she allowed herself to be exposed; but the issue of deception, and the private sphere in which it occurred, needs to be brought into consideration when deciding whether this is a suitable case for criminalisation.

Related policy issues

Bearing in mind those fundamental issues – too wide-ranging to be argued to a conclusion here – we must now consider the more focused questions that need to be answered when resolving the fundamental policy issues. First, a group of harm questions: what might be the characteristics of a disease that would present the strongest case for criminalisation? Is the mode of transmission

---

19 Houlihan (n 17); Weait (ibid); and J Loveless, 'Criminalising Failure to Disclose HIV to Sexual Partners: a short note on recent lessons from the Canadian Supreme Court' [2013] 3 Crim LR 214.
20 D Gurnham, 'What role should criminal justice play in the fight against STIs?' (2012) 88(1) Sexually Transmitted Infections 4.
21 Cf Canada, where failure to disclose a serious infection may constitute a fraud that vitiates consent to sexual intercourse for a charge of sexual assault, even where D take precautionary measures (*R v Mabior* (2012) SCC 47).

relevant here? And if we are discussing levels of harm, how should these be matched to the existing structure of non-fatal offences against the person? Would a new structure for offences of personal violence alter the argument? Second, and relatedly, causation questions: is it established how these diseases can be communicated? How widely do members of the public, or those who have been medically advised, know about the potential for transmitting the disease to others by various means? Third, and again relatedly, how should culpability be constructed if there is to be criminalisation? Should an intent to cause harm be proved, or is it sufficient to establish that the transferor was subjectively reckless as to the risk of transmitting the disease by the chosen activity? These issues are discussed one by one, although their inter-connections will also be noted.

What level of harm should be required for criminalisation?

If the transmission of disease is to be criminalised, what level of harm should be required? Perhaps in an ideal world the criminal law would incorporate a list of diseases capable of causing serious harm to the transferee, and the court would simply read them off. This is unattainable for at least three reasons – one is that many of the diseases vary in their impact on health, so that sometimes they cause really serious harm and in other contacts the consequences may be no more than mildly inconvenient; another is that the potential seriousness of the consequences may depend on the vulnerability of the other people involved, as where a community nurse goes to work knowing that he or she has influenza and realising that already sick patients might contract it; a third is that any such list would have to be related, using expert opinion, to the degree of harm specified by the different levels of criminal offence. Thus the question in *Golding* was whether there was (as the Court found) a sufficient basis for the jury to consider whether the consequences of the transmission amounted to 'grievous bodily harm', or whether they merely amounted to the lesser offence (although with the same maximum penalty of 5 years' imprisonment) of assault occasioning actual bodily harm, contrary to section 47 of the Offences Against the Person Act 1861. Herpes simplex may cause a recurrent, painful, blistering genital rash, or may go unnoticed. Those with HSV-2 have an 80–90% chance of recurrence within 12 months, with typically around four recurrences in a lifetime.[22] Treacy LJ affirmed that the judgment is one for the jury rather than experts,[23] the necessary basis for their verdict being provided by the experts describing herpes as an 'unpleasant and painful acute illness',[24] causing 'soreness' and 'excruciating pain' to CS,[25]

---

22 K Dunphy, 'Herpes genitalis and the philosopher's stance' (2014) 40 (12) J Med Ethics 793.
23 *Golding* (n 10) [77].
24 Ibid [20].
25 Ibid [57].

as an 'incurable and recur[ring]' and 'devastating condition'.[26] The judgment goes on to recall that 'grievous' means 'really serious'[27] and to affirm that an assessment of the degree of harm takes into account the particular circumstances of and impact upon the victim both at the time of first presenting and projected into the future, applying 'contemporary social standards'.[28]

Since the offences concerned are result-crimes (specifying the degree or type of harm caused), the mode of transmission should not be a determinative issue. There is, however, the difficulty with the word 'inflicting' in section 20 of the Offences Against the Person Act 1861, and we should consider this in the present context. The Court of Appeal's decision that the jury was entitled to find that Golding did 'inflict' herpes on the complainant (and furthermore that he was 'reckless' in doing so – see below) crucially turns on the contrast between the defendant and complainant on the question of their relative knowledge, sexual behaviour and honesty – providing the necessary *prima facie* case for a verdict.[29] It is well-known that it is very difficult to ascertain with a great deal of accuracy the exact source and timing of herpes transmission, and thus very difficult for genitourinary experts to provide a criminal court with the kind of certainty on this matter to secure a conviction.[30] It is unsurprising then that the Court placed a comparatively heavy emphasis on their positive impression of the female complainant (CS) and their preference for her testimony that she had not had any other sexual relations at the relevant time.[31] As a legal question, that transmitting a disease by way of sexual intercourse can be understood to satisfy the meaning of 'inflicts' for the purposes of s 20 is no longer particularly controversial. Judge LJ's overturning in the landmark judgment in *R v Dica*[32] of the *Clarence*[33] principle that grievous bodily harm could not be 'inflicted' by consensual sexual intercourse is now well established, as *Golding* confirms.

One important issue for the criminalisation of herpes is the transmissibility of that type of infection, because this is relevant to the magnitude of the risk posed by sexual intercourse with an infected person. In addressing this issue, we might compare it with the criminalisation of HIV transmission and with judgments on HIV handed down by the Court of Appeal roughly a decade ago at time of writing. In those cases (*Dica* and also *R v Konzani*[34]), exposing a sexual partner to the risk of HIV infection was judged to pass the threshold of an unjustifiable risk, even though a) the risk of infection arising from any single

---

26 Ibid [59].
27 *DPP v Smith* [1961] AC 290.
28 *Golding* (n 10) [64], citing *R v Bollom* [2003] EWCA Crim 2846.
29 *Golding* (n 10) [62], [76].
30 E Clarke, J Green and R Patel, 'Sex post Golding: Time for a debate on whether the criminal law is the best way to deal with infectious diseases' (2014) 349 BMJ:g4457.
31 *Golding* (n 10) [16], [10], [30]–[31], [46].
32 [2004] EWCA Crim 1103.
33 *Clarence* (n 15).
34 [2005] EWCA Crim 706.

act of unprotected heterosexual vaginal sex is known to be as low as 1 in 1000 to 1 in 2000 (or 0.1–0.05%) (allowing for the various contingent factors[35]) and b) HIV is no longer fatal, provided that antiretroviral treatment is available and taken properly.[36] The latter consideration is not crucial here, because the question concerns grievous bodily harm. However, in *Dica* and *Konzani* the Court did at least demonstrate awareness that in applying s 20 to sexually transmitted infections they were taking the law into a new territory, even if they did not attend to the specific details of the transmissibility or healthcare implications of HIV. If we accept that the courts were right in those cases to deem a single act of unprotected vaginal heterosexual intercourse where one party is HIV positive an 'unjustifiable' risk when the infected person fails to disclose and transmission actually occurs, then it is not inconsistent to take the same line with herpes. The available information suggests that the likelihood of transmission of herpes is certainly no lower than is the case with HIV. It also suggests that, in the absence of any precautionary measures taken by the infected party (i.e. no disclosure, no condoms), the risk of HSV-2 exposure is 20% per episode. In a long-term relationship it is 18% per annum for M>F and 5% for F>M.[37] Although the status of herpes as 'incurable' is contested (HVA 2014 puts this belief down to misinformation from drugs companies in the 1980s), it is taken as fact by the Court of Appeal in *Golding* that CS would require lifelong treatment.

How, if at all, does the seriousness of genital herpes relate to the legal categories of offence? Some sexual health experts maintain that herpes (HSV-2) is in general terms insufficiently severe to attract the label of 'grievous' bodily harm.[38] Others have argued that it is on the contrary a very serious infection indeed.[39] It seems evident that the symptoms actually experienced by individual infected persons are highly variable, ranging from barely being aware of having been infected to very severe pain and flare-ups of sores that reoccur throughout one's life. If the disease has to be categorised once and for all, there would seem to be a strong case for herpes as *actual* bodily harm in the present structure of offences, because even the more minor cases would be likely to qualify as interfering with the 'health or comfort' of the victim.[40] However, this throws up a further problem: that whereas it is established (since Lord Steyn's judgment in

---

35 See B Knauper and R Kornik, 'Perceived transmissibility of STIs: lack of differentiation between HIV and chlamydia' (2004) 80 Sexually Transmitted Infections 74.
36 L Gable, L Gostin and JG Hodge Jr., 'A global assessment of the role of law in the HIV/AIDS pandemic' (2009) 123 Public Health 260.
37 Dunphy (n 22).
38 Herpes Viruses Association: 'We are appalled at the court's failure to overturn the guilty verdict. Herpes virus transmission should not be in the legal arena at all' (Press release, 8 May 2014).
39 S D Sallen, 'HERPES-A Legal Cure-Can the Law Succeed Where Medicine has Failed?' (1983–4) 61 U Det J Urb L 273.
40 *R v Donovan* [1934] 2 KB 498.

Burstow[41]) that 'inflicting' grievous bodily harm for the purposes of s 20 simply means 'causing' and hence does not require an 'assault' by D, no such width of interpretation has ever been applied to the 'occasioning' of actual bodily harm under s 47. An assault must be proved, because it is integral to the offence.

The reasons why this is so speak to the question of the criminal law's reach, raised above: grievous bodily harm is considered serious enough to warrant a more flexible approach to the means by which it is caused so that cases of serious harm do not escape punishment too easily; actual bodily harm on the other hand is much less serious (and more common) and hence the stricter prosecution threshold serves to deter over-criminalisation. In 1861 Parliament did not have in mind sexually transmitted infections when it enacted the Offences Against the Person Act, and probably intended both *inflict* (s 20) and *occasion* (s 47) to involve an act of violence. While the generally accepted seriousness of HIV/AIDS (even in the age of effective and accessible antiretroviral treatment) can be brought within the widening of the *actus reus* of s 20, no such general acceptance exists in the case of herpes.

The Court in *Golding* failed to examine the context and implications of holding that genital herpes falls within s 20, although its judgment signals that herpes (and possibly a range of other yet to be determined ills and diseases too) is indeed henceforth to be considered serious enough to qualify as grievous bodily harm, despite considerable doubt about this amongst sexual health experts (it is likely that the reaction to the judgment by the Herpes Viruses Association (HVA) – that 'herpes virus transmission should not be in the legal arena at all' (2014) – represents the opinion of a large community of sexual health practitioners). Of course, the Court of Appeal does not have the authority to depart from the established common law requirements under s 47: the need is for a bolder, more authoritative ruling from the Supreme Court, or a full examination by the Law Commission. Any argument in favour of the criminalisation of transmitting infections – herpes included – ought to engage closely with the issues of transmissibility and short- and long-term effects,[42] in relation to the structure of the relevant offences against the person.

What evidence of causation is required?

Any proper examination of the issues must have a basis in expert opinion. Whether it is the Law Commission analysing the issues, scholars making arguments about them, or indeed a court dealing with a particular case, there needs to be a foundation in expert medical opinion. One question is how harmful a particular communicable disease can be: are the consequences always of the same order, or do they vary considerably? If they vary, are patients informed about this? It is certainly not for medical experts to state that certain

---

41 [1998] AC 147.
42 Cf. Sallen (n 39) 280–1 in particular.

consequences amount to the 'really serious injury' required for grievous bodily harm, as they purported to do in *Golding* and which the Court of Appeal rightly discounted.[43] It seems that it is not the normal consequences of a given disease that are determinative but the actual consequences in the particular case (see *Bollom*, cited above), and this of course has to do with the culpability question.

A particular difficulty in *Golding* was that it could not be determined from Golding's medical records whether his particular strain of herpes was type 1 (HSV-1 – which may be transmitted from the mouth) or type 2 (HSV-2 – the strain CS contracted, transmissible realistically only by sexual intercourse). Apart from the issue of causation (on which, as we have said, the Court simply preferred CS's evidence over Golding's), this implies that the criminal law now extends to herpes cases in which HSV-1 is transmitted by kissing. Given that there is a fault element in liability (on which see below), it is important to consider the sort of behaviour we are deeming it proper to target. If the *Golding* judgment is to be taken as authority for the notion that prosecutions based on 'reckless kissing', if not envisaged now, may at least in theory be possible in the near future, then it will be important to consider whether we find that 'encouraging',[44] 'appalling',[45] 'absurd'[46] or something in between. It is a question that furthermore makes our brief consideration above of the transmissibility of herpes relevant. The ends of criminal justice might be best served by pursuing and punishing bodily harm wherever we find it and without prioritising or excluding any particular means by which it is caused, or it may be preferable to limit its reach by excluding activities and behaviours that are trivial or are otherwise too routine to deem criminal. This policy matter deserves a much fuller treatment than it receives in this judgment.

How should the fault element be interpreted?

It is on the question of the fault requirement that the reluctance of Treacy LJ to go into more depth on policy and the proper 'reach' of criminal sanction becomes more problematic. If (unusually) it can be proved that the defendant intended to infect the transferee, knowing of the potentially serious effects of infection, the route to liability is clear. But what about the more usual case, where the prosecution has to prove recklessness? The *Golding* judgment confirms that, in the context of s 20, the test for recklessness is primarily a subjective one to the extent that the defendant must have been aware of an unjustifiable risk of causing 'some harm to some person, albeit of a minor character' and go on to take that risk.[47] The Court held that the jury were entitled to find

---

43 *Golding* (n 10) [77].
44 Mawhinney (n 7) 213.
45 Herpes Viruses Association (n 38).
46 Clark, Green and Patel (n 30).
47 *Golding* (n 10) [66]–[67]; *Mowatt* [1968] 1 QB 421 (CA); see also *R v Savage; R v Parmenter* [1992] 1 AC 699 (HL) (Lord Ackner).

recklessness on the evidence of Golding's 'state of mind': his knowledge of his infection from his own diagnosis and advice given to him prior to his relationship with CS, and thus that he had done wrong in not telling her about it before it was too late.[48]

Expert testimony confirmed that Golding *ought* to have been given explicit advice to inform partners and that he could still be infectious even if not showing symptoms.[49] However, it is widely acknowledged in medical circles that such advice may not always 'get through' if the patient is struggling to deal with their own diagnosis,[50] and the Court of Appeal noted that Golding's medical records could not definitely show that he was given this advice. Additionally, herpes presents at least three particular challenges for infected individuals who want to reduce the risk of infecting others, and thus some significant difficulties in determining fault for the purposes of criminal sanctions. The first of these is that condoms, far from being an effective and reliable barrier to infection, only reduce the transmissibility of HSV-2 by 50%, and the infection can be spread by activity short of penetrative sex (such as oral sex). This makes the notion of 'protected sex' a misnomer (let alone '*safe* sex') and removes the possibility of gaining sexual satisfaction in ways that avoid the risks.

Second, herpes can show itself in the form of lesions on the genital area, but in fact carriers can be infectious both on days when lesions are evident *and* when they are not. There is no reliable way of determining on *which* of the non-lesion days the carrier is infectious. Third, while there do exist dating websites for people living with herpes that allow for sexual interactions that do not pose a risk of transmission, this will only work as a means of preventing transmission when both parties are infected with the same type (HSV-1 or HSV-2). This presents a practical obstacle for individuals' chances of minimising the risk of transmission. Are people with herpes to be told that abstinence or disclosure are the only ways to ensure that others are not exposed to an unjustifiable risk of harm? The difficulties for risk-reduction pose a challenge for sexual health experts called upon to testify that D has been reckless in not following advice. To put this another way, if we cannot agree on what constitutes an acceptable minimum standard of responsibility, how can we confidently determine the point at which an infected person crosses over into criminal recklessness?[51]

It is at this point that it is helpful to return to Brazier's own words and to consider their implications. George Mawhinney uses Brazier's stated view – that 'people have ethical responsibilities which do not disappear simply because they are ill' – to argue for a much broader recklessness test even than that adopted in the HIV judgments.[52] Mawhinney advocates for making explicit the

---

48 *Golding* (ibid) [78]–[83].
49 Ibid [21].
50 See Clark, Green and Patel (n 30) and N Narouz, P S Allan and A H Wade, 'Genital herpes: general practitioners' knowledge and opinions' (2002) 78 Sexually Transmitted Infections 198.
51 Dunphy (n 22).
52 Mawhinney (n 7).

implication of the subjective test for recklessness as laid down in *R v Parker*,[53] *R v Cunningham*[54] and *R v G and another*:[55] that even those who *suspect* but *close their minds to the possibility* that they are infected should be included in its net.[56] After all, he argues, anyone who recently has had risky, unprotected sex knows there is a chance that he or she may have been infected, and thus it is to take an unreasonable risk to then have risky, unprotected sex with someone else. There is some justification for this attempt to apply Brazier's argument as endorsing a widening of the scope of criminalisation in this way. Brazier does remind us that there is nothing novel about the criminalisation of disease: it was 'not solely an invention in *Dica* or exclusively a response to HIV'.[57] However, there is nothing in Brazier's work that suggests that she is unaware of the harms that criminalisation can do. Where she has endorsed the use of criminal sanctions in medical and healthcare contexts, whether for patients or professionals, and, furthermore, whether in the 2006 article we are focusing on here or in her work much more broadly, she has always been hesitant, reserved and reluctant. Even while suggesting that insofar as *Dica* imposes a legal duty on infected persons to disclose prior to sexual intercourse 'enforces the fundamental principle of do no harm' for example, Brazier warns that the ramifications of this '*at the same time* illustrat[e] the difficulties inherent in translating ethical responsibilities into legal obligations'.[58] It is important to appreciate that those two statements, which at the very least stand in some tension, appear within the same sentence in Brazier's article.

The *Golding* judgment does not question at all the *objective* aspect to the recklessness test, namely whether having unprotected sex without disclosing the fact that one is infected with herpes is an *unreasonable* risk, all things considered, for the purposes of the criminal law. Since 2004, the courts seem to have assumed that any exposure by D to V of infection (namely HIV) in circumstances where that risk has in fact manifested in transmission is also an *unreasonable* risk. But we would argue that the application of the law to herpes indicates that this assumption must be considered afresh in determining the crossing point between mere moral failure and criminal sanction. This compounds our regret that Treacy LJ put most of his energy into considering whether the parties' testimonies seem to present a case to answer rather than into whether this prosecution was a proper use of the criminal law.

---

53 [1977] 1 WLR 600.
54 [1957] 2 QB 396.
55 [2003] UKHL 50.
56 Mawhinney (n 7) 205. If D's 'wilful blindness' as regards his being infected is consistent with the law as set down in *R v Konzani* (n 34) then this is as-yet a theoretical and untested possibility. See Law Commission (n 9) [6.24].
57 Brazier (n 1) 409.
58 Ibid 408, emphasis added.

Conclusions

There is no doubt that a return to Brazier's contribution to the question of patients' responsibilities and to her view that the vulnerabilities associated with being ill does not erase these responsibilities is timely now, given the latest foray into the criminalisation of disease transmission by the Court of Appeal. We have attempted here to explore some of the myriad controversies that arise in attempting to give legal effect to ethical responsibilities to disclose a herpes infection by attaching criminal sanctions to non-disclosure when transmission occurs. While we would not pretend to be in any sense 'applying' Brazier's work in so doing (indeed Brazier herself may well disagree with our conclusions), we hope at least that our call for a more considered and serious judicial handling of these controversies than that offered by the Court of Appeal pays some sort of homage to Brazier's own discomfort on the subject of the risks of over-criminalisation.

24 Maternal responsibility to the child not yet born

Emma Cave and Catherine Stanton

Introduction

The fetus lacks a legal personality but is valued and protected in a variety of ways in both criminal and tort law.[1] As Amel Alghrani and Margaret Brazier have pointed out, these protections can render the law's 'bright line between the fetus and the baby 'born alive''[2] both blurred and difficult to sustain.[3] As we shall see, third parties may be liable for harming the fetus which is later born alive, but to extend this principle to mothers whose actions in pregnancy harm the born alive child is ethically and legally problematic.

The 2014 Court of Appeal case of *CP v Criminal Injuries Compensation Authority*[4] has reignited the debate as to whether the criminal law has any role to play in regulating the conduct of pregnant women. A child with Fetal Alcohol Spectrum Disorder (FASD) was refused compensation from the Criminal Injuries Compensation Authority (CICA) in the Administrative Upper Tribunal on the ground that the child was not a person in law when the harmful act took place.[5] As a result it was not possible to establish the 'crime of violence' necessary for an award under the scheme. Attracting intensive publicity in the mass media, the case came before the Court of Appeal in November 2014. Around 80 other cases of children and young people with FASD awaited the outcome.[6] In its judgment, the Court of Appeal upheld the decision of the CICA that the child was not entitled to compensation.

Not all jurisdictions are so reluctant to criminalise acts in pregnancy that harm the born alive child. In July 2014, the state of Tennessee introduced a new state law criminalising 'narcotic drug' consumption in pregnancy.[7] The

---

1 R Scott, 'The English Fetus and the Right to Life' (2004) 11(4) EJHL 347.
2 A Alghrani and M Brazier, 'What is it? Whose it? Re-Positioning the Fetus in the Context of Research?' (2011) 70 CLJ 51, 52.
3 Ibid.
4 [2014] EWCA Civ 1554.
5 *CICA v First-Tier Tribunal and CP* [2013] UKUT 638 (AAC). Accessible at <http://s.conjur.com.br/dl/uk-feto-alcool-gestante.pdf> (accessed 10 Mar 2015).
6 [2014] EWCA Civ 1554, [3] (Treacy LJ).
7 Bill SB1391. Accessible at <http://wapp.capitol.tn.gov/apps/BillInfo/Default.aspx?BillNumber=SB1391)>; Pub. Ch. 820 amends the Tenn. Code Ann. § 39–13–107.

Criminal Code's prohibition on the prosecution of a woman for assault – if her fetus is harmed by any 'act or omission' she commits while she is pregnant – is now subject to an exception in the case of illegal drug use which harms another.[8] According to the media,[9] the first person to be charged under the statute was 26-year-old Mallory Loyola. When her baby tested positive for amphetamine, she was reportedly charged with assault.

Tennessee's position is highly controversial,[10] but it is one of a number of similar examples. In the US there have long been a variety of civil and criminal measures designed to protect the fetus and child born alive from harm imposed by the mother.[11] In the UK, the House of Lords made clear in *Attorney-General's Reference (No 3 of 1994)*[12] (*A-G's Reference*) that a father can be liable for manslaughter having injured his child *in utero*, the child being born alive and dying shortly after birth. The case concerned a pregnant woman who was stabbed by her boyfriend. The knife penetrated the fetus. As a result of the attack the baby was born prematurely and died 121 days later due to the effects of this premature birth. The House of Lords, applying the 'born alive rule' which dates back to 1680, held that the father was guilty of 'dangerous act manslaughter'. Commentators expressed concern that, by extension, the born alive rule might be extended to apply to mothers whose actions in pregnancy harm the born alive child.[13]

---

8 §39–13–107(c) states the following:

> (1) Nothing in subsection (a) shall apply to any lawful act or lawful omission by a pregnant woman with respect to an embryo or fetus with which she is pregnant, or to any lawful medical or surgical procedure to which a pregnant woman consents, performed by a health care professional who is licensed to perform such procedure. (2) Notwithstanding subdivision (c)(1), nothing in this section shall preclude prosecution of a woman for assault under § 39–13–101 for the illegal use of a narcotic drug, as defined in § 39–17–402, while pregnant, if her child is born addicted to or harmed by the narcotic drug and the addiction or harm is a result of her illegal use of a narcotic drug taken while pregnant. (3) It is an affirmative defense to a prosecution permitted by subdivision (c)(2) that the woman actively enrolled in an addiction recovery program before the child is born, remained in the program after delivery, and successfully completed the program, regardless of whether the child was born addicted to or harmed by the narcotic drug.

9 N Feeney, 'First Woman Charged Under Tennessee's Controversial Drugs-During-Pregnancy Law', (2014) *Time*, 14 July.
10 L Bassett, 'ACLU Seeks To Challenge Law Targeting Pregnant Drug Addicts', (2014) *The Huffington Post*, 11 July.
11 E Cave, *The Mother of All Crimes: Human Rights, Criminalization and the Child Born Alive* (Ashgate 2004), ch 3; L Paltrow and J Flavin, 'Arrests of and Forced Interventions on Pregnant Women in the United States (1973–2005): The Implications for Women's Legal Status and Public Health' (2013) 38(2) J Health Pol, Pol'y & L 299.
12 *Attorney-General's Reference (No 3 of 1994)* [1997] All ER 936, [1998] AC 245.
13 S Fovargue and J Miola, 'Policing Pregnancy: Implications of the Attorney-General's Reference (No 3 of 1994)' (1998) 6 Med L Rev 265, 293; E Cave (n 11) ch 4.

Nearly 20 years on, as the outcome of the Court of Appeal decision in *CP v CICA* was eagerly awaited, there were indications that such an extension remained a very real possibility. Vic Larcher and Joe Brierley argue that the growing compensation culture threatens to extend parental liability for their acts and omissions which lead to harm to the child. They point to arguments that children should be able to sue where they are harmed by failure to vaccinate, passive smoking and wrongful birth.[14] Arguing against criminalisation for acts and omissions in pregnancy which cause harm to the child born alive, Larcher and Brierley fear that it would make the paediatrician 'a kind of moral policeman for parental behaviours'.[15] Nonetheless, the growing prevalence of FASD[16] and increased willingness to claim in law for injury meant that the outcome of *CP v CICA* was by no means a foregone conclusion.

This chapter considers the judgment of the Court of Appeal and revisits Brazier's exploration of the issue in 'Liberty, Responsibility, Maternity' in 1999 in which she argues that parents have a *moral* responsibility to the child not yet born.[17] Brazier argues that *legal* responsibility should only follow where there are 'cogent reasons' for prioritising the child's interests and 'the law could do so in a manner which will realistically achieve that aim'.[18] Did the facts of *CP v CICA* provide the 'cogent reasons' for legal responsibility to which Brazier refers? On the one hand, if the Court of Appeal in *CP v CICA* had recognised that the mother's alcohol consumption in pregnancy constituted a 'crime of violence', this could have paved the way for the criminalisation of maternal acts and omissions in pregnancy that harm the child born alive and led to the imposition of a standard of reasonableness in pregnancy. On the other hand, *CP v CICA* was a civil case and it would not necessarily have led to prosecution in the immediate or analogous cases. Allowing a compensation claim in *CP v CICA* would have given legal recognition to the maternal moral duty to the fetus by recognising resulting harm as a 'crime of violence', but criminal prosecution would not necessarily have followed and the state would have borne the cost of compensation. So restricted, the implications for maternal liberty would be minimal. Within these narrow confines, is the case for reasserting the born alive rule successfully made? We will argue that it is not and that the strength of our case lies in the nature of the moral and legal maternal responsibility outlined by Brazier.

---

14 V Larcher and J Brierley, 'Fetal Alcohol Syndrome (FAS) and Fetal Alcohol Spectrum Disorder (FASD) – Diagnosis and Moral Policing; An Ethical Dilemma for Paediatricians' (2014) 99(11) Archives of Disease in Childhood 969, 969.
15 Ibid 970.
16 E Elliott, J Payne, E Haan et al., 'Diagnosis of Fetal Alcohol Syndrome and Alcohol Use in Pregnancy: A Survey of Paediatricians' Knowledge, Attitudes and Practice' (2006) 42 Journal of Paediatrics and Child Health 698.
17 M Brazier, 'Liberty, Responsibility, Maternity' (1999) 52(1) CLP 359, 375.
18 Ibid.

Moral responsibility

In law, the fetus is not a person and does not have human rights.[19] In practice, the option of abortion is open to the pregnant woman. Brazier does not duck the problem this poses for her assertion that future parents owe a moral responsibility to the child: '[I]f, to put it dramatically, a woman may kill her "child", on what basis can there be an obligation not to do lesser harm?'[20]

Brazier's answer lies in the distinction between the choice to terminate pregnancy and the choice to carry the child to term, assigning to the latter a 'much more onerous set of *moral* constraints on maternal liberty'.[21] In fact, Brazier goes so far as to argue that: 'If a human child is to acquire at birth those same fundamental rights we assert for ourselves, recognition of her own and independent interest in avoiding prenatal harm is essential.'[22] In a characteristically colourful example, Brazier argues that a refusal to recognise the prenatal interests of those who will be born is:

> equivalent to saying that at a dinner party my host may not poison my wine at dinner. Yet should he be so apparently kind as to send me a bottle of port for my birthday with instructions that it will not be ready to drink until 2021, he has not acted wrongfully, even though his poisoned port kills both me and my young nephew when we celebrate his twenty-first birthday in 2021. Would anyone contend that because on the day the port was poisoned no wrong is done against my nephew simply because on that fateful day in 1999 he was naught but an embryo?[23]

The same reasoning might be applied to a third party who causes harm to the fetus, and it will also, Brazier argues, apply to the mother, who can pose 'the most direct threat to the welfare of her child'.[24]

Maternal liability

Brazier has argued that third parties owe a moral duty to the fetus and the law correspondingly recognises both civil[25] and criminal liability.[26] Brazier's position vis-à-vis the pregnant woman who has decided to become a mother is equally clear: 'the woman is required by morally responsible motherhood to consider the interests of the child she has chosen to mother.'[27] And yet, the

---

19 *Re F (In Utero)* [1988] 2 All ER 193.
20 Brazier (n 17) 364.
21 Ibid 365.
22 Ibid 366.
23 Ibid 366.
24 Ibid 367.
25 Congenital Disabilities (Civil Liability) Act 1976.
26 *A-G's Reference* (n 12).
27 Brazier (n 17) 367.

law has been slower to recognise corresponding liability. The mother is immune from civil liability[28] and no UK court has yet applied the born alive rule to harm caused by a mother. This does not, however, demonstrate a parting of the ways between Brazier's position and the law. The strong moral responsibility a woman owes to her future child does not countenance the law restraining maternal choices in pregnancy.[29] Her moral responsibility is for her to weigh the 'future interests of her child' against her other fundamental interests – in health, privacy and liberty.[30] Compulsion is not the appropriate means of recognising the value of the fetus. Brazier recognises that the moral responsibility might be translated into liability 'only if cogent reasons could be advanced for prioritising the child's interests, and the law could do so in a manner which will realistically achieve that aim'.[31] In resolving this conflict of interests Brazier suggests that three considerations are vital. First, that society cannot demand that a pregnant woman 'subordinate her interests to the potential child's, where in the case of a child already born no such demand could be made'.[32] Therefore, if a parent is under no legal obligation to donate blood to a dying child, a woman cannot be deemed to have an obligation to undergo a procedure such as an enforced obstetric intervention. Second, the woman's obligation is to make judgements based on what is best for herself, her child and any other children. Quoting Sheila McLean, Brazier recognises that it is important to avoid the assumption that a recommendation by a clinician is 'effectively value free'.[33] Finally, Brazier suggests that a protection of the child's interests at the expense of the mother's must be 'proportionate and practical and able to be defined within agreed limits'.[34] In the context of the Tennessee statute outlined above, this legislation is likely to turn women who need help for their addiction away from the healthcare system (particularly if they are reluctant to enrol on a recovery programme which provides a defence to prosecution) and thus not be 'proportionate' or 'practical'. The British compensation case was quite different. It is to this we now turn.

The case of CP

CP's claim was for compensation for criminal injury. Since 1964 the UK government has run a scheme to compensate victims of 'crimes of violence'. There have been various incarnations of the scheme, which is currently administered by the CICA. CP's case falls under the '2008' version which was replaced in

---

28 Congenital Disabilities (Civil Liability) Act 1976, s 1(1), subject to s 2 where negligent driving by a pregnant woman results in prenatal injury.
29 Brazier (n 17) 374.
30 Ibid 374.
31 Ibid 375.
32 Ibid 375.
33 Ibid 376, quoting S McLean, *Old Law, New Medicine* (Pandora 1999) 67.
34 Ibid 376.

2012.³⁵ There is no legal definition of the term 'crime of violence', though annex B of the 2012 scheme³⁶ gives examples of the type of crime envisaged. A 2012 consultation³⁷ contained proposals to clarify the term and narrow its ambit, with the primary aim of making financial savings.³⁸ It recommended excluding from the scheme 'injuries sustained by children in utero injured by the consumption of alcohol by their mother' and stated that this was the current policy.³⁹ The Guide to the Criminal Injuries Compensation Scheme 2012 went a step further, denying compensation not only for FASD but also in wider circumstances where injury 'was sustained *in utero* as a result of harmful substances willingly ingested by the mother during pregnancy, with intent to cause, or being reckless as to, injury to the foetus'.⁴⁰

The Court of Appeal recognised that 'past applications for criminal injuries compensation for victims for FASD have been accepted under previous schemes',⁴¹ but it is not clear how many were successful. *The Sunday Times* reported in May 2014 that the CICA awarded £500,000 in criminal injuries compensation to a 16-year-old called Molly in September 2013.⁴² According to the report, the Authority considered that a crime was committed when the mother persisted in heavy drinking regardless of warnings from professionals about the risks to her unborn child. It seems that the payment was made pursuant to an original £44,000 interim award in which the CICA recognised that Molly had been a victim of a crime, prior to the change in policy.

In 2009, a local authority made a claim on behalf of CP, born in 2007. The claim predates the change in the rules. CP's mother engaged with maternity services, cut down her drinking and stopped recreational drug use.⁴³ However, she still 'consumed grossly excessive quantities of alcohol' despite discussing with healthcare professionals the dangers of consuming alcohol.⁴⁴ CP was diagnosed at birth with FASD.

Eligibility for compensation depended on CP being able to establish that she was the victim of a 'crime of violence'. For the purposes of paragraph 9 of the 2008 Scheme, the injury suffered must constitute 'personal injury' for which

---

35 Ministry of Justice, *The Criminal Injuries Compensation Scheme 2012* (London: The Stationery Office, 2012) <https://www.gov.uk/government/uploads/system/uploads/attachment_data/file/243480/9780108512117.pdf> (accessed 10 Mar 2015).
36 Ibid.
37 Ministry of Justice, *Getting it Right for Victims and Witnesses* (Cm 8288, 2012).
38 See Ministry of Justice, *Getting it Right for Victims and Witnesses: The Government Response* (Cm 8396, 2012) [161].
39 Ministry of Justice (n 38) 54. Approved by the Commons by 275 votes to 231. Pursuant to s 11 of the Criminal Injuries Compensation Act 1995.
40 Criminal Injuries Compensation Authority, *A Guide to the Criminal Injuries Compensation Scheme 2012* (2013) s 2, [8].
41 [2014] EWCA Civ 1554, [3] (Treacy LJ).
42 S-K Templeton, 'Girl Harmed by Drink in Womb Wins Payout', (2014) *The Sunday Times*, 18 May.
43 *CICA v First-Tier Tribunal and CP* (n 5), [3].
44 Ibid.

all agreed that FASD sufficed. The meaning of 'crime of violence' is specific to the Scheme, so evidence of prosecution or conviction (or lack of such evidence) neither defeats nor proves the claim. The dispute centred on whether or not a crime had been committed.

In 2009, the CICA determined that no award could be made under the scheme as no crime had been committed. Upon appeal, however, the First-Tier Tribunal held that CP was the victim of a crime of violence on the basis that an offence had been committed under section 23 of the Offences Against the Persons Act 1861 (OAPA)[45] which criminalises 'maliciously administering poison so as to endanger life or inflict grievous bodily harm'. The fetus is not recognised in law as a person, and the necessary coincidence of *mens rea* and *actus reus* posed a hurdle which the tribunal overcame by applying the House of Lords decision of *A-G's Reference*.[46]

The Upper Tribunal disagreed and quashed the decision of the First-Tier Tribunal. In *CICA v First-Tier Tribunal and CP*,[47] it was held that no offence was committed under section 23. Levenson J accepted that there had been administration of poison, and the infliction of grievous bodily harm, but held that the harm had not resulted to 'another person'.[48] The rule in *A-G's Reference*, he held, applied to dangerous act manslaughter and could not be extended to apply to section 23 of the OAPA.

Court of Appeal decision

In the Court of Appeal, the appellant sought to argue that passages in the judgment in *A-G's Reference* supported the contention that the criminal law could protect a fetus from deliberate conduct causing foreseeable harm, where the harm became evident after birth. Counsel drew for support on passages from Lord Mustill's judgment, such as where he opined that:

> Violence towards a foetus which results in harm suffered after the baby has been born alive can give rise to criminal responsibility even if the harm would not have been criminal . . . if it had been suffered in utero.[49]

However, the court rejected these arguments and upheld the decision of the Upper Tribunal that no offence had been committed under section 23. The court held that the harm occurred while CP was in the womb. At this time, the child was not a legal person and so the requirement that the poison be administered to 'any other person' could not be made out. The court distinguished this from the circumstances in *AG's Reference* where the harm was

---

45 (2011) reference 9/256563.
46 *A-G's Reference* (n 12).
47 *CICA v First-Tier Tribunal and CP* (n 5).
48 Ibid [14].
49 *A-G's Reference*, (n 12) 942.

ongoing from when the fetus was in the womb until the child's death after birth 'by which stage the child had undoubtedly achieved legal personality'.[50] In the case of CP, the harm had all occurred prior to birth. The fact that some of this harm could not be identified until certain milestones in development were missed 'does not constitute fresh damage. It merely means that the damage was already done but has only then become apparent.'[51]

The implications of the Court of Appeal decision

As set out above, Brazier argues that parental moral responsibility predates the birth of the child and that this might translate into liability 'only if cogent reasons could be advanced for prioritising the child's interests, and the law could do so in a manner which will realistically achieve that aim'.[52] The discussion above highlighted the statute introduced in Tennessee and suggested that it was neither 'proportionate' nor 'practical'. Three features of CP's compensation case contrasted starkly with the Tennessee statute. First, application of the statute might damage the relationship between mother and child, but the family relationship in the case of CP had in any event broken down. CP was cared for by the local authority. Second, while the criminalisation statute would not benefit the injured child, compensation of up to £500,000 would undoubtedly have proved beneficial to CP and made a significant difference to her quality of life. Third, the criminalisation statute provides a defence where the woman is 'actively enrolled in an addiction recovery program before the child is born, remained in the program after delivery, and successfully completed the program'[53] which might amount to compulsion where the alternative is prosecution. In the compensation case, on the other hand, there can be a 'crime of violence' under the scheme, even where prosecution is not possible. And even if the Crown Prosecution Service sought to prosecute, the higher criminal standard of proof would apply. The spectre of 'criminalisation of addiction' and even 'criminalisation of pregnancy' which loom large in Tennessee might be avoided even if the compensation case had been successful.

However, if successful, CP's claim would have created a precedent which could have led inexorably to criminalisation. Birthrights (a UK organisation dedicated to protecting women's rights in pregnancy and childbirth) and the British Pregnancy Advisory Service (BPAS) intervened[54] in the CP appeal case. Birthrights stated in a press release:

> If the court were to interpret the law as requested by the council, it would establish a legal precedent which could be used to prosecute women who

50 [2014] EWCA Civ 1554, [40].
51 Ibid [43].
52 Brazier (n 17) 375.
53 See above (n 8).
54 See <http://www.birthrights.org.uk/wordpress/wp-content/uploads/2014/11/BPAS-Birthrights-CP-v-CICA-Intervention.pdf> (accessed 10 March 2015).

drink while pregnant. Similar developments in the US have resulted in the incarceration of women.[55]

If the appeal had succeeded, the CPS would – provided there was sufficient evidence and prosecution was in the public interest[56] – have had the option to prosecute in future cases of alcohol consumption in pregnancy. Contravention of section 23 might have also occurred when other substances were imbibed in pregnancy, but questions would then arise regarding the types and amounts of relevant 'poisons'. The CPS might have provided guidance, but the ambits of such guidance would have been likely to prove controversial, as has been demonstrated by the CPS guidance on assisted suicide.[57]

Could criminalisation have been kept within the narrow confines of the facts before the court in *CP v CICA*? While it is acknowledged that 'slippery slope' arguments are subject to philosophical criticism,[58] if the claim had been successful, there was a clear risk of extension by analogy. While a law such as that in Tennessee only criminalises certain *acts* of the mother (i.e. taking drugs), why then, in principle, should *omissions* which cause a child to be born harmed not also be criminalised? As novel treatments including *in utero* stem cell therapy are developed,[59] could pregnant women have faced the spectre of criminal prosecution for the failure to undertake treatment to their child *in utero*, which would have prevented their child suffering future harm?

If the narrow confines of *A-G's Reference* had been extended, then there might have been scope to prosecute women for such omissions under section 20 of the OAPA, which criminalises those who 'unlawfully and maliciously wound or inflict any grievous bodily harm upon any other person'. Notably, case law has established that to 'inflict' does not require any violence to be used.[60] However, in order for any offence to be made out, it would have to be established that it could be committed by omission.[61] However, such a possibility would have highlighted the danger, foreseen by Brazier, that a pregnant woman's 'reflective choice' about whether or not to undergo a certain treatment, could be trumped by considerations of the fetal interest:

> The fact that in refusing to agree a woman may have made a reflective choice centred on her judgment of the potential benefit of the therapy

---

55 Birthrights, 'Birthrights Applies to Court of Appeal to Intervene in Fetal Alcohol Case' (26 July 2014) <http://www.birthrights.org.uk/2014/07/birthrights-applies-to-court-of-appeal-to-intervene-in-fetal-alcohol-case/> (accessed 10 Mar 2015).
56 CPS, *The Code for Crown Prosecutors* (January 2013) [4.1–4.12].
57 CPS, *Policy for Prosecutors in Respect of Cases of Encouraging or Assisting Suicide Issued by The Director of Public Prosecution* (February 2010, updated October 2014).
58 A Miller, 'The "Slippery Slope" Argument: Uses and Misuses' (2007) 14(5) Think 43.
59 For example see: C Götherström, M Westgrem, SW Shaw et al., 'Pre- and Post Natal Transplantation of Fetal Mesenchymal Stem Cells in Osteogenesis Imperfect: A Two-Center Experience' (2014) Feb 3(2) Stem Cells Transl Med 255.
60 *R v Burstow* [1998] AC 147.
61 D Ormerod, *Smith and Hogan's Criminal Law* (13th edn, OUP 2011) 69.

proposed, to her and the child she bears, may equally disappear in a purportedly scientific evaluation of foetal interests.[62]

Such a development would threaten a woman's liberty to make responsible choices about the conduct of her pregnancy.

No maternal criminal liability?

Although it is only recently that the courts have been called upon to consider the possible impact on maternal criminal liability of *A-G's Reference*, it is notable that Brazier and other commentators questioned the potential scope of the decision considerably earlier. Brazier, writing in 1997, referred to Lord Mustill's words noted above. She pointed out that although this case related to manslaughter, his words could suggest a more general criminal responsibility for prenatal harm.[63] As she stated, with characteristic prescience, over a decade and a half ago: 'the ambit of such general criminal responsibility remains unexplored. The class of women whose conduct becomes potentially criminal would inevitably be extended.'[64] Fovargue and Miola also noted the potential impact of this case.[65] In *A-G's Reference*, the baby's father had been found guilty of unlawful act manslaughter. Therefore, by analogy, a woman could be prosecuted for any unlawful act in pregnancy which caused the subsequent death of her child (e.g. heroin use).[66] Fovargue and Miola also highlighted the potential for the use of the offence of gross negligence manslaughter, which would broaden the scope of the criminal law to include manslaughter not just due to unlawful acts, such as drug-taking, but also negligent ones such as excessive alcohol consumption.[67]

Does the Court of Appeal's decision now make such concerns redundant? Can pregnant women now be assured that the spectre of the criminal law will not appear in their lives in relation to any prenatal harm they may cause their unborn child? The decision provides some clarity. A pregnant woman who drinks excessively in pregnancy will not be subject to prosecution under section 23 (or for causing harm under section 20). However, it does not appear to close the door completely on any possibility for criminal maternal liability. As the Master of the Rolls acknowledged, there are certain circumstances where

---

62 Brazier (n 17) 377–378.
63 See Alghrani and Brazier (n 2) 65. Consider, for example, potential application of section 27 of the Offences Against the Person Act 1861, 'Exposing children whereby life is endangered': see E Cave (n 11) 72.
64 M Brazier 'Parental Responsibilities, Foetal Welfare and Children's Health' in C Bridge (ed), *Family Law Towards the Millennium: Essays for PM Bromley* (Butterworths 1997) 263–293, 291.
65 Fovargue and Miola (n 13).
66 Ibid 289.
67 Ibid 289.

Parliament has legislated so that a woman will be criminally liable for harm caused to the fetus before birth. These include where a woman administers a poison to herself with the intent to cause a miscarriage (section 58 OAPA). In addition, it is an offence to destroy the life of a child who is capable of being born alive (section 1 Infant Life (Preservation) Act 1929). Nevertheless, the Court of Appeal's decision does not discount the possibility for criminal charges whereby, as in Miola and Fovargue's example, a woman causes the death of her child due to her actions in pregnancy. For example, could a pregnant woman who takes heroin during pregnancy be charged with gross negligence manslaughter when her baby dies of sudden infant death syndrome (SIDS) six weeks after birth?[68] Unlike the case of CP, the harm is not just caused in the womb, but continues after birth, since drug use in pregnancy can leave the baby vulnerable to SIDS. In this respect, such an example is more clearly analogous to the situation in *AG's Reference*, where death is caused by an act before the child's birth, the effects of which continue after birth, thus creating a causal link between the act and the harm (i.e. death). However, before any prosecution could be brought, the CPS would have to determine that there was sufficient evidence to link the woman's actions with the death of the child. Furthermore, any prosecution would have to be deemed in the public interest.[69] Once at trial, the prosecution would have to establish that the offence had been committed 'beyond reasonable doubt'. Such hurdles may make prosecutions unlikely.

The Master of the Rolls considers that, because Parliament has legislated to a limited extent in this area, the courts should therefore be slow to apply general criminal legislation in this context.[70] He also commented that the law would be incoherent if it allowed compensation by establishing the commission of a criminal offence when the civil law does not allow a child to claim compensation from her mother for prenatal harm (as per the Congenital Disabilities (Civil Liability) Act 1976[71]):

> It is true that tort and crime are conceptually distinct. But the policy reasons underlying the state's view that a child should not be able to claim compensation from her mother for what is done (or not done) during pregnancy should rationally also lead to the conclusion that, save in the exceptional circumstances expressly recognised by Parliament, there should be no criminal liability for what a mother does (or does not do) during pregnancy.[72]

---

68 S Kandall, J Gaines, L Habel et al., 'Relationship of Maternal Substance Abuse to Subsequent Sudden Infant Death Syndrome in Offspring' (1993) 123(1) The Journal of Pediatrics 120.
69 See above (n 56).
70 [2014] EWCA Civ 1554, [66].
71 See above (n 28).
72 [2014] EWCA Civ 1554, [67].

However, given that there remains, as we have argued, some potential scope for application of the criminal law in addition to those areas on which Parliament has legislated, we believe these should be addressed. One means would be to propose legislation to clarify that a woman will not face criminal sanction for her actions (or omissions) during pregnancy which harm the unborn child (and which may also lead to additional harm following birth) save in the circumstances set out in statute.[73] Such a measure would have the advantage of mirroring the certainty which a woman already has in relation to her potential liabilities in civil law for prenatal harm. This is important because use of the criminal law raises additional concerns beyond those raised by the civil law. As Brazier argues:

> Criminal sanctions, even more than civil liability will place very many pregnant women under others' control. Successful prosecution may in reality be limited to the truly 'egregious case', but the threat of criminal liability will hover over every woman confronting difficult choices in pregnancy and at odds with her partner or her doctors . . . Criminal sanctions could be used to coerce women, and to punish women who, if disaster has ensued to their child, will in most cases have long ago punished themselves. They offer nil benefit to the child. If the child remains with the mother, criminalizing and stigmatizing her does him no good. If the child is removed from her care, is not that loss sufficient retribution?[74]

Conclusion

Success for the claimant would have brought much needed compensation. Yet it is not a result we would have celebrated. Brazier's recognition of maternal moral responsibility comes with an important caveat: 'maternal conduct, maternal choices which may injure the fetus cannot be restrained by the law.'[75] There are no cogent reasons for translating maternal moral responsibility into liability for the simple reason that the criminal law should not be used to regulate maternal conduct and choices in pregnancy. The threat of its use could lead to coercion in pregnancy and would not benefit mother or child. Compensation in the case of CP would have come at too high a price, for it would have brought with it the recognition that those who drink excessively in pregnancy are committing a criminal offence and the slippery slopes and public health connotations that entails. However, this case has highlighted some remaining uncertainty surrounding the scope of maternal criminal liability, which we suggest needs to be addressed.

---

73 See Fovargue and Miola (n 13) 293.
74 Brazier (n 17) 383–384.
75 Ibid 374.

25 Compromise medicalisation

Roger Brownsword and Jeffrey Wale

Introduction

In *Bioethics, Medicine and the Criminal Law*,[1] Margaret Brazier and Suzanne Ost 'tell a story about the ways that the criminal process engages with medicine and bioethics' – a story designed to explore and 'to explain the interaction between the three when they meet in the theatre of the courts, the legislature and public opinion'.[2] In fact, Brazier and Ost tell several stories, two of which inspire this chapter. The first is a story about the use of 'medicalisation' ('compromise medicalisation' as we will term it) as a strategy for dealing with bioethical conflicts that divide communities. So, for example, Brazier and Ost present the Abortion Act 1967 in this light;[3] and, putting the point more generally, they suggest that 'medicalisation plays a useful if often criticised role in mediating between the polarized extremes of bioethical debate . . . offer[ing] a way forward that is less than intellectually first class, but better than the practical alternatives'.[4] The second story highlights the 'kindly'[5] treatment typically accorded by prosecutors, juries and judges to doctors who follow their conscience and try to do the right thing (even when this might fly in the face of the law) – for example, 'doctors who seek to practise compassionately at the end, or beginning, of life, [or] who seek to honour their patients' wishes'.[6]

Against the backcloth of these stories, we suggest that when the United Kingdom (UK) Parliament introduces a measure of 'compromise medicalisation', this does more than change the law; crucially, it changes the responsibilities of both doctors and legal actors. Post-enactment, the medical profession, as a trusted third party, is charged with safeguarding the terms of the compromise;

---

1 M Brazier and S Ost, *Bioethics, Medicine and the Criminal Law Volume III: Medicine and Bioethics in the Theatre of the Criminal Process* (CUP 2013).
2 Ibid 255.
3 Ibid 194, 198–9; cf A Grubb, 'Abortion Law in England: The Medicalization of a Crime' (1990) 18 J L M & E 146.
4 Brazier and Ost (n 1) 262–3.
5 Ibid 15.
6 Ibid 5.

and where doctors fail to discharge their new responsibilities, it is quite wrong for those legal actors who play a leading role in the theatre of the criminal justice system to default to a kindly attitude.

This chapter is in three main parts. First, we identify three distinct types of 'medicalisation' before specifying the nature of the special responsibilities that go with 'compromise medicalisation'. Second, looking back at nearly half a century's experience with the explicit statutory medicalisation of abortion in the UK, we consider whether there is any evidence that doctors are *not* taking their special responsibilities seriously, and whether the key legal actors continue (inappropriately) to treat doctors kindly. Third, learning from the experience with abortion, we focus on the possible medicalisation of assisted suicide, as proposed recently by Lord Falconer's Assisted Dying Bill. In short, our question is whether we can be confident that the medical profession (and, no less importantly, the leading legal actors) would hold the legislative line and safeguard the terms of the compromise. Or, are opponents of the Bill right to fear that this might be the thin end of an unauthorised wedge?

Our conclusions are as follows. First, our experience in relation to the medicalisation of abortion is that the terms of the compromise have not stuck. Second, this experience rightly gives a cause for concern to those who oppose the Falconer Bill. Third, if 'compromise medicalisation' is the intended strategy of the Bill, then it needs to be made absolutely clear that the medical profession stands in the position of a trusted third party with a special responsibility to adhere to the terms of the compromise. Fourth, because – if the Bill succeeds in changing the law – there is a distinct possibility that public opinion in relation to the ethics of assisted suicide might also change, there needs to be a strategy for keeping the law and practice in alignment with reasonable public views. Fifth, where the original strategy is one of compromise medicalisation, it cannot be the medical profession that has the responsibility for keeping the law and practice aligned with public opinion. Finally, if the Falconer Bill survives the parliamentary process, it will be a controversial but legitimate development of the law. We suggest that, if the terms of this latest exercise in compromise medicalisation are to be modified, a similar process should be engaged – that is to say, a process that requires nothing less than a positive act of parliamentary approval; and there should certainly be no change in the practice of assisted dying without proper legislative authorisation.

The special responsibilities associated with 'compromise medicalisation'

Broadly speaking, the term 'medicalisation' signifies that a particular kind of decision or procedure is entrusted to the medical profession. However, we can differentiate between three particular instances of this phenomenon. First, there is 'exclusionary medicalisation'. Here, in the belief that some decision or procedure is uniquely within the range of expertise of the medical profession and that it would be unsafe for other persons to make the decisions or to undertake the procedures, we entrust the matter exclusively to the former, excluding those who are not members of the profession from making the decisions or undertaking the procedures in question.[7] Second, there is 'evolutionary medicalisation', entrusting to the medical profession the task of adjusting medical practice so that it, and the law that authorises it, aligns with public opinion and reasonable patient needs and expectations. Third, there is 'compromise medicalisation', which entrusts the medical profession with granting patients access to an ethically controversial procedure but if, and only if, the terms and conditions set by the legislative compromise are satisfied. While there is much to be said about both exclusionary and evolutionary medicalisation, our interest is in teasing out the special responsibilities that attach to 'compromise medicalisation' in this chapter.

To locate 'compromise medicalisation' in a larger regulatory context: where communities are divided about the ethics of some matter – for example, about the ethics of divorce, or using human embryos for medical research, or abortion or euthanasia – a compromise might be brokered. Against a restrictive background, a degree of relaxation is introduced. However, the permission is subject to carefully specified conditions (a list of approved reasons, grounds, purposes, and the like) together with an appropriate process for authorisation by independent and accountable persons (whether judges, the members of a regulatory agency, or doctors). *Ex hypothesi*, the medicalisation of such contested issues as abortion and assisted suicide is controversial, sensitive, and above all a compromise: for pro-choice advocates, the permission will be too narrow; for pro-life advocates, the permission will be too broad.[8] Nevertheless, it is of the essence of democratic politics that the compromise sticks in practice; and, to this end, there are safeguards and limits that operate both *ex ante* and *ex post*. *Ex ante*, doctors are required conscientiously and in good faith to assess whether a relevant application falls within the terms of the permission; and *ex post*, they are required to report the acts that they have authorised.

Clearly, post-enactment, it is not for doctors to follow their convictions in the way that they might when participating in pre-enactment debates; rather, it is now their (possibly unwelcome) responsibility to ensure that the terms of the regulatory compromise are faithfully observed.[9] To be sure, this might put some doctors in a position that strains their commitment to the compromise. Nevertheless, in their *ex ante* practice, doctors should act in a way that is compatible with their position as trusted third parties, neither stretching nor

---

7   Cf M Thomson, 'Abortion Law and Professional Boundaries' (2013) 22 S & L S 191.
8   See Brazier and Ost (n 1) 103–4 for the 'uneasy compromise' in relation to abortion; and the chapter by McLean in this collection for the distorted shape of the law in relation to end-of-life issues.
9   Subject to any right of conscientious objection: see Abortion Act 1967, s 4 (as interpreted by *Janaway v Salford AHA* [1989] 1 AC 537 and *Greater Glasgow Health Board v Doogan* [2014] UKSC 68); and the Assisted Dying Bill 2014 (ADB 2014), s 5.

squeezing the sphere of legal permission in order to satisfy their pro-choice or pro-life inclinations. Similarly, it is important, too, that legal actors are compliant so that, in the event that a doctor is found to have wilfully departed from the compromise, the response should be to enforce the law.

Yet, there surely must be some margin for both doctors and judges where they are faced with particular cases that expose some lack of clarity in the legislative scheme or that have simply not been anticipated.[10] Where doctors have in good faith sought to respect the spirit and intent of the compromise, a kindly response is appropriate. However, more difficult questions are raised where the medical profession takes it upon itself to adjust the compromise so as to align it with what is perceived to be changing public opinion. The concern is not that doctors might misread public opinion; the point is that, if the scheme is one of 'compromise medicalisation', doctors simply should not be engaging in this exercise. Of course, if the legislation contemplates the profession being entrusted with an 'evolutionary' role, then that is a different matter; this is not 'compromise medicalisation', and the profession's new guidance and practice might well be legitimate.

However, in the absence of express authorisation, the profession's licence to act this way might be at best implicit (possibly with encouragement from, or at least acquiescence by, the relevant government department) and its scope might be uncertain. This raises broader questions of transparency and accountability that go well beyond the particular interests of the pro-choice and pro-life lobbies.[11] Moreover, if the standard criminal justice response is to show a kindly attitude to those doctors who defend their actions on the basis that it is broadly in line with general practice – whether their initial decision or their subsequent administration of the relevant procedure or treatment – then legal actors risk becoming complicit in unlicensed adjustment of the compromise.[12]

Ex post, it is the special responsibility of doctors to report their authorising actions. Reporting is no mere bureaucratic requirement. At a general level,

---

10 In this chapter, we cannot elaborate on this 'margin'. In the place of literal or mechanical interpretation, we are advocating an intelligent purposivism that is sensitive to the context in which the compromise was struck (cf R Brownsword, *Rights, Regulation and the Technological Revolution* (OUP 2008) ch 6). That said, it might be thought appropriate to try to constrain departure from the terms of the compromise by drafting appropriate guidance for the benefit of both doctors and key legal actors. We emphasise, however, that it is important that any such guidance should be subject to positive endorsement by Parliament: cf A Mullock, 'Overlooking the Criminally Compassionate: What are the Implications of Prosecutorial Policy on Encouraging or Assisting Suicide?' (2010) 18 Med L Rev 442.
11 Cf the recent history in the United Kingdom (UK) of the regulation of human fertilisation and embryology (particularly the criticism of the regulatory agency).
12 Cf Brazier and Ost (n 1) 103, 116–7.

reporting enables the impact of the compromise to be monitored;[13] and it provides an evidence base for any tweaking of, or more radical revision to, the compromise.[14] At a specific level, reporting functions as a prompt for whatever checks and further inquiries need to be made as to the propriety of the doctors' actions. It follows that, even though reporting obligations might be viewed as tiresome, they are an important part of the compromise package. As Brazier and Ost recognise, these packages might not always be 'intellectually first class' but they almost always reflect a delicate balance; it is of the essence of compromise medicalisation that the balance – that is to say, the balance struck between opposing ethical views – is maintained.

Abortion and 'medicalisation'

Although the common law recognised that, if a doctor undertook an abortion in good faith for the purpose of preserving the life of the mother, then they would not have acted unlawfully,[15] the Abortion Act 1967 (1967 Act) reset the framework for lawful terminations in a way that makes it an exemplar of 'compromise medicalisation'. At the time of the 1967 Act, there was much that was not anticipated – not least, the development of modern abortion techniques[16] and the fact that there would be a significant change in the delivery mechanism for abortion services (i.e. from NHS to independent sector delivery). Most strikingly, in 1967, it would have been absurd to have suggested that the legislation licensed 'abortion on demand'; this would have been a sell-out to the pro-choice group and no kind of compromise. At the time, the Act was a hesitant endorsement of 'the position that abortion *could* be acceptable medical treatment';[17] and it was recognised that a 'great social responsibility' had been placed by the law 'on the shoulders of the medical profession'.[18] Nearly 50 years later, the big picture looks very different; the landscape of abortions has been transformed.[19] Nowadays, abortions have been normalised; from allowing that abortions *could* be acceptable in limited circumstances, abortion on demand is available in all but name. While it can be argued that practice has simply evolved

---

13 Although there are important questions to be asked about the identity of the monitoring body – is it to be Parliament or a government department or both (as envisaged by clause 9 of the ADB 2014)?
14 However, it will only be a useful evidence base for tweaking if it is publicly accessible, or at least accessible to Parliament: see for example *R (Department of Health) v Information Commissioner* [2011] EWHC 1430 (Admin).
15 *R v Bourne* [1939] 1 KB 687 (CCC).
16 See for example, M Brazier, 'Unfinished Feticide: a Legal Commentary' (1990) 16 JME 68.
17 See Brazier and Ost (n 1) 116 (emphasis in original).
18 *R v Smith (John)* [1974] 1 All ER 376 (CA) 378f (Scarman LJ).
19 See Brazier and Ost (n 1) 116–7.

to reflect changes in public opinion,[20] and while this might be consistent with 'evolutionary medicalisation', it is deeply problematic relative to 'compromise medicalisation'.

The normalisation of abortion is reflected in many ways, not least in the fact that there have been very few prosecutions under the 1967 Act and hardly any successful ones against doctors.[21] Reverend Jepson's well-publicised attempt to challenge the supremacy of medical decision-making ultimately failed,[22] although the litigation may have had some impact on the medical approach to abortions based solely on the ground of disability.[23] The Jepson litigation also highlights the importance of the reporting provisions in the context of medical accountability.[24] In this regard, it is noteworthy that a recent UK Parliamentary Inquiry expressed concern at 'the lack of transparency of decision-making in cases of fetal disability'.[25] Meanwhile, the professional medical bodies have continued to resist any attempt to delimit or prescribe the scope of the disability ground.[26]

More recently, we have seen concern expressed in the media over abortions allegedly carried out on the basis of gender but reported by doctors as being on lawful grounds.[27] The subsequent Care Quality Commission (CQC) Inspections,[28] the Department of Health Guidance[29] and the decision of the Director of Public Prosecutions (DPP) not to prosecute the individual doctors involved[30]

---

20 However, there is some evidence that there may be a divergence of views in respect of abortions carried out on the grounds of disability (pursuant to section 1(1)(d) of the Act): see for example the findings of the UK Parliamentary Inquiry into Abortion on the Grounds of Disability (July 2013). It has also been suggested that the wider (so-called social) ground for a lawful abortion (under section 1(1)(a) of the Act) may have been used by the medical profession to sidestep the more restrictive grounds elsewhere in the Act: see Department of Health, *Matching Department of Health Abortion Notifications and Data from the National Down's Syndrome Cytogenetic Register & Recommendations for Improving Notification Compliance* (London May 2014) 11.
21 *R v Smith (John)* [1974] 1 All ER 376 (CA) is a rare example of a successful conviction.
22 *Jepson v Chief Constable of West Mercia Police Constabulary* [2003] EWHC 3318 (Admin).
23 See the Royal College of Obstetricians and Gynaecologists (RCOG), *Guidance on Termination of Pregnancy for Fetal Abnormality in England, Scotland & Wales* (London 2010) 8.
24 A failure to report can result in a summary conviction to a fine not exceeding level 5 on the standard scale.
25 See UK Parliamentary Inquiry into Abortion on the Grounds of Disability (July 2013) 4.
26 RCOG (n 23).
27 For example 'The abortion of unwanted girls taking place in the UK', (2013) *The Telegraph*, 10 January <www.telegraph.co.uk/news/uknews/crime/9794577/The-abortion-of-unwanted-girls-taking-place-in-the-UK.html> (accessed 6 November 2014).
28 See Department of Health, *Guidance in Relation to Requirements of the Abortion Act 1967* (May 2014) 6–7.
29 Letters from the Chief Medical Officer, Department of Health to Registered Medical Practitioners (23 February 2012 and 22 November 2013).
30 The Director of Public Prosecutions (DPP) publishes fuller reasons for decision not to prosecute doctors over abortion (CPS, 7 October 2013) <http://www.cps.gov.uk/news/latest_news/dpp_abortion_case_fuller_reasons/> (accessed 9 February 2015).

revealed a number of potential issues regarding the *bona fides* of the decision-making and notification process, as well as highlighting practical and evidential difficulties in mounting any legal challenge to medical decisions in this context. In particular, the absence of any clear medical guidance about the law was highlighted by the DPP,[31] raising the question why it has taken the medical profession and the Department of Health so long to rectify any ambiguity either in the law or in professional understanding of the statutory regime.

We can also learn from compliance with the reporting requirements laid down by the 1967 Act[32] and subsequent regulations.[33] These requirements were put in place to provide some measure of *ex post* external scrutiny. There are two aspects to the statutory provisions that require separate consideration: (i) the method of recording abortion procedures and (ii) external notification compliance. Both aspects have come under close scrutiny in recent years and the findings from various investigations have revealed some worrying practices and trends. For example, the CQC carried out inspections on a number of NHS abortion providers in 2012 and found that a number of doctors were pre-signing the abortion record form HSA1 (i.e. before referral and assessment of the pregnant woman),[34] as well as signing these forms based solely on decisions/assessments made by other practitioners.[35] According to the Department of Health, these practices call into 'question whether doctors have acted in accordance with their legal obligations under the Abortion Act'.[36]

Under the 1967 Act and the Abortion Regulations 1991, the registered medical practitioner who terminates a pregnancy must provide notification of the procedure to the relevant Chief Medical Officer (CMO).[37] Any person who 'wilfully contravenes or wilfully fails to comply' with these requirements is liable on summary conviction.[38] Although 'wilfully' is not defined, it seems that the provision has been interpreted as requiring a deliberate failure.[39] In recent years, both Parliament[40] and the Department of Health[41] have highlighted notable discrepancies in data reporting (i.e. differences between the procedures carried out, recorded and notified to the CMO). The Royal College of Obstetricians

---

31 The Guidance (n 28) is intended to remedy that deficiency.
32 Abortion Act 1967, s 2.
33 Abortion Regs 1991, SI 1991/499; Abortion (Amendment) (England) Regs 2002, SI 2002/887; Abortion (Amendment) (Wales) Regs 2002, SI 2002/2879.
34 Department of Health (n 28) 6, [10]. See also Department of Health, *Consultation: Procedures for the Approval of Independent Sector Places for the Termination of Pregnancy* (November 2013).
35 Department of Health (n 28).
36 Ibid.
37 See specifically Abortion Act 1967, s 2(1)(b).
38 Abortion Act 1967, s 2(3).
39 See Department of Health, *Matching Department of Health Abortion Notifications and Data from the National Down's Syndrome Cytogenetic Register & Recommendations for Improving Notification Compliance* (May 2014).
40 UK Parliamentary Inquiry (n 25) 4.
41 Department of Health (n 39).

and Gynaecologists (RCOG) were commissioned by the Department of Health to undertake a fact-finding mission as a result of the discrepancies found in data reporting. Of particular concern is the RCOG's suggestion that a possible explanation for the under-reporting of abortion procedures may be not so much a 'wilful failure to comply with the law, but rather a lack of understanding of the statutory requirements, which in turn produced a lack of organisation and accountability'.[42]

Yet, not only has the medical profession had plenty of time to consider the statutory provisions, their own guidance requires doctors to be familiar and up to date with the guidelines and law relevant to their work.[43] It is also notable that the Department of Health chose to utilise the RCOG (which has a representative function for the medical profession) rather than a truly independent body to undertake the inquiry. Arguably, a highly deferential approach to the medical profession has been adopted by the Department, both in terms of the process of investigation and the subsequent response to the discovery of the data reporting issue.

Pulling together these threads, we can see two very different perspectives on the compromise effected by the 1967 Act and subsequent practice. From one perspective, that of 'compromise medicalisation', the medical profession has failed to confine conduct and practice within the terms of the compromise. By contrast, from the perspective of 'evolutionary medicalisation', the medical profession has done pretty well in keeping practice in touch with public opinion (which is now much more comfortable with the idea of termination)[44] and making minimal demands on legislative time.[45] In other words, the verdict on the last 50 years might well be that the medical profession has failed to discharge the responsibilities that it was given by the 1967 compromise but, instead, has done rather well in discharging responsibilities that it was not given.

Assisted suicide and 'medicalisation'

Where secular views dominate end-of-life debates, the principal argument against relaxing the legal prohibition against assisted suicide is that there is too great a risk that unwilling and vulnerable persons will succumb to pressure to take steps to end their lives. Famously, this was the central objection expressed by Chief Justice Rehnquist in the leading United States case of *Washington v Glucksburg*.[46]

---

42 Ibid 11.
43 General Medical Council, *Good Medical Practice* (2013), domain 1, [12].
44 However, note the caveat at (n 20).
45 Notably, the amendments made to the Abortion Act 1967 via the Human Fertilisation and Embryology Act 1990, s 37.
46 *Washington v Glucksburg* (1997) 521 US 702, esp at 731–2.

It is found in the jurisprudence of the European Court of Human Rights, where national prohibitions against acts of assistance with suicide are protected by a margin of appreciation that gives particular weight to the potential vulnerability of the unwilling.[47] It is also seen in the judgments in the UK Supreme Court hearing of the joint appeals of *Nicklinson*, *Lamb* and *Martin*, which are full of references to this critical concern.[48]

While pro-life supporters will not miss the opportunity to plead this concern, its real significance is that it must be taken extremely seriously by any *pro-choice* advocate. This is because, for such an advocate, the choice to be defended has value only so long as it is free and informed. Accordingly, if assisted suicide is to be 'medicalised', it is imperative that the compromise regime puts the condition of free and informed choice firmly in the foreground. To be sure, it is also important that the other qualifying conditions are carefully and clearly specified; but, without assurance that assistance will be given only where there has been a truly hard look at whether the relevant person's choice is free and informed, no concession should be made.[49] In this light, what is striking about Lord Falconer's Assisted Dying Bill is that it presents a proposal for medicalisation that seeks to give precisely the assurance that those who are vulnerable will not be tricked or coerced or otherwise pressurised into seeking assistance that they do not actually wish to have.[50]

At the core of the Bill is the requirement that the person who seeks assistance has a clear and settled intention to end their life. By restricting permissible assistance to cases where the person has been diagnosed as terminally ill and with a life expectation of no more than six months,[51] the Bill invites the obvious criticism that it misses too many of the target cases (such as that of the late Tony Nicklinson);[52] but, of course, this restriction increases the plausibility of the claim that only those persons who really do want to end their lives will be assisted. However, the key assurance in the Bill is given by the provision that requires an independent doctor (together with the person's attending physician) to countersign the person's statutory form declaration. However, they can do so only if satisfied that the person 'has a clear and settled intention to end their

---

47 See *Pretty v United Kingdom* (2002) 35 EHRR 1 [74].
48 *R (on the application of Nicklinson and another) v Ministry of Justice; R (on the application of AM) (AP) v The DPP* [2014] UKSC 38, [2014] 3 WLR 200. For just a few of the many examples, [85]–[89], [172], [228]–[229], [349]–[351] and especially at [350] where Lord Kerr points out a devastating disconnection between permitting assistance for those who are unable to assist themselves and increasing the vulnerability of those who are able to assist themselves.
49 Cf the argument in R Brownsword, P Lewis and G Richardson, 'Prospective Legal Immunity and Assistance With Dying' (2012) 23 King's LJ 181.
50 In this chapter, our references are to the Bill as it stood as at 30 November 2014.
51 ADB 2014, ss 2 and 3(3)(a).
52 See *R (on the application of Nicklinson) v Ministry of Justice* [2012] EWHC 2381 (Admin).

own life which has been reached voluntarily, on an informed basis and without coercion or duress.'[53] This introduces a very particular kind of special responsibility for the medical profession.

In July 2014, when the Falconer Bill was presented to the House of Lords for its second reading, there was a long and impassioned debate, drawing out all shades of opinion. However, with a strong signal from the Supreme Court in *Nicklinson* that a declaration of incompatibility is hanging over the legislative prohibition on assisted suicide unless Parliament takes a hard look at the issues,[54] it was no surprise that it was unanimously agreed that the Bill should proceed to the next stage. Moreover, there are significant supportive statements in *Nicklinson*, recognising the good sense of an *ex ante* inquiry into the state of mind of a person who seeks assistance.[55] Nevertheless, a compromise of the kind proposed by the Falconer Bill presents major challenges both for the criminal justice system and for the medical profession.

First, if the only lawful acts of assistance are those permitted by the compromise, then there is no reason why the criminal justice system should look kindly on doctors who give unlawful acts of assistance, albeit on compassionate grounds. We can be quite sure that there will be many such cases that fall outside the authorised ambit of assistance but which invite a merciful act; and, no doubt, there will be pressure to extend the sphere of permitted acts of assistance. Yet, as Brazier and Ost chronicle in their discussion of end-of-life cases, the record of the criminal justice system is to find any number of ways of looking kindly on doctors (such as Cox[56] and Moor[57]) who, on compassionate grounds, ease the passing of their patients.[58] The question is whether, following a medicalised compromise, with very strict limits, the leading legal actors would see the unlawful acts of doctors in a different light. If not, the opponents of the Bill would have a reasonable ground *ex ante* for concern and correction and *ex post* for complaint.

Second, for the medical profession, the challenge is not quite like that facing doctors after the 1967 Act, when abortions needed to be legitimated by reference to the particular statutory grounds. It is not a matter of exercising restraint in stretching or squeezing the limiting conditions. Rather, the challenge is to

---

53 ADB 2014, s 3(3)(c).
54 The legislative provisions are in s 2 of the Suicide Act 1961 as repealed and re-enacted by s 59(2) of the Coroners and Justice Act 2009. For some of the relevant remarks in the *Nicklinson* appeal, see [2014] UKSC 38, [113]–[118], [190], and [293].
55 See [2014] UKSC 38, [108] (Lord Neuberger), [186] (Lord Mance), and [314]–[316] (Lady Hale).
56 Dr Cox was actually convicted of attempted murder, although his subsequent treatment via sentencing and the GMC can certainly be regarded as 'kindly': R Hannaford, 'Euthanasia: An overview', (1999) *BBC News*, 12 May <http://news.bbc.co.uk/1/hi/health/background_briefings/euthanasia/331255.stm> (accessed 26 January 2015).
57 (unreported) Newcastle Crown Court 11/5/1999 <http://news.bbc.co.uk/1/hi/health/343257.stm> (accessed 26 January 2015).
58 Brazier and Ost (n 1) 140–3.

prove the doubters wrong: to demonstrate that the profession is capable of making robust judgements about whether a person who seeks assistance does so on a free and informed basis. Even though free and informed consent is the fulcrum of modern medical law, and even though in their daily clinical practice doctors seemingly make judgements with complete confidence about the free and informed decisions of their patients, some might question whether – at any rate, in the context of assisted suicide – doctors are the best persons to make such judgements.

So, for example, in her incisive speech in *Nicklinson*, Lady Hale says that while it might not always be easy to make such judgements, this is what judges in the Court of Protection or the Family Division are sometimes required to do;[59] moreover, it is something that those judges are required to do in cases that involve 'sensitive life and death questions'.[60] That said, Lady Hale does not insist that it is only judges who are equipped for such a task: what matters is that the judgement is made by persons who are 'sufficiently neutral and independent of anyone involved with the applicant, and skilled at assessing evidence and competing arguments'.[61] If the Falconer Bill completes its legislative passage, it will be a surprise if its 'medicalising' strategy is abandoned – doctors surely must be responsible, at the very least, for confirming the terminal diagnosis. However, it will not be a complete surprise if the task of determining that the applicant is acting on a free and informed basis is not left to doctors alone.[62]

Conclusion

In the UK, we have lived for half a century with the medicalisation of abortions; in contrast, the medicalisation of assisted suicide is still an unknown quantity. However, the lessons of the former are relevant to the debates that currently rage around the latter. The key lesson is this. Brazier and Ost's 'medicalisation' argument implies that the terms of the compromise should be strictly observed by the professions – primarily by the doctors but also by the key legal actors in the theatre of the criminal justice system. To put it bluntly, the medical profession is entrusted with holding the line and the legal actors are charged with ensuring that the doctors discharge their special responsibilities. However, the world does not stand still; public opinion, technologies, and economies change; and, in practice, the 'medicalisation' of abortions has proved to be anything but conservative. In practice, we have had 'evolutionary medicalisation'. Viewed retrospectively, this might seem to be no bad thing: it has enabled doctors and lawyers to go with the flow of public opinion, and it has meant

---

59 *Nicklinson* (n 48) [314].
60 Ibid [315].
61 Ibid [315].
62 Cf Brownsword et al. (n 49). Significantly, Lord Falconer conceded at the Committee Stage of the Bill that doctors alone might not be able to deal with all the relevant questions (see the Committee Stage of ADB 2014, cols 1880–1).

that there is no great gap between the law and public opinion. However, viewed prospectively, at the time of the compromise embodied in the 1967 Act, these developments would seem to be quite unacceptable: the terms of the compromise are not respected and the norms are changed without the medical profession being held to account.

As the latest attempt to change the law on assisted suicide runs its course, we again face the challenge of finding a way of facilitating the compromise (which also means, respecting the compromise), but also of finding a mechanism *ex post* for reflecting whatever changes in public opinion might take place. The obvious answer is that we need both 'sunset' and 'sunshine' so that, after a specified period of years, the compromise legislation is brought to Parliament to be openly reviewed and then renewed or revised by *positive* act.[63] Of course, for the opponents of the Bill, no guarantee can be given that the terms of the compromise will never be changed – in this sense, the Falconer Bill might prove to be the thin end of the wedge. However, in the interests of transparency, accountability, democracy and the integrity of the compromise, it will not do to leave any adjustment of the law either to unauthorised medical discretion or to low visibility governmental 'guidance' or codes of practice. Any adjustment to the compromise needs the positive imprimatur of Parliament.

---

63 Cf the provision in ADB 2014, s 13(4).

Index

abortion: medicalisation, and 296–9
acts and omissions distinguished 58–9
adolescence: nature of 22
adolescent autonomy 21–2
Artificial Nutrition and Hydration (ANH) 47
assisted dying: criminalisation 58–61; harms, form of 62; human rights, and 65; legalisation 61–3; religious doctrine, and 62
assisted suicide: medicalisation, and 299–302
Australia: genetic information 29
autonomy 6–7, 19–30; context 19; end of life, and 56–7; parent-child relationship, and 21–4; scope of notion of 20; tyranny of 26

blame 113–15; tropes 114–15
Brazier, Margaret: academic scholarship 3–5; autonomy, on 3–4; autonomy and responsibility, on 19–21; contribution to healthcare law 3–5; humanity, on 4; key areas in research 6; methodological approach 4–5; public service engagement and leadership 5–6

circumcision 181
child incapax 24–5
clinical ethics committees (CECs) 123–8
complaints: trust, and 112
compromise medicalisation 292–303; abortion and medicalisation 296–9; special responsibilities 293–6
compulsion: public health sphere, within 37–8
compulsory vaccination 31–42 *see also* vaccination; constraining individual interests 37–9; herd immunity, and 40; mandatory 39; moral responsibility, and 40–1; programmes 39–41; state intervention 36–7
courts: costs of 122–3
criminal law 13–14; bioethical conflict, and 267; Brazier on 264–7; gross negligence 191; ill treatment and neglect 263; individuals, and 265; maternal responsibility 280–91; regulatory force 79; role of 44–5, 258; sexual boundary breaches 92, 101; transmission of disease 268–79; vulnerability, and 257–67
criminal offences: sexual boundary breaches 101
critically ill infants 116–28; best interests 119–20; Clinical Ethics Committees (CECs) 123–4; costs of courts 122–3; critical decisions 116–28; ethical questions 116–17; intractable disputes 117–18; parent-clinician conflict 118–19; parental authority 120–1; parental influence 121; principles 116–28; problems 116–28; processes 116–28; shared decision-making 120
Curtis, Dr Richard 186–7

data protection 27–8
death: choice of 57
deceased organ donation 138–9
disclosure procedures: sexual boundary breaches 99–100
donor conception 231–42; consent of prospective parents to information disclosure 236–8; family implications 238–41; information disclosure, and 231–42; non-identity problem

234–5; prospective parents 238–41; prospective parents' right to respect for private life 235–6; reproductive ethics 234–5; treatment options 238–41; welfare of child clause 232–4
donor gametes 219–22

embryos 11–12, 199–210; categorising 199–210; constructions 200–1; legal controversies 201–5; politics of muddling through 205–9
empowerment 103–15; competence gap, and 106–7; influence of 104; role of 105–8
end of life 55–66; acceptable decisions 64; autonomy, and 56–7; criminalisation of assisted dying 58–61; future developments 65–6; intention, and 60; liberalism, and 56
Endocrine Treatment of Transsexual Persons (ETTP) guidelines 182–3, 184, 188
EU health law 67–77; CJEU, and 72; clinical trials legislation 75–6; future 67–77; global health, and 76–7; global trade patterns, and 75; healthcare as consumer service 72; human organs 76; human rights, and 73; organising category, as 74–5; past 67–77; present 67–77; reduction of risk of harm 74; relevant provisions 68; status quo, and 70; themes 71
euthanasia 55 *see also* assisted dying; assisted suicide

family, role of 129–40; autonomy, and 130–2; best interests 135–8; deceased organ donation 138–9; eccentric decisions 134–5; end-of-life situations 135–8; family ties 25–6; futility 135–8; incompetent adults 132–5; informal representatives 133; Spanish model 133; undue influence, and 130–1
female genital mutilation 181–2
foetal health, responsibility for 244–7

genetic information 26–8; Australia 29
Gillick 22–3
global health law 86–7
good death 63

harassment 101
healthcare law: development 1–3; evolution 1–3; future of 8
herd immunity 40
Human Bodies Human Choices 151–2
Human Fertilisation and Embryology Act 2008 212–15
Human Fertilisation and Embryology Authority (HFEA) 203–4
human life, value of *see* value of human life
human rights 27; assisted dying, and 65
Human Tissue Act 1961 157–9
Human Tissue Authority 153
humane autonomy 21

ill health: changes in conceptions 69
individual interests: constraining 37–9
individual patient choice 79–80
infants, decisions for critically ill *see* critically ill infants
information disclosure: consent of prospective parents, and 236–8; donor conception, and 231–42; welfare of child clause, and 232–6
informed consent: aim of 130
intention: evidence of 59–60
inviolability of life 44–6

Judging Best Interests in Paediatric Intensive Care 117, 124, 127
judiciary: value of human life, and 43–54

key principles and themes 6–8
King, Ashya 25
knowledge asymmetry 109–11

law and humanity 168–80
law, ethics and the human body 9–11
liberalism: essence of 56–7

manslaughter 192
maternal responsibility to child not yet born 280–91; maternal liability 283–4, 289–91; moral responsibility 283
measles, mumps and rubella (MMR) vaccine 32
medical law: growth of 78–9; pre-Brazier era 169–70; shift to health law 69; theoretical development 79
medicalisation: abortion, and 296–9; assisted suicide, and 299–302

Medicine, Patents and the Law xxiv–xxv; 78
Mental Capacity Act 2005 246
Mill, John Stuart 229
mitochondria replacement 219–22
moral responsibility for foetal health 244–7

notifiable diseases 38

omissions: acts distinguished 58–9
organ donation 168–80; Brazier method 168–80; commitment to rule of law 171–2; embracing complexity 174–5; failure to recognise different stakeholders 178–9; law and life 174–5; *Murnaghan* case study 176–8; recognising humanity 172–4; revised policy as mediating solution 179–80
outcome-based approach to competence 134

parent-child relationship: autonomy, and 21–4
parental influence: scope 121
paternalistic attitudes 109
patient-doctor relations 8–9
patient harm 103–15
patient responsibility 103–15; differing conceptions 106; patients as co-producers 105
patients: sexual boundary breaches by 91–102
policing pregnancy 243–54; newer caesarean cases 248–54
political context: relevance of 85
pregnancy: criminal responsibility for maternal conduct during 247
procreative responsibility 223
property interests in human tissue 156–67; Australian cases 164–6; bailment 164–6; current law 157; fetus 162; lawful possession 161–2; legal evolutions 163–6; no property rule 159–60; questioning old rules 160–2; work/skill exception 163
Public Health and Private Lives 31
public health law: definitions 82–4; justifications for concepts 84–5

regulating reproduction 11–13, 211–22, 223–30
Reid, Dr Russell 187

relational advocates 110
religious doctrine: assisted dying, and 62
Retained Organs Commission 9–10, 143–55; advocacy for families 148–9; aims 146; background 144–5; challenges 145–50; dangers of lessons lost 153–5; law reform, and 150–3; legacy of 143–55; lessons learned 153–5; public face 147; role 145–50
responsibilities to autonomous others 25–9
reverence for life 7–8

sanctity of life 44–5
sex change surgery for transgender minors 181–8; balancing exercise 185–6; deferring until adulthood 183–5; offering 185; surgeries in the shadows 186–8
sexual boundary breaches 91–102; definition 91–2; doctor, responsibility of 95; patients, responsibilities of 96
state intervention: vaccination, and 36–7
suicide: assisted, medicalisation, and 299–302 *see also* assisted dying
surrogacy 215–19

tobacco products 75
transgenderism 182
transmission of disease 268–79; causation 275–6; Court of Appeal's approach 269–70; criminal law 268–79; fault element 276–8; fundamental policy issues 270–1; level of harm required for criminalisation 272–5; related policy issues 271–2
trust 111–13; complaints, and 112

undue influence 130–2

vaccination 31–42; autonomy 34–5; benefits 33; burdens 34; effect 32–3; encouragement 32; programmes 31–2; public good, and 34–5; reciprocity 34–5; risks 34; routine 36
value of human life 43–54: accommodation 46–8; *Aintree* 49–51; ANH 47; conceptual difficulties 44–6; exception 46–8; future developments 52–3; moral and ethical questions 43–4; *Nicklinson* 51–2; rebuttable presumption 46–8; recent judicial interpretations 48–52; terminology 44;

W v M 49; withdrawal of treatment cases 47–8
vulnerability 108–11; autonomy, and 260–4; Brazier's critique of autonomy and consent 258–60; criminal law, and 257–67; disempowerment, and 110–11; knowledge asymmetry 109–11; liberty, and 260–4; paternalistic attitudes, and 109; relational advocates 110; symptoms, and 108

World Professional Association for Transgender Health's Standards of Care (WPATH guidelines) 182–3, 184, 188